BOTANY AND GARDENS IN EARLY MODERN IRELAND

Botany and Gardens
in Early Modern Ireland

Elizabethanne Boran, E. Charles Nelson
& Emer Lawlor

EDITORS

PUBLISHED FOR THE TRUSTEES OF
THE EDWARD WORTH LIBRARY, DUBLIN
BY FOUR COURTS PRESS

Set in EhrhardtPro 10.5pt/13pt by
Carrigboy Typesetting Services for
four courts press ltd
7 Malpas Street, Dublin 8, Ireland
www.fourcourtspress.ie
and in North America for
four courts press
c/o IPG, 814 N Franklin St, Chicago, IL 60610

© The various contributors and Four Courts Press 2022

A catalogue record for this title is available
from the British Library.

ISBN 978-1-84682-023-3

All rights reserved. No part of this publication may be reproduced,
stored in or introduced into a retrieval system, or transmitted, in any form
or by any means (electronic, mechanical, photocopying, recording, or otherwise),
without the prior written permission of both the copyright
owner and publisher of this book.

Printed in Spain by Castuera.

Foreword

As a trustee of the Edward Worth Library, Dublin, it is my pleasure to write the foreword for our publication *Botany and gardens in early modern Ireland*. This book includes chapters many of which were previously presented at a conference jointly organized by the Edward Worth Library and the Dublin Naturalists' Field Club on 'Botany in early modern Ireland' (2017), and a second conference which concentrated on the topic 'Gardens and gardening in early modern Ireland' (2018). Both conferences were inspired by the wonderful botanical collection of Dr Edward Worth (1676–1733), an early eighteenth-century Dublin physician who left his library of uniquely well preserved rare books to Dr Steevens' Hospital, Dublin, where they are still housed in their original eighteenth-century setting.

The Worth Library Trust set up under the High Court Scheme in 1995 has as one of its main objects promoting greater knowledge and awareness of this rare and beautiful library by both the public and scholarly community. The Trust is committed to sharing Worth's extraordinary collections via tours of the Library, an annual lecture series, a research fellowship scheme, publications such as this, and our myriad of online exhibitions which are hosted on our website www.edwardworthlibrary.ie. Our online exhibitions explore the many subjects which fascinated Edward Worth, and enable us to share his collections both nationally and internationally.

Finally, I would like to acknowledge the support of my fellow trustees, and the support of the HSE, whose headquarters the hospital now is. In particular, I wish to thank my co-editors, Dr E. Charles Nelson, Associate Editor, *Archives of Natural History*, and Dr Elizabethanne Boran, the Librarian of the Edward Worth Library, who with their great editorial experience shouldered the bulk of the work and without whose commitment this publication would not have been possible.

DR EMER LAWLOR
Trustee, Worth Library Trust

Contents

LIST OF CONTRIBUTORS	9
LIST OF ILLUSTRATIONS	11
LIST OF ABBREVIATIONS	15
ACKNOWLEDGMENTS	16
PREFACE, *Elizabethanne Boran and E. Charles Nelson*	17

BOTANY IN SEVENTEENTH-CENTURY IRELAND

1   Recollecting Ireland's flora: botanical information in the 'Zoilomastix' (*c.*1626) of Philip O'Sullivan Beare
E. Charles Nelson   25

2   Irish wild plants before 1690
E. Charles Nelson   45

3   The Molyneux brothers, the New Science and the Dublin Philosophical Society in the late seventeenth century
Patrick Kelly   58

CALEB THRELKELD AND BOTANY IN EIGHTEENTH-CENTURY IRELAND

4   Caleb Threlkeld: dissenting minister, physician and botanist
Emer Lawlor   80

5   Caleb Threlkeld's plant records
Declan Doogue   100

6   Caleb Threlkeld, Dublin's earliest plant ecologist
Declan Doogue   116

Contents

PAPER GARDENS: COLLECTING BOOKS ON BOTANY AND GARDENS IN
EARLY MODERN IRELAND

7   Botany and gardens at the Edward Worth Library, Dublin
    Elizabethanne Boran   157

8   'If you have a garden in your library, nothing will be wanting': botany
    and gardens in the collections of Marsh's Library, Dublin
    Susan Hemmens   174

9   Pleasure gardens and gardening for pleasure in the Fagel collection at
    Trinity College Dublin
    Regina Whelan Richardson   193

GARDENS AND LANDSCAPES IN EARLY MODERN IRELAND

10 The Physic Garden at Trinity College Dublin, in the early eighteenth
    century
    E. Charles Nelson   213

11 Gardening at Mitchelstown: John K'Eogh's *Botanalogia universalis
    Hibernica* (Cork, 1735)
    E. Charles Nelson   231

12 Gothic features in eighteenth-century Irish landscapes
    Vandra Costello   249

13 The nursery and seed trade in Dublin before 1800
    Terence Reeves-Smyth   263

14 Ellen Hutchins (1785–1815), botanist in West Cork: how did her garden
    grow?
    Madeline Hutchins   286

INDEX OF PLANT NAMES   305

GENERAL INDEX   320

Contributors

ELIZABETHANNE BORAN is the Librarian of the Edward Worth Library. She is the Secretary General of the International Commission for the History of Universities and has published extensively on the history of ideas in the early modern period.

VANDRA COSTELLO is an independent scholar, an historic gardens and landscape historian and garden writer. She is the author of *Irish demesne landscapes, 1660–1740* (Dublin, 2015), and she regularly publishes articles on garden and landscape history in peer reviewed and popular journals.

DECLAN DOOGUE's interests include the biogeography and conservation of Ireland's habitats and the history of Irish botany. He has co-authored *The wild flowers of Ireland* (with Carsten Kreiger) and is the Hon. Vice President of the Dublin Naturalists' Field Club.

SUSAN HEMMENS is the Deputy Director of Marsh's Library, Dublin. Her research interests in the history of science include the dissemination and reception of natural philosophy within the knowledge networks of the early modern period, and the development of modes of scientific enquiry.

MADELINE HUTCHINS is a researcher, writer and events organizer for the Ellen Hutchins Festival, Bantry, Co. Cork.

PATRICK KELLY is an Emeritus Fellow of Trinity College Dublin. His publications include editions of *Locke on money*, 2 vols (Oxford, 1991) and *William Molyneux's The case of Ireland's being bound by acts of parliament in England, stated* (Dublin, 2018), as well as articles on Locke and Irish political and intellectual history of the seventeenth and eighteenth centuries.

EMER LAWLOR, a Trustee of the Worth Library, is a retired medical practitioner who was awarded an M. Litt. by Trinity College Dublin in 2016, for her thesis 'Enquiries into vegetables: botanists in Ireland and their sources, 1680–1775'.

E. CHARLES NELSON, FLS, VMM, was horticultural taxonomist in the National Botanic Gardens, Glasnevin (1976–95). His research publications include books and numerous papers relating to the history of Irish horticulture and botany, and he was co-author of *'The brightest jewel'. A history of the National Botanic Gardens, Glasnevin, Dublin* (Dublin, 1987).

TERENCE REEVES-SMYTH is an archaeologist, specializing in architectural and garden history.

REGINA WHELAN RICHARDSON is an independent scholar.

Illustrations

E. Charles Nelson

1.1   First page of the botanical section of 'Zoilomastix'.   27
1.2   Jacques Daléchamps, *Histoire generale des plantes* (Lyon, 1615), title page.   29
1.3   Map of Ireland published by Abraham Ortelius in *Theatrum orbis
        terrarum* (Antwerp, 1603).   32
1.4   Philip O'Sullivan Beare's 'seamrog' (*Trifolium repens*, white clover,
        seamair bhán). Watercolour by Bridget Flinn.   35
1.5   *Cydonia oblonga*, 'Membrillo' in Spanish, quince in English.
        Watercolour by Wendy F. Walsh.   37
1.6   Distribution of *Arbutus unedo* (strawberry tree) in Munster.   39

E. Charles Nelson

2.1   John Parkinson, *Theatrum botanicum: the theater of plants* (London, 1640),
        title page.   46
2.2   *Arbutus unedo*, caithne, strawberry tree.   48
2.3   *Drosera anglica*, cailís Mhuire mhór, great sundew.   49
2.4   *Dryas octopetala*, leaithín, mountain avens.   50
2.5   *Epipactis helleborine*, ealabairín, broad-leaved helleborine.   51
2.6   *Euphorbia hyberna*, bainne caoin, Irish spurge.   52
2.7   *Gentiana verna*, ceadharlach Bealtaine, spring gentian. Éire €10 stamp.   53
2.8   *Juniperus communis*, aiteal, juniper.   54
2.9   *Pyrola rotundifolia*, glasluibh chruinn, round-leaved wintergreen.   54
2.10   *Rubus saxatilis*, sú na mban mín, stone bramble.   56
2.11   *Scilla verna*, sciolla earraigh, spring squill.   56

Patrick Kelly

3.1   Hermann Moll's 1714 map of Dublin, detail.   60
3.2   Portrait of William Molyneux (1698), attributed to Sir Godfrey
        Kneller, Bt.   63
3.3   Sir Thomas Molyneux, Bt., F.R.S. by unknown artist.   65
3.4   Hortus Botanicus Leiden in 1610.   68
3.5   *Vicia faba* (broad bean); extract from Nehemiah Grew, *The anatomy
        of plants* (London, 1682).   73
3.6   *Arbutus unedo* (strawberry tree), woodcut from Adam Lonicer,
        Naturalis historiae opus novum (Frankfurt, 1551).   75

Emer Lawlor

4.1   Caber Farmhouse, Kirkoswald, Cumbria.   81
4.2   Caleb Threlkeld's application for a licence to preach at Huddlesceugh.   83

Illustrations

4.3	'Ranunculus Tlammeus ... Aliis Flammula. The Lesser Spearwort ... In Ulster' (*Ranunculus flammula*, lesser spearwort).	88
4.4	Caleb Threlkeld's handwriting.	89
4.5	'Spring herbs' from William Laffan (ed.), *The cries of Dublin &c. Drawn from the life by Hugh Douglas Hamilton, 1760* (Dublin, 2003).	91
4.6	*Lythrum salicaria* (purple loosestrife).	93
4.7	Signature of Thomas Molyneux on Caleb Threlkeld, *Synopsis stirpium Hibernicarum* (Dublin, 1727).	95

Declan Doogue

5.1	Caleb Threlkeld, *Synopsis stirpium Hibernicarum* (Dublin, 1726), title page.	101
5.2	John Ray, *Catalogus plantarum circa Cantabrigiam nascentium* (London, 1660), title page.	103
5.3	Threlkeld's account for the early-flowering *Ficaria verna* (formerly *Ranunculus ficaria*) (lesser celandine).	105
5.4	Detail from Charles Brooking's map of Dublin, 1728, showing Mark's Alley.	107
5.5	*Anacamptis pyramidalis* (pyramidal orchid) drawn by Johann Jakob Dillenius, from John Ray, *Synopsis methodica stirpium Britannicarum* (London, 1724).	109
5.6	*Saxifraga tridactylites* (rue-leaved saxifrage) from John Gerard's *The herball or generall historie of plantes* (London, 1633).	109
5.7	*Anthriscus caucalis* (hedge parsley) from Caspar Bauhin, *Prodromus theatri botanici* (Basle, 1671).	110

Declan Doogue

6.1	Charles Brooking's map of Dublin (1728).	118–19
6.2	'The Harbour of Dublin actually survey'd by Capt. Thomas Phillips'.	120
6.3	*Armeria maritima* (thrift, sea pink).	121
6.4	*Silene uniflora* (sea campion).	122
6.5	*Ulex europaeus* (gorse).	127
6.6	*Centaurea nigra* (knapweed).	129
6.7	*Caltha palustris* (marsh marigold).	132
6.8	*Stachys palustris* (marsh woundwort).	134
6.9	*Pinguicula vulgaris* (common butterwort).	136
6.10	Anonymous annotation recording 'lords-and-ladies' in the Phoenix Park, from Otto Brunfels, *Herbarum vivae eicones ad naturae imitationem* (Strassburg, 1532).	140
6.11	*Malva sylvestris* (common mallow).	143
6.12	*Narthecium ossifragum* (bog asphodel).	147

Elizabethanne Boran

7.1	Dr Edward Worth (1676–1733): portrait in oils, artist unknown.	158
7.2	Otto Brunfels, *Herbarum vivae eicones ad naturae imitationem* (Strasburg, 1532), p. 96: *Primula veris* (cowslip).	160

Illustrations

7.3	'Lilio-Narcissus Africanus platycaulis humilis ...' (*Ammocharis longifolia* (L.) Herb.). Jan Commelin, *Horti Medici Amstelodamensis rariorum* (Amsterdam, 1697–1701).	164
7.4	Caspar Bauhin (1560–1624), portrait from Pietro Andrea Mattioli, *Opera quæ extant omnia: hoc est, commentarij in VI. libros Pedacij Dioscoridis Anazarbei de medica materia* (Basle, 1598).	167
7.5	The garden of the Villa Sagredo at Marocco, from Paolo Bartolomeo Clarici's *Istoria e coltura delle piante ...* (Venice, 1726).	170

Susan Hemmens

8.1	Ground plan of the Library contained in the Visitations Book, Marsh's Library.	175
8.2	Fourteenth-century Montpellier manuscript: Marsh's Library, MS Z4.4.4, fo. 38r.	180
8.3	Poppies as illustrated in Mathias de L'Obel, *Icones stirpium* (Antwerp, 1591), p. 273.	181
8.4	Paul Contant, *Le bouquet printanier* (La Rochelle, 1600), introductory plate.	184
8.5	Daniel Rabel, *Theatrum florae* (Paris, 1620), engraved frontispiece.	185
8.6	John Worlidge, *Systema horti-culturae or the art of gardening* (London, 1677), p. 17.	190

Regina Whelan Richardson

9.1	*Beschouwende en werkdadige hovenier-konst* (Leeuwarden, 1753), tab. III following p. 310.	196
9.2	*Tractaat der Lusthoff* (Leiden, 1720), plate III.	198
9.3	The estate of Clingendael near The Hague.	200
9.4	Sections of the plan of the ground floor and garden of the Fagel house in The Hague (*c*.1706), showing two of the four planting beds.	202
9.5	Johan Barents (?), 'Viceroy', Fagel tulip catalogue (*c*.1637–41), watercolour and gouache.	204
9.6	Magdalena Poulle's orangery and greenhouse at Gunterstein.	210

E. Charles Nelson

10.1	Detail of a 'bird's-eye view' (isometric drawing) by Samuel Byron of the south-western corner of Trinity College campus in 1780.	214
10.2	Henry Nicholson, *Methodus plantarum, in horto medico, Collegii Dublinensis* (Dublin, 1712), title page.	216
10.3	Advertisement for botany lectures at the Physic Garden in *The Dublin Weekly Journal*, 23 April 1726.	218
10.4	William Stephens, portrait in oils, artist unknown	219
10.5	The first page of William Stephens's 'Catalogus Plantarum in Horto Dublinensis'.	220
10.6	*Aloe variegata* (now *Gonialoe variegata*), from Jan and Maria Moninckx's *Altas, c.*1699–*c.*1706.	223
10.7	William Stephens, *Botanical elements* (Dublin, 1727), title page and p. 11.	228
10.8	*Euphorbia hyberna*, Irish spurge: hand-coloured engraving by Johann Jacob Dillenius, *Hortus Elthamensis* (London, 1732)	229

Illustrations

E. Charles Nelson

11.1	John K'Eogh, *Botanalogia universalis Hibernica* (Cork, 1735), title page.	232
11.2	The restored eighteenth-century orangery at Marino Point, Cork.	235
11.3	'*Aloes Vulgaris sive Sempervivum marinum*' (*Aloe vera*), from John Gerard's *Herball* (London, 1633), p. 507.	236
11.4	*Crocus sativus*, saffron.	237
11.5	'Great Dragons … Dracontium majus', called '*Geiredarrig*' in Irish.	239
11.6	*Aegopodium podograria* (bishopsweed or goutweed).	243

Vandra Costello

12.1	Leixlip Castle on the River Liffey.	250
12.2	View of Muckross Abbey, on the Lake of Killarney, Co. Kerry.	253
12.3	Adare Manor and ruins.	255
12.4	Slane Castle, Co. Meath.	256
12.5	Rathfarnham Castle gate, July 1952.	257
12.6	The Jealous Wall at Belvedere, Co. Westmeath.	260

Terence Reeves-Smyth

13.1	John Speed's map of Dublin, 1610.	266
13.2	John Johnson, *A catalogue of garden seeds and flower roots*, c.1705.	275
13.3	Map of Dublin seed and nursery shops, 1740–1800.	279
13.4	Map of Dublin's nursery grounds, 1760–1800.	281
13.5	'A list of forest trees, fruit trees, shrubs, and evergreens. Nursery Garden of the Hibernian Hospital, 1781'.	283

Madeline Hutchins

14.1	Silhouette of woman writing, in the style of the early 1800s.	287
14.2	Ballylickey House, photograph c.1910.	289
14.3	*Fucus capillaris*, now *Gloiosiphonia capillaris*.	292
14.4	*Jungermannia hutchinsiae*, a leafy liverwort, now *Jubula hutchinsiae*.	295
14.5	*Arabis hirsuta* (hairy rock-cress), from J.E. Smith and James Sowerby, *English botany* (London, 1807).	299
14.6	*Ramalina farinacea*.	303

TABLES

1.1	Concordance of foliation in the 'Zoilomastix'.	42
1.2	Plants named in the 'Zoilomastix'.	42–4
6.1	Concordance of plant names.	150–6
7.1	Scientific subject divisions in the Edward Worth Library.	157
11.1	Localities (by county) for wild plants published in John K'Eogh's *Botanalogia*.	246–8

Abbreviations

BSBI	Botanical Society of Britain and Ireland
DIB	*Dictionary of Irish biography*
IHS	*Irish Historical Studies*
NLI	National Library of Ireland
ODNB	*Oxford dictionary of national biography*
OED	*Oxford English dictionary*
OPW	Office of Public Works
PRONI	Public Record Office of Northern Ireland
RCB	Representative Church Body Library
RIA	Royal Irish Academy
TCC	Trinity College Library, Cambridge
TCD	Trinity College Dublin

Acknowledgments

GRATEFUL THANKS ARE DUE to the Trustees of the Edward Worth Library, Dublin for facilitating the publication of this collection. The editors would also like to thank the members of the Dublin Naturalists' Field Club, both for their involvement in the 2017 conference on botany in early modern Ireland, and for the illustrations provided by members for this volume. We are grateful to the staff of all the many libraries and archives, and to the various individuals, who provided images for this book. Special thanks are due to Ms Nuala Canny (Farmleigh House), Dr Lydia Ferguson (TCD), Ms Francesca Halfacree (Cumbria Archive Centre), Dr Susan Hemmens (Marsh's Library), Ms Barbara Mc Cormack (RIA), Mr Antoine Mac Gaoithín (Edward Worth Library), Ms Dervla McAleese (Dublin), Ms Meadhbh Murphy (RIA), and Ms Sharon Sutton (TCD).

Preface

THE HISTORY OF IRISH BOTANY – in the sense of recording and interpreting the wild plants that occur throughout Ireland at different historical periods – is relatively well chronicled. Since the early eighteenth century, 'hand books' (although not necessarily small enough to fit in a pocket) almost always contain acknowledgments to those, both living and deceased, who contributed records not just in previous decades but also in previous centuries. The accumulation of information has always been important, as each new publication represented an accretion of collections or sightings of the plants occurring on the island. Each new flora was a new base-line for future investigators. Caleb Threlkeld's handy, pocketable *Synopsis stirpium Hibernicarum* (Dublin, 1726), published the same month as *Gulliver's travels*, while not the ultimate starting point, laid the foundation for James Townsend Mackay's *Flora Hibernica* (Dublin, 1836), for David Moore and Alexander Goodman More's *Cybele Hibernica* (Dublin, 1866), and for all their successors including, in the twentieth century, David Allardice Webb's *An Irish flora* (Dundalk, 1943) which, through various succeeding editions, still serves twenty-first-century botanists, amateur and professional.

At the start of the last century, a comprehensive bibliography of Irish botany was compiled by Robert Lloyd Praeger (1865–1953) for his magisterial 'Irish topographical botany' published in the *Proceedings of the Royal Irish Academy* (Dublin, 1901); this is as much a roll-call of workers as it is of their publications. Praeger is famous for his evocative and readable book *The way that I went* (Dublin, 1937) and he also provided thumb-nail biographies of the principal naturalists who were of Irish birth or who worked in Ireland in his compendium *Some Irish naturalists* (Dundalk, 1949).[1] As well as listing the sources for the records quoted, many post-nineteenth-century works about the flora of Ireland, especially those dealing with provinces or counties, provide historical overviews of the progress of floristic botany since about 1800.

Other modern works dealing with botanical history have included the individual histories of the scholarly bodies that supported and published research as far back as the late seventeenth century: the Dublin Philosophical Society, Trinity College Dublin, the Royal Dublin Society, the Royal Irish Academy and the Belfast Natural History and Philosophical Society being the most significant.[2]

---

1 E.C. Nelson, '[Review] "A good man's sin", or *Some Irish naturalists* revisited', *Irish Naturalists Journal*, 22:7 (1987), 323–4. 2 See also, *inter alia*, M.E. Mitchell, 'Irish botany in the seventeenth century',

Our knowledge of Ireland's native and naturalized plants before the modern period is axiomatically much more fragmentary and partial. Very few herbarium specimens – the pressed, dried and labelled fragments of plants that serve as vouchers for scientific purposes – from before 1800 survive. Likewise, little in the way of field notebooks are known in archives.[3] While Irish literary sources contain a remarkable wealth of allusions to the natural world, including vernacular names of plants, for scientific purposes these are of little value.[4]

The same can be stated about gardens and gardening in Ireland. Like icebergs, gardens that are not maintained melt away and become invisible, their footprints obscured by the subsequent history of the landscape.[5] Yet, as Thomas McErlean has noted, 'The Irish landscape is filled with abandoned parks and gardens. In a short drive through any part of the countryside the eye is drawn to ruined demesnes walls, the shells of gatehouses, relic plantations and the shadows of former landscape parks and features of a past era of large-scale gardening and landscaping'.[6] The plants that were cultivated in ancient gardens, unless they were long-lived trees, will have reached their prime, senesced and died.[7] Thus, we largely rely on pictorial and written records to chronicle the changing fashions espoused by gardeners in Ireland, and as with the wild flora, that archive becomes more sparse the longer ago the gardens were actively cultivated. On maps and plans of Irish towns and fortified dwellings made before 1700 there are sometimes scant indications of gardens, at least rows of trees in enclosures that may indicate planted spaces.[8] Correspondence and business records rarely record importations of plants other than common agricultural crops. Garden

---

Proceedings of the Royal Irish Academy 75, section B (1975), 275–84; James White, 'A history of Irish vegetation studies', *Journal of Life Sciences of the Royal Dublin* Society, 3 (1982), 15–42; D.M. Synnott, 'Botany in Ireland' in J.W. Foster and H.C.G. Chesney (eds), *Nature in Ireland: a scientific and cultural history* (Dublin, 1997), pp 157–83; Christopher Moriarty, 'The early naturalists' in Foster and Chesney (eds), *Nature in Ireland*, pp 71–90. Another recent history of Irish natural history as a whole is David Cabot, 'Naturalists and their works' in David Cabot, *Ireland* (The New Naturalist Library) (London, 1999), pp 14–49, especially pp 15, 23–9. **3** It is to be hoped that the exciting project 'Beyond 2022' which has found a wealth of unpublished material relating to the history of Ireland may provide more material of botanical interest. To find out more about this digital initiative which seeks to reclaim the material lost in the 1922 Four Courts fire, see https://beyond2022.ie/, accessed 5 May 2022. **4** Moriarty, 'The early naturalists' in Foster and Chesney (eds), *Nature in Ireland*, pp 71–90; Christopher Moriarty, 'Plant references in translations from Irish etc.' (file: nhiplant.xls, not published). **5** Christopher Thacker, *The history of gardens* (London, 1979), p. 7. **6** Thomas McErlean, 'The archaeology of parks and gardens, 1600–1900, an introduction to Irish garden archaeology' in Audrey Horning et al. (eds), *The post-medieval archaeology of Ireland, 1550–1850* (Dublin 2007), pp 279–88. **7** Dating ancient trees such as *Taxus baccata* (yew) is problematic, and whether such yews as those at Muckross Abbey, Co. Kerry, and Crom Castle, Co. Fermanagh, were deliberately planted, and so represent the remnants of planted gardens, is debatable. The Muckross Abbey yew is variously dated (without any contemporary evidence or tree-ring data) to the fifteenth century (e.g. Martin Gardner et al., 'Conservation hedges – modern-day arks', *Sibbaldia, the Journal of Botanic Garden Horticulture*, 17 (2019), 71–100; Jeremy Harte, 'How old is that yew', *At the Edge*, 4 (1996), 1–9; Ben Simon, 'A review of notable yew trees in Ireland', *Arboricultural Journal*, 24 (2000), 97–137); or the late seventeenth century (Terence Reeves-Smith, 'Irish gardens and gardening before Cromwell', *The Barryscourt Lectures*, IV, (1997), 97–144, at 118, 139–40). **8** Sheila Pim, 'History of gardening in Ireland' in E.C. Nelson and Aidan Brady (eds), *Irish gardening and horticulture* (Dublin, 1979), pp 45–69, at p. 47; Reeves-Smith, 'Irish gardens

Preface

catalogues are very rare before the publication of that for the Dublin Society's Botanic Gardens at Glasnevin – now the National Botanic Gardens – in 1800.

Little was published about Ireland's garden history before the late twentieth century, when the ground-breaking study, *Lost demesnes* by Edward Malins and the Knight of Glin, was produced.[9] Malins's and Glin's book laid a solid foundation for subsequent work on the larger planted spaces – the 'lost demesnes' of the title – in the past four centuries and stimulated interest in the unique history of gardening and gardens in Ireland. Terence Reeves-Smith's essay on gardening 'before Cromwell' epitomized the gardens of earlier centuries as far as archives and archaeology permitted.[10] T.C. Barnard's paper on 'Gardening, diet and "improvement" in later seventeenth-century Ireland' extended details further into the early modern period.[11] *A history of gardening in Ireland* by Keith Lamb and Patrick Bowe summarized our knowledge of Irish garden history up to 1995.[12] The Heritage Gardens Committees active since the late 1970s both in the Republic of Ireland and Northern Ireland facilitated research and documentation as did many in-depth surveys of individual gardens undertaken under a variety of heritage, conservation and restoration schemes.[13] Building on pioneering studies of Irish nurseries by Dr Eileen McCracken (1920–88) and work on significant individual nurseries, a compendium providing the histories of Ireland's unique cultivars (varieties) of garden plants was published under the aegis of the Irish Garden Plant Society.[14]

The chapters in this book stand on the shoulders of these giants. Chapter 1 focuses on a manuscript, unpublished until the twentieth century, written by Philip O'Sullivan Beare (1590–1636) in the period 1625–6. The manuscript of his 'Zoilomastix', now in Uppsala University Library, was a work written in exile, for

---

and gardening before Cromwell' at 124.   **9** Edward Malins and the Knight of Glin, *Lost demesnes: Irish landscape gardening, 1660–1845* (London, 1976). Its sequel was Edward Malins and Patrick Bowe, *Irish garden and demesnes from 1830* (London, 1980). For an invaluable bibliography on Irish garden history to 2010, see Terence Reeves-Smyth, 'Published sources for Irish garden history research', http://www.nihgt.org/resources/images/SOURCES%20STUDY%20IRISH%20GARDEN%20HISTORY%202.pdf, accessed 30 March 2022. On this topic see also Vandra Costello, *Irish demesne landscapes, 1660–1740* (Dublin, 2015), and Finola O'Kane and Robert O'Bryne (eds), *Digging new ground: the Irish country house garden, 1650–1900* (Dublin, 2022).   **10** Reeves-Smith, 'Irish gardens and gardening before Cromwell', 97–144.   **11** T.C. Barnard, 'Gardening, diet and "Improvement" in later seventeenth-century Ireland', *Journal of Garden History*, 10 (1990), 71–85. For discussion of plants cultivated in Ireland before 1800, see E.C. Nelson, '"This garden to adorne with all varietie" – the garden plants of Ireland in the centuries before 1700', *Moorea*, 9 (1990), 37–54.   **12** Keith Lamb and Patrick Bowe, *A history of gardening in Ireland* (Dublin, 1995).   **13** Knight of Glin and Patrick Bowe (eds), *Gardens of outstanding historic interest in the Republic of Ireland* (Dublin, n.d.); Northern Ireland Heritage Gardens Committee (eds), *Northern garden. Gardens and parks of outstanding historic interest in Northern Ireland* (Belfast, [1982]); Belinda Jupp, *Heritage gardens inventory* (Belfast, 1992); Belinda Jupp, 'Sources for the Heritage Gardens Inventory of Northern Ireland' in Terence Reeves-Smith and Richard Oram (eds), *Avenues to the past. Essays presented to Sir Charles Brett on his 75th year* (Belfast, 2003), pp 197–212. See Terence Reeves-Smith, 'Published sources for Irish garden history research', and Thomas MacErlean, 'The archaeology of parks and gardens, 1600–1900', for references to reports about individual gardens and demesnes.   **14** E.g. E.M. McCracken, 'Nurseries and seedshops in Ireland' in E.C. Nelson and Aidan Brady (eds), *Irish gardening and horticulture* (Dublin, 1979), pp 179–90; E.C. Nelson, *A heritage of beauty:*

O'Sullivan Beare had left Ireland in 1602. As Nelson notes, the botanical section of his text was therefore a work written from memory, and what we might now call crowd-sourced information from other exiled colleagues. The 'Zoilomastix' is thus a useful reminder of the impact of colonization on the study of botany in early modern Ireland. It is a reminder in two ways, for the circumstances of its production were a direct result of the colonial process underway in Ireland; and, at the same time, O'Sullivan Beare's motivation in writing the entire text was to refute colonial perceptions of Ireland, most notably Gerald of Wales' famous and oft-repeated *Topographica Hiberniae*.[15]

Botanical research in early modern Ireland was directly affected by and reflected the uneasy political status of the country. Two important vectors of botanical investigation on the continent, universities and the press, while not absent in early seventeenth-century Ireland, were focused on colonial concerns rather than exploration of the native flora. Trinity College, Dublin (TCD), founded in 1592 by Elizabeth I (1533–1603), was a university designed to foster colonization and concentrated (at least until the 1660s) on the provision of teaching in the faculties of arts and theology, in an endeavour to strengthen the reformation in Ireland, while at the same time provide a skilled bureaucracy for the colonial administration.[16] True, the early seventeenth-century members of TCD purchased a handful of botanical works (mainly herbals), but these were few in number and there was hardly any botanical teaching on the campus during the first half of the seventeenth century.[17] The wars of the 1640s and 1650s did little to aid botanical research and even in the later seventeenth century, botany was considered to be of far less interest to members of TCD than mathematics, astronomy, physics or chemistry.[18]

Equally the press in Ireland was far more restricted that its English counterpart which had been producing herbals since the sixteenth century.[19] For much of the seventeenth century in Ireland there was little press competition and the King's Printer concentrated on the provision of state proclamations and theological texts necessary for disputations with Roman Catholics.[20] In fact, during the early

---

the garden plants of Ireland. An illustrated encyclopaedia (Dublin, 2000).   **15** In the 'Zoilomastix' (of which the botanical section forms just one part), O'Sullivan Beare not only took aim at Giraldus Cambrensis (*c.*1146–*c.*1223), but also at a late sixteenth-century reworking of the *Topographia* by Richard Stanihurst (1547–1618): Hiram Morgan, 'O'Sullivan Beare, Philip (1590–1636), writer, soldier, and exile', *DIB*. **16** Elizabethanne Boran, 'Perceptions of the Role of Trinity College, Dublin, from 1592 to 1641' in Andrea Romano (ed.), *Università in Europa. Le istituzioni universitarie dal Medio Evo ai nostro giorni; strutture, organizzazione, funzionamento* (Messina, 1995), pp 257–66.   **17** James Ussher (1581–1656), a major figure in the history of TCD in the first half of the seventeenth century, references nearly all the major authors of sixteenth-century herbals in a list of recommended authors: TCD, MS 790, fo. 37r lists Otto Brunfels (1488–1534), Leonard Fuchs (1501–66), Rembert Dodoens (1571–85) and Pietro Andrea Mattioli (1501–77).   **18** On this point see Elizabethanne Boran, 'Science in Trinity College Dublin in the seventeenth century' in Anna Marie Roos and Gideon Manning (eds), *Collected wisdom of the early modern scholar: essays in honor of Mordechai Feingold* (Forthcoming 2022, Springer).   **19** On botanical printing in England see Leah Knight, *Of books and botany in early modern England: sixteenth-century plants and print culture* (Aldershot, 2009). See also Sarah Neville, *Early modern herbals and the book trade: English stationers and the commodification of botany* (Cambridge, 2022).   **20** On the history of printing in early

seventeenth century it was known as 'the Protestant Press' and Roman Catholics looked to the Continent to publish their works, again concentrating on religious debate.[21] Clearly in seventeenth-century Ireland botany was not regarded by printers as a subject that would attract a large readership and the economic costs involved in producing highly illustrated botanical works were not attractive to Irish printers.

The first section of this volume reflects this intertwining of colonization and botanical research in seventeenth-century Ireland in a number of ways. O'Sullivan Beare's 'Zoilomastix' is, to date, one of the few instances of a native Irish author commenting on botany in Ireland in the first half of the seventeenth century. As chapter 2 makes clear, the principal commentators on botany in mid- to late-seventeenth-century Ireland were English botanists, clergymen such as Richard Heaton (1601–66), who had travelled to Ireland and who communicated their findings to English colleagues such as William How (1620–56). The linkage between botanical research and colonization is particularly obvious in one of the few publications commenting on the natural history of Ireland – Gerard Boate's *Ireland's naturall history* (London, 1652). The epistle dedicatory (which was written by Samuel Hartlib (*c.*1600–62) who published the text after Gerard Boate's death in 1650) dedicated the work to Oliver Cromwell (1599–1658) and Charles Fleetwood (*c.*1618–92), while the title page proclaimed that the book was intended 'For the Common Good of *Ireland*, and more especially, for the benefit of the Adventurers and Planters theirin'.

Though the text included discussions of the bogs of Ireland, the focus was on how these might be reclaimed to encourage the Cromwellian plantation. As Mitchell pointed out, the text lacked botanical material.[22] However, as Gerard Boate's brother Arnold (who had in fact provided much of the material for the book) commented in his letter 'To the Reader', the published text was conceived as being but the first part of a much larger work:

> For to make it a compleat Naturall History, there should be joined to that which my Brother hath gone through, two Books more, the one of all kind of Plants, and the other of all sorts of living Creatures; which also might have been expected of him if God had given him longer life.[23]

Hartlib and Arnold Boate (1606–53) had hoped to rectify this deficiency, and Hartlib approached a number of colleagues based in Ireland in the 1650s to undertake research. However, as Toby Barnard has demonstrated, the deaths in quick succession of many of these men, coupled with the overly ambitious plans of the projectors,

---

modern Ireland see Mary Pollard, *Dublin's trade in books, 1550–1800* (Oxford, 1989); Tony Sweeney, *Ireland and the printed word* (Dublin, 1997); J.W. Phillips, *Printing & bookselling in Dublin 1670–1800* (Dublin, 1998) and T.C. Barnard, *Brought to book: print in Ireland, 1680–1784* (Dublin, 2017). **21** Elizabethanne Boran, 'Printing in early seventeenth-century Dublin: combating heresy in serpentine times' in Elizabethanne Boran and Crawford Gribben (eds), *Enforcing Reformation in Ireland and Scotland, 1550–1700* (Aldershot, 2006), pp 40–65. **22** Mitchell, 'Irish botany in the seventeenth century', 276, fn. 7. **23** Gerard Boate, *Irelands naturall history* (London, 1652), Sig. A6v.

meant that this plan never came to fruition.[24] Thus the plans of Hartlib and the Boate brothers, while they included botanical research within a raft of Baconian-inspired scientific projects, not only viewed botany through colonial lens but were, in the mid-century, defeated by the scope of their many interests.

Barnard has noted that many of the Hartlib's circle's plans had much in common with the later Dublin Philosophical Society, a sister society of the Royal Society, which was founded in Dublin in 1683 and whose first president was one of the 1650s projectors, Sir William Petty (1623–87).[25] Chapter 3 examines the botanical investigations of this group and, in particular, focuses on the work of Thomas Molyneux (1661–1733). Molyneux would later provide material for the first Irish flora, Caleb Threlkeld's *Synopsis stirpium Hibernicarum*, published in Dublin in 1726. This seminal work is the subject of the second section of volume, which explores Threlkeld's life and the influences on his *Synopsis*, as well as a detailed investigation of what his work can tell us of plant ecology in early eighteenth-century Dublin.

Threlkeld (1676–1728) was a committed botanist whose *Synopsis* was among the first botanical publications of the Dublin printing presses. As Máire Kennedy has demonstrated, the beginning of botanical printing in Ireland was ushered in by entrepreneurial printers who, particularly in the 1720s, began to use subscriptions to finance the publication of works, most of which had previously been printed in London.[26] As the third section of this volume indicates, these were not the only books available to Irish readers interested in botany – and in fact the libraries of clergymen such as Narcissus Marsh (1638–1713), archbishop of Armagh, and John Stearne (1660–1745), bishop of Clogher, and the Dublin physician Edward Worth (1676–1733), reflect the fact that most of their books on botany and gardening were imports from London and the continent. The 'paper gardens' available to such readers provide windows into the collecting activities of learned men in the early eighteenth century and their tastes in such matters as garden layout and design. Chapters 7, 8 and 9 investigate the motivations behind their collecting of works on botany and gardening. As chapter 7 relates, the botanical collection of Edward Worth, who, like Thomas Molyneux, received his medical education at the University of Leiden, was clearly influenced by the botanical explorations of the Dutch East India Company. This is a theme reflected in chapter 8 also, which explores the botanical collections of Marsh's Library, Dublin, the first public library in Ireland, and it is a theme unsurprisingly found in chapter 9 which explores the outstanding botanical collections of the Dutch Fagel dynasty, whose printed collections were purchased for Trinity College Dublin in 1802.

---

24 T.C. Barnard, 'Miles Smyner and the New Learning in seventeenth-century Ireland', *The Journal of the Royal Society of Antiquaries of Ireland*, 102: 2 (1972), 134.   25 T.C. Barnard, 'The Hartlib circle and the origins of the Dublin Philosophical Society', *Irish Historical Studies*, 19:73 (1974), 56–71, at 62. 26 Máire Kennedy, 'Botany in print: books and their readers in eighteenth-century Dublin', *Dublin Historical Record*, 68:2 (2015), 193–205. One of the earliest publications was a pamphlet by Samuel Waring, *A short treatise of firr-trees: containing plain and particular directions (with observations) for the planting and improving thereof* (Dublin, 1705). On this see E.C. Nelson, 'A short treatise of firr-trees …

As Boran argues, the possession of botanical books might not always indicated the presence of a keen gardener. Luckily we have other information on early modern gardening techniques, and the last section of this volume explores the factors influencing planting and garden design in different types of gardens in early modern Ireland. Chapter 10 investigates the institutional teaching garden of Trinity College Dublin, reconstructed from the unique eighteenth-century manuscript catalogue compiled by William Stephens (1696–1760). Chapter 11 brings to life the gentry gardens reflected through the lens of John K'Eogh's *Botanalogia* (Cork, 1735). Chapter 12 moves the focus away from plants to the other types of structures that adorned eighteenth- and nineteenth-century gardens – gothic-style ruins; while chapter 13 investigates the seed trade on which such gardens were dependent.

The final chapter moves away from the male-dominated history of botanical endeavour in seventeenth- and eighteenth-century Ireland to tell the story of one of the few known female gardeners who has left records, the indefatigable Ellen Hutchins (1785–1815), whose garden and gardening at Ballylickey House in Bantry, Co. Cork, may be re-imagined from her surviving correspondence. Her letters to other amateur and professional botanists remind us of the importance of scribal communication in the study of botany for botanical research in the early modern period was dependent on scholarly communication in the republic of letters.[27] As her correspondence, and those of earlier botanists such as Heaton and the members of the Dublin Philosophical Society demonstrate, letters might include not only information but also seeds.

Like many of her botanical antecedents she too created a portable reference collection of pressed and dried specimens of plants, some of which are now in the Herbarium of Trinity College Dublin. Such *horti sicci* (literally, dried gardens) preserved plant specimens and, at the same time, could be used in scholarly exchange networks to augment the words and pictures in printed books and the living plants in the gardens of correspondents. They could collect and store the dried specimens in ordered and documented collections called herbaria (singular, herbarium). They were no longer limited by ephemeral specimens but could preserve an invaluable record of the world's flora for future research.

Thus, words and pictures, books and libraries, gardens and herbaria, permeate the essays in this volume about botany and gardens in early modern Ireland. Together, these chapters demonstrate that Ireland, although situated on the periphery of Europe, was closely connected to neighbouring lands whether as a source of novel plants for gardens or novel ideas about the scientific study of plants.

E. CHARLES NELSON AND ELIZABETHANNE BORAN, 2022

(Dublin, 1705) by Samuel Waring', *Archives of Natural History*, 19:3 (1992), 305–6. **27** On the republic of letters see Howard Hotson and Thomas Wallnig (eds), *Reassembling the republic of letters in the digital age* (Göttingen, 2019).

CHAPTER ONE

Recollecting Ireland's flora: botanical information in the 'Zoilomastix' (*c*.1626) of Philip O'Sullivan Beare

E. CHARLES NELSON

WHILE WRITTEN, or at least commenced, around 1626, the 'Zoilomastix' of Philip O'Sullivan Beare (Pilib Ó Súilleabháin Bhéarra) was essentially unknown until the manuscript was brought to the attention of Irish scholars in 1932.[1] Since then parts of the 'Zoilomastix' has been transcribed, translated and published.[2] Although its existence was mentioned as early as 1629, the 'Zoilomastix' cannot have played any part in informing students of Irish history and natural history before the last half of the twentieth century.[3] From a botanical point of view, the 'Zoilomastix' is especially informative about indigenous vernacular names used in Ireland during the late 1500s and early 1600s.[4]

The manuscript comprising 370 folios is generally accepted as having been composed solely by Philip O'Sullivan Beare (*fl.* 1590–1636) while living in Spain.[5] Philip and other members of his extended family had been forced into exile in February 1602 following the battle of Kinsale when the Gaelic Irish clans and their Spanish allies were defeated by forces loyal to the English Queen Elizabeth (1533–1603). Philip was twelve years old when he arrived in Galicia. He was subsequently enrolled in the University of Santiago de Compostela, gaining a degree in canon law before he was expelled for opposing the takeover of the Irish College in Santiago by the Jesuits. Don Philip, as he is known, then served in the Spanish navy and remained in Spain for the rest of his life living variously in Madrid and Cadiz, dying before the end of 1636. Thus, the zoological, botanical and geological information in the 'Zoilomastix', a polemical work written to counter disparaging accounts of Ireland by Gerald de Barry (Giraldus Cambrensis) (*c*.1146–1223) and Richard Stanihurst (1547–1617) in particular, was not directly based on the author's own natural history observations as an informed adult residing in Ireland. Undoubtedly Don Philip's

---

1 The full name of the manuscript is 'Hiberni Vindiciae contra Giraldum Cambrensem et alios vel Zoilomastigis liber primus, 2, 3, 4 et 5 et contra Stanihurstum'. The shortened title 'Zoilomatix' will be used throughout this chapter.   2 T.J. O'Donnell (ed.), *Selections from the Zoilomastix* (Dublin, 1960); D.C. O'Sullivan (trans. and ed.), *The natural history of Ireland: included in book one of the Zoilomastix of Philip O'Sullivan Beare* (Cork, 2009).   3 Jorge Mendoza Afranca, 'In authorem laudis elegia' in Philip O'Sullivan Beare, *Patritiana decas* (Madrid, 1629), Sig. ¶¶3r.   4 For a list of most of the Irish names used by O'Sullivan Beare, see Tomás de Bhaldraithe, 'Appendix A. Irish names of birds, animals, fishes and

E. Charles Nelson

work contains fragments of his childhood experiences but these are unlikely to have been extensive in any sense and cannot be disentangled.

THE MANUSCRIPT

The structure of the botanical portion of the 'Zoilomastix' is simple and consistent (Fig. 1.1.).[6] Divided into six chapters, Don Philip's neatly inscribed text occupies a central column on each folio allowing wide margins into which he placed numbered, quadrilingual glosses giving the names for the principal plants. These glosses follow a set pattern with four names for each plant: Latin, Greek (usually but not always in Greek script), Spanish and Irish, in that order. Almost all the plants were provided with a name in each language. The neatness of the handwritten main text and numbered glosses suggests that the extant manuscript was at least a 'fair copy' although it could well have been the original script. Whatever its chronology, Don Philip certainly amended and corrected his work as there are innumerable insertions and deletions that often make the text difficult to read or comprehend.[7] Clearly, he annotated the 'Zoilomastix' after he had completed this manuscript – if it was a 'fair copy', it appears to have become the 'master copy', and no later 'fair copy' of the edited text is known. As well as amendments, he added material in the margins and between lines and paragraphs after the initial composition and sometimes he directed attention to these additions by abbreviated notes such as 'Vid. Annot'. The bulk of

minerals' in O'Donnell, *Selections*, pp xxxvii–liv. **5** Many older sources give inaccurate dates for Philip O'Sullivan Beare: for the most recent biographical summaries, see Toby Barnard, 'O'Sullivan Beare, Philip (*b. c.*1590, *d.* in or after 1634), historian and writer', *ODNB*, and Hiram Morgan, 'O'Sullivan Beare, Philip (1590–1636)', *DIB*. The foliation in MS H248 has also presented problems for the manuscript has two different pagination/foliation systems. What may well be the author's own pagination scheme is represented on the recto of each leaf, toward the lower left corner of the page, by a neat numeral written in black ink by a broader nibbed pen than that used for the text. This set of numerals is very clear and should not be confused with another set of numerals numbering the entries about each different plant. Thus, on the opening page of the botanical section the number 51 is written towards the lower left of the page (see Fig. 1.1). Modern foliation is represented by a number in pencil at the upper right edge of each page. To complicate foliation, MS H248 has two transposed folios, fos. 52 and 53, within the section about plants. Folio 53 should come *before* fo. 52, and this is clearly indicated by the catchwords 'generi' (fo. 51r), 'e flore' (fo. 51v), 'nux' (fo. 53r), 'Tilia' (fo. 53v); there are no catchwords on fos. 52r or 52v. Neither de Bhaldraithe nor Denis O'Sullivan recognized this. So, some of the sections of the text in O'Sullivan, *Natural history*, are out of sequence, particularly regarding trees. There are other flaws in O'Sullivan's transcription including text omissions and mis-readings that affect his translation. De Bhaldraithe and O'Sullivan used the modern (pencil) numbers but the fact folios are out of sequence mean that their treatment of the botanical text can be chaotic. The original broader ink numbers are here preferred. **6** My analysis is based on study of the original manuscript, as represented by a photographic reproduction of the photostat copy, made in 1932, now in the National Library of Ireland, Dublin. I am grateful to the National Library of Ireland for making this photocopy available in the 1980s. It was this copy that also provided Mary Brennan with the text that she translated, at my invitation, for me to use in E.C. Nelson and W.F. Walsh, *Trees of Ireland: native and naturalized* (Dublin, 1993). I have also consulted O'Donnell, *Selections* (especially Appendix A, edited by de Bhaldraithe), and O'Sullivan, *Natural history* (but see fn. 5). **7** Aubrey Gwynn, 'An unpublished work of Philip O'Sullivan Beare', *Analecta Hibernica*, 6

12

de Sbernie
boribg

C. ~~LXXVII~~.

Viuentia, quæ sensu carent.

Cuiusq́ naturas animantium, quæ
in Shernia locali motu agitantur, senti-
endiq́ vi pollent, enarrauimus. Alia viuentia, quæ animam quidem, non tamen
mouentem loco, vel sensitiuam, at nutri-
entem habent, dispersunt, ut arbores fru-
tices, herbæ. Quibus est ea indula copiosis-
sima.   Quamobrem singulorum vel no-
mina comprehendere longissimum & quæ
quam unius scriptoris opus fuisset. Ne
verò a tam uberi & amœno memora-
bilium rasforoso ieiuni egrediamur no
nihil dicere, putaui ab arboribg frugi-
feris auspicans.

Principio in Shernia ires, uinaq́ gigni
arbores frugiferas prisci scriptores memoriæ prodiderant.
nostra tamen tempestate illæ perquam
paucæ creantur. horum vero uberrimus est
prouentus, sed peregrè, ut ex Hispania
Gallia, & insulis fortunatis adueciarum.

Malg autem, siue pomus hic varia ma-
lorum genera producit, alia dulcia, alia
acria.

Pyri quoque pyra proferunt inde
dicta quod ad similitudinem flammæ
e lato in acumen tendant. utroum

generi.

*Die de labrusca.
i vite sylustri cp
Plin.l.14.c.15.*

C. ~~LXXVIII~~.

*Die de oliua quæ
est in Shernia seu
coepta. Vide orchas
in an: st.C*

g. funxis. 51

*Die de ficu quæ est
sata Pontana in
horto.*

Portis, q̄

L. Malg Pomus, g.
no.L. abhall
3 āuñes
L. Pyrus. g.
Peral. l. Peii.

1.1 First page, originally numbered '51', of the botanical section of 'Zoilomastix'.
© Uppsala University Library, H. 248, 41r.

the text on folios 53v, 52r and v and 54r clearly comprises a mixum-gatherum of extra information, mainly about plants, as on these folios the manuscript departs from the set structure of the main text and the handwriting is much less uniform.

Assessing how much of the text and glosses in the 'Zoilomastix' comprise original, indigenous information is often difficult, except in the case of the Irish vernacular names for animals and minerals as well as plants. As Tomás de Bhaldraithe pointed out not only is there no evidence in the 'Zoilomastix' that Don Philip availed of 'any written Irish source' but also he cannot have had 'literary training in the language'. In other words, O'Sullivan Beare spoke Irish, probably with a distinctive West Munster inflection, and the plant names that he and his associates used were written phonetically.[8] Besides, there were no published works about the natural history of Ireland available to him apart from scant, often inaccurate chapters in the books he disparaged by De Barry, Stanihurst and a few others, none of which included Irish names.

Don Philip occasionally acknowledged his sources for Latin or Spanish names, and undoubtedly used the same works for the Greek names. It is certain he had an excellent education that is very likely to have been conducted in Latin, and he was more than competent in composing Latin text. He must have learned Greek too and was able to write the names for plants using the Greek alphabet. Obviously, having come to Spain as a boy, he learned to speak and write Spanish, although there are no extensive passages in Spanish in the botanical part of the 'Zoilomastix'.

PHILIP O'SULLIVAN BEARE'S SOURCES

In common with his contemporaries, Don Philip availed of Pliny the Elder's (Gaius Plinius Secundus, AD 23–79) encyclopaedic *Naturalis historia* and frequently cited it by book and chapter – he certainly relied for zoological information on a translation by Jerónimo Gómez de la Huerta (1573–1643), published in Madrid in 1624.[9] Citations among the annotations added to the main text also indicate that he consulted at least one botanical work, the two-volume *Historia generalis plantarum* by the French botanist and physician Jacques Daléchamps (1513–88). Various Latin editions had been issued before 1625 as well as a French one that was published in Lyon in 1615 (Fig. 1.2). Don Philip also cited the Italian lexicographer Ambrogio Calepino (*c.*1440–1510); the edition of his *Dictionarium undecim linguarum* published in Basle (1627) contained information that Don Philip extracted – this may appear anachronistic but the annotations can date from any time during the last decade of O'Sullivan Beare's life after the original text of the 'Zoilomastix' had been written. Another book indicated by annotations in both the zoological and botanical chapters

(1934), 1–11. 8 de Bhaldraithe, 'Appendix A', p. xxxvii. 9 See, for example, 'Zoilomastix', chapter XXXVII, Pisces longi, marginal glosses no. 12, 15; O'Sullivan, *Natural history*, pp 174–5. Pliny the Elder, *Historia natural ... traduzida por ... Geronimo de Huerta ... Y ampliada por el mismo, con escolios y anotaciones, en que aclara lo oscuro y dudoso, y añade lo no sabido hasta estos tiempos* (Madrid, 1624–29?).

HISTOIRE
GENERALE
DES PLANTES,
CONTENANT XVIII. LIVRES
EGALEMENT DEPARTIS
EN DEVX TOMES:

Sortie Latine de la Bibliotheque de M. IAQVES DALECHAMPS, puis faite
Françoise par M. IEAN DES MOVLINS, Medecins
tres-fameux de leur Siecle.

OV SONT POVRTRAITES ET DESCRIPTES INFINIES PLANTES,
par les noms propres de diuerses Nations, leurs especes, forme, origine, saison, temperament
naturel, & vertus conuenables à la Medecine.

AVEC VN INDICE CONTENV AV COMMENCEMENT DV SECOND
Tome, tres-vtile & tres-necessaire pour monstrer les proprietez des Simples, & donner
guerison à toutes les parties du Corps humain.

ENSEMBLE LES TABLES DES NOMS EN DIVERSES LANGVES.

TOME PREMIER.

A LYON.
Chez les Heritiers Guillaume Rouille.
M. DCXV.

1.2 Jacques Daléchamps, *Histoire generale des plantes* (Lyon, 1615), title page. By permission of the Trustees of the Edward Worth Library, Dublin. © Edward Worth Library.

was the *Diccionario de romance en latin,* probably the Seville 1610 edition, by Elio Antonio de Nebrija (1444–1522) (Aelius Antonius Nebrissensis), a Spanish humanist and lexicographer. One of Don Philip's inserted notes was to remind himself to find other books by Nebrija. There is a single reference in the botanical section (an annotation about *Veratrum*) to Aulus Cornelius Celsus (*c.*25BC–*c.*AD50), the Roman author, quoted by Pliny, known for his encyclopaedia *De medicina.*[10]

PLANTS IN THE ZOILOMASTIX

The section of the 'Zoilomastix' headed 'Viventia quæ sense carent' (Living things that are devoid of feeling) that contains Don Philip's summary of the plants of Ireland is subdivided into six chapters as follows:

xliii: 'arbores frugiferae' (fruit-bearing trees) comprises eighteen plants.

xliv: 'Alliae arbores' (other trees 'which, although they do not bear fruits suitable for human consumption, nevertheless are very useful for many purposes') includes a further twelve plants.

xlv: 'frumenta' (grains) enumerates only three crop plants that yield grains (all Poaceae, in modern terminology).

xlvi: 'Legumina' (legumes) has four plants, all members of the pea and bean family (Leguminosae, in current botanical terminology).

xlvii: 'Herbae' (herbs) is a miscellany of forty-six plants useful for sustaining human beings.

xlviii: 'Flores' (flowers) originally had five entries.

Thus, in the original text of chapters forty-three to forty-eight, Don Philip specified eighty-eight plants (Table 1.2, pp 42–4) and he was explicit that this was just a selection that he hoped subsequent authors would extend. Through annotating his text, Don Philip added many more names. Some of the additions and annotations are essentially synonyms so it is difficult to compute the total number of different plants mentioned in the 'Zoilomastix'.

xliii arbores frugiferae: *Vitis, Malus pomus, Pyrus, Ficus, Prunus, Spinus, Cerasus, Cornus, Lentiscus, Arbutus, Fragum, Rubus, Rhamnus, Robur, Castanea, Pinus, Nux juglans, Corylus.*

It is notable that some of these 'arbores frugiferae' never grow as trees: *Vitis vinifera* (grape) and *Rubus* spp. (brambles) become woody so would be termed shrubs, while '*Fragum*' (*Fragaria vesca,* strawberry) is a diminutive short-lived perennial herb. On the other hand, most of the plants yield quantities of edible fruits: grapes, both sweet and sour apples, pears, plums, damsons and sloes, cherries, blackberries, walnuts and

---

10 O'Sullivan Beare was somewhat inconsistent in his abbreviations of authors' names, but most can easily be recognized. However, O'Sullivan, *Natural history,* often did not recognize these abbreviated names,

hazel nuts. Except perhaps in time of famine, acorns from native oaks (*Quercus robur* and *Q. petraea*) are unlikely to be used for human food because of their extreme bitterness, and under Irish conditions *Castanea sativa* (sweet chestnut) rarely produces edible seeds.[11] The seeds of *Pinus sylvestris* (Scots pine), the only native *Pinus* (pine) species, are insubstantial and not worth harvesting, unlike the edible 'pine nuts' of *P. pinea* (stone pine) that O'Sullivan Beare would have encountered in Spain. The inclusion of *Lentiscus* (lentisc or mastic; *Pistacia lentiscus*), which is not native and is very unlikely to have been cultivated in Ireland in the seventeenth century, is puzzling, as is *Rhamnus* (buckthorn) for different reasons. The fruits of *R. cathartica*, the native buckthorn, are poisonous; if eaten, they are violently purgative.

Concerning vines, Don Philip implied that these were not planted in Ireland as frequently as some authors had said, nor was wine produced in quantity. However, abundant wine was imported from Spain, France and the 'Fortunate Isles' (the Canary Islands). A few decades earlier, Peter Lombard (*c*.1554–1625), created archbishop of Armagh in 1601, had written in *De regno Hiberniae*, published in 1632, that when carefully cultivated in the south and west of Ireland vines yielded grapes that compared favourably with any produced in Germany and France.[12] The earliest reference to vines in Ireland was made by the Venerable Bede (673–735) who referred to the climate of Ireland being milder and more healthy than that of Britain, and noted that milk and honey were plentiful and that there was 'no lack of vines'.[13] However, changes in the climate, leading to the so-called Little Ice Age that was at its height after 1600 (about the time of Don Philip's exile), caused vineyards to vanish from the Irish landscape.[14]

Ficus carica (fig) likewise is not a native Irish species, although it thrives and fruits in Irish gardens and has occasionally been found as a self-sown casual. In one of his annotations, on the page before the numbered gloss, Don Philip stated 'dic de ficu quae est sata Pontanæ in horto': 'tell of the fig which is sown in a garden in Drogheda'.

Two more of the list of fruit-bearing trees are also not native plants – *Castanea* (sweet chestnut) and *Nux juglans* (*Juglans nigra*, walnut). O'Sullivan makes no comment about the walnut's presence, only that its seed is protected by an outer 'cup' and an inner woody shell. The walnut is likely to have been an early introduction into Irish gardens, possibly with continental monastic orders. *Castanea sativa* is more enigmatic, especially given Don Philip's statement that 'Castanea sunt in Ultonia sylvii apud Claūn ath bui': 'there are chestnut trees in the forest of Ulster at

---

and thus does not always expand the abbreviations. **11** See P.W. Jackson, *Ireland's generous nature. The past and present uses of wild plants in Ireland* (St Louis, Missouri, 2014). **12** Sheila Pim, 'The history of gardening in Ireland', chapter 4 in E.C. Nelson and Aidan Brady (eds), *Irish gardening and horticulture* (Dublin, 1979), pp 44–69, at p. 44; E.C. Nelson, '"This garden to adorne with all varietie" – the garden plants of Ireland in the centuries before 1700', *Moorea*, 9 (1990), 37–54. **13** Venerable Bede, *Historia ecclesiastica gentis Anglorum*, ed. Michael Lapidge, *Bede: Storia vi degli Inglesi*, 2 vols (Rome, 2010), I.1: 'Diues lactis ac mellis insula, nec uinearum expers, piscium uolucrumque, sed et ceruorum caprearumque uenatu insignis'. **14** E.C. Nelson et al., *The virtues of herbs of Master Jon Gardener* (Dublin, 2002), p. 99;

1.3 Map of Ireland published by Abraham Ortelius in *Theatrum orbis terrarum* (Antwerp, 1603). By permission of the Governors and Guardians of Marsh's Library. © Marsh's Library.

Clannaboy' (Clann Aodha Buí) by which he meant the territory of the O'Neill clan in north-east Ulster, a kingdom that came to an end with the flight of the earls in September 1607.

Illustrating the fact that Don Philip obtained information about parts of Ireland he is most unlikely to have known as a boy, the next plant enumerated is *Pinus* (pine).[15] 'Pinus non deest, maxime in Conkeinia sylva': 'there is no shortage of pine, especially in Glenconkeyne'. It is doubtful that the young O'Sullivan ever went to Glenconkeyne which is situated on the north-western shoulder of Lough Neagh (in the present county of Derry/Londonderry) (Fig. 1.3), more than 500 kilometres from his family home on Dursey Island in the far south-west of Ireland, so he must

E.C. Nelson, 'This garden to adorne', 39.   15 See also, for example, T.G. Ó Canann, 'Ó Domhnaill's inauguration according to Pilib Ó Súilleabháin Bhéarra', *Journal of the Royal Society of Antiquaries of Ireland*, 137 (2007), 101–16.   16 On Glenconkeyne, see, for example, E.M. McCracken, *Irish woods since*

have heard about this woodland from one of the exiles that had come from the north of Ireland. Famously, the dense, 'impenetrable' woodland of Glenconkeyne was the refuge of Hugh O'Neill (*c*.1550–1616), 2nd earl of Tyrone, and his men towards the end of the Nine Years War after they had abandoned and destroyed Dungannon in June 1602. Yet, Glenconkeyne was principally composed of oak with small quantities of ash and elm – pine was not one of its components according to standard accounts. The woodland was the principal source of timber for the building of Derry/ Londonderry by the English settlers.[16]

xliv **Alliae arbores**: *Fraxinus, Acer, Buxus, Populus alba, Laurus, Sambucus, 'Agrifolium', Tilia, Salix, Alnus, Arundo, Hedera*.

This rather random list of plants includes several more non-trees, notably the last two enumerated, *Arundo* (reed) and *Hedera* (ivy). Don Philip probably intended the spectacular giant reed of southern Europe, *Arundo donax*, but that does not grow wild in Ireland and is too frost-sensitive to be naturalized. His description does not match the native *Phragmites australis* (common reed) of riverbanks and lough shores because it is not woody. Otherwise, *Fraxinus excelsior* (ash), *Sambucus nigra* (elder), numerous *Salix* species (willow, sally) and *Alnus glutinosa* (alder) are accepted native plants, as is *Ilex aquifolium* ('*Agrifolium*', holly). Both *Acer pseudoplatanus* (sycamore) and *A. campestre* (field maple), as well as various *Tilia* species (lime) and their hybrids and poplars including *Populus alba* (white poplar) are regarded as introduced although their dates of introduction are not known, while the two evergreen shrubs, *Buxus sempervirens* (box) and *Laurus nobilis* (bay laurel), are only known from gardens. Regarding box, Don Philip commented that the dense wood sinks in water but does not decay, adding 'ex ea in Ibernia ~~rosariam~~, vel lapilli pecatoris fiebant': 'from it ~~rosary~~ or prayer beads were made in Ireland'.[17]

The final entry in the chapter about 'Alliae arbores', no. 30 *Hedera*, is lightly scored through but not heavily struck out, as if Don Philip was uncertain about its inclusion among 'Alliae arbores', perhaps because it was not a tree. Some pages later, in the chapter headed 'Herbae' (fo. 58r), an unnumbered quadrilingual gloss for *Hedera* was added apparently indicating a more appropriate position for ivy. The new gloss included a slightly revised sentence about ivy: 'Hedera cum se sustinere non possit murisque arboribus innixa surgit': 'Ivy, since it cannot support itself, climbs by leaning against walls and trees'.

xlv **frumenta**: *Triticum aestivum* (wheat), *Secale cereale* (rye), *Hordeum vulgare* (barley) and *Avena sativa* (oats) were and are common field crops in Ireland. They are not native plants but introduced either deliberately for food or, as in the case of rye ('Tipha') and oats, accidentally as weeds in other cereal crops. All four belong, according to current botanical classification, to the Poaceae (Graminae).

Tudor times. Distribution and exploitation (Newton Abbot, 1971); V.A. Hall, 'Woodlands of the Lower Bann valley in the seventeenth century: the documentary evidence', *Ulster Folklife*, 38 (1992), 1–11.   **17** The word 'rosariam' (rosary) is deleted in the manuscript.

xlvi Legumina: four legumes (Leguminosae) were enumerated alongside the original text and were named as *Faba*, *Phaseolus*, *Lens* and *Ervum*. *Faba* probably meant *Vicia faba* (broad bean), while *Lens* is likely to be *Lens culinaris* (lentil), but it is unwise to be dogmatic about the use of these Latin names; their modern, post-Linnaeus application may be different.

xlvii Herbae: forty-six 'herbs' were named in this chapter representing a selection of mainly useful plants ('in varios humanae vita usus utilissimas procreat'). It is notable that about half of the enumerated 'herbs' are not native to Ireland, although they may have become naturalized following introduction into cultivation. Their present-day uses include flavouring and seasoning food, and the same herbs had similar uses in the seventeenth century. Don Philip's roster contained *Rosmarinus* (rosemary), *Mentha* (mint), *Origanum* (marjoram), *Sinapis* (mustard) and *Thymus* (thyme).[18] He also noted numerous kitchen-garden denizens, edible vegetables and fodder plants for animals including grass in general ('*Gramen*') and *Trifolium repens* (white clover). Counted among the 'Herbae' were ferns ('*Filix*') without specifying individual species, as well as two organisms once classified as plants but now known to belong to separate kingdoms: no. 29 '*Fungus*', for which he gave the Irish name pucapeill (toadstool), and no. 42 seaweed ('Alga herba in aquis marinis nascens'). The culinary vegetables, all of which must have been cultivated, vary from *Pastinaca* (parsnip) and *Rapum rapulum* (turnip) to *Lactuca* (lettuce) and *Brassica* (cabbage), and several different cultivars of *Allium* that probably included onions ('*Caepa*'), leek ('*Porrum*') and garlic ('*Allium*'). Two different members of the squash family (Cucurbitaceae) also are enumerated, *Cucurbita* (pumpkin) and probably *Cucumis* (cucumber). Several of the listed plants would have provided fibres, particularly *Linum* (flax), *Cannabis* (hemp) and *Urtica* (nettle). Hops (then named *Lupulus*) were for brewing beer.

A number of the plants were esteemed for medicinal purposes – no. 36 is glossed with Latin *Veratrum* and Greek ἑλλέβορος (helleboros) as well as Spanish vedegambre, while the Irish name that was struck out is 'Meacabui' (meacan buí). That conflicting cocktail of names is not easy to equate with modern scientific nomenclature, although the 'true' *Veratrum* (Melianthaceae: *V. album* is commonly called white hellebore, and *V. niger* is known as black hellebore) was probably intended rather than a species of *Helleborus* (Ranunculaceae) which include *H. niger* (Christmas rose). The Irish name 'Meacabui' (meacan buí) that Don Philip also applied to *Daucus carota* (carrot; meacan dearg, cairéad) later was commonly used for an entirely different plant, yet one that has the same reputed purgative property as *Veratrum* ('insignem vim purgandi habet'). From the mid-1600s, makenboy, the Englished version of meacan buí, meant *Euphorbia hyberna* (Irish spurge) and it continued in use for it well into the nineteenth century. Today, the 'official' Irish name for

---

18 There are many similarities between Don Philip's list of herbs and that contained in the medieval poem 'The virtues of herbs'. The Loscombe manuscript (Wellcome Library, London, MS 406) contains a version of this written in south-eastern Ireland around 1300: see E.C. Nelson et al., *The virtues of herbs*.

1.4 Philip O'Sullivan Beare's 'seamrog' (*Trifolium repens*, white clover, seamair bhán). Watercolour by Bridget Flinn. © reproduced by permission, from E.C. Nelson, *Shamrock: botany and history of an Irish myth* (Aberystwyth and Kilkenny, 1991), plate 3.

E. hyberna is bainne caoin.[19] Although as a boy he could have been familiar with the spurge because it occurs in south-west Cork, Don Philip does not apparently include it in his enumeration.

Two other Irish names in this part of the 'Zoilomastix' are of special interest. No. 32 *Plantago* is glossed by 'cuach phadrig' (cuach phádraig, meaning Patrick's drinking vessel), today used as the vernacular name for *Plantago major*.[20] No. 26 *Trifolium*: 'hic abundat album florem producens': 'here it abounds, producing a white flower' (Fig. 1.4). Thus white-blossomed clover, unmistakably *Trifolium repens*, was known to Philip O'Sullivan Beare as 'seamrog' (shamrock).[21] He later added 'seámur' to the gloss.

xlviii Flores: the final botanical chapter, xlviii, contained only five entries for plants, the characteristics of which included attractive, sometime perfumed blossoms or scented foliage: *Rosa* (rose), *Lilium* (lily), *Viola* (violet), *Crocus* and chamomile that the Spaniards call manzanilla and the Greeks χαμαιμηλον (chamaimelon, meaning ground apple) because it smells of apples. Whereas there are numerous native species of both *Rosa* and *Viola* in Ireland, *Lilium* is only known as a garden plant – at that time probably only *Lilium candidum* (Madonna lily) would have been familiar. As for crocus, Don Philip explained that it was more commonly cultivated in former times in Ireland, but how he knew this is not explained. The crocus that was deliberately grown during the early seventeenth century in southern Europe was *Crocus sativus* (saffron) but it is not a native Irish plant.[22]

Concluding the description of Ireland's flora, Philip O'Sullivan Beare wrote:

> Quid referam plures flores. tot in Ibernia hortos, atque campos, ornat, ut, eorum nomina comp'hendere, longissimum fuisset. Unde de cadici posset:

> *Tot fuerant illic, quot habet natura colores*
> *Pictaque dissimili flora nitebat humus.*

Why refer to more flowers? So many embellish the gardens and fields of Ireland that a comprehensive list of their names would be very long, so he has missed out many. Besides, he explained, he was not a botanist so he could not provide a very exact account of Ireland's botanical riches.

ANNOTATIONS, AMENDMENTS AND ADDITIONS

It is clear from the innumerable additions and crossings-out that Don Philip returned to his 'Zoilomastix', perhaps on many occasions, to augment and amend the botanical

---

19 On makenboy – there are various different attempts at spelling this, see E.C. Nelson, 'Irish wild plants: before 1690' in this volume (p. 52). **20** D.M. Synnott, 'Folk-lore, legend and Irish plants', chapter 3 in Nelson and Brady (eds), *Irish gardening and horticulture*, at p. 42. **21** E.C. Nelson, *Shamrock: botany and history of an Irish myth* (Aberystwyth and Kilkenny, 1991), p. 17. **22** These are all plants long known to gardeners in Ireland: see E.C Nelson et al., *The virtues of herbs*.

1.5 *Cydonia oblonga*, 'Membrillo' in Spanish, quince in English: native in the Caucasus and Kurdistan, but long cultivated. Watercolour by Wendy F. Walsh, reproduced by permission of the executor of the estate of Wendy Felicité Walsh.

section at least. One frequent amendment was to replace the Greek plant names that were originally written in the Latin alphabet with the same names, or sometimes a different one, in the Greek alphabet. Also, he made notes to himself about doing more research and writing additional material, but he seems never to have achieved those aims. For example, on the first page (Fig. 1.1.), he inserted three short glosses commencing with the Latin phrase 'Dic de …' meaning 'What about …?': 'Dic de Labrusca'; 'Dic de Olivia quae est in Ibernia seri coepta'; 'dic de ficu quæ est sata Pontanæ in horto'. There is no extended gloss with additional information about the grape named Labrusca that was mentioned by Pliny. The second annotation, 'What about the olive that has begun to be planted in Ireland' – included the note 'Vide Orchas in annot^c.': 'See Orchas in the annotations'. This clearly refers to the series of random, usually one- or two-line notes written after the thirtieth entry (*Hedera*) of the chapter headed 'Alliae arbores' and extending over three pages (fos. 52r and v, 54r). Among these are lines about 'Orchas' referencing entries in Nebrija's *Diccionario* as well as reporting that olives were being planted in Thomond ('olivia in Iberniae est coepta serim Tomonia'). The third 'dic de' annotation referred to a fig tree that had been planted in a garden in Drogheda (Pontana). The few place names or records of plants in gardens are almost confined to these additions, suggesting that Don Philip inserted much of this information after he had spoken to fellow exiles who told him about plants they knew – for example, about the quince (membrillo in Spanish) that had borne fruit in John Burke's garden in Connacht where it had been planted by a doctor (Fig. 1.5). This is also the only instance of Don Philip giving an English plant name in the 'Zoilomastix': 'quince ex Anglo sermone'. Some of the added notes refer to plants that are unlikely to have been in Ireland in the early 1600s, including orange and lemon, both of which require greenhouse protection: he had no Irish names for these citrus fruits, only the Spanish ones – 'limon & naranja nascuntur in Ibernia'.[23]

Another recurring annotation was the insertion of new or different Irish names, or amending those used in the original draft. Sometimes these comprised nothing more than a name: 'Aitin francach', for example, is not explained nor does it have any synonyms although it is indubitably a name for one of the species of *Ulex* (gorse or furze), which genus was mentioned very briefly by Don Philip a few lines above where he wrote the inexplicable phrase 'Aitin vide erica': gorse see heather.

Regarding additions to his original text, there are only two extra quadrilingual entries but they are not numbered. Both are positioned in the left margin of the 'Herbae' section. A revised gloss, as previously mentioned, for the lightly cancelled gloss for no. 30 *Hedera* (ivy) was inserted here too, again without any number. The two additions were 'Lappa' (*Arctium* spp.) and 'Serratula' (*Stachys officinalis*). A major interpolation was written on the final page of the botanical section, before the chapter

---

23 Indoor cultivation of plants such as lemon or orange is most unlikely to have been practiced in Ireland until the late seventeenth century when the earliest orangeries were constructed: see E.C. Nelson, 'Some records (*c*.1690–1830) of greenhouses in Irish gardens', *Moorea*, 2 (1983), 21–8. See also E.C. Nelson, 'Gardening at Mitchelstown: John K'Eogh's *Botanalogia universalis Hibernica* (Cork, 1735)' in this volume, especially pp 235–6.

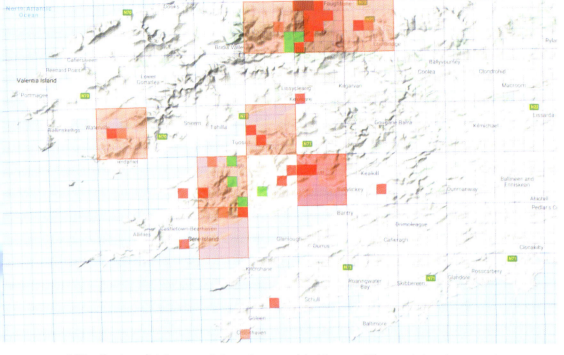

1.6 Distribution of *Arbutus unedo* (strawberry tree) in Munster. The map is based on records mainly collected by BSBI members and recorders and is reproduced with the permission of the Botanical Society of Britain and Ireland.

on salts. This concerned *Solaris herba* – solar herb or sunflower – and he questions whether this is what the Irish called 'Nonín', a daisy. Don Philip's text closely follows Daléchamps's, although the French botanist used 'Heliotropium' rather than 'Helioscopium' and referred not just to a relative of the daisy but also to another unrelated plant that is still known as heliotrope (*Heliotropium arborescens*).

***Arbutus unedo*, caithne, strawberry tree**: *Arbutus unedo* is unique among the plants enumerated by Philip O'Sullivan Beare because of its presence, yet very restricted distribution in Ireland in the general hinterland of his home (Fig. 1.6).

In the seventeenth and early eighteenth centuries, and earlier, only individuals who lived in those parts of south Munster where the tree grew are likely to have known any name for it and its fruits – and there were local variants. Most outsiders would have been completely ignorant not just about the plant's appearance and characteristics but also about its Irish name unless they were well-versed in the 'Laws of Neighbourhood' (Bretha Comaithchesa), an eight-century law tract that laid out penalties for damaging trees. Caithne, the strawberry tree, was named in this as one of the third-rank trees. The earliest report and description known of the strawberry tree in Munster occur in the survey of the Desmond forfeitures of 1584, particularly the lands around Killarney and islands in Lough Leane owned by Rory O'Donoghue Mór.[24]

That Don Philip knew not just a Latin, Greek and Spanish name for the plant he called 'caithni' is significant. However, he was not entirely confident as can be deduced from his crossing out of words. For example, he had originally included 'comaron' and 'memecylon' (in the Roman alphabet), names mentioned by Pliny, in the quadrilingual gloss, as well as 'madroño' and 'caithni' – respectively two Greek names with the Spanish and an Irish synonym – but scored out all of these, substituting only the first of the Greek names in Greek characters – χομαρος – plus subhcraobh (sú craobh), that is the current Irish vernacular name for the unrelated *Rubus idaeus* (raspberry).

Inexplicably, in the right-hand margin opposite the main numbered gloss for *Arbutus*, O'Sullivan Beare added 'Dic de caorrhann carrha vid. Lotos … Unedo madrono caithni [… illeg.] l. 3. lat. c.19'. It is not at all clear what this means especially the reference to 'Lotos' but the next three names are, respectively, Latin, Spanish and Irish names for the strawberry tree (*Arbutus unedo*) whereas caorthann curraigh is generally the name given to *Valeriana officinalis* (valerian).

Don Philip does not give any information about where *Arbutus unedo* grew in Ireland but there is every possibility he knew it from the small isolated stands that occur near the coast on the southern Iveragh Peninsula, or he may have been into the Macgillicuddy Reeks and seen it around Lough Leane (see Fig. 1.6). One mysterious annotation is the single line, unattached to any plant, 'Inis faithlinn insula in Leno Lacu': Innisfallen, an island in Lough Leane.

CONCLUSION

O'Sullivan Beare's 'Zoilomastix' was undoubtedly intended for publication, but it never reached the press and, as noted, remained unknown to Irish scholars until the early 1930s. As noted, its existence had been alluded to by Don Philip's Portuguese friend Jorge Mendoza Afranca who wrote the laudatory Latin verse that prefaced *Patritiana decas* published in 1629:

> Notitiâ variâ pulchrum, sermone politum,
> Zoilomastix & dicitur illud opus.[25]

> [That work adorned with diverse ideas and
> polished speech is called the 'Zoilomastix'.]

---

24 See, for example, E.C. Nelson and W.F. Walsh, *Trees of Ireland*, pp 86–94. 25 Jorge Mendoza Afranca, 'In authorem laudis elegia' in Philip O'Sullivan Beare, *Patritiana decas* (Madrid, 1629), Sig. ¶¶3r.

It was also referred to obliquely in *Cambrensis Eversus* by John Lynch (*c.*1599–*c.*1677), who wrote under the pen name of Gratianus Lucius.[26]

The manuscript of the 'Zoilomastix' was acquired, presumably after Don Philip's death, by the Marques de Astorga and was in his collections until 1690 when it was bought by the Swedish diplomat Johan Gabriel Sparwenfeldt (1655–1727), who had been sent to Madrid to look in Spanish archives for materials about the Goths and Visigoths. Thus the 'Zoilomastix' has resided for more than three centuries neither in Ireland nor Spain but in Sweden: it is manuscript H248 in the library of the University of Uppsala.[27] Irish scholars were alerted to it in January 1932 and shortly afterwards the Irish Manuscript Commission obtained a photostat copy, which was deposited in the National Library of Ireland. The 'Zoilomastix' was studied by Father Thomas Joseph O'Donnell (1906–83) who transcribed the Latin text for his masters' thesis. Subsequently extracts were published in 1960, with an appendix listing 'Irish names for birds, plants, animals, fishes and minerals' edited by Tomás de Bhaldraithe (1916–96). In 2009, for the first time an English translation by Dr Denis C. O'Sullivan (1928–2019) of those parts of Don Philip's 'Zoilomastix' dealing with natural history was published.[28]

A notable characteristic of Don Philip's text about plants is its entirely factual nature. There is nothing that can be termed 'folklore' apart from the wealth of names. He does not record medicinal properties nor the uses of plants in treating illnesses. This contrasts starkly with the earliest botanical works published in Ireland by Caleb Threlkeld (1676–1728) and John K'Eogh (*c.*1681–1754), written more than a century later.[29] Indeed, Don Philip is almost silent about the uses of the plants that he enumerated, with the exception of a few garden plants, and he makes no comments about the economic value of those plants.

While the natural history content of the 'Zoilomastix' is arguably the most interesting part of this polemical work, the plants, animals and minerals recorded by Philip O'Sullivan Beare are not, or were not necessarily Irish. It is a work done from memory – almost certainly more than one person's memory – and is not reliable in all its information. When specific place names were attached to his entries about plants, we may be more certain that the records were real: John Burke had a garden in Connacht and a quince bush grew in it! Another garden in Drogheda contained a fig. There were pine trees in the great woods of Glenconkeyne. These places are very unlikely to have been visited by Don Philip, so he must have relied on fellow exiles for these facts and, axiomatically, for correctly identifying the plants.

---

26 John Lynch, *Cambrensis Eversus* (St Malo?, 1662), cap. xxv, ii, 662. **27** I acknowledge the assistance of the staff of Uppsala Universitetsbibliotek in clarifying particulars of the botanical section of the Uppsala manuscript. **28** See fn. 5 for a discussion on the foliation of the manuscript. **29** Caleb Threlkeld's *Synopsis stirpium Hibernicarum* (Dublin, 1726) is explored elsewhere in this volume, as is John K'Eogh's *Botanalogia* (Cork, 1735).

42   E. Charles Nelson

Table 1.1. Concordance of foliation in the 'Zoilomastix'.

Original (broad ink)	Modern (pencil), [quoted by de Bhaldraithe and O'Sullivan]
51[r + 51v]	41[r + 41v]
53[r + 53v]	43[r + 43v] [*recte* 42]
52[r + 52v]	42[r + 42v] [*recte* 43]
54[r] verso blank	44[r] verso blank
55[r + 55v]	45[r + 45v]
56[r + 56v]	46[r + 46v]
57[r + 57v]	47[r + 47v]

At this point a folio has been excised but is represented by a narrow stub with text from the inner edge of the verso of the excised leaf (the text on the stud was rewritten and is on 59v).

58[r + 58v]	48[r + 48v]
59[r + 59v]	49[r + 49v]
60[r]	50[r]

Table 1.2. Plants named in the 'Zoilomastix'.

Original folio number	Latin name [numeral in ms]	Irish name	Modern scientific name (cv = cultivar)
xliii	arbores frugiferae		
51r	*Vitis* [1]	finuir	*Vitis vinifera*
51r	*Malus Pomus* [2]	abhall	*Malus* cultivars 'alia dulcia, alia acria'
51r	*Pyrus* [3]	peri	*Pyrus communis*
51v	*Ficus* [4]	figi	*Ficus carica*
51v	*Prunus spinus* [5]	droin	*Prunus spinosa* etc. 'alia acria, alia dulcia'
51v	*Spinus* [6]	[skeach]	*Crataegus monogyna*
51v	*Cerasus* [7]	selin	*Prunus cerasus*
51v	*Cornus* [8]	[carthin] carrhinn	? *Sorbus aucuparia*
51v	*Lentiscus* [9]	[freachain]	*Pistacia lenticus* [entry deleted]
51v	*Arbutus* [10]	[?] subh croabh	*Arbutus unedo*
51v	*fragum* [11]	sombh talbhuin	*Fragaria vesca*
51v	*Rubus* [12]	Dris	*Rubus fruticosa*
51v	*Rhamnus* [13]	spin [spineog]	? *Rhamnus alaternus*
53r	*Robur* [14]	daer	*Quercus* spp.
53r	*Castanea* [15]	castanna	*Castanea sativa*
53r	*Pinus* [16]	craunn rosin, giumhuis	*Pinus sylvestris*
53r	*Nux juglans* [17]	cno fhrancach	*Juglans nigra*
53v	*Corylus* [18]	Coll	*Corylus avellana*

Recollecting Ireland's flora

Table 1.2. Plants named in the 'Zoilomastix'. *(continued)*

Original folio number	Latin name [numeral in ms]	Irish name	Modern scientific name (cv = cultivar)
xliv	**Alliae arbores**		
53v	*Fraxinus* [19]	foin seoig	*Fraxinus excelsior*
53v	*Acer* [20]	fiorus	*? Euonymus europaeus*
53v	*Buxus* [21]	busc	*Buxus sempervirens*
53v	*Populus alba* [22]	crithir	*Populus tremula*
53v	*Laurus* [23]	lauruis	*Laurus nobilis*
53v	*Sambucus* [24]	troim & tromin	*Sambucus nigra*
53v	~~*Agrifolium*~~ [25]	Cuilinn	*Ilex aquifolium*
52r	*Tilia* [26]	limbhain & limh	*Tilia europaea*
52r	*Salix* [27]	saileach	*Salix* spp.
52r	*Alnus* [28]	fearnoig	*Alnus glutinosa*
52r	*Arundo* [29]	bearrach, goaleach	*Phragmites australis*
52r	*Hedera* [30]	faith helinn	*Hedera helix*
xlv	**frumenta**		
55r	*Triticum* [1]	crothneacht	*Triticum aestivum*
55r	*Tipha* [2]	[hordeum], siagail	*Secale cereale*
55r	*Hordeum* [3]	orna	*Hordeum vulgare*
	Avena [4]	coirke	*Avena sativa*
xlvi	**Legumina**		
55v	*Faba* [1]	poinri	*? Faba* spp.
55v	*Phaseolus* [2]	frisolas arvesa	
55v	*Lens* [3]	pisean	*? Lens culinaris*
55v	*Ervum* [4]		
xlvii	**Herbae**		
55v	*Linum* [1]	llin	*Linum usitatissimum*
55v	*Cannabis* [2]	cnaib	*Cannabis sativa*
55v	*Spartum* [3]		*? Spartium junceum*
55v	*Iuncus* [4]	luachair	*? Juncus* spp.
55v	*foeniculum* [5]	fineil	*Foeniculum vulgare*
55v	*cucumer cucumis* [6]		*? Cucumis*
56r	*Cucurbita* [7]	calabas pompin	*Cucurbita* spp.
56r	*Rapum rapulum* [8]	tornaps	*Brassica rapa*
56r	*Rhaphanus radix* [9]	rabuin	*Raphanus sativus*
56r	*Pastinaca* [10]	meaca dearg	*Pastinaca sativa*
56r	*Gingidium* [11]		*Daucus* sp.
56r	*Siser* [12]	caisearbhan	*? Sium sisarum*
56r	*Beta* [13]	biatas	*Beta vulgaris*
56r	*Caepa* [14]	innium	*Allium* cv
56r	*Porrum* [15]	linis	*Allium* cv
56v	*Allium* [16]	gairleog	*Allium* cv [cf. *Allium sativum*]

Table 1.2. Plants named in the 'Zoilomastix'. *(continued)*

Original folio number	Latin name [numeral in ms]	Irish name	Modern scientific name (cv = cultivar)
xlvii	**Herbae** *continued*		
56v	*Lactuca* [17]	leituis	*Lactuca* cv
56v	*Brassica* [18]	coil, cabsisti	*Brassica* cv
56v	*Nasturtium* [19]	Ribui riogas Biulta	*? Rorippa*
56v	*Origanum* [20]	origanum	*Origanum vulgare*
56v	*Mentha* [21]	miuntuis, mismin	*Mentha* spp.
57r	*Malva* [22]	Hocuis, leamhin	*? Malva sylvestris*
57r	*Carduus* [23]	hardechoc	*? Cirsium* spp.
57r	*Ruta* [24]	rut	*Ruta graveolens*
57r	*'radices longa'*	daith Duimhi. priamh gdhaithi	
57r	*Trifolium* [26]	seamrog, seamur	*Trifolium repens*
57r	*Thymus* [27]	tim, toim	*Thymus praecox*
57r	*Gramen* [28]	Irthinn	grass
57v	*fungus* [29]	pucapeill	fungus (toadstool)
57v	*Absinthium* [30]	mormotir	*Artemisia absinthium*
57v	*Artemisia* [31]	buachallan, Hansae, luis na fhbhainc	*? Tanacetum vulgare*
57v	*Plantago* [32]	cuach phadrig, Slan luis [?]	*Plantago* spp.
57v	*Buglossus* [33]	borraiste	*Borago officinalis*
57v	*Salvia* [34]	saiste	*Salvia* sp.
58r	*Hyssopus* [35]	hyssoip	*Hyssopus officinalis*
58r	*Veratrum* [36]	[~~Meaca bui~~]	*? Helleborus*
58r	*Rosmarinus* [37]	rosmarinum	*Salvia rosmarinus*
58r	*Sinapis* [38]	mostaird	*Sinapsis alba* or *Brassica nigra*
58r	*Acetaria* [39]	samhbha	*? Rumex acetosa*
58v	*Apium* [40]	persil	*? Petroselinum crispum*
58v	*Petroselinum* [41]	creiric	*? Crithmum maritimum*
58v	*Alga* [42]	raibh locha	*? algac*
58v	*Urtica* [43]	neantoig	*Urtica dioica*
58v	*Gladiolus* [44]	elistruim	*? Iris pseudacorus*
58v	*Filix* [45]	raithneach	ferns
58v	*Lupulus* [46]	hoip	*Humulus lupulus*
xlviii	**Flores**		
59r	*Rosa* [1]	ros, scearagdhis, ros muchoir	*Rosa canina*
59r	*Lilium* [2]	lil	*Lilium* sp.
59v	*Viola* [3]	sail chuach	*Viola* spp.
59v	*'humile malum'*	comain miull	*? Chamaemelum nobile*
59v	*Crocus* [5]	croich	*? Crocus sativus*

CHAPTER TWO

Irish wild plants before 1690

E. CHARLES NELSON

THE FIRST 'scientific' records of the native plants of Ireland can be traced to a few botanical tomes published in the seventeenth century.[1] None of these were written or printed in Ireland – the first indigenous published records of the native flora were contained in the Reverend Dr Caleb Threlkeld's pocketable book titled *Synopsis stirpium Hibernicarum*, published first in Dublin during October 1726.[2]

Wild and cultivated plants were often named in legal and literary works composed or compiled in Ireland before the production of printed books. Dr Christopher Moriarty estimated that the names of around fifty plants can be traced in Irish legal tracts, epic tales and poetry.[3] However, no matter how interesting these are they are not generally deemed adequate for scientific purposes given there is no certainty about the applications of vernacular and Latin names in early Christian and medieval times.

THE BOOKS

'Scientific' recording basically requires mention in a work that was primarily botanical in intent and content. While a name alone may suffice, usually the scientific record includes more information, at best with a place and date of collection or direct observation as well as the name of the person who found the plant.

John Parkinson (1567–1650) was a London apothecary, the 'Kings Herbarist', famous for his herbal with the punning title *Paradisi in sole paradisus terrestris* (it translates into English as 'Park in sun's earthly paradise'), issued in London in 1629.[4] His book containing reports of Irish plants – *Arbutus unedo* (strawberry tree) and

---

1 M.E. Mitchell, 'Irish botany in the seventeenth century', *Proceedings of the Royal Irish Academy*, 75 B 13 (1975), 275–84; E.C. Nelson, 'Records of the Irish flora published before 1726', *Bulletin of the Irish Biogeographical Society*, 3 (1979), 51–74.   2 See chapters in this volume and also Caleb Threlkeld, *The first Irish flora. Synopsis stirpium Hibernicarum*, ed. E.C. Nelson (facsimile with annotations by E.C. Nelson and D.M. Synnott) (Kilkenny, 1988); E.C. Nelson, 'The publication date of the first Irish flora, Caleb Threlkeld's *Synopsis stirpium Hibernicarum* 1726', *Glasra*, 2 (1978), 37–42.   3 Christopher Moriarty, 'The early naturalists' in J.W. Foster and H.C.G. Chesney (eds), *Nature in Ireland: a scientific and cultural history* (Dublin, 1997), pp 71–90, at p. 87. Christopher Moriarty, 'Plant references in translations from Irish etc.' (file: nhiplant.xls, not published).   4 John Parkinson, *Paradisus in sole paradisi terrestris* (London, 1629).

45

THEATRUM BO-
TANICVM:
THE
THEATER OF PLANTS.
OR,
AN HERBALL OF
A
LARGE EXTENT:

Containing therein a more ample and
exact History and declaration of the Physicall Herbs
and Plants that are in other Authours, encreased by the accesse of
many hundreds of new, rare, and strange Plants from all the parts of
the world, with sundry Gummes and other Physicall materials, than hath beene hitherto published by any before ; And
a most large demonstration of their Natures and Vertues.

Shewing vvithall the many errors, differences, and
oversights of sundry Authors that have formerly written of
them ; and a certaine confidence, or most probable con-
jecture of the true and genuine Herbes
and Plants.

Distributed into sundry Classes or Tribes, for the
more easie knowledge of the many Herbes of one nature
and property, with the chiefe notes of D^r. Lobel, D^r. Bonham;
and others inserted therein.

Collected by the many yeares travaile, industry, and experience in this
subject, by *John Parkinson* Apothecary of *London*, and the
Kings Herbarist.

And Published by the Kings Majestyes especiall priviledge.

LONDON,
Printed by *Tho. Cotes.* 1640.

2.1 John Parkinson, *Theatrum botanicum: the theater of plants* (London, 1640), title page. By permission of the Trustees of the Edward Worth Library, Dublin. © Edward Worth Library.

Irish wild plants before 1690

Drosera anglica (great sundew) – is his later, more monumental *Theatrum botanicum: the theater of plants* published in London in 1640 (Fig. 2.1). *Theatrum botanicum* is profusely illustrated and comprises more than 1,750 pages. The book was described by the author himself as a 'Manlike Worke of Herbes and Plants'.[5] Parkinson's portrait adorns the allegorical title page that includes four female figures representing the four then-known continents, each one surrounded by suitable plants.

In stark contrast to John Parkinson's lavish herbal is the anonymous, pocket-sized *Phytologia Britannica* of 1650, also published in London.[6] This has been reliably attributed to William How (1620–56), an English physician. Criticized as 'very hasty and defective' and lacking illustrations, How's *Phytologia* nonetheless contains numerous new records of the flora of these islands.[7] The Irish ones are mostly, if not entirely, based on plants observed by the Reverend Richard Heaton (1601–66), a Yorkshire man, graduate of the University of Cambridge and one-time Anglican rector of Birr in Co. Offaly.[8]

THE PLANTS

Arbutus unedo, caithne, strawberry tree

> The Strawberry tree with dented leaves … in *Ireland*, where they have beene found growing of their owne accord … hath beene of late dayes found in the West part of *Ireland*, of a reasonable bigge sise for a tree … it hath come to us from *Ireland*, by the name of Cane Apple, with a great judgement and reason as many other vulgar names are.[9]

John Parkinson's published account was not the first reliable report of *Arbutus unedo* (Fig. 2.2) from western Ireland, but the earlier ones were contained in such manuscripts as an inquisition of the estates of Rory O'Donohoe about 1584 that were not published until many decades later.[10] Other manuscripts report that sapling strawberry trees were exported from Co. Kerry in the late 1580s for cultivation in English gardens.[11] 'Cane Apple' was not a real English name but an attempt to render the Irish phrase *úlla caithne* (literally apples of *Arbutus* – that is *caithne*) in English, but Parkinson clearly misunderstood its significance. According to William Petty's *Political anatomy of Ireland*, published in 1691 but written two decades earlier, 'the *Arbutus*-Tree groweth in great numbers and beauty … in that part of *Kerry* call'd *Desmond*'.[12]

---

5 John Parkinson, *Theatrum botanicum: the theatre of plants* (London, 1640), epistle dedicatory.   6 William How, *Phytologia Britannica* (London, 1650).   7 C.E. Raven, *English naturalists from Neckam to Ray: a study of the making of the modern world* (Cambridge, 1947), p. 299.   8 Laurence Walsh, *Richard Heaton of Ballyskenagh 1601–1666: first Irish botanist* (Roscrea, 1978). This biography is not faultless; see E.C. Nelson, '[Review of] L. Walsh: *Richard Heaton of Ballyskenagh, 1601–1666*', *The Naturalist*, 105 (1980), 162–3.   9 Parkinson, *Theatrum botanicum*, pp 1489–91.   10 *Arbutus unedo* is mentioned by Philip O'Sullivan Beare in his unpublished 'Zoilomastix' (*c.*1626). See my chapter in this volume.   11 E.C. Nelson and W.F. Walsh, *Trees of Ireland* (Dublin, 1993), pp 89–94.   12 William Petty, *The political anatomy of Ireland* (London, 1691), p. 111. Thomas Molyneux made a similar observation, presumably independently, in his communication to the Royal Society of London (see Kelly, chapter 3: p. 76 in this volume).

2.2 *Arbutus unedo*, caithne, strawberry tree: confined to Cos. Cork, Kerry and Sligo. © E. Charles Nelson.

Drosera anglica, cailís Mhuire mhór, great sundew

> *Ros Solis sylvestris longifolius*. Long leafed Rosa solis. This was sent me by M[r]. *Zanche Silliard* an Apothecarie of *Dublin* in *Ireland*.[13]

Thus wrote John Parkinson, so the great sundew (Fig. 2.3) must have been found in Ireland before 1640. A decade later William How quoted Richard Heaton: 'Plentifully on a Bogge by *Edenderry*. … I gave some of the Plant to *Zanchie Sylliard*, *Apoth*[ecary]. of *Dublin*, which he sent to Mr. *Parkinson*, who in his description mentions the said *Zanchie* as if he had found it'.[14] In 1726 Caleb Threlkeld repeated that the great sundew grew 'Plentifully on a Bogg by *Edenderry*'.[15]

---

13 Parkinson, *Theatrum botanicum*, p. 1053.   14 How, *Phytologia Britannica*, p. 105.   15 Caleb Threlkeld, *Synopsis stirpium Hibernicarum* (Dublin, 1726), Sig. I4v.

Irish wild plants before 1690

2.3 *Drosera anglica*, cailís Mhuire mhór, great sundew: frequent in suitable habitats particularly in north and west. © V. Macartney.

Sankey Silliard (or Zanche, or Sullyard) was apothecary general to the army in Ireland. In 1629 he was one of the sheriffs of the city of Dublin, and in June 1649 he succeeded Thomas Pemberton who had died, as mayor of Dublin.[16]

Dryas octopetala, leaithín, mountain avens

> Teucrium Alpinum Cisti flore. *Alpine Germander with a Cistus flower*: In the mountaines betwixt *Gort* and *Galloway*. It makes a pretty shew in the Winter with his rough heads like *Viorna*. Mr. *Heaton*.[17]

There can be no doubt that Richard Heaton visited south-western Co. Galway and Co. Clare. He found juniper (see below) at Kilmacduagh, the ancient ecclesiastical

---

16 James Ware, *The antiquities and history of Ireland* (Dublin, 1705), p. 171; Walter Harris, *The history and antiquities of the city of Dublin* (Dublin, 1766), p. 506.   17 How, *Phytologia Britannica*, p. 120.

2.4 *Dryas octopetala*, leaithín, mountain avens: restricted to widely scattered habitats in west and north, always on limestone. © E. Charles Nelson.

site situated on the eastern edge of the Burren. Throughout the Burren, mountain avens (Fig. 2.4) are abundant, carpeting substantial areas. In early summer their white flowers are spectacular, and these are soon succeeded by fluffy heads composed of plumed fruits that do indeed look like those of 'Viorna', an old name used for species of *Clematis*, especially *C. vitalba* (traveller's joy, or old man's beard). Heaton's other discovery between Gort and Galway was spring gentian (see below), a species that often accompanies mountain avens and juniper in the Burren.

Epipactis helleborine, ealabairín, broad-leaved helleborine

> Helleborine flore atro rubente. *Park*[*inson*]. *Wild white Hellebore with dark red flowers*: found by *Lysnegeragh*. Mr. *Heaton*.[18]

Lysnegeragh is indubitably the townland of Lisnageeragh, Lios na gCaorach, in Co. Offaly, a short distance north-west of the town of Roscrea. Heaton purchased

---

18 Ibid., p. 57.

2.5 *Epipactis helleborine*, ealabairín, broad-leaved helleborine: especially in west and north in woods and scrub. Photo © John Fogarty.

property in the adjacent townland Baile Sceanach (Ballyskenagh) that is now known in English as Mountheaton.[19] There are wooded areas within these townlands so Heaton's finding of this orchid is consistent with what we know of its ecology although there are no modern observations for *Epipactis helleborine* (Fig. 2.5) within the hinterland of Lisnageeragh.

In the past this record was interpreted as *Epipactis atrorubens*, a species entirely confined in Ireland to the limestones of Cos. Clare and Galway.[20] It is indeed possible that Heaton saw that species during a journey through the Burren, although it is not usually in bloom when spring gentians and mountain avens are in full flower.

19 Walsh, *Richard Heaton*, pp 97–8. 20 For example, Walsh, *Richard Heaton*, p. 59, fn. 26; Nelson, 'Records of the Irish flora', p. 63; E.C. Nelson and Brendan Sayers, *Orchids of Glasnevin: an illustrated history of orchids in Ireland's National Botanic Gardens* (Dublin, 2002), pp 85–6; David Pearman, *The discovery of the native flora of Britain and Ireland* (Bristol, 2017), p. 188.

2.6 *Euphorbia hyberna*, bainne caoin, Irish spurge: abundant in west Cork and Kerry, very rare elsewhere. © E. Charles Nelson.

Euphorbia hyberna, bainne caoin, Irish spurge

Tithymalus Hibernicus.[21]

William How was the first botanist to list '*Tithymalus Hibernicus*'. Whether he coined this Latin name or obtained it from someone else is impossible to tell and he did not indicate a source. However, information about the plant evidently was circulating in learned circles in Britain during the mid-1600s for Samuel Hartlib (*c.*1600–62), a Polish polymath who had settled in England, spelling the name 'Maccamboy', asked for information about it in his *An interrogatory relating more particularly to the husbandry and naturall history of Ireland* issued in 1652: 'Whether there be such a thing at all, that this herb should purge the body meerly by external touch, or whether it be a fable, what particular observations have been taken for or against it, the shape of the herb, and in what place it groweth?'[22]

By 1658, 'Tith[ymalus]. hibernus tuberosus sive Makimboy, *Irish knotty rooted sp[urge]*.*' was cultivated in the botanic garden at the University of Oxford, presumably having been brought over from Ireland. The asterisk after its name

---

21 How, *Phytologia Britannica*, p. 121. 22 [Samuel Hartlib], *An interrogatory relating more particularly to the husbandry and naturall history of Ireland* in *Samuel Hartlib, his legacie* (London, 1652), Sig. S3v.

indicated that it was one of the 'non descripts', defined as a plant that had not been found 'upon our best enquiry' in the work of any other botanical author.[23] Thus, the identification of 'Makimboy' or 'Makenboy' (as it was rendered by Dr Christopher Merrett (1614–95) in 1667) as *Euphorbia hyberna* (Fig. 2.6) should be credited to Dr Philip Stephens (*c.*1620–79) and the Reverend William Browne (1629/30–78), compilers of *Catalogus horti botanici Oxoniensis* of 1658.[24] The first person to provide in print a definite locality for Irish spurge was William Petty (1623–87), in 1691: 'there are vast quantities in that part of *Kerry* call'd *Desmond*, where the *Arbutus*-Tree groweth in great numbers and beauty'.[25] *Meacan buí* is the modern form of this Irish name, meaning yellow root.

Gentiana verna, ceadharlach Bealtaine, spring gentian

> Gentianella Alpina verna. *Alpes Felwort of the spring time*. In the Mountaines betwixt *Gort* and *Galloway*, abundantly. Mr. *Heaton*.[26]

We can be certain, given how relatively inconspicuous spring gentian (Fig. 2.7) is when not in bloom, that Richard Heaton was in the mountains 'betwixt' Galway and Gort – in other words the Burren – at least once between late April and early June,

2.7 *Gentiana verna*, ceadharlach Bealtaine, spring gentian: abundant only in Clare, infrequent in adjacent parts of Galway into Mayo. Éire €10 stamp – illustration by Susan Sex, from the Wild flowers of Ireland definitive stamp series. Reproduced by kind permission of An Post ©

23 Philip Stephens and William Browne, *Catalogus horti botanici Oxoniensis* (Oxford, 1658), p. 178. 24 Christopher Merrett, *Pinax rerum naturalium Britannicarum* (London, 1667), p. 118. 25 Petty, *Political anatomy*, p. 111. As P.H. Kelly's paper on the Molyneux brothers and the Dublin Philosophical Society in this volume makes clear (p. 73), this plant was also discussed by its members. 26 How, *Phytologia Britannica*, p. 46.

2.8 *Juniperus communis*, aiteal, juniper: mainly in west and north in rocky or heathy places. © E. Charles Nelson.

2.9 *Pyrola rotundifolia*, glasluibh chruinn, round-leaved wintergreen; eastern counties, bogs, fens. Heaton may have collected a different species. © Zoë Devlin. www.wildflowersofireland.com

which period is its only flowering time. We do not know how often he visited the area, including Kilmacduagh, but he may have done so annually on parochial business for as well as being rector of Birr, Heaton was also prebendary of Iniscattery. That island parish situated at the mouth of the River Shannon was then at least three days' journey from Ballyskenagh.

Juniperus communis, aiteal, juniper

> Iuniperus repens. *Creeping Iuniper:* Upon the Rocks neer *Kilmadough*. Mr. *Heaton*.[27]

Shrubs of juniper (Fig. 2.8), both prostrate and upright, occur throughout the eastern Burren. Female plants are often laden with glaucous fleshy fruits, for although *Juniperus* belongs to the Cupressaceae (cypress family) its cones are fleshy and oily rather then woody. They are the principal 'botanical' in gin! Heaton stipulated Kilmacduagh as the place where he found juniper; it is close to Gort on the eastern boundary of the Burren.

Pyrola minor, glasluibh bheag, common wintergreen

> Pyrola vulgaris. ... *Winter Green*. It growes ... also in a Bogge, by *Roscre* in the *Kings County*. Mr. *Heaton*.[28]

The wintergreens are not particularly conspicuous plants even when in bloom and so are easy to overlook. They are also not abundant in Ireland and moreover are somewhat tricky to identify – fresh flowers are essential so that the length of the style can be measured. As no specimen collected by Richard Heaton is known to be extant, equating How's name with a current scientific name is at best a guess. However, some quite recent discoveries of *Pyrola* populations near Roscrea strongly suggests that Heaton found *Pyrola minor* and not *P. rotundifolia* (Fig. 2.9) as had hitherto be presumed.[29] It is noteworthy that when the Roscrea plants were first reported they were named *P. media*.[30]

Rubus saxatilis, sú na mban mín, stone bramble

> Soon-a-man-meene: In English, The *juyce of a faire Woman*: In a Wood neer Eddenderry. I referred it to the *Rubus Saxatilis*, But the berries of this Plant were yellow. Mr. *Heaton*.[31]

---

27 Ibid., p. 64.   **28** Ibid., p. 100.   **29** Nathaniel Colgan and R.W. Scully, *Contributions towards a Cybele Hibernica*, 2nd edition Dublin, 1898 were emphatic (p. 227): 'Though the record for the King's Co. station given by How has never been verified, there can be little doubt that the plants gathered was *P. rotundifolia*'. The authors of the previous edition listed How's record under *Pyrola minor*: David Moore and A.G. More, *Contributions towards a Cybele Hibernica* (Dublin, 1866), p. 187.   **30** T.G.F. Curtis, R.A. Fitzgerald and J. Green, '*Pyrola media* Sw. in North Tipperary (H10): the sequel to an old botanical puzzle', *Irish Naturalists Journal*, 24 (1993), 332–5; Aideen Austen, Fiona Devery and D.W. Nash, '*Pyrola minor* L. in Offaly (H18) and North Tipperary (H10)', *Irish Naturalists Journal*, 27 (2002), 143–5.   **31** How, *Phytologia Britannica*, p. 116.

2.10 *Rubus saxatilis*, sú na mban mín, stone bramble: rocky places, as its scientific name indicates, and sand dunes, throughout Ireland. © E. Charles Nelson.

2.11 *Scilla verna*, sciolla earraigh, spring squill: only on eastern and northern coasts, in rocky or sandy habitats. © Pat Lenihan.

Su na mban mín (Fig. 2.10), the Irish name recorded phonetically by Richard Heaton, remains the name for this diminutive bramble. It has not been recorded recently from the vicinity of Edenderry, but Heaton could have seen it in the Burren where it is relatively common and is particularly conspicuous when the ripe fruits are bright ruby red. The comment in How's *Phytologia Britannica* that 'the berries ... were yellow' is enigmatic – none of the native *Rubus* have yellow fruits.

Scilla verna, sciolla earraigh, spring squill

> Hyacinthus stellarius vernus pumilus. *Lob[el]. The small spring starred Hyacinth*: At the Rings-end neere *Dublin*. Mr. *Heaton*.[32]

The spring squill is a native plant but has not survived at Ringsend, unsurprising given the intensive urbanization of the area – it had vanished by 1904. However, it does continue to flourish on the Dublin coast to the south of the River Liffey at Dalkey Island and at Coliemore. To the north of the Liffey estuary there are populations on Howth Head, Lambay Island and Ireland's Eye.[33] The species' range extends northwards along the coast, disjunctly, through Cos. Louth, Down and Antrim into Derry/Londonderry.[34] In Heaton's day, Ringsend was a narrow peninsula projecting into the estuary of the River Liffey and separated from the city of Dublin by the River Dodder. It was where ships from Britain would dock to disembark passengers. A bridge over the Dodder linked Ringsend directly to Dublin in 1640.

* * *

The Reverend Richard Heaton is likely to have made his observations of the Irish flora before 1641 when he seems to have departed and returned to Britain.[35] Half a century elapsed before there was any enlargement of published inventory of the Irish flora. The individuals who botanized in the last decade of the seventeenth century left a materially different set of records – they pressed samples of the plants and created herbarium specimens so the identity of each extant example can be determined beyond doubt.

---

32 Ibid., pp 60–1.   **33** Nathaniel Colgan, *Flora of the County Dublin* (Dublin, 1904), p. [xix]; Declan Doogue et al., *Flora of County Dublin* (Dublin, 1998), pp 27, 425.   **34** Paul Hackney (ed.), *Stewart and Corry's flora of the north-east of Ireland*, 3rd edition (Belfast, 1992), p. 323.   **35** Walsh, *Richard Heaton*, p. 61.

CHAPTER THREE

The Molyneux brothers, the New Science, and the Dublin Philosophical Society in the late seventeenth century

PATRICK KELLY

THE FIRST IRISH FLORA, Caleb Threlkeld's *Synopsis stirpium Hibernicarum* (Dublin, 1726), covers a wider range of topics than would be found in such a list today. As its title page proclaims, it is at once 'A Short Treatise of Native plants, especially such as grow spontaneously in the Vicinity of Dublin; with their *Latin*, *English* and *Irish* Names: And an Abridgment of their Vertues, With Several new Discoverys'. In addition, it included 'An Appendix: Containing, The Names and Observations on such Plants as grow spontaneously in *Ireland*, Communicated chiefly by that eminent *Botanist* Dr. *Thomas Molyneux*, Physician to the State'. The latter comprises observations of plants Molyneux had made twenty-six years prior to the publication.[1]

Molyneux (1661–1733) was influential not only because of his position as 'Physician to the State' but also, and perhaps even more importantly, as a result of his involvement in the Dublin Philosophical Society. The society had been founded in 1683 by his brother, William Molyneux (1656–98), and both the Molyneux brothers had played leading roles in developing it as an important focus for inquiry into nature.

---

1 Caleb Threlkeld, *Synopsis stirpium Hibernicarum* (Dublin, 1726), Sigs. M1r and Preface (Sig. c3r). Little seems to be known of Threlkeld's association with the elderly Thomas Molyneux beyond the statement in the preface of *Synopsis stirpium Hibernicarum* that the communication of the Observations 'came too late to be inserted in the Body of the Book': Sig. c3r. Threlkeld went on to say that such of Molyneux's plants as he (Threlkeld) had not described in his own text were included in an appendix so 'that he [Thomas Molyneux] may have the Praise due to his Merit.' At the beginning of the appendix (Sig. M1r) he mentions that the names and observations of the plants had been communicated 'chiefly' by Molyneux, suggesting that others had also provided material. Molyneux identified several informants in the text of the appendix: 'Mr Sherard' on Antrim plants (p. 1); 'Mr Bennet Apothecary at Athy' for 'Hemlock Dropwort' (p.7); and 'Captain Stewart', 4 May 1696, for 'Muscus erectus ramosus saturate viridis' (p. 16). He also draws comparisons with how the same plant grew in England, commenting on whether it was larger/smaller; fruiting/flowering later/earlier, etc. On the topic of botany in Ireland in the later seventeenth century see M.E. Mitchell, 'Irish botany in the seventeenth century', *Proceedings of the Royal Irish Academy*, 75 B 13 (1975), 275–84; E.C. Nelson, 'Records of the Irish flora published before 1726', *Bulletin of the Irish Biogeographical Society*, 3 (1979), 51–74 and E.C. Nelson's chapter 2 in this volume (pp 45–57). A facsimile of the 1727 Dublin issue is available: Caleb Threlkeld, *The first Irish flora. Synopsis stirpium Hibernicarum*, ed. E.C. Nelson (facsimile with annotations by E.C. Nelson and D.M. Synnott)

It had ceased to function, even in its final etoliated form of 1707–8, well before before Threlkeld first arrived in Dublin in 1713, but elements of its afterlife are visible in Threlkeld's text. Threlkeld's reminiscence that 'During the Summer Months [he] used to perambulate in Company of ingenious Men, both of the Clergy and Laity, to have ocular Demonstration of the Plants themselves in their native Soil' is reminiscent of the collaborative nature of much of the work of the society and it seems likely the 'Ingenious Communicator' Molyneux may have been one of those 'Ingenious Men' in whose company Threlkeld had botanized in Dublin. Equally, an indirect reference to the Dublin Philosophical Society and its achievements may perhaps lie behind the concluding exhortation in Threlkeld's preface to 'Let the polite World know, that Arts and Sciences flourish here [in Ireland], and are encouraged, as much as in any other Parts of Europe'.[2]

THE NEW SCIENCE

Scant though these links are, they pose the question who 'that worthy antiquary and Naturalist' Thomas Molyneux was and what was the nature of the society that had caused 'the Arts and Sciences [to] flourish here, as much as in any other Parts of Europe'.[3] The Dublin Philosophical Society is claimed by Theodore Hoppen to have been a fairly typical manifestation of a phenomenon particularly characteristic of the seventeenth century, namely the scientific society or grouping dedicated to the promotion of useful knowledge, obtained through collaborative observation and experiment, that emerged in different states in Europe as far apart as Berlin and Dublin, Stockholm and Naples.[4] Though many of these societies were short-lived and depended on the enthusiasm and commitment of single individuals, or members of a single family, others had a wider membership and proved more enduring, surviving in the case of the Royal Society of London to the present day, with ever-increasing distinction. Although in most instances, the ideal of advancing scientific knowledge through collaborative effort in jointly undertaken experiments proved at best aspirational, the achievements of the more distinguished members of these societies working initially in isolation, reported and publicized through the vehicle of the societies, conferred well-merited lustre on them – the outstanding, early example being the connection between the Royal Society of London and Isaac Newton's work on the composition of light.[5] Indeed, the most significant practical impact of such

(Kilkenny, 1988). **2** Threlkeld, *Synopsis*, Preface, Sig. c3r and v. **3** Ibid., Sig. c3r. **4** On the Dublin Philosophical Society see K.T. Hoppen, *The common scientist in the seventeenth century: a study of the Dublin Philosophical Society, 1683–1708* (London, 1970) and his wonderful edition of the *Papers of the Dublin Philosophical Society, 1683–1709* (Dublin, 2008). See also Martha Ornstein, *The role of scientific societies in the seventeenth century* (rev. edn, Chicago, 1938). Though it is well over a century since this pioneering work first appeared in 1917, no comparable overall survey has yet replaced it. **5** H.W. Turnbull (ed.), *The correspondence of Isaac Newton, volume 1, 1661–1675* (Cambridge, 1959), pp 92–102, and further A.I. Sabra, *Theories of light from Descartes to Newton* (Cambridge, 1981), chapters ix–xi.

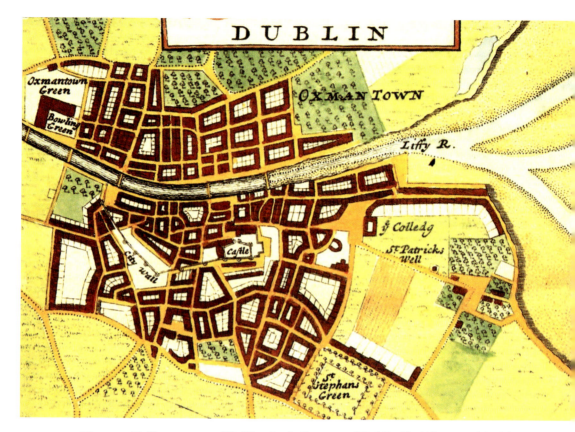

3.1 Hermann Moll's 1714 map of Dublin, detail. Courtesy of Dublin City Library and Archive.

societies was probably their role in publicizing new scientific ideas, and in the cases of the Royal Society and the French Académie des Sciences establishing runs of serial publications making otherwise obscure discoveries easily available internationally, as in the case of those of the Dutch microscopist Antonie van Leeuwenhoek (1632–1723).[6]

As one would expect, the fortunes of individual societies were much influenced by conditions in the places where they were established, and the evolution of the Dublin Philosophical Society certainly reflected the society of late Restoration Dublin. Despite the devastation of the wars of the 1640s and upheaval of the 1650s, late Restoration Dublin was a surprisingly thriving and confident society.[7] The second city (Fig. 3.1) in the three Stuart kingdoms in terms of population with some 30,000 inhabitants in the early 1660s, rising to well over 60,000 by the mid-1680s, it possessed a university, which, if its formal curriculum was still rather old-fashioned

---

[6] Hand-indexed runs of both journals were included in the 1730 Molyneux family library sale: Patrick Kelly, 'The one that got away, or almost: the Molyneux family library and Trinity College, Dublin' in *The Old Library, Trinity College, Dublin 1712–2012*, ed. W.E. Vaughan (Dublin, 2013), p. 96. [7] As observed by William Molyneux to John Flamsteed, 8 April 1684: E.G. Forbes et al. (eds), *The correspondence of*

(though probably no more so than contemporary Oxford or Cambridge), contained a number of individuals (including three successive provosts) interested in the New Science, together with a student body whose number of matriculations had doubled since 1660.[8] With its two cathedrals and numerous parishes, the city possessed a large Anglican clerical establishment, as well as a recently established College of Physicians, and other medical practitioners including apothecaries and surgeons; a range of mathematically based skills and professions, from the military establishment with its knowledge of fortification, military engineering and ballistics, through architects, surveyors, gaugers and excise officials to jewellers, spectacle-makers and clock-makers – though, as Thomas Molyneux's brother William complained, no skilled scientific instrument makers; printers and booksellers, as well as theatres, inns, taverns and coffee-houses – places of public resort where ideas were exchanged, and news disseminated.[9]

By comparison with England and even Scotland, the penetration of the New Science into seventeenth-century Ireland had been relatively slow; little beyond a few isolated instances predated the civil wars of the mid-century. Once the wars ended, however, the situation evolved comparatively rapidly. Cromwellian Ireland offered vast opportunities for what the seventeenth century characterized as reform – often along Baconian lines – as various groups competed for government backing, particularly the members of the London-based Hartlib circle embracing such substantial figures as William Petty (1623–87), Benjamin Worsley (1618–73) and for a short while even Robert Boyle (1627–91) himself. The survey of the whole country initiated by Worsley and completed by Petty in 1655 had been a remarkable achievement, particularly in its successful adaptation of surveying techniques to the capacity of private soldiers. The extent to which the Dublin Philosophical Society drew on these earlier 'scientific' interests and activities has been much disputed between Theo Hoppen and Toby Barnard, who asserted that Hoppen failed to give adequate credit to the influence and activities of the Hartlib circle (now much better known thanks to the exploitation of Hartlib's enormous archive at Sheffield University), though Hoppen was able to point out that these earlier manifestations of scientific interest were for the most part the work of transient visitors to Ireland, and lacked any institutional framework.[10]

Part of the difficulty in maintaining momentum in the scientific field after 1660 was political; paradoxically the would-be reformers of the 1650s had often been both too obscure and at the same time too openly identified with the Commonwealth regime to retain credibility after the Restoration, though a few prominent figures such

---

John Flamsteed, first Astronomer Royal, 3 vols (London, 1995–2001), ii, pp 155–8. 8 Cf. David Dickson, *Dublin: the making of a capital city* (London, 2014), pp 77–97 passim. 9 On lack of artificers, see Molyneux to John Flamsteed, 17 September 1681, cited in J.G. Simms, *William Molyneux of Dublin, 1656–1698*, ed. P.H. Kelly (Blackrock, 1982), p. 18. 10 Toby Barnard, 'The Hartlib circle and the origins of the Dublin Philosophical Society', *IHS*, 19 (1974–5), 56–70, and 'Myles Symner and the New Learning in seventeenth-century Ireland', *Journal of the Royal Society of Antiquaries in Ireland*, 102 (1972), 129–42. For Hoppen's rejoinder, see 'T.C. Barnard, 'The Hartlib circle and the Philosophical

as Petty and eventually Worsley managed to carve out new careers under the restored monarchy. Another problem in assessing the debt arose from the propagandist claims of the Dublin Philosophical Society itself. In keeping with the Baconian ideology projected by the Royal Society in London, Molyneux and his associates chose to represent the Dublin of their youth as an intellectual desert and the teaching at the university as a farrago of scholastic verbalizing, in contrast to the new learning based on observation and experiment and directed towards utility and the 'reliefe of man's estate'.[11] In the dedication to the Royal Society that prefaced his *Dioptrica nova* (London, 1692) William Molyneux called for educational reform to eradicate philosophic errors, in the way that the Reformation had dispelled errors in religion, an aspiration that he himself made good in 1692 by persuading his friend St George Ashe (1657–1718), by then provost of Trinity College Dublin, to place John Locke's *Essay concerning human understanding* (London, 1689) on the college curriculum.[12]

WILLIAM MOLYNEUX

The brothers William (Fig. 3.2) and Thomas Molyneux (Fig. 3.3) were among the most serious adherents of the New Science in later seventeenth-century Ireland, and William in particular played a crucial role in the establishment of an informal scientific society here in late 1683, which acquired a formal structure and fourteen original members the following January with rules and methods of procedure along the lines of the Royal Society of London – though there is a danger of exaggerating his importance and presenting the affair as a one-man band.[13] William was also responsible for the most distinguished publication to come out of the Dublin scientific milieu of the 1680s and 1690s, namely his *Dioptrica nova: a treatise of dioptricks, in two parts* of 1692. The first practical treatise on optics to appear in English, *Dioptrica nova* retained a dominant position in its field until the appearance of Robert Smith's *Optics* nearly half a century later in 1738 – though of course eclipsed on the theoretical front by Isaac Newton's *Optics* (1704).[14]

Almost as important as William Molyneux in establishing the Dublin Philosophical Society were his friend and college contemporary the Trinity fellow, St George Ashe (later bishop of Clogher), a man, as Hoppen says, perhaps more remarkable for the range of his scientific interests than for any specific scientific achievement; the physician Allen Mullen (1654–90), famous for his account of the

---

Society', *IHS*, 20 (1975–6), 40–8.   **11** Francis Bacon, *The advancement of learning* (London, 1605), Sig. G3v.   **12** William Molyneux, *Dioptrica nova* (London, 1692), dedication.   **13** Though generally referred to as 'The Dublin Philosophical Society', its proper designation was 'The Dublin Society for the Improving Naturall Knowledge, Mathematicks and Mechanics'. For the biographical details of the Molyneux brothers see *ODNB* and *DIB*; Simms, *William Molyneux*; Hoppen, *The common scientist* and *Papers of the Dublin Philosophical Society*.   **14** For an illuminating synopsis of *Dioptrica nova,* see entry for William Molyneux by James G. O'Hara in *ODNB*; Isaac Newton, *Opticks* (London, 1704); Robert Smith, *A compleat system of opticks* (Cambridge, 1738).

3.2 Portrait of William Molyneux (1698), attributed to Sir Godfrey Kneller, Bt.
© National Portrait Gallery, London.

dissection of an elephant in Dublin in 1681, published in London the following year; the well-known physician, Charles Willoughby (*c.*1630–94), possessor of a notable library; and finally the renowned Sir William Petty, former president of the Royal Society of London and first president of the Dublin body (once formally established). All these were – in varying degrees – serious inquirers into nature, and had in most cases established links with prominent scientific figures in England and further afield, links that would prove crucial in getting the Dublin group off the ground. Nonetheless the view that William Molyneux was the moving spirit behind the Dublin Philosophical Society enshrines an important measure of truth, and understanding the Society's fortunes requires consideration of the Molyneux family and how they came to engage so deeply with the New Science.

THE MOLYNEUX FAMILY

William and Thomas Molyneux were the fourth-generation of a family originally from Calais, who had come to Ireland in the 1570s under the patronage of Archbishop Adam Loftus (1533–1605). In the next generation, the Molyneuxs had married into the powerful Ussher family and were therefore kin to many prominent figures in Ireland's protestant elite. Samuel Molyneux the elder (1616–93), the father of Thomas and William, had trained as a lawyer but changed as a result of the wars of the 1640s to a military career, becoming chief gunner of Ireland, while his brother Adam was a military engineer (as had been their great uncle, an earlier Samuel Molyneux). Samuel subsequently developed a theoretical and experimental interest in ballistics and published an account of his artillery trials in 1681.[15] He also facilitated the family's scientific take-off through the acquisition of extensive landed estates in the 1660s that provided the money to build up a substantial library and collection of scientific instruments, and allow his sons to pursue studies not merely at Trinity College Dublin but also in London, and in Thomas's case Leiden as well. By the next generation the family's standing had sufficiently increased to permit William's son Samuel (1689–1728) to marry Elizabeth Capel, eldest daughter of Algernon Capel (1670–1710), second earl of Essex, a substantial heiress who subsequently inherited Kew House, the place where Samuel and his collaborator James Bradley (*d.* 1762), conducted their astronomical observations. Out of these came Bradley's discovery of the aberration of starlight and thus confirmation of stellar parallax, which at last provided physical corroboration of the Copernican theory.[16]

According to the autobiography that William drew up in 1694, the event that first turned his attention seriously to the New Science was a family tragedy. Shortly after their marriage in 1678 his wife, Lucy Domville (*d.* 1691), became blind; visits to

---

15 Samuel Molyneux, *Practical problems concerning the doctrine of project[ile]s, design'd for great artillery and mortarpieces* (Dublin, 1681).   16 See *Dictionary of scientific biography*, ed. C.C. Gillespie, 16 vols (New York, 1970–2); see also A.M. Clerke, 'Samuel Molyneux (1689–1728)', *ODNB*.

3.3 Sir Thomas Molyneux, Bt., F.R.S. by unknown artist. © Armagh County Museum.

oculists in England having proved futile, William applied himself to the study of vision and optics, a particularly active field of inquiry in the later seventeenth century. What, however, transformed him from an interested amateur – not very different to scores of similar figures across Europe – into a serious student of nature was the patient tutoring by correspondence that he received from the English Astronomer Royal, John Flamsteed (1646–1719).[17] This vital contact starting in 1681 was later supplemented by the help and encouragement of Edmund Halley (1656–1742), and both these mentors contributed generously to *Dioptrica nova*.

Quite how Thomas (Fig. 3.3) developed his interest in the New Science is not known. There would seem to be reason to think it was partially through the influence of William, though Thomas's choice of medicine as a profession was probably equally important. Seventeenth-century medicine with its emphasis on botany, anatomy and to a growing extent chemistry was a particularly fruitful field for scientific interest, and though Galenic influences would appear to have been strongly prevalent in what Thomas studied for his bachelor of medicine degree at Trinity College Dublin, they would not have excluded more recent ideas. Much of what is known of William's and Thomas's scientific interests in the 1680s, and the personal scientific contacts they made, comes from a tantalizing source, namely an account of Thomas Molyneux written by Sir William Wilde (1815–76), for *Dublin University Magazine*'s 'Gallery of Illustrious Irishmen' in 1841, that drew on surviving letters between the brothers.[18] And though Hoppen asserted these letters (and other family papers) no longer survive, I am not entirely convinced that this is the case.[19] Initially William sought to play the experienced elder sibling by instructing Thomas to keep a careful record of his travels with full details 'of such things as you would publish', stressing the importance of identifying 'such curiosities that may relate more particularly to *my* [i.e. William's] fancy', advice at which at Thomas rather bridled. As a younger brother, Thomas had to make his own way in the world, and subsequently did so with spectacular success becoming Ireland's first medical baronet, building a remarkable mansion in Great Peter Street, Dublin in 1711, and establishing notable collections of pictures and natural curiosities. The list of prominent men of science whom Thomas met in London on his way to further medical studies at Leiden in 1683 was impressive. It included Flamsteed; Boyle (whose conversation struck Thomas as as

---

17 See E.G. Forbes et al. (eds), *The correspondence of John Flamsteed*. A lasting breach occurred, however, on the publication of *Dioptrica*, when Flamsteed objected (with good reason) that Molyneux had failed to give proper credit to William Gascoigne (*d.* 1644) for key material that Flamsteed had passed on for inclusion in the book.   **18** [Sir William Wilde], 'Gallery of illustrious Irishmen, no.XIII: Sir Thomas Molyneux, Bart. M.D., F.R.S.', *Dublin University Magazine*, 18 (1841), 305–27, 470–90, 604–19, 744–64. **19** Despite the dispersal of the contents of the family house at Castle Dillon by auction in 1923, as recently as 2013 deeds relating to Castle Dillon and other Molyneux properties were acquired at auction by Maynooth University Library (now accessible as Molyneux archive (PP15), Special Collections, Maynooth University Library). In 1981, Mrs C.C. Molyneux (*d.* 1980) of Trewyn, Abergavenny, Wales, bequeathed the portrait of William Molyneux to the National Portrait Gallery, London; see further John Ingamells (ed.), *National Portrait Gallery: later Stuart portraits, 1685–1714* (London, 2009), and https://www.npg.org.uk/collections/search/portraitExtended/mw07687/William-Molyneux, accessed

convoluted as his writings); the botanist and physician Nehemiah Grew (1641–1712), and Theodore Haak (1605–90), founder of one of the scientific clubs of mid-1640s that fed into the Royal Society; as well as Sir William Petty; the pioneer geologist Thomas Burnet (*d.* 1715); the Royal Society's previous secretary, Robert Hooke (1635–1703); Isaac Newton (1643–1727); John Evelyn (1620–1706); and 'young Mr Haley the astronomer'. An important theme in the letters was the brothers' pride in their native city, and the satisfaction that they felt on discovering that the name of Dublin was now known in the world of learning in Amsterdam, as William wrote: 'Let the polite World know, that the Arts and Sciences are encouraged here [in Dublin], as much as in any other parts of Europe'[20] – a sentence that would, as we have seen, be echoed four decades later in Threlkeld's preface.

THE UNIVERSITY OF LEIDEN

In July 1683 Thomas crossed over to Holland together with St George Ashe, and after a brief tour of Dutch cities settled at Leiden (Fig. 3.4). In November Thomas provided an account of the university and of his studies there (which indirectly illuminates his earlier experience at Trinity College Dublin). Though reputed to be the 'worst university in the world', Leiden with its 150 students of medicine was, he recounted, 'one of the best societies in Europe' for physic. He warmly praised the botany professor Paul Hermann (1646–95), 'who in this part of learning is accounted as knowing as any man whatever, not even Dr Morrison himself to be excepted'.[21] And, though he criticized Dr Charles Drelincourt (1633–97), the professor of anatomy, as too 'addicted to the authority of the ancients', Thomas subsequently took his 'private college', that is the course delivered to small paying classes which medical professors provided for advanced students as a supplement to their public lectures.[22] By the end of December he had moved into lodgings in the house of Dr Christiaan Marggraf (1626–87), the professor of chemistry, with whom he had already taken an instructive private course.[23] Another letter shows Thomas already interested in a subject on which he would contribute to the third edition of Gerard Boate's *Natural history of Ireland* more than forty years later, namely that of 'Danish mounts' in Ireland. He reported a discussion with a Danish gentleman named Scheldorp, grandson of the great scholar Ole Worm (1588–1654), who rejected Thomas's claim that the 'Danish mounts' (that is, earthworks or tumuli Molyneux and his associates believed were associated with the Vikings) in Ireland were bigger than those in Denmark and that they served as burial mounds rather than watch-towers.[24]

1 March 2022. **20** Wilde, 'Gallery of illustrious Irishmen', 314; 314–20; and 485. As noted above, Threlkeld echoed these sentiments in his *Synopsis*, Preface, Sig. c3v. **21** The Scot Robert Morison (1620–83) was the first professor of botany at Oxford (1669), and compiler of the Morisonian herbarium – one of the most important early modern herbaria. See further *ODNB*. **22** Wilde, 'Gallery of illustrious Irishmen', 473. **23** Hermann and Margraf are identified in Kenneth Dewhurst, *John Locke (1632–1704) physician and philosopher: a medical biography* (London, 1963), p. 227. **24** Wilde, 'Gallery of illustrious

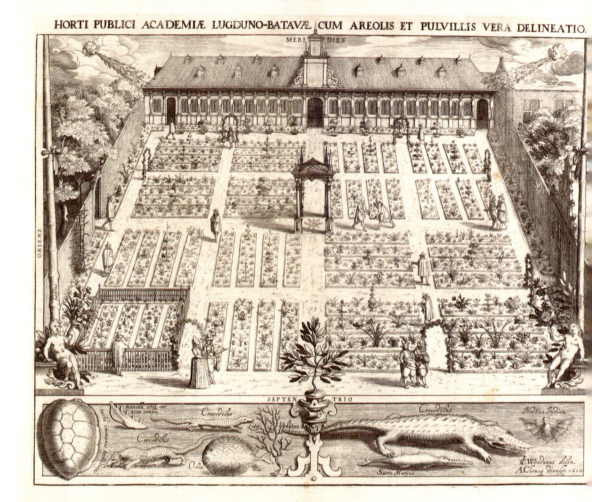

3.4 Hortus Botanicus Leiden in 1610. Print designed by Jan Cornelisz. Woudanus and engraved by Willem Isaacsz. van Swanenburg. By kind permission of the Rijksmuseum, Amsterdam.

While Thomas kept William abreast of his Leiden experiences, William provided occasional glimpses of the development of the Dublin Philosophical Society. Whatever about the need for modesty in more public pronouncements on his role in keeping the society going, William felt no such restraint in writing to Thomas. Before the society had got off the ground he had proposed that he and his brother-in-law, John Madden (1649–1703/4), the husband of their sister Mary, should visit Leiden the following summer, but in the spring of 1684 agreed with his brother that the

Irishmen', 483; Gerald Boate, *Natural history of Ireland* (Dublin, 1726), part III. On Gerard Boate see Robert Armstrong, 'Boate (De Boote, Boet, Bootius, Botius), Arnold (1606–53) and Gerard (1604–50)', *DIB*.

The Molyneux brothers

Dublin Philosophical Society would collapse if he left Dublin.[25] By 1685, however, William felt sufficient confidence in the society's capacity to survive without him to undertake a trip to the Continent, travelling this time in an official capacity to undertake a survey of European fortifications in his role as joint Surveyor General of the King's Buildings, a post recently acquired through the patronage of the viceroy, the duke of Ormonde.[26] Meeting up in Leiden in May, the brothers set off on a three-month journey that would bring them through the Netherlands, parts of present-day Germany and finally to Paris. What was notable was the number of distinguished scientists they made contact with *en route*, including Christiaan Huyghens (1629–95) at The Hague, Antonie van Leeuwenhoek in Delft, and the Bolognese astronomer Giovanni-Domenico Cassini (1625–1712), newly appointed head of the Paris observatory.[27] These encounters were not, however, just complimentary visits but involved serious exchanges of scientific ideas, as William's *Dioptrica nova* records several instances of practical information that he obtained in these meetings, such as Cassini's directions for grinding lenses.[28]

One acquaintance of Thomas's whom William did not encounter on his trip to Leiden was the English philosopher, John Locke (1632–1704), then in exile in Holland. At this point Locke was not yet the leading figure in the Republic of Letters that he would become through publishing his celebrated *Essay concerning human understanding* in 1689. When William sent him a copy of his newly published *Dioptrica nova* in June 1692, with its fulsome praise of the *Essay*, Locke responded with a letter of thanks that initiated the celebrated exchange of letters between them, that was such an important element in Molyneux's philosophic reputation in the eighteenth century. A postscript to Locke's first letter added that he had known

> … one of your name at Leyden, about seven or eight years since. If he be any relation of yours and now in Dublin, I beg the favour of you to present my humble service to him.[29]

The publication of their correspondence in *Some familiar letters between Mr. Locke and several of his friends* (London, 1708) revealed not only William but also Thomas as an intimate of the great man. Back in November 1684 Locke, who was not only a qualified physician but, as Peter Anstey has recently shown, also had a deep interest in botany, both practical and theoretical, had come to Leiden to meet members of the medical faculty. His most important contact there was Paul Hermann from whom he recorded extensive information about the flora of Ceylon, where the latter had resided

---

25 Wilde, 'Gallery of illustrious Irishmen', 471, 477 and 478. Madden, John (bap. 1649, *d.* 1703/4), physician and manuscript collector, *ODNB*. There are herbarium specimens associated with Madden in TCD: E.C. Nelson, 'A late seventeenth-century Irish herbarium in the library of Trinity College Dublin', *Irish Naturalists' Journal*, 20 (1981), 334–5.   26 Butler, James (1610–88), 1st duke of Ormonde, *DIB*.   27 Wilde, 'Gallery of illustrious Irishmen', 486–8; 476, 606.   28 For example, Molyneux, *Dioptrica nova* (London, 1692), pp 223–4.   29 *The correspondence of John Locke*, ed. Esmond de Beer (8 vols, Oxford, 1976– series incomplete, vol. viii published 1989, 2 vols forthcoming), letter no. 1515.

for several years.[30] Hermann may well have introduced Locke to Thomas Molyneux, who by then was acting more like an assistant to the professor than a mere student.[31] After he left Leiden, Locke wrote a brief letter to Thomas in December, thanking him for his company on a visit to Utrecht and asking him to inquire after some papers that Locke had left behind in Leiden, papers that were the kernel of his later *Thoughts on education*, a book that William would subsequently use as the model for bringing up his by-then-motherless son, Samuel. Thomas's becoming acquainted with Locke was, as he later acknowledged to him, 'among the most Fortunate Accidents of my Life' for it was thanks to this connection that the renowned physician, Thomas Sydenham (*d.* 1689), had accepted him as his medical clerk, when Thomas returned to further studies in London on leaving Leiden in 1686.[32]

THE DUBLIN PHILOSOPHICAL SOCIETY

A notable feature of the formally established Dublin Philosophical Society was the way in which it modelled its activities on the Royal Society of London in keeping regular minutes of its meetings, registers of letters sent and received by the society, lists of papers read, and in many cases the actual papers. Fortunately, a substantial part of this archive still survives and has been superbly edited for the Irish Manuscripts Commission by Hoppen.[33] In passing it may be noted that developments in the historiography of science in the half century since the publication of *The common scientist* have meant that Hoppen's 1970 monograph did not give what we would now consider adequate attention to certain aspects of the society's work, notably chemistry – a lacuna that has been made good by Susan Hemmen's important article, 'Crow's Nest, and beyond' in the *Intellectual History Review* of 2015.[34] Accounts of the society's proceedings were sent regularly to both the parent body in London and a sister society established in 1683 at Oxford, thanks to the initiative of Robert Plot (1640–96). Despite going through a difficult period in its own history, the Royal Society of London proved remarkably supportive, and indeed without its encouragement the Dublin society might well have withered away after a few months, an outcome not dissimilar to the roughly contemporary, failed attempts to set up similar institutions in Edinburgh and Cambridge.[35] The link between London and Dublin was strengthened by the election of the Molyneux brothers and St George

---

30 Kenneth Dewhurst, *John Locke physician* (London, 1963), pp 263–6; Peter Anstey, 'John Locke and botany', *Studies in History and Philosophy of Science Part C*, 37 (2006), 151–71. Locke's own herbarium survives as MS Locke d. 9 in the Bodleian Library, Oxford, with its plants mounted on paper recycled from themes (theses) written by his Oxford pupils in the early 1660s.   **31** For example, in sending a list of Hermann's collection of rarities to the Royal Society, as a flier for the detailed description that the latter was preparing for publication; see Thomas Molyneux to Theodore Haak, 24 November 1684; to Francis Aston, 29 December 1684, 16 March 1684/5: Hoppen (ed.), *Papers of the Dublin Philosophical Society*, ii, 524, 533, 550–3.   **32** *Locke corr.*, letters nos. 1515, 800, 1531.   **33** For bibliographical details, see n. 4 above.   **34** Susan Hemmens, 'Crow's Nest and beyond: chymistry and the Dublin Philosophical Society, 1683–1709', *Intellectual History Review*, 25 (2015), 59–80.   **35** Hoppen, *Common scientist*

Ashe to the Royal Society in February 1686, though the initiative in doing so had had to come from William himself rather than their London contacts.[36]

While the first informal meetings were held in rooms in a tavern, the formally constituted Dublin Philosophical Society soon acquired more permanent premises in Robert Crow's house off Dame Street, known as Crow's Nest, part of which was occupied by the apothecary Robert Witherall. Here the society established rooms for meetings, a library, a laboratory, and accumulated instruments and a cabinet of curiosities, even setting up a herb garden, and starting a herbarium.[37] While such facilities were very much the norm for later seventeenth-century scientific societies, they proved expensive to maintain, and the Dublin Philosophical Society's subscriptions were rather higher than those in London, while both societies struggled to survive without the benefit of official patronage such as had funded the Florentine Accademia del Cimento in the 1650s and 1660s or the Paris Académie des Sciences. What the Dublin Philosophical Society did not aspire to was its own journal, its more significant papers appearing in the long-established *Philosophical Transactions of the Royal Society*, which published material from across Britain, Ireland and continental Europe. The Dublin Philosophical Society did, however, make use of the services of the Dublin printer Joseph Ray (*d.* 1709), who would subsequently publish William Molyneux's celebrated political pamphlet *The case of Ireland's being bound by acts of parliament in England, stated* which appeared in 1698, the year after the second phase of the society's activities had come to an end.[38] William Molyneux, who in 1681 had published a translation of Descartes's *Meditationes de prima philosophia*, also assisted the society in making translations of important Italian mathematical texts, notably Galileo Galilei's *Discorsi e dimostrazioni matematiche intorno a due nuove scienze* (*Discourses on two new sciences*), which still survive in manuscript in the Pitt collection, Southampton.[39]

The total number of those involved with the Dublin Philosophical Society in its earliest and most scientifically productive phase from 1683 to 1687 amounted to about eighty people; some of these, however, only attended once, while others participated marginally without formally becoming members. The social range of the society was rather more homogenous than that of the London body, for the Dublin group never attracted the aristocratic and courtier membership (drawn in by an appetite for scientific toys rather than serious experimental interest) that had marked the early stages of the London society.[40] While Trinity graduates provided a large portion of

---

(London, 1970), pp 210–11.　**36** Cf. Michael Hunter, *The Royal Society and its fellows, 1660–1700: the morphology of an early scientific institution*, 2nd edition (Oxford, 1994), catalogue of members, nos. 428–30.　**37** Hemmens, 'Crow's Nest and beyond', 60. The premises had earlier served as the headquarters of Petty's Down Survey.　**38** For Ray, see Mary Pollard (ed.), *A dictionary of the members of the Dublin book trade, 1550–1800* (London, 2000), pp 479–82. See the critical edition by P.H. Kelly, *William Molyneux's The case of Ireland's being bound by acts of parliament in England, stated* (Dublin, 2018). **39** René Descartes, *Six metaphysical meditations wherein it is proved that there is a God*. Trans. from the Latin, together with a Preface by William Molyneux (London, 1680). For his translations from Italian, see Pitt collection, MS 14, Southampton Dept. of Archives, Southampton.　**40** See Hoppen, *Common scientist*, ch. 2 passim. The small number of aristocrats who did figure such as Hon. Francis Robartes, and

the Dublin Philosophical Society members, there was no formal link with the college (though some early meetings were held there in Provost Robert Huntington's lodgings). As was the case in Oxford, a considerably higher proportion of the Dublin Philosophical Society were members of the clergy than in London, and included many present and future bishops. The other significant professional grouping were physicians whose academic training had involved scientific disciplines such as anatomy, botany and chemistry. Dublin Philosophical Society members with medical backgrounds did not of course confine themselves to matters relating to their profession, many became interested in a variety of technologies, including in Petty's case transport in the form of various (unsuccessful) experiments with 'double-bottomed' boats, that is catamaran-type vessels.[41]

The Dublin Philosophical Society's most significant strictly scientific activities were in the field of astronomical observations and speculations in which William Molyneux was very much to the fore, though even from 1687, as he recounted in his autobiography, declining health forced him to give up night-time observations and sell off many of his larger instruments.[42] The 1694 autobiography listed various forms of instruments that he possessed (which were no doubt available to the society), having at one stage a thirty-foot telescope, microscopes, prisms, magic lanterns and pendulum clocks, as well as an extensive range of tools. A more detailed picture of the family's instruments emerges from the catalogue of the sale of the Molyneux family library in London in 1730 following the death of William's son, Samuel the younger (1689–1728).[43] Much of what is listed had probably been acquired by the latter, who was skilled enough to produce some of his own instruments, including a modified Newtonian reflector telescope, an example of which had been acquired by the king of Portugal in 1725, while both William and his father, the elder Samuel (1616–93), evinced a similar mechanical bent.[44]

BOTANY AND THE DUBLIN PHILOSOPHICAL SOCIETY

As Hoppen pointed out in his ground-breaking exploration of the Dublin Philosophical Society and its works, *The common scientist in the seventeenth century* (1970), botany was not a field to which the society made many significant contributions in its early period.[45] The first botanical exploration was a lengthy paper, read to the society on 10 March 1684 by Samuel Foley (1655–95), who recounted his experiments on *Vicia faba* (commonly known now as broad bean). As Foley himself made plain, these were based on the discussion of the 'great *Garden-Bean*' (Fig. 3.5)

the fourth and fifth Viscounts Mountjoy were serious virtuosi, Robartes serving as president in 1693–4: Hoppen (ed.), *Dublin Philosophical Society papers*, ii, biographical list of members.   **41** See further Hoppen (ed.), *Dublin Philosophical Society papers*, ii, pp 490–5.   **42** *An account of the family and descendants of Sir Thomas Molyneux, Kt., Chancellor of the Exchequer in Ireland to Queen Elizabeth* (privately printed, Evesham, 1820), p. 75. Several volumes of his astronomical observations were included in the 1730 family library sale.   **43** For details, see Kelly, 'The one that got away', pp 97–8.   **44** *Account of the family and descendants of Sir Thomas Molyneux*, p. 39.   **45** Hoppen (ed.), *The common scientist*, passim, esp. pp 141–2.

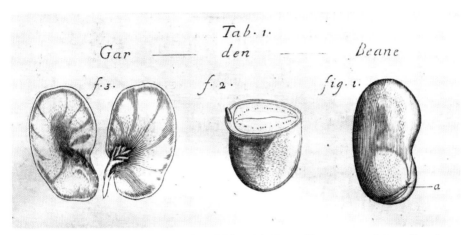

3.5 *Vicia faba* (broad bean); extract from Nehemiah Grew, *The anatomy of plants* (London, 1682), Book 1, tab. 1, figs 1–3. 'Gar–den–Beane'. By permission of the Trustees of the Edward Worth Library, Dublin. © Edward Worth Library.

in Nehemiah Grew's *The anatomy of plants* (London, 1682).[46] Using a microscope, Foley examined the broad bean before dissecting it to reveal the various layers beneath, for, as Foley observed, 'the way of discovering it is by dissection'.[47] As Mitchell noted, Foley's account was one of the first to discuss an experiment to demonstrate geotropism.[48]

A month later, on 22 April 1684, Thomas Molyneux wrote to a fellow physician and antiquary, William Musgrave (1655–1721), to comment on a report of the minutes of the Royal Society for their meeting on 26 March of that year. He noted that 'the Irish mackenboy is nothing but a *Tithymalus montanus Hibernicus* or mountain spurge' (now *Euphorbia hyberna*, Irish spurge), proximity to which was said to act as a purge.[49] Thomas related that hearsay evidence strongly suggested otherwise though noted that it would certainly act as a purgative if taken inwardly. His colleague Allen Mullen who, like Thomas, seems to have had a professional medical interest in botany, displayed an interest in the same plant three years later, this time debunking the spurious claim not by hearsay but with direct experience:

> Doctor Mullen tried lately an experiment upon the famous Irish herb called mackenboy or *Tithymalus Hybernicus*, which is by the natives reported to be so strong a purge that even the carrying it about one in their clothes is sufficient to produce the effect. This fabulous story, which has long prevailed, he proved false by carrying its root for 3 days in his pocket without any alternation of that sort.[50]

46 Nehemiah Grew, *The anatomy of plants* (London, 1682), Book 1, chapter 1, pp 1–10.   **47** Hoppen, (ed.), *Dublin Philosophical Society papers*, i, p. 169.   **48** Mitchell, 'Irish botany in the seventeenth century', 276.   **49** Hoppen, (ed.), *Dublin Philosophical Society papers*, ii, p. 493. *Euphorbia hyberna* is illustrated in chapter 2 in this volume.   **50** Ibid., ii, p. 649. Previously, on 23 March 1685, Allen Mullen had shared

It seems clear that Thomas was heavily influenced by the instruction he received at the University of Leiden from botanists such as Paul Hermann. Hermann had been made professor of botany at Leiden in 1679 and became the director of the university's botanic garden.[51] Writing to Theodore Haak in December of 1684, Thomas Molyneux reported that Hermann's 'Hortus Lydensi' was due to be finished in the following spring.[52] This was the first of a number of works by Hermann (many published posthumously). One of his most important creations was his herbarium.[53] It seems more than likely that Thomas Molyneux's decision to purchase a Dutch herbarium while at Leiden was guided by the teaching he received there from such a renowned botanist.[54]

The members of the Dublin Philosophical Society not only reported such individual findings to their fellow members, either in person or via correspondence; they also reported findings to the Royal Society. This traffic was two-way for they in turn learnt of new developments and discoveries from their sister society. This could be about new publications or just simply random experiments or gifts. An example of the latter was reported on 4 June 1685 by Francis Aston (1645–1715), who served as the Secretary of the Royal Society from 1681 to 1685. Writing to St George Ashe, Aston mentioned that Esprit Cabart de Villermont (1617–1707), a Fellow of the Royal Society, had recently presented it with 'a West Indian honeycomb, the cavities whereof were oval, a piece of West India cinnamon and clove bark, natural shagreen'.[55]

The ending of the first phase of the society's activities with the arrival of Tyrconnel (1630–91) as viceroy in February 1687 did not mean that individual Dublin Philosophical Society members abandoned their scientific pursuits; exile in Chester in 1689–90, for example, enabled William Molyneux to complete his *Dioptrica nova*,

---

another botanical experiment with his Irish colleagues when he reported that 'the root *Allium ursinum*, commonly called ramsons, being rubbed and pressed hard against one end of a small stick of cherry tree, apple tree, pear tree etc. newly cut off, makes the sap of the branch issue out of the other end of the stick, as if one end thereof had been put in the fire' (ibid., i, p. 54).   **51** On the influence of the University of Leiden on another Irish physician's botanical collecting see Elizabethanne Boran's chapter on Edward Worth in this volume (pp. 157–73). See also E.C. Nelson, 'The influence of Leiden on botany in Dublin in the early eighteenth century', *Huntia*, 4:2 (1982), 133–46.   **52** Hoppen, *Dublin Philosophical Society papers*, ii, 524. As Hoppen notes, Molyneux is undoubtedly referring to Hermann's *Horti Academici Lugduno-Batavi catalogus* (Leiden, 1687).   **53** Pieter Baas, 'The golden age of Dutch colonial botany and its impact on garden and herbarium collections' in Ib Friis and Henrik Balslev (eds), *Tropical plant collections: legacies from the past? Essential tools for the future?* (Copenhagen, 2017), pp 53–61. **54** Molyneux's *hortus siccus*, a herbarium compiled by Antoni Gaymans (*c.*1630–80), is now in the National Botanic Gardens, Glasnevin; see M.J.P. Scannell, 'A 17th century hortus siccus made in Leyden, the property of Thomas Molyneux, at DBN', *Irish Naturalists Journal*, 19 (1979), 320–1; E.C. Nelson, 'A contribution towards a catalogue of collectors in the foreign phanerogam section of the herbarium, National Botanic Gardens, Glasnevin (DBN)', *Glasra*, 4 (1980): 31–68; M.S.M. Sosef et al., *Catalogue of the herbaria of Antoni Gaymans (1630–1680) and a comparison with the plant collection of the Leiden Hortus Botanicus in 1668* (Leiden, 1987); J. Heniger and M.S.M. Sosef, 'Antoni Gaymans (ca 1630–1680) and his herbaria', *Archives of Natural History*, 16 (1989), 147–68; E.C. Nelson, 'Tracking Antoni Gaymans's seventeenth-century horti sicci', *Archives of Natural History*, 45 (2018), 149–52.   **55** Hoppen (ed.), *Dublin Philosophical Society papers*, ii, p. 564.

ARBVTVS.
Κόμαρ<mark>ος</mark>.   Memecylos.

NOMINA ET DESCRIPTIO.

ARbutum Latini uocant,quam Græci,teste Plinio, Comaron & Memecylon. Arbor, describente Dioscoride, est Cotoneæ malo non dissimilis, folio tenui, cuius fructus pruni magnitudinem implet, nullo intus nucleo. Fructus eius eodem cum arbore nomine , Memecylos uidelicet, appellatur, qui maturus flauet aut rubescit, esu acetosus. Plinius autem lib. 15. cap. 24. fructum eius Vnedonem uocat. Vnedo, inquiens, pomum inhonorum, ut cui nomen ex argumento sit, unū tantùm edendi, duobus tamen hoc nominibus appellāt Grçci, ex quo apparet totidem esse genera & apud nos: alio nomine Arbutus dicit̃. Ex quo loco Plinij constat, Plinium similitudine quadam deceptum diuersas arbores confudisse. Siquidem Vnedo nõ est fructus Arbuti, sed alterius quæ Epimelis Græcis dicitur, ut Galenus lib.6.Pharm. simp. scribit. Epimelis, inquiens, acerba planta est, & ut dicere possis, syluestris malus, cuius fructus ὄνεδωρ in Italia appellatur, ac plurimum in Calabria nascitur: fructus eius acerbus, stomacho incōmodus, & caput dolore grauans. Vnde liquet. Vnedonem proprie fructum esse Epimelidis arboris: Arbuti uero fructum esse Memecylon. Plinius itaq; uel ab alijs Græcis sua hæc descripsit, uel ex facultatis quadam conuenientia inter utrasq; arbores falsus, eandem credidit esse Comaron & Vnedonem.

TEMPERAMENTVM ET VIRES.

Comaros qualitatis est acerbæ. Stomacho, Diosco. testimonio, aduersatur, capitis dolorem mouet. Quod idem Galenus etiā perhibet.

k 2

3.6 *Arbutus unedo* (strawberry tree), woodcut from Adam Lonicer, *Naturalis historiae opus novum* (Frankfurt, 1551), fol. 56r. By permission of the Trustees of the Edward Worth Library, Dublin. © Edward Worth Library.

while Mullen and Ashe established fresh scientific contacts in London and on the Continent. Indeed, Ashe, travelling in Austria and Hungary in 1690, wrote to Edmond Halley of his intention to build up 'a pretty good collection of the rarer plants that grow hereabouts or in Hungary'.[56] With the re-establishment of English control in Ireland following the Jacobite surrender at Limerick in 1691 intellectual life in Dublin began slowly to recover, though Trinity College, which had suffered the depredations of army occupation, had to defer its first centenary celebrations till January 1694. At the ceremony Ashe, now provost of the college, delivered a sermon that set out a Baconian vision for its future development (remarkably similar to that advanced in Molyneux's dedication in *Dioptrica nova*), in which the New Learning would serve the three-fold function of fostering true religion through revealing the wonders of God's creation; advancing knowledge of the natural world through observation and experiment; and, third, producing utilitarian benefits for society and the state.[57] This reference to religion recalls the fact that in the 1680s, the Dublin Philosophical Society had on occasion heard papers dealing with both religious and political subjects, topics that the London society had found it necessary to ban as potentially too inflammatory after the Restoration.[58]

Meetings of the Dublin Philosophical Society resumed in 1693 and continued until 1697; however, the records for this second period of the society's activities are very much sparser than those of the 1680s, and the meetings would appear eventually to have just petered out – as had happened with some of the earlier continental groupings. William Molyneux's declining health forced him to take a much reduced role, and the lead passed to his brother Thomas who, as Hoppen felicitously put it, had previously functioned merely as 'a corresponding member'.[59] In the 1690s less attention was devoted to purely scientific matters, the emphasis being on technology and antiquarian pursuits such as Thomas Molyneux's continuing interest in Danish mounts.

It was, however, during this period, that Thomas Molyneux began commenting in more detail on the natural history of the island. He certainly responded to Sir Richard Cox's paper on the 'geographical and natural history of the county of Londonderry', read at a meeting on 3 May 1693, but unfortunately the briefness of the relevant minute does not relate whether he included botany in his remarks.[60] However, a wide-ranging paper communicated by Molyneux to the Royal Society on 29 April 1697 included a number of significant observations on 'some of our more rare spontaneous plants' which he said grew only in the west of Ireland. Among these was *Arbutus unedo* (strawberry tree) (Fig. 3.6):

> the *Arbutus sive Unedo*, or the *Strawberry Tree*; not to be found any where of *Spontaneous Growth* nearer than the most Southern Parts of *France, Italy, Sicily*; and there too, 'tis never known but as a *Frutex* or *Shrub*: whereas in the Rocky Parts of the County of *Kerry* about *Loughlane*, [*sic*] and in the

---

56 Ibid., ii, pp 168–9; 664.　**57** See Helga Robinson-Hammerstein, '"With great solemnity": celebrating the first centenary of the foundation of Trinity College, Dublin, 9 January 1694', *Long Room*, 37 (1992), 27–38, though she does not refer to the parallels with *Dioptrica nova*, dedication.　**58** See Hoppen, *Common scientist*, pp 88, 155.　**59** Ibid, p. 51.　**60** Hoppen (ed.), *Dublin Philosophical Society papers*, i,

Islands of the same *Lough*, where the People of the Country call it the *Cane Apple*, it flourishes naturally to that Degree, as to become a large tall *Tree*.[61]

His second plant, called by him 'Cotyledon sive Sedum serratum Latifolium Montanum guttato flore Parkinsoni et Raii, vulgarly call'd by Gardners London Pride', derived its name, he suggested, from 'its pretty elegant Flower: that viewed near at hand and examined closely, appears very beautiful'. Thomas conceded that it had been described by the Reverend John Ray (1627–1705) in his *Historia plantarum*, despite Ray never having come across it himself in the wild, and confirmed Ray's suspicion that it was a mountain plant by pointing to many instances of it on Mangerton mountain in Co. Kerry.[62]

Thomas's account is of interest not only because it displays what botanical sources were at his disposal, but also because it sheds light on the networks of knowledge to which he had access. Continuing his survey of plants found in Kerry, he notes that his knowledge of '*Sabina vulgaris*, or *Common Savin*' (generally accepted to be *Juniperus communis*, juniper) was thanks to an apothecary based in Killarney who had assured him that he had 'gathered *Savin* growing wild as a native shrub in one of the islands of Lough-*Lane* [*sic*] in the *County* of *Kerry*'.[63]

It was at this time that Thomas undertook his investigation of plants in the neighbourhood of Dublin and Meath, the results of which appeared in the appendix to Threlkeld's *Synopsis stirpium Hibernicarum*. Interestingly the details that Thomas provided showed that his wife, Katherine, assisted him in his plant-hunting at Clontarf beach and elsewhere.[64] Like William, Thomas also corresponded with the Welsh savant Edward Lhuyd (1660–1709), receiving from him a wide range of botanical information, procured during Lhuyd's lengthy tour of Ireland in 1697–8.[65] On 7 May 1700 Lhuyd provided Molyneux with important information about over twenty plants he found during his sojourn in Sligo:

p. 102. Cox, Sir Richard, first baronet (1650–1733), *ODNB*. **61** Thomas Molyneux, 'A discourse concerning the large horns frequently found underground in Ireland, concluding from them that the great American deer, call'd a moose, was formerly common in that island, with remarks on some other things natural to that country', *Philosophical Transactions of the Royal Society*, 19 (1695), 489–512, at 510. See also E.C. Nelson, this volume pp 47–8. **62** Ibid. John Ray, *Historia plantarum species hactenus editas aliasque insuper multas noviter inventas & descriptas complectens*, 3 vols (London, 1686–1704), ii, p. 1046. The plants found in Kerry are not the same as the cultivated London pride (*Saxifraga × urbium*) which is of hybrid origin. **63** Hoppen (ed.), *Dublin Philosophical Society papers*, i, p. 282. In the appendix of Threlkeld's *Synopsis* (p. 7), Thomas mentions that *Smyrnium olusatrum* (alexanders) also grew by Lough Leane. **64** Katherine subsequently copied her brother Hugh Howard's drawing of the skull of the Irish giant deer as an illustration to Thomas's paper on the subject in *Philosophical Transactions*, 1702. For Howard, see Nichola Figgis, ed., 'Painting, 1600–2000' in *Art and architecture in Ireland*, ed. Andrew Carpenter, 5 vols (New Haven & London, 2014), pp 317–18. **65** The Molyneux-Lhuyd correspondence in the papers of the Dublin Philosophical Society contains botanical information: see Hoppen, ii, pp 658–9; 709–12; 715–17; 720. Also important for understanding the extent of the influence of the Molyneux brothers are the letters Thomas exchanged with John Locke between 1692–9, which have tended to be overlooked, because they are far fewer in number and less personally revealing than those with William. However, as Kenneth Dewhurst pointed out, their correspondence includes Locke's most explicit exposition of his medical credo, in which he argued for adopting Sydenham's empirical method in

1. Caryophyllata Alpina Chamædryos Mosisini [recte Morisoni] folio sive Teucrium Alpinu[m] Cisti flore, Gerardi, formerly observed by Mr Heaton on the mountains betwixt Gort and Gallway. 2. Lychnis minima Alpina Serpilli folio wch for ought I know yet is a plant wholy undescrib'd. 3. Caryophyllus pumilio Alpinus Clusij. 4. Rhodia Radix. 5. Sedum alpin[um] flore luteo pallido Raij. 6. Lonchitis Aspera Matthioli sive Aspera Maior. 7. Trichomanes montanu[m] costa viridi. 8. Bistoria minima Alpina. 9. Geranium mont[anum] batrachoides. 10. Juniperus Alpina. 10. Thlaspi vel Lunaria vasculo Sublongo intorto Raij. 11. Sedum Alpinu[m] trifido folio. 12. Lysimachia Chamænerion dicta Alpina sive Augusti folia minor. 13. Thalictrum minus. 14. Hierarcium montanum villosum 15. Hieraciu[m] montanu[m] maculatum 16. Ignota Alpina Cicutæ folio together with some sea plants though at five miles Distance such as 17. Caryoph[yllus]. marinus; 18. Lychius marina Anglica 19. Plantago marina 20. Cochlearia rotundifolia.[66]

Lhuyd not only provided Molyneux with information about plants, he also provided plants themselves, though, as Molyneux ruefully admitted in a letter dated 10 August 1702, most did not survive replanting in Dublin.[67]

The final revival of the society came in 1707–8 at the initiative of William's son, Samuel Molyneux the younger, then a student at Trinity College Dublin, who became its first secretary, supported by his uncle Thomas, who both presented papers at the meetings and served on the council.[68] In this last period the Dublin Philosophical Society acquired its most intellectually distinguished member in the person of the philosopher George Berkeley (1685–1753), then a Fellow of Trinity College Dublin, who read a paper on 'Infinites' in November 1707, and who may also have presented an account of the cave of Dunmore near Kilkenny, which Hans Sloane (1660–1753) had earlier declined to publish in *Philosophical Transactions*.[69] However, interest in the society was on the wane. John K'Eogh (*c*.1650–1725), the father of the author of

---

preference to either of the dominant theories of the day, namely the Galenic and the chemical or Paracelsian: Locke to Thomas Molyneux, 20 January 1694/4: *Locke corr.*, letter no. 1539.   **66** TCD, MS 888/2, fo. 312. Mitchell, 'Irish botany in the seventeenth century', 282, provided the modern names of these plants: 1: *Dryas octopetala* (mountain avens); 2: probably *Arenaria ciliata* (fringed sandwort); 3: *Silene acaulis* (moss campion); 4: *Sedum rosea* (roseroot); 5: *Saxifraga aizoides* (yellow saxifrage); 6: *Polystichum lonchitis* (holly-fern); 7: *Asplenium viride* (green spleenwort); 8: *Persicaria vivipara* (alpine bistort); 9: *Geranium* sp. (crane's-bill); 10: *Juniperus communis* (juniper); 10 [*sic*]: *Draba incana* (hoary whitlowgrass); 11: *Saxifraga hypnoides* (mossy saxifrage); 12: *Chamerion angustifolium* (rosebay willowherb); 13: *Thalictrum minus* (lesser meadow-rue); 14: *Hieracium* sp. (hawkweed); 15: cf. *Hieracium maculatum* (a spotted hawkweed); 16: unknown; 17: *Armeria maritima* (thrift); 18: *Silene uniflora* (sea campion); 19: *Plantago maritima* (sea plantain); 20: *Cochlearia officinalis* (common scurvygrass). **67** Hoppen (ed.), *Dublin Philosophical Society papers*, ii, pp 715–16: Molyneux relates that of all the plants Lhuyd sent him from Galway, the only one to survive was '*Sedum serratum latifolium*' (*Saxifraga spathularis*, St Patrick's cabbage). Molyneux also sought information from Lhuyd about Jacob Bobart's edition of the third part of Robert Morison's *Plantarum historiæ universalis Oxoniensis* (Oxford, 1699): ibid., ii, p 730.   **68** See Hoppen (ed.), *Papers of the Dublin Philosophical Society*, ii, pp 725–890.   **69** This assumption rests on the presence of a copy of Berkeley's description of Dunmore in the Molyneux

Botanalogia universalis Hibernica, or, a general Irish herbal (Cork, 1735), writing to Samuel Molyneux the younger from Strokestown in late December 1707, opined that 'There are no men very curious in this neighbourhood'.[70] By 1709 the society was no longer in existence and though Samuel declared his wish to publicize the natural history collections kept by his family, nothing came of the scheme.[71] The decision of Caleb Threlkeld to publish Molyneux's findings in an appendix to his *Synopsis stirpium Hibernicarum* in 1726 thus preserved Molyneux's botanical notes, which harkened back to a more illustrious past of scientific investigation in late seventeenth-century Ireland.[72]

Papers: ibid., p. 721, n.1.   **70** Hoppen (ed.), *Papers of the Dublin Philosophical Society*, ii, 807. K'Eogh noted that one of the few exceptions was a fellow member of the society, Sir Arthur Shane of Kilmore (near Athlone), 'who has a green house for exotic plants'.   **71** Ibid., ii, 882.   **72** It is now increasingly appreciated how much Berkeley owed to William Molyneux's *Dioptrica nova* as a source for his first major philosophic publication, *A new theory of vision* of 1709. Charles J. McCracken also credits Molyneux's 1680 translation of *Meditationes de prima philosophia* as the source of Berkeley's early knowledge of Descartes; 'Berkeley and Descartes' in Bertil Belfrage and Richard Brook (eds), *The Bloomsbury companion to Berkeley* (London, 2017), p. 247.

CHAPTER FOUR

Caleb Threlkeld: dissenting minister, physician and botanist

EMER LAWLOR

DR CALEB THRELKELD (1676–1728), the author of the first Irish flora, *Synopsis Stirpium Hibernicarum* (Dublin, 1726), came from rural Cumberland to the crowded Dublin Liberties in April 1713.[1] He lived in Dublin until his death from a 'violent' fever, dying at his house in Mark's Alley on 28 April 1728. We owe the details of his death to an anonymous commentator, whose short note on Threlkeld was written in the front pages of a copy of the *Synopsis* purchased by the botanist Richard Pulteney (1730–1801). The unknown writer ascribed the reason for Threlkeld's move to Dublin, following his qualification as MD in Edinburgh in 1713, as 'a strait income and a large family' but the real reasons for Threlkeld's move to Dublin were more complicated.[2] This contribution, building on the extensive work of E. Charles Nelson, and aided by the digitization of many sources and increased access to archival material, seeks to throw further light on Threlkeld's life before he came to Ireland, aspects of his *Synopsis*, and his medical practice in Ireland.[3]

DISSENTERS

Caleb was born on 31 May 1676 in Keibergh, now Caber Farmhouse (Fig. 4.1), in the village of Kirkoswald in Cumberland, in north-west England.[4] He was the third child and youngest son of a well-off yeoman farmer, Thomas Threlkeld (1646–1712), and his wife Bridget Brown (*c*.1654–1712). There is no record of Caleb's baptism in St Oswald's, the Kirkoswald parish church.[5] This may be due to a lacuna in the baptismal registers of the church, for notes on baptisms or dates of birth in the first

---

1 Caleb Threlkeld, *Synopsis stirpium Hibernicarum* (Dublin, 1726), Appendix, p. 19. A facsimile of the 1727 Dublin issue is available: Caleb Threlkeld, *The first Irish flora. Synopsis stirpium Hibernicarum*, ed. E.C. Nelson (facsimile with annotations by E.C. Nelson and D.M. Synnott) (Kilkenny, 1988). 2 Richard Pulteney, 'Letter to Mr Urban', *The Gentleman's Magazine*, 47 (Feb. 1777), 63–4, at 63. 3 On Threlkeld's life see Nelson, *The first Irish flora*, pp xiii–lii; E.C. Nelson, '"In the contemplation of vegetables": Caleb Threlkeld (1676–1728), his life, background and contribution to Irish botany', *Journal of the Society for the Bibliography of Natural History*, 9:3 (1979), 257–73; and E.C. Nelson and Marjorie Raven, 'Caleb Threlkeld's family,' *Glasra*, 3 (1998), 161–6. 4 Threlkeld, *Synopsis*, Sig. B4v. 5 Nelson,

80

4.1 Caber Farmhouse, Kirkoswald, Cumbria. Reproduced with permission from *Victoria county histories short: Kirkoswald and Renwick* (London, 2019). © University of London.

two pages between 1659 and 1684 are incomplete.[6] Certainly the registers hold records of baptisms, marriages and burials of many of the Threlkeld family, including the baptisms of some of Caleb's own children, which would at first suggest that the Threlkeld family were members of the Church of England.[7] The family were, however, staunch Dissenters and their practice of baptizing children into the Established Church was due to the more secure maintenance of baptismal registers by the Church of England, registers which might subsequently be needed to ensure property rights.[8] Marriages also had to be conducted in the parish church and Dissenters did not have separate burial grounds.[9] That the Threlkeld family were Dissenters is clear: Threlkeld's grandfather John and his father Thomas were fined as Nonconformists twice in late 1670 and again in 1671 along with their wives. During the brief period of tolerance instituted by the Declaration of Indulgence from March 1672 to February 1673, a licence to hold religious meetings was granted to 'The howse of Thom: Threkeld'. In April and November 1675, his family were on a list of over fifty persons who 'separate from ye Church and seeme to discourse agt it'.[10]

'"In the contemplation of vegetables"', 258.   6 Cumbria Archive Centre, Carlisle: PR9/2 Kirkoswald, St Oswald Parish, 1577–2015.   7 Nelson, '"In the contemplation of vegetables"', 258.   8 Amicus Rusticus, B., 'On the neglect of baptismal registers among Dissenters', *The London Christian Instructor or Congregational Magazine*, 5 (1822), 416–18.   9 D.A. Spaeth, *The church in an age of danger: parsons and parishioners, 1660–1740* (Cambridge, 2000), p. 169.   10 Benjamin Nightingale, *The ejected of 1662 in Cumberland & Westmorland: their predecessors and successors*, 2 vols (Manchester, 1911), ii, pp 1338–9;

EDUCATION

We have no information on Caleb's schooling although the 1675 list mentions a Catherine Walton who was also fined for 'teaching a Schoole, being a Nonconformist'.[11] This school may still have been in existence when Caleb was of school age but there was also a school run by the curate of Kirkoswald, John Romney (*fl.* 1723).[12] Dissenting families educating their sons for the ministry often had their sons privately tutored or sent them to one of the dissenting academies that prepared many students for the dissenting ministry.[13] The best-known academy in the north of England at the time was Richard Franklin's school at Rathmell, near Settle, North Yorkshire. Although a list of the students who attended Rathmell exists, Caleb Threlkeld's name is not listed.[14] He may instead have been tutored locally by George Nicholson (1636–97), the dissenting minister in Kirkoswald. Nicholson had been a student in Magdalen College, Oxford, between 1657 and 1661, but had left Oxford without a degree shortly before the Act of Uniformity of 1662 was passed.[15] Whichever route Caleb followed, it was sufficient to allow him enter as an undergraduate student into the third class in the University of Glasgow on 9 March 1696.[16] In the preface to his *Synopsis* he ascribes the beginning of his interest in botany to this year as a student in Glasgow.[17] Threlkeld's time there was short: though a family manuscript states that he married his wife Elizabeth Dalrymple on 7 March 1698 while at the 'Colledge of Glasco', his name is not listed in any of the student lists for that year and nor is there any record of his graduation.[18] This was not unusual for generally, at Glasgow, the numbers graduating were very small and it was common for students to attend the university for only one year.[19]

MINISTER OF THE INDEPENDENT CHURCH AT HUDDLESCEUGH

The death of George Nicholson, the long serving dissenting minister, in August 1697, paved the way for Threlkeld to become minister in his place. Describing himself as a dissenting preacher, he applied at the Carlisle midsummer sessions in 1698 to take the oath for licence to preach at Huddlesceugh, Cumberland.[20]

1367; 1339. **11** Ibid., p. 1339. **12** Richard Brockington with Sarah Rose, *The Victoria history of Cumberland: Kirkoswald and Renwick*, (London, 2019), p. 59. A 'Johannes Romney' is mentioned in the 'Clergy of the Church of England Database': https://theclergydatabase.org.uk/jsp/persons/index.jsp, accessed 9 March 2022. **13** D.L. Wykes 'The dissenting academy and rational dissent' in Knud Haakonssen (ed.), *Enlightenment and religion: rational dissent in eighteenth-century Britain* (Cambridge, 1996), pp 99–139; at pp 105, 111. **14** Dissenting Academies Online: https://dissacad.english.qmul.ac.uk/sample1.php?parameter=Surnamest&alpha=T, accessed 9 March 2022. **15** Nightingale, *The ejected of 1662*, i, pp 337–9. **16** Nelson, '"In the contemplation of vegetables"', 258. **17** Threlkeld, *Synopsis*, Preface, Sig. c2v. **18** Nelson and Raven. 'Caleb Threlkeld's family,' 164. Cosmo Innes (ed.), *Munimenta alme universitatis Glasguensis: records of the university of Glasgow, from its foundation till 1727*, 3 vols (Glasgow, 1854), iii, pp 162, 164. **19** A.L. Brown and Michael Moss, *The university of Glasgow: 1451–1996* (Edinburgh, 1996) pp 9–11, 17–18. **20** Cumbria Archive Centre, Carlisle: Q11/1/47/34 MIDS.

4.2 Caleb Threlkeld's application for a licence to preach at Huddlesceugh.
Image courtesy of Cumbria Archive Centre, Carlisle: Q/11/1/47/34.

The minutes of the Congregational Fund Board record that in July 1698 consideration of the case of 'Mr. Threlkeld' was being adjourned until Mr John Nesbitt (1661–1727), a dissenting minister and a correspondent for the Congregational Fund for a number of counties including Cumberland, was present.[21] There is a further record in March 1699 that 'Tho. Threlkelde' was to be allowed £6 for the coming year. It is unclear whether this reference to Thomas was in mistake for Caleb or whether the allowances were to his father while Caleb was undertaking further education for the ministry. In April 1700, there was a further record that 'Mr. Threscall' be allowed £6.[22] On 4 July 1700, Caleb was ordained to the church at Huddlesceugh.[23] Huddlesceugh was also known as Parkhead, and most of what we know of Threlkeld's ministry in Cumberland may be found in his own hand in the Parkhead Register.[24]

---

21 On Nesbitt see Alexander Gordon (ed.), *Freedom after ejection: a review (1690–1692) of Presbyterian and Congregational nonconformity in England* (Manchester, 1917), p. 316. On financial support of ministers mentioned in the minutes of the Congregational Fund Board see Michael Watts, *The Dissenters; from the Reformation to the French Revolution* (Oxford, 1978), p. 289. Wykes, 'The dissenting academy and rational dissent', p. 107, mentions that students were also given financial support.   22 See Nightingale, *The ejected of 1662*, ii, pp 1259–60 for the minutes of the Congregational Fund Board for 4 July 1698, 20 March 1698/9 and 22 April 1700.   23 National Archives, UK: RG4/566, Parkhead Register, fo. 6v.   24 National Archives, UK: RG4/566, Parkhead Register.

The church appears to have been a flourishing one. Threlkeld listed the names of the 191 members of the congregation since the church was set up in 1653, supplemented by the nineteen new parishioners admitted since his ordination and the names of the sixty parishioners who regularly attended during 1711, the last full year of his ministry.[25] Between June 1700 and September 1712, a total of 140 children were baptized. Based on the baptismal register figures from 1703 to 1712 and the birth rate at the time Watts estimates that the community at Huddlesceugh numbered 373.[26]

Glimpses of Threlkeld in his role as minister include a testimonial, dated 26 July 1710 and signed by John Atkinson, dissenting minister at Stainton and Threlkeld, stating that as 'ministers of Cumberland' they affirmed that a Co. Durham preacher, James Paul, was 'sound in judgement and sober in life'.[27] In addition, Consistory Court and probate records demonstrate that Caleb acted as a scribe and a witness to the will, dated 26 January 1707/8, of one of his parishioners, Leonard Whitesmith.[28]

'PROGRESS IN THE STUDY OF PHYSIC'

At the same time, Threlkeld continued to follow his interest in botany for in his *Synopsis* he records seven plants from Cumberland, and a number from the neighbouring counties of Yorkshire and Northumberland.[29] Indeed, he mentions in his preface that, while clambering on rocks at Tynemouth Castle near Newcastle upon Tyne in 1707, he had been arrested as a spy.[30]

Threlkeld's interest in plants, an important source of medicinal remedies of the time, also appears to have led him into the study of medicine. According to the handwritten record in Pulteney's copy of the *Synopsis*, he had made 'considerable progress in the study of physic' during his time in Kirkoswald.[31] Dissenting ministers often had other occupations to support themselves and their families, notably farming and medicine.[32] While Dissenters did not always approve of their ministers practising medicine, it was an economic necessity in many cases.[33] In the Parkhead Register, Threlkeld notes that the amount of land (including the minister's house with its outbuildings, gardens and the chapel or 'oratory') was somewhat less than four acres and required the addition of some extra land nearby to make up the four acres. While an additional five acres had been acquired in 1706 through a bequest of £20 from a local landowner to buy land to support the minister, this might not have been enough to support his family.[34]

25 National Archives, UK: RG4/566, fo. 6v, fo. 7r.   26 Watts, *The Dissenters*, p. 502.   27 National Records of Scotland, Correspondence of the Dukes of Hamilton, 1563–1712: GD 406/1/5638; for Atkinson see Nightingale *The ejected of 1662*, ii, p. 1289.   28 Cumbria Archives, Carlisle: Consistory Court Act book DRC/3/7 and PROB/1712/WX153. See Fig. 4.4, p. 89.   29 See, for example, Threlkeld, *Synopsis*, Sig. B1r (silverweed near Settle); K7r (yew at Sedbergh); on this see E.C. Nelson, '"The long tradition" – Caleb Threlkeld's British plant records', *BSBI News*, 44 (1986), 8–9. 30 Threlkeld, *Synopsis*, Preface, Sig. B2r.   31 Pulteney, 'Letter to Mr Urban', 63–4.   32 Watts, *The Dissenters*, p. 344.   33 David Harley, '"Bred up in the study of that faculty": licensed physicians in north-west England, 1660–1760', *Medical History*, 38:4 (1994), 398–420, at 409.   34 National Archives, UK:

Caleb Threlkeld: dissenting minister, physician and botanist

Medical practitioners in remote areas in the seventeenth and eighteenth centuries did not all have university medical degrees. Some were licensed under the diocesan licensing system, which allowed the bishop to issue a licence, usually on the recommendation of two university trained medical practitioners. We know of two licensed physicians practising in Kendal in 1695, some 40 miles from Kirkoswald, and another, Miles Atkinson from Windermere, was licensed in January 1709, supported by a testimonial by the local magistrates and on the recommendation of John Archer of Kendal. Apprenticeship to either university trained or diocesan licensed medical practitioners was a recognized way of receiving medical training.[35] Threlkeld may therefore have been able to arrange some practical training with a practitioner in the area.

DIFFICULTIES WITH HIS CONGREGATION

To meet the needs of the congregation, the old meeting house was torn down on 29 May 1711 and a new church was built in its place with Threlkeld preaching the first sermon on 5 August 1711.[36] However, the following year brought a breach between Threlkeld and his congregation that ended his ministry in Kirkoswald. 1712 was a year of upheaval for the Threlkeld family: on 2 February his father died suddenly without leaving a will, at a time when his wife Bridget and Caleb were away from Kirkoswald. Caleb's subsequent unsuccessful petition to the chancellor of Carlisle, asking for letters of administration to be granted to his mother and himself in addition to his brothers John, Joshua and Thomas Threlkeld, his cousin, states that he and his mother were away 'upon weighty reasons'.[37] Family reasons were unlikely to have been the cause of their absence as Bridget Brown's family lived in Kirkoswald, so it is possible that Bridget's and Caleb's journey was to seek medical advice and treatment as she died eight months later in October 1712 aged fifty-eight.[38]

The sudden death of his father in early 1712 may have unsettled Threlkeld but it is clear from outbursts in his *Synopsis*, written fourteen years later, that Threlkeld had a temper and was prone to expressing himself in colourful and acerbic language.[39] At some point in 1712 a bitter quarrel broke out between Threlkeld and a new parishioner, James Tolson, as well as some other members of the Tolson family.[40] The background to the quarrel is unclear but in a petition entered to the Cumberland Midsummer Quarter Sessions in Carlisle in July 1712, James Tolson requested that Threlkeld be bound to the peace. Tolson (who was blind) alleged that Threlkeld had threatened him in violent language on several occasions, including saying that he would get him knocked on the head and, on another occasion, stating that 'that blind

---

RG4/566, fo. 7v.   **35** On these points see Harley, '"Bred up in the study of that faculty"', 409, 412; 418; 410 and 413.   **36** National Archives, UK: RG4/566, fo. 7v.   **37** Cumbria Archive Centre, Carlisle: PROB/1711/AINVX18, 8 February 1712.   **38** Cumbria Archive Centre, Carlisle: PR 9/2 DRC /6/93 Burials 1712 Kirkoswald.   **39** Nelson, '"In the contemplation of vegetables"', 265.   **40** National Archives, UK: RG4/566, fos. 6v and 7r for records of James Tolson as a parishioner in Threlkeld's church; the

wretch' would not die in his bed.[41] Tolson also claimed that Threlkeld had expressed similar threats against him in a letter to the dissenting Presbyterian minister, Mr Peter Seddon (1689–1731), of Penrith.[42] In addition, James's brother, Joshua Tolson, requested that Threlkeld keep the peace towards Joshua's wife Elizabeth.[43] Joshua and Elizabeth were not listed by Threlkeld as parishioners during his time at Huddlesceugh, though they clearly became members of the church after Threlkeld had left since their daughter Mary was baptized there in 1713.[44] Threlkeld was bound to the peace on his own recognisance of £40 and recognisances of £20 each from two of his parishioners to be of good behaviour especially towards James Tolson.[45] Joshua opted to have his defence sent forward to the next session but unfortunately the court records for the Michaelmas sessions were destroyed by water damage and it is not possible to determine the outcome.

'Unseemly' disagreements between ministers and their congregations both in the Established Church and among Dissenters were not uncommon but rarely ended in court as in this case.[46] The scandal meant that Threlkeld's position as minister was no longer tenable. The last baptism recorded by him, that of his niece, was in September 1712.[47] His mother Bridget was buried on 5 October and his ministry at Huddlesceugh was terminated by mutual agreement on 9 November 1712.[48] The elders' certification of the dissolution states that they had lived in peace and order for 'twelve years last past' under Threlkeld's ministry but 'now dissatisfactions arising to our Pastor and us' had led to an agreed parting of the ways. The elders 'heartily' recommended him in his labours 'wherever Divine Providence shall cast him' and prayed that he might be 'further useful as a burning and shining light'.[49]

We have two clues to the cause of the dispute: the first comes from a short angry paragraph in Latin, written by Threlkeld above this entry, which suggested that the disputes had led to vile imputations thrown at him by some women in the congregation. Joshua Tolson's request that Threlkeld stay away from his wife Elizabeth Tolson at first suggests that this might have been the reason for the termination of Threlkeld's ministry at Huddlesceugh. However, there may have been another reason for tension between Threlkeld and the Tolsons and James Tolson inadvertently drew attention to it in his petition to the court. In his petition he alleged that Threlkeld had written to Peter Seddon that if Tolson died in his bed 'of the common death of men, Let it never be said that the Lord spoke by him meaning the said Caleb Threlkeld'.[50] Threlkeld's alleged reference is to a biblical episode, where Moses confronts rebellious

---

quarrel is referenced on fo. 8r. **41** Cumbria Archive Centre: Q/11/1/104/15 Cumberland Quarter Sessions Midsummer petitions 1712: 'Petition of James Tolson of Huddlesceugh … that Mr. Caleb Threlkeld …'. **42** On Seddon at Penrith see Nightingale, *The ejected of 1662*, ii, p. 1278. **43** Cumbria Archive Centre: Q/1/2 Minute Book (19), Michaelmas 1696 – Midsummer 1738, p. 356. **44** National Archives, UK: RG4/566, fo. 23r: Mary Towlson, daughter of Joshua and Elizabeth Towlson, was baptized on 26 November 1713. **45** Cumbria Archive Centre: Q/1/2 Minute Book (19), Michaelmas 1696 – Midsummer 1738, p. 356. **46** On this see Spaeth, *The church in an age of danger*, pp 22–9, and Watts, *The Dissenters*, p. 298. **47** National Archives, UK: RG4/566, fo. 12r. **48** Cumbria Archives, Carlisle: PR9/2, DRC /6/93; National Archives, UK: RG4/566, fo. 8r. **49** National Archives, UK: RG4/566, fo. 8r. **50** Cumbria Archive Centre: Q/11/1/104/15.

Caleb Threlkeld: dissenting minister, physician and botanist

followers saying 'if these men die the common death of all men … then the Lord had not sent me', before uttering words which cause an earthquake which engulfs them.[51] If this quotation is accurate, then perhaps the quarrel originated in some rejection by James Tolson of Threlkeld's ministerial authority.

Threlkeld's final entry in the register was on the 24 November 1712. Six days before he had written a short four-line lament, partially reworked from lines from Virgil's *Aeneid* and Ovid's *Fasti*, on the uncertainty of what fate would bring on leaving his native land and praying God for calm after misfortunes.[52]

Threlkeld's decision to apply to the University of Edinburgh for the MD degree was made shortly afterwards: the university wrote to the Royal College of Physicians of Edinburgh on 6 January 1713 asking the college to examine him as this was the arrangement between the university and the college.[53] The Edinburgh college's examinations consisted of three separate sections, usually held on separate days: an examination on the *Institutiones medicae*, another on two *Aphorisms* of Hippocrates, and, finally, two practical cases.[54] By including a practical examination, Edinburgh's curriculum provided a more testing exercise than in many other universities of the time but Threlkeld satisfied the examiners and was awarded the degree of MD in the University of Edinburgh on 16 January 1713.[55]

THRELKELD IN DUBLIN

Threlkeld moved to Dublin with his wife and family, arriving on Good Friday, 3 April 1713.[56] Mary, their last child, was born in Maiden Lane, off Thomas Street in the Liberties, probably shortly after they arrived in Dublin, as a family manuscript records her age at death from smallpox in February 1715 at nearly three years of age. By that time, they were living in Back Lane.[57]

His reasons for coming to Ireland may have been due to links established when he was at the University of Glasgow where, of the eighty-eight students in his class, twenty-two were listed as 'Hibernus' including five 'ScotoHibernus'.[58] More importantly, Dublin was a bustling capital city, second only to London in size with an estimated population of 66,000 of whom about 42,000 were Protestant.[59] Many of these were members of the dissenting traditions, notably Huguenots, Presbyterians and Quakers and a number of dissenting physicians who moved to Dublin from Scotland or England established flourishing practices.[60] Some dissenting ministers in Ireland also practised medicine.[61]

---

[51] The biblical reference is to Numbers 16: 29–31. [52] National Archives, UK: RG4/566, fos. 12r and 14r. [53] Nelson, *The first Irish flora*, xx–xxi. [54] R.P. Ritchie, *The early days of the Royal College of Physicians, Edinburgh* (Edinburgh, 1899), pp 280–2. [55] Ibid., p. 96. [56] Threlkeld, *Synopsis*, Appendix, p. 19. [57] Nelson and Raven, 'Caleb Threlkeld's family', 163. [58] Innes (ed.), *Munimenta alme universitatis Glasguensis*, iii, pp 159–60. [59] Toby Barnard, *A new anatomy of Ireland: the Irish protestants, 1649–1770* (New Haven & London, 2003), p. 2. [60] Toby Barnard, 'The wider cultures of eighteenth-century Irish doctors' in James Kelly and Fiona Clark (eds), *Ireland and medicine in the seventeenth and eighteenth centuries* (London, 2016), p. 184. [61] Barnard, *A new anatomy of Ireland*, p. 129.

4.3 'Ranunculus Tlammeus ... Aliis Flammula. The Lesser Spearwort ... In Ulster' (*Ranunculus flammula*, lesser spearwort), a sheet (no. LXV) from an eighteenth-century *hortus siccus*, most probably assembled and personally annotated by Caleb Threlkeld. Compare the handwriting with Threlkeld's script in Fig. 4.4. Image courtesy of The Herbarium, Botany Department, Trinity College Dublin.

Information on his life in Dublin, except for comments in the *Synopsis*, is sparse. The unnamed memorialist in Pulteney's copy of the *Synopsis* says that he initially practiced both as a physician and a dissenting preacher but that he concentrated solely on medicine as his practice grew.[62] There is no evidence that he was licensed to preach or involved with the Plunket Street Meeting House attached to the Synod of Ulster, but he may have been associated with the Meeting Houses in Wood Street,

---

62 Pulteney, 'Letter to Mr Urban', 63.

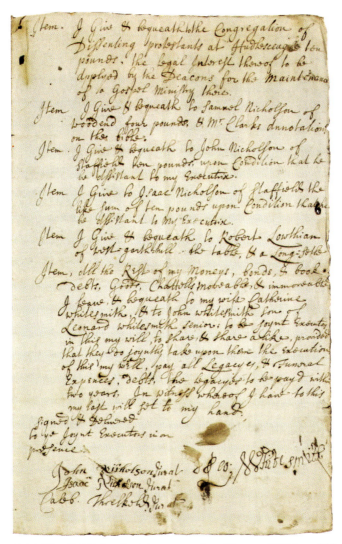

4.4 Caleb Threlkeld's handwriting: transcript of Leonard Whitesmith's will. Image courtesy of Cumbria Archive Centre, Carlisle: PROB/1712/WX153.

New Row Without-Newgate or Cook Street, which were later attached to the Synod of Munster.[63] Threlkeld's interest and pursuit of botany continued when he settled in Dublin. In the preface to his *Synopsis*, where he sets out the method he applied when compiling the book, he describes botanical walks during the summer months in the company of 'ingenious Men, both of the Clergy and Laity' observing plants growing in their native habitats.[64] He had undertaken similar botanical expeditions in

[63] Presbyterian Church in Ireland, *Records of the General Synod of Ulster from 1692–1820*, 3 vols (Belfast, 1890); S.C. Smyrl, *Dictionary of Dublin dissent: Dublin's Protestant dissenting meeting houses 1660–1920* (Dublin, 2009), p. 18.   [64] Threlkeld, *Synopsis*, Preface, Sig. c3r.

Cumberland but the context suggests Threlkeld was referring to walks around Dublin.[65] His further remark that 'now I have reduced our plants into the Model you here see' suggests that he is talking about his Irish walks. Threlkeld's use of the pronoun 'we' in the plant records in the *Synopsis* for *Lathraea squamaria* (toothwort) 'Found upon a moist Acclivity, as we came up the Sea Shore from *Dunlary* to *Newton*,' and *Parentucellia viscosa* (yellow bartsia) 'beneath *Cardiff's-bridge*' suggests these Dublin records were some of the fruits of this communal activity.[66]

Threlkeld also stated he had started an herbarium or *hortus siccus* of specimens twelve years previously, setting out where they grew. As the preface of his *Synopsis* is dated 8 July 1726, this suggests that he started his herbarium in 1714, shortly after he settled in Ireland.[67] An early eighteenth-century herbarium in the Department of Botany, Trinity College Dublin, was identified in 1992 as likely to be Threlkeld's from both internal evidence in the *Synopsis* and comparison of the writing on the herbarium sheets (Fig. 4.3) with his signature when graduating as MD in the University of Edinburgh.[68] My researches into his life in Cumbria have unearthed a number of examples of his handwriting that support this attribution, notably Leonard Whitesmith's will transcribed and witnessed by Threlkeld (Fig. 4.4).[69]

Threlkeld's *Synopsis* followed the herbal tradition with its inclusion of information on the uses or 'virtues' of plants.[70] He states that he derived this information principally from the works of John Ray (1627–1705), Samuel Dale's *Pharmacologia*, and the apothecary Joseph Miller's *Botanicum officinale*, with some additions from other authors.[71] Miller's recently published *Botanicum officinale* (1722) was a simplification of Dale's *Pharmacologia* and was intended to describe all the plants used in apothecaries' shops, listing them in alphabetical order by Latin name.[72] Miller's stated purpose was to make available in English the information in Dale's *Pharmacologia* and expand the plant descriptions, which were brief and based on Ray's classification, which he noted few understood. This was intended to improve the knowledge of both customers and apothecaries, many of whom had little botanical knowledge, and to save them from the impositions of the herb sellers who often substituted one herb for another 'directly contrary to the Intention of the Prescriber'.[73] Threlkeld made frequent references to herb sellers, often women, who

---

65 See Declan Doogue's chapters in this volume. 66 Threlkeld, *Synopsis*, Sigs. D1r (toothwort); D4v (yellow bartsia). 67 Threlkeld, *Synopsis*, Preface, Sig. c3v. 68 For example, see Threlkeld's spelling of 'Ranunculus Tlammeus …' in *Synopsis*, Sig. I2v. Declan Doogue and John Parnell, 'Fragments of an eighteenth-century herbarium, possibly that of Caleb Threlkeld in Trinity College, Dublin (TCD)', *Glasra*, new series, 1 (1992), 99–109. See also E.C. Nelson, '"In the contemplation of vegetables"', figure 2, at 261. 69 Cumbria Archives, Carlisle: PROB/1712/WX153. 70 Declan Doogue, 'History of the study of the flora of County Dublin' in Declan Doogue et al. (ed.), *Flora of County Dublin* (Dublin, 1998), p. 28. 71 Samuel Dale, *Pharmacologia, seu, manuductio ad materiam medicam* (London, 1693), 2nd ed. 1710 with supplements in 1705 and 1718; Joseph Miller, *Botanicum officinale* (London, 1722); Threlkeld, *Synopsis*, Preface, Sig. c2r. On Dale, who was John Ray's friend and executor, see G.S. Boulger, revised by Juanita Burnby, 'Dale, Samuel (*bap.* 1659, *d.* 1739), apothecary and physician', *ODNB*; *English short title catalogue* gives Joseph Miller's dates as (1668/9–1748). 72 Blanche Henrey, *British botanical and horticultural literature before 1800*, 3 vols (London), ii, p. 5. 73 Miller, *Botanicum officinale*, Sig. *4r–v.

4.5 'Spring herbs' from William Laffan (ed.), *The cries of Dublin &c. Drawn from the life by Hugh Douglas Hamilton, 1760* (Dublin, 2003), p. 61. Private collection.

cried their seasonal wares such as watercress or spring leaves for salads, or medicinal herbs through the Dublin streets.[74] One of these was captured in this drawing (Fig. 4.5) by Hugh Douglas Hamilton (1740–1808) made several decades later.[75]

The market for this type of popular vernacular medical text was considerable.[76] Threlkeld's reason for including information on the '*Vertues of the plants*' was to make the book appealing to purchasers, as he was well aware that a bare listing of plant

---

74 Threlkeld, *Synopsis*, Sig. G8r (water cress). Nelson, *The first Irish flora*, at p. xiv.   75 William Laffan (ed.), *The cries of Dublin &c. Drawn from the life by Hugh Douglas Hamilton, 1760* (Dublin, 2003), pp 60–1.
76 M.E. Fissell, 'The marketplace of print' in M.S.R. Jenner and Patrick Wallis (eds), *Medicine and the market in England and its colonies, c.1450–c.1850* (London, 2007), pp 110–13.

names without information of the uses of the plant, 'would please few Buyers'. He hoped to sidestep any criticism from his medical colleagues by pointing out that knowledge of a few remedies did not replace the practice or skilled knowledge of physicians. Threlkeld stated that his desire was that his '*Treatise*' would be of use to those who could not obtain the advice of physicians, by giving information on the use of plants which formed the '*greatest Part of our Foods and the safest Part of our Physick*'. He expressed the hope that his readers would find their time well spent and that a buyer would find '*his Money well laid out, in getting a Knowledge of Simples*'.[77]

Threlkeld seems to have thrived in Dublin, practising as a 'Physician in Ordinary' (the equivalent of a modern general practitioner). In addition to information on plant uses derived from herbal and medical sources, the *Synopsis* gives snapshot pictures of his practice as a physician in the teeming district of the Liberties with its diverse population of native Irish, English and Huguenot patients, of differing social classes, including the poor, skilled craftsmen and merchants. Physicians needed a knowledge of Irish to treat their poorer patients and Threlkeld's knowledge and interest in Irish is clear from a perusal of his *Synopsis* where he supplies the Irish name of plants on a number of occasions.[78]

Women and children made up a considerable part of his practice. Under the entry for *Fraxinus* (ash), he noted the use of Manna Calabrina, a dry exudate from a species of ash tree from Calabria, as the best purgative for children after measles and, dissolved in hyssop water, as the only medicine he used to treat the many hundreds of children with 'Chincough' or Whooping Cough that he has seen. He described his experience with the successful use of *Hypericum hirsutum* (hairy St John's wort) for worms but also pointed to the dangers posed by the use of some folk medicines by recounting a Dublin mother's tragic story of the deaths of her two young sons as a result of their treatment for worms with *Helleborus foetidus* (stinking hellebore) by a country practitioner. He recommended to charitable ladies the use of seven or eight drops of oil extracted from juniper, diluted in liquid, to help their poor neighbours 'in such a dreadful Pinch', where labour has stalled, in order to induce progression of labour.[79]

Threlkeld provided snatches of case histories in the *Synopsis*: he noted that *Geranium robertianum* (herb Robert) was useful for kidney stones or gravel and that a decoction of it had been the only remedy to relieve some cases of renal colic. His comment on the use of juice from crushed leaves of *Allium ursinum* (ramsons) in wine or ale, for the cure of kidney stones, has perhaps a more personal ring, suggesting he used it on himself as he states that 'it is very good against Gravel as I have experienced' and that it could not be sufficiently praised for its efficacy.[80]

---

77 Threlkeld, *Synopsis*, Preface, Sig. c2r–v.   **78** Ibid., Sig. G1r. On Threlkeld's use of Irish names see, for example, Sigs. A4r; B1r; B5r–v; B7v; B8r; C1r; C3r; C4r–v; C6r–v; C7r; C8v. See D.M. Synnott, 'Commentary on Irish names used by Threlkeld' in Nelson (ed.), *The first Irish flora*, pp 120–35. **79** Ibid., Sigs. D6v (ash); E8r (hairy St John's wort); E6r (stinking hellebore); I6v (juniper).   **80** Ibid., Sigs. E3v (herb Robert); A4r (ramsons).

4.6 *Lythrum salicaria* (purple loosestrife). © Zoë Devlin. www.wildflowersofireland.com

One of the most interesting case histories is his account of the recovery of one of his patients, a sixty-year-old man, dying of 'dysentery', which had not responded to Threlkeld's standard treatment. Coming to his deathbed, he found the man drinking a strong tea made of the dried leaves of an unknown plant laced with white sugar; this led to his recovery and the patient was still living five years later at the time of the writing of the *Synopsis*. Threlkeld subsequently identified the plant from a fresh specimen he was shown as *Lythrum salicaria* (purple loosestrife) (Fig. 4.6). He noted the use of *Lythrum* as a wound plant and listed three names in Irish for it but had not

94   *Emer Lawlor*

been aware of its use in diarrhoeal illnesses.[81] John K'Eogh (*c*.1681–1754), writing in the early 1730s, does not mention this usage and there is apparently no evidence of its usage for diarrhoea in more recent Irish folk medicine.[82]

Whether Threlkeld grew purple loosestrife himself is unknown: at one time it was assumed that he had a private botanic garden but this claim is likely to be unfounded.[83] Threlkeld did, however, have an interest in gardening and garden plants slipped into the *Synopsis* under entries of native plants: examples include the double forms of *Caltha palustris* (marsh marigold), *Lychnis flos-cuculi* (ragged robin), and *Silene dioicia* (red campion). He also included non-native trees such as *Acer pseudoplatanus* (sycamore), which he noted was planted on landed estates to form walks and avenues and for walks in St Stephen's Green, Dublin. It is likely that the sixteen varieties of holly, which Threlkeld noted were grown in gardens, some of which he named, were taken from a list in Philip Miller's recently published *The gardener's and florist's dictionary*, which had appeared in 1724. Threlkeld evidently either owned or had access to a copy of this work belonging to Sir Thomas Molyneux (1661–1733).[84]

THRELKELD AND MOLYNEUX

One of the interesting aspects of the *Synopsis* is the support the leading Irish physician of the time, Sir Thomas Molyneux, provided to Threlkeld. The wealthy Molyneux, the first state physician in Ireland, four times president of the Royal College of Physicians of Ireland, and the professor of physic in Trinity College Dublin, had built a magnificent house in Peter Street in 1711 near St Patrick's Cathedral and had amassed a large collection of natural history specimens.[85] Shortly before the *Synopsis* was published, Molyneux gave Threlkeld his notes on plants, compiled some twenty-six years previously, as well as access to his collections.[86] Plants were arranged in alphabetical order in the *Synopsis*, and, as most of the sheets down

---

81 Ibid., Sig. F8r–G1r (purple loose-strife); Synnott, 'Commentary on Irish names used by Threlkeld', 128.   82 John K'Eogh, *Botanalogia universalis Hibernica or, a general Irish herbal* (Cork, 1735), p. 72; D.E. Allen and Gabrielle Hatfield, *Medicinal plants in folk tradition: an ethnobotany of Britain & Ireland* (Portland and London, 2004), p. 164; Peter Wyse Jackson, *Ireland's generous nature: the past and present uses of wild plants in Ireland* (St Louis, Missouri, 2014), p. 393. On John K'Eogh see E.C. Nelson's chapter in this volume.   83 J.C. Loudon, *An encyclopaedia of gardening* (London, 1835), p. 354; Nelson, *The first Irish flora*, p. xxiii.   84 Threlkeld, *Synopsis*, Sigs. B8r (marsh marigold); F7v (ragged robin); F8r (red campion); A2v (sycamore); A3v (holly); I1v (oak). Threlkeld's oak reference mentions Philip Miller's *The gardener's and florist's dictionary: or a complete system of horticulture*, 2 vols (London, 1724), p. 85 on the subject of honeydew on the leaves of oaks.   85 P.M. Byrne, 'Molyneux, Sir Thomas (1661–1733), physician, natural historian, and antiquarian', *DIB*. See also P.H. Kelly's chapter in this volume. 86 Threlkeld, *Synopsis*, Preface, Sig. c3r; Threlkeld, on p. 15 of the Appendix, states of 'Muscus erectus abietiformis' (*Huperzia selago* (fir clubmoss)), that there was 'a very fair Specimen of this *Moss* preserved by the Doctor, not in the least decay'd these 26 Years', and on p. 19 he refers to 'Corallina alba nodosa' (an unidentified marine organism, probably a coralline alga: Nelson, *The first Irish flora*, 119), which he had found 'among the Drs. Collections either without a Name, or the Label lost off it'. On p. 7 of the Appendix Threlkeld explains the printing history of the additional information he received from Molyneux.

Synopsis Stirpium

HIBERNICARUM

Sponte Nascentium,

ALPHABETICE DISPOSITA.

A.

ABIES SCOTICA, Hortulanis nostris perperam dicta, *The Scotch Firr-tree* grows plentifully in the *Highlands* of *Scotland*, and is really the *Pinus Sylvestris folijs brevibus glaucis, Conis parvis albentibus.*

Found by Mr. *Harrison* in *Ireland* in the County of *Kerry* where the *Arbutus* grows. Dr. *Richardson* proves by strong Arguments

A   that

4.7 Signature of Thomas Molyneux on Caleb Threlkeld, *Synopsis stirpium Hibernicarum* (Dublin, 1727), Sig. A1r. © The Board of Trinity College Dublin.

to the letter 'P' had already been printed, Molyneux's additions could not be inserted in the main text and were therefore included in an appendix. The appendix consists mainly of brief plant entries, not in alphabetical order, mostly in English with a small number in Latin. As has been pointed out by Nelson, the authorship of the appendix is complex and disentangling Molyneux's contributions from those of Threlkeld is sometimes difficult.[87] Some entries are composite, with Threlkeld's additions and interpolations indicated by quotation marks or commonplace marks. It is probable that the pressures of meeting the printer's deadlines were responsible.

PUBLICATION OF THE *SYNOPSIS*

Threlkeld included a fulsome six-page dedication to Hugh Boulter (1672–1742), who had become archbishop of Armagh in 1724. This might suggest that he had moved away from dissent but the more likely reason was that Boulter was one of the most powerful men in Ireland.[88] Threlkeld's remark in the preface that 'Your Grace's Approbation of this Attempt ... is still a further Demonstration of Your great Beneficence to this Kingdom' suggests that Boulter gave some financial support towards its printing.[89] This is supported by an entry in the records of the Medico-Philosophical Society.[90] These contain a transcription of a paper on the 'Present State of Natural History in Ireland' by Dr John Rutty (1698–1775), written to the editor of the *Universal Advertiser*.[91] Rutty notes that 'the first essay towards an account of the vegetables of this Kingdom' (identified in the margin as Threlkeld's *Synopsis*), although 'imperfectly executed yet as being the first attempt was encouraged by the munificence of the late Primate Boulter'.[92] Boulter was more tolerant of Dissenters than many of his bishops, recommending to his clergy that they should try to instruct them and correct their errors with kindness and gentleness, and that there should also be a 'Readiness to do them all good Offices'.[93] Molyneux's input and support for the *Synopsis* may also have had an influence on the archbishop.

The *Synopsis* was published in Dublin in late October 1726 and a second issue appeared in 1727.[94] Nelson noted that some copies of the Dublin 1727 issue contained a subscription list. Of the fourteen copies I have checked, two have a subscription list.[95] The subscription list has ninety-nine subscribers of whom forty-three are listed as being from Galway. The Galway subscribers include the governor of Galway, George St George, first Baron St George (*c.*1658–1735), George Staunton, who was

---

87 Nelson, *The first Irish flora*, p. xxiii. 88 Ibid. 89 Threlkeld, *Synopsis*, Dedication, Sig. A3v. 90 Royal College of Physicians of Ireland: Medico-Philosophical Society Archive, MPS/1 Memoirs, 3 February 1757, pp 111–2. 91 *Universal Advertiser*, 8 Jan. 1757. 92 Royal College of Physicians of Ireland: Medico-Philosophical Society Archive, MPS/1 Memoirs, 3 February 1757, pp 111–12. 93 Hugh Boulter, *The charge given by Hugh, lord archbishop of Ardmagh and primate of all Ireland to his clergy* (Dublin, 1725), p. 15. 94 E.C. Nelson, 'The publication date of the first Irish flora, Caleb Threlkeld's *Synopsis stirpium Hibernicarum* 1726', *Glasra*, 2 (1978), 37–42. 95 Nelson, *The first Irish flora*, pp xxv, lii. I have examined twelve original copies and a digital copy from the British Library on ECCO. I am very grateful to the staff of Armagh Public Library for checking their copy for me.

Caleb Threlkeld: dissenting minister, physician and botanist

mayor of Galway in 1725, and two aldermen. Three were army officers. There is also a Patrick Molyneux, possibly a relation of Thomas Molyneux's. The considerable number of Galway plant records, a county that Threlkeld does not seem to have visited himself, may have been added in view of the number of Galway subscribers. It is likely that Molyneux was responsible for mustering the majority of these subscribers, most of whom cannot have been known to Threlkeld himself.

Six women are listed as subscribers, three of whom were from the landed gentry: 'Lady Dorathea Royden' who was almost certainly Lady Dorothy Rawdon (d. 1733), widow of Sir John Rawdon of Moira, Co. Down, third baronet, who had died in 1724, and the mother of John Rawdon (1720–93), first earl of Moira. Dorothy was also the daughter of the lawyer and politician Sir Richard Levinge (1656–1724) and she was joined by her sister-in-law, Lady Isabella Levinge of Monelea (d. 1731) and a Lady McCarthy.[96] There were four clergymen and four apothecaries, including a William Johnston in Glaslough, Co. Monaghan, and one surgeon and only one physician, Thomas Molyneux himself. There was one MP, Colley Lyons (d. 1741), of River Lyons, who was elected in the 1727 Irish parliament for King's County (now Co. Offaly).

The success of the two Dublin issues of 1726 and 1727 appears to have encouraged Threlkeld to bring out a London edition.[97] This London edition was probably published later in 1727 and advertisements for it ran in the *Dublin Weekly Journal* between 6 January 1728 and 3 February 1728. Unlike the advertisements in the previous year for the Dublin issue, which did not mention a price, the London edition in bound form was 'Three British Shillings and a half'.[98]

Threlkeld died at the end of April 1728, two months later, and Pulteney's unnamed source said he was buried in the new plot belonging to St Patrick's Cathedral, attended by children from a charitable school, to which he was probably physician. This plot, known as the Cabbage Garden Cemetery, is now a public park, and to date no records of his burial or grave has been found. The memorialist gives him a fitting epitaph, adding that he was much regretted by the poor 'to whom he had been both as a man, and as a physician, a kind benefactor'.[99]

RECEPTION AND AFTERLIFE OF THE *SYNOPSIS*

In a letter from William Sherard (1659–1728) to Richard Richardson (1663–1741) of 5 August 1727, Sherard noted that Johann Jakob Dillenius (1687–1747), the editor of the third edition of Ray's *Synopsis*, was going to go to Dublin to meet 'the professor'

96 On the family connections of the Rawdons see D.W. Hayton, 'Thomas Prior, Sir John Rawdon and "improvement"' in Raymond Gillespie and Roy F. Foster (eds), *Irish provincial cultures in the long eighteenth century* (Dublin, 2012), p. 109.   **97** See Nelson, *The first Irish flora*, pp xxvi–xxx, for discussion of the three issues.   **98** *Dublin Weekly Journal*, 1727/8, pp 438, 438, 442, 458, 570, 574, 578, 582, 585. The value of the British shilling was set at 13 Irish pence since 1700: Patrick Honohan, 'Using other people's money: farewell to the Irish pound,' *History Ireland*, 10:1 (2002), 34.   **99** Pulteney, 'Letter to

and a botanist, 'author of a synopsis stirpium [Hibernicarum]'.[100] Threlkeld's criticisms of Dillenius in the *Synopsis*, in which he took him to task for what Threlkeld considered unnecessary multiplication of plant names, had, however, caused considerable offence and there is no evidence that Dillenius came to Dublin. Threlkeld's attacks on Dillenius harmed him in the eyes of English commentators such as Pulteney.[101] However, Robert Brown (1773–1858), the eminent Scottish botanist, who spent five years in Ireland between 1795 and 1800 as an army surgeon, mainly in the north of Ireland, clearly did not share that opinion.[102] Brown later called a plant, which he found on the coast of Tasmania in December 1803, *Threlkeldia diffusa* in his memory.[103]

Threlkeld's work has rightly been celebrated by Irish botanists but as well as for his plant records he deserves recognition in the history of medicine for his case description of dysentery cured by *Lythrum salicaria* noted above. While the use of *Lysimachia* for 'fluxes' goes back to Dioscorides and is included in many of the sixteenth- and seventeenth-century herbals, there was often no clear distinction between the virtues of the yellow-flowered *Lysimachia vulgaris* (Primulaceae), and the purple-flowered *Lythrum salicaria* (Lythraceae). The noted herbalist, John Gerard (*c.*1545–1612), at the end of his chapter (112) 'On Willow herbe, and Loosestrife', which includes *Lythrum salicaria*, described the virtues of the yellow forms of *Lysimachia* and says the 'others have not beene experimented, wherefore until some matter woorthy the noting doth offer it selfe unto our consideration, I will omit further to discourse hereof'.[104] Threlkeld's report was certainly 'some matter woorthy the noting' and the Swedish German physician Johann Andreas Murray (1740–91) would later credit Threlkeld with the first report on the plant as a remedy for diarrhoeal illnesses in Ireland.[105] This report entered the European medical literature of the eighteenth century through Samuel Dale's entry for *Salicaria* in the third and fourth editions of his *Pharmacologia*, which references Threlkeld's *Synopsis*.[106] Most of the references tabulated in a recent review of the chemical compounds and medical uses of *Lythrum salicaria* are in the French or German literature with only one listed from the British literature, the *Edinburgh new dispensatory* (1818).[107] This included

Mr Urban', 63–4; Nelson, *The first Irish flora*, p. xxiii. **100** G.C. Druce, *The Dillenian herbaria* (Oxford, 1907), pp lx–lxi, includes a summary of a letter (Early Modern Letters Online: http://emlo.bodleian. ox.ac.uk/ profile/image/66bcadd2-f02b-455b 8548-c5aa9f7a105c, accessed 15 April 2022) from Dillenius to the botanist Samuel Brewer (1670–1743), in which, it appears that perhaps it was Brewer who intended to travel to Ireland. The 'professor' with whom they were in contact was probably Dr William Stephens (1696–1760), who was, at the time, lecturing in botany at Trinity College Dublin, who had been exchanging seeds with William Sherard. On Stephens see E.C. Nelson's chapter on Trinity College's physic garden in 1726 in this volume. **101** Richard Pulteney, *Historical and biographical sketches of the progress of botany*, 2 vols (London, 1790), ii, pp 165–6. **102** D. J. Mabberley, 'Brown, Robert (1773–1858), botanist', *ODNB*. **103** Robert Brown, *Prodromus florae Novae Hollandiae et Insulae Van-Diemen … 2* vols (London, 1810), i, pp 409–10: 'Dixi in memoriam CALEB THRELKELD, MD, synopsis stirpium Hibernicarum auctoris'. **104** John Gerard, *The herball or general historie of plantes* (London, 1597), p. 388. **105** Johann Andreas Murray, *Apparatus medicaminum tam simplicium quam praeparatorum et compositorum in praxeos adiumentum*, 3 vols (Göttingen, 1784), iii, p. 511. **106** Dale, *Pharmacologia*, 3rd edition (London, 1737), p. 240; *Pharmacologia*, 4th edition (Leiden, 1739), p. 264. **107** Jakub Piwowarski et al., '*Lythrum salicaria* L. –

information from the latest London, Edinburgh and Dublin dispensatories, listing this plant as an entry from the Dublin Dispensatory and noting that 'the decoction of this plant has been long celebrated in Ireland for diarrhoeas'.[108] Threlkeld said that he was making knowledge of the cure by *Lythrum salicaria* freely available, hoping it might be useful 'to the Poor in such desperate Circumstances'.[109] If extracts of *Lythrum salicaria* return to therapeutic use, he deserves due recognition for his observation. Threlkeld rightly has a place in Irish botanical history but he also deserves to be celebrated in Irish medical history as a kind and caring physician whose *Synopsis* gives a valuable insight into general medical practice in Dublin in the early eighteenth century.

underestimated medicinal plant from European traditional medicine: a review', *Journal of Ethnopharmacology*, 170 (2015), 226–50, Table 4 at 230. **108** Andrew Duncan, *The Edinburgh new dispensatory*, 7th edition (Edinburgh, 1813), p. 176. **109** Threlkeld, *Synopsis*, Sig. G1r (purple loosestrife).

CHAPTER FIVE

Caleb Threlkeld's plant records

DECLAN DOOGUE

THE PUBLICATION OF Caleb Threlkeld's *Synopsis stirpium Hibernicarum* in Dublin in 1726 must have come as something of a surprise to those with an interest in Irish botany.[1] Previously, most botanical exploration of Ireland had been conducted far from the capital, by explorers seeking new and unusual species in the further reaches of the kingdom. A small number of spectacular species had been recorded, mainly from the north-east and west of Ireland and had been brought to the attention of the botanical community through the efforts of the collectors Edward Lhuyd (1660–1709), Gédéon Bonnivert (1651–1703), William Sherard (1659–1728) and Richard Heaton (1601–66), and thence through the publications of botanists based in England, particularly William How (1620–56) and John Ray (1627–1705).[2]

Threlkeld's work stands in the long-established tradition of published herbals, detailing the medicinal uses of plants, but also comprises a substantial check-list of the flora of the greater Dublin area with much topographical content. An expanded commentary on the title page ('A Short Treatise of Native Plants, especially such as grow spontaneously in the Vicinity of *Dublin*; with their *Latin*, *English* and *Irish* Names; And an Abridgement of their Vertues. With several new Discoverys') sets out his stall. As a result, an illuminating summary of the state of the flora of Dublin during the first quarter of the eighteenth century emerges, with *inter alia* insights into the art of the practitioner-herbalist, academic botanist and religious minister.

The purported medicinal value of many plant species was well known and transmitted both in the oral tradition and in manuscript form. Later, printed herbals originated in the late fifteenth century, incorporating elements of botanical identification, including illustrations, herbal medicine, gardening and culinary uses.[3] In published form, this evolving knowledge was widely disseminated, aided by the adoption of Latin as a common language. In some cases the arrangement of species within books was simply alphabetical or was related to their functionality or growth forms. Later, with increased appreciation of the need for a classification based on

---

1 Caleb Threlkeld, *Synopsis stirpium Hibernicarum* (Dublin, 1726). 2 E.C. Nelson, '"In the contemplation of vegetables" – Caleb Threlkeld (1676–1728), his life, background and contribution to Irish botany', *Journal of the Society for the Bibliography of Natural History*, 9:3, (1979), 257–73. 3 Agnes Arber, *Herbals, their origin and evolution. A chapter in the history of botany, 1470–1670* (Cambridge, 1912), pp 10–34. The text was expanded in the second edition of 1938.

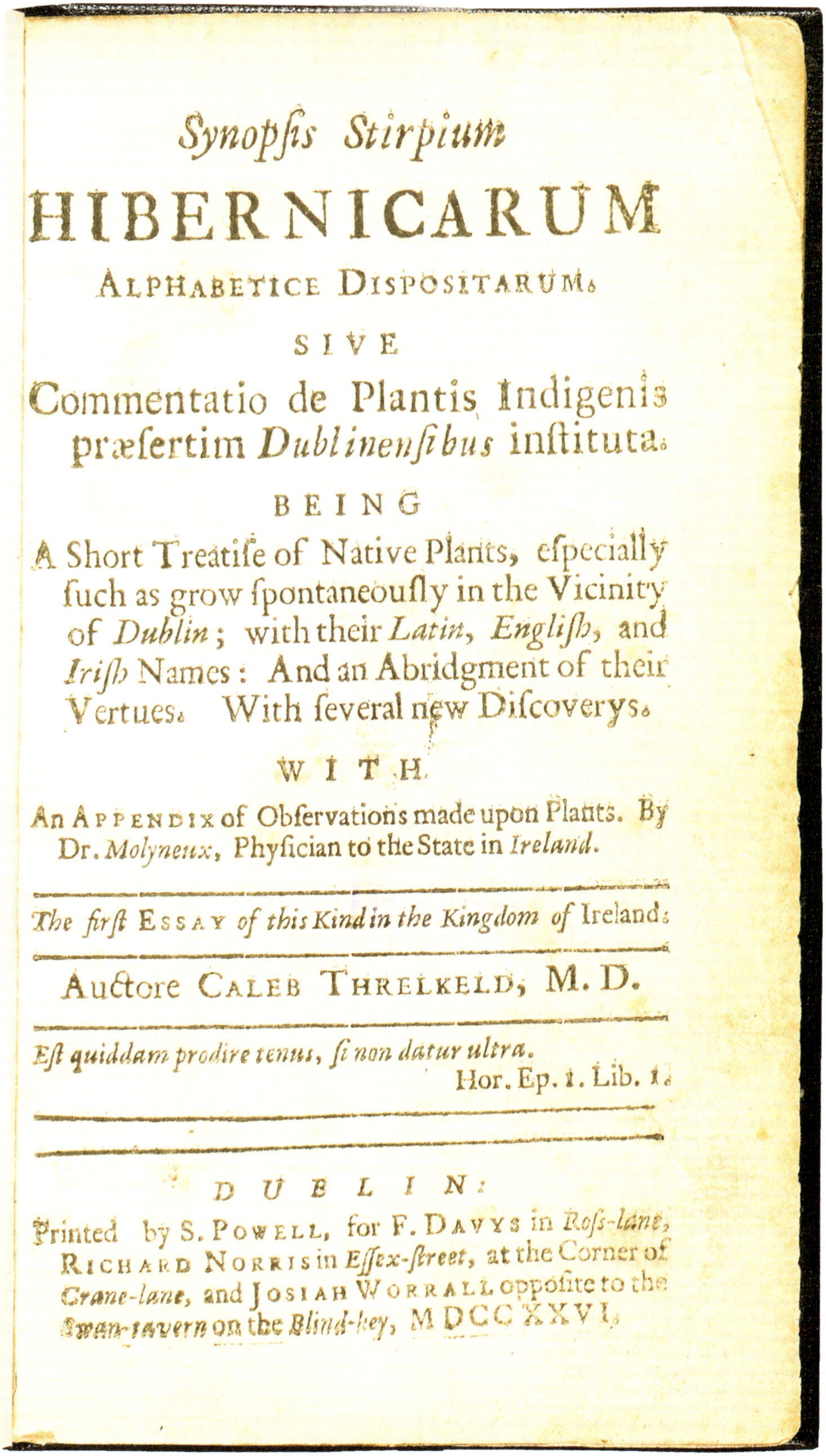

Synopsis Stirpium

HIBERNICARUM

ALPHABETICE DISPOSITARUM,

SIVE

Commentatio de Plantis Indigenis
præsertim *Dublinensibus* instituta.

BEING

A Short Treatise of Native Plants, especially
such as grow spontaneously in the Vicinity
of *Dublin*; with their *Latin, English*, and
Irish Names: And an Abridgment of their
Vertues. With several new Discoverys.

WITH

An APPENDIX of Observations made upon Plants. By
Dr. *Molyneux*, Physician to the State in *Ireland*.

The first ESSAY *of this Kind in the Kingdom of* Ireland.

Auctore CALEB THRELKELD, M.D.

Est quiddam prodire tenus, si non datur ultra.
Hor. Ep. 1. Lib. 1.

DUBLIN:

Printed by S. POWELL, for F. DAVYS in *Ross-lane*,
RICHARD NORRIS in *Essex-street*, at the Corner of
Crane-lane, and JOSIAH WORRALL opposite to the
Swan-tavern on the *Blind-key*, MDCCXXVI.

5.1 Caleb Threlkeld, *Synopsis stirpium Hibernicarum* (Dublin, 1726), title page. Image
courtesy of the National Library of Ireland, LO 13501.

discernible physical attributes, alternative classifications evolved in Europe. These ideas found expression in the British and Irish context in the researches of John Ray, whose *Synopsis methodica stirpium Britannicarum* in its various editions was to stimulate botanical fieldwork for many decades.[4] It was some years later (1732), before the young Carl Linnaeus (1707–78) was to embark on his epic tour of Lapland where his ideas on classification, influenced strongly by Ray, based on floral parts, began to take form. He was still refining his natural system of generic and specific classifications which were not to surface for some time.[5]

The taxonomy and nomenclature adopted by Threlkeld was thus of its time. To modern botanical readers (setting aside unfamiliar spelling and typography) the most obvious difference was the employment of the polynomial phrase-names that preceded the binomial system developed by Linnaeus. Polynomials were condensed word-strings illustrating the salient points of agreement and difference in closely related species. Thus, the species we know as *Primula vulgaris* (primrose) appears as 'PRIMULA VERIS MINOR VULGARIS' (to contrast and distinguish it from *Primula veris* (cowslip) 'PRIMULA VERIS MAJOR').[6]

THRELKELD'S SOURCES

Threlkeld had acquired his botanical skills in the north of England and applied them as a herbalist in Dublin. He was part of a tradition of field naturalists who found interest in the search for wild plants in their natural habitats. The fruits of these discoveries were published in local lists or preserved as specimens in *horti sicci* (herbaria, or reference collections of pressed and dried plants). John Ray's prototypical *Catalogus plantarum circa Cantabrigiam nascentium* (London, 1660) had fostered the concept of the local flora, which listed not just the English name of each species occurring in the Cambridge area, with their formal polynomials and synonyms but also included details of the nature and occurrence of the relevant species in the locality.[7]

Details of Threlkeld's early life and studies have been explored by Nelson and Lawlor.[8] In his 'Preface' Threlkeld speaks of botanizing with 'ingenious men' where he had enjoyed first-hand encounters ('ocular Demonstration') with the various wild species in their natural habitats ('in their native Soil').[9] He noted the geographical

---

4 John Ray, *Synopsis methodica stirpium Britannicarum* (London, 1680, 1696, 1724).   **5** Carl Linnaeus, *Critica botanica* (Leiden, 1737) and *Genera plantarum* (Leiden, 1737); *Species plantarum* (Stockholm, 1757).   **6** Threlkeld, *Synopsis*, Sig. H8r.   **7** See English translations by A.H. Ewen and C.T. Prime (eds), *Ray's flora of Cambridgeshire* (Codicote, 1975) and P.H. Oswald, and C.D. Preston, *John Ray's Cambridge catalogue (1660)* (London, 2011).   **8** See E.C. Nelson and M. Raven, 'Caleb Threlkeld's family', *Glasra*, new series, 3 (1998), 161–6, and Emer Lawlor's chapter on Caleb Threlkeld's life and sources in this volume. See also E.C. Nelson, '"In the contemplation of vegetables"', and Caleb Threlkeld, *The first Irish flora. Synopsis stirpium Hibernicarum*, ed. E.C. Nelson (facsimile with annotations by E.C. Nelson and D.M. Synnott) (Kilkenny, 1988), pp [xiii]–l.   **9** Threlkeld, *Synopsis*, Preface, Sig. c3r.

CATALOGUS
PLANTARUM
CIRCA
CANTABRIGIAM
naſcentium :

In quo exhibentur
Quotquot hactenus inventæ ſunt, quæ
vel ſponte proveniunt, vel in
agris ſeruntur;

Unà cùm
Synonymis ſelectioribus, locis natalibus
& obſervationibus quibuſdam
oppidò raris.

Adjiciuntur in gratiam tyronum,
Index Anglico-latinus, Index locorum,
Etymologia nominum, & Explicatio
quorundam terminorum.

CANTABRIGIÆ:
Excudebat *Joann. Field*, celeberrimæ
Academiæ Typographus.
Impenſis Gulielmi Nealand, *Bibliopolæ.*
Ann Dom. 1660.

5.2 John Ray, *Catalogus plantarum circa Cantabrigiam nascentium* (London, 1660), title page.
By permission of the Governors and Guardians of Marsh's Library. © Marsh's Library.

positions of the plants where they were encountered and prepared a *hortus siccus*.[10] He had realized the significance of the circumstances governing the geographical occurrence of certain species in natural habitats and incorporated these insights into his later commentaries regarding their soil and habitat preferences in Dublin. These comments are explored in the next chapter of this volume.

He came from that vigorous field tradition, then current in the north of England and exemplified by the botanical researches of polymath William Nicolson (1655–1727), bishop of Carlisle, who moved from that diocese in 1718 to Ireland, having been promoted to the bishopric of Derry.[11] Nicolson (a regular correspondent of botanist and antiquarian Edward Lhuyd) had worked with Thomas Lawson (1630–91), a Quaker and the main botanist in Cumberland, and collected many specimens from the Salkeld area.[12] A shared interest in field botany bridged the social divide between religious conformists and nonconformists, the latter of which included Threlkeld and may have facilitated his later contacts with the Dublin establishment.

ANATOMY OF A THRELKELD SPECIES ACCOUNT

Threlkeld followed closely the species concepts of Ray, supplementing many of the accounts with listings of their medicinal values. The species accounts are laid out in alphabetical order, adhering to the presentation style and content adopted by Ray in his *Catalogus plantarum circa Cantabrigiam nascentium*, employing the polynomial nomenclature of the time, and conforming closely to more general works such as the second edition of his *Catalogus plantarum Angliae*, thus sidestepping the systematic or method-based arrangement of Ray's later classification.[13]

As Threlkeld provided no descriptions of the plants themselves, the book had little use as a means of identification. Its users would have acquired the necessary identification skills by other means or would have relied on named material supplied by others, by having access to other illustrated works, by having the use of volumes of identified pressed specimens (*horti sicci*), or by engagement in an oral tradition where plant lore was passed from one practitioner to another.

Each species account (see Fig. 5.3 for an example) comprises elements relating to the polynomial of the species (cited in block capitals), with some synonyms in lower case.[14] This is followed by a contemporary English name (italics), an Irish name where available (Gothic script), some topographical and ecological references with place

---

10 Declan Doogue and J.A.N. Parnell, 'Fragments of an eighteenth-century herbarium – possibly that of Caleb Threlkeld in Trinity College Dublin (TCD)', *Glasra*, new series, 1 (1992), 99–109. 11 On Nicolson's botanizing in Cumbria see William Nicolson, *A seventeenth-century flora of Cumbria. William Nicolson's catalogue of plants, 1690*, edited by E.J. Whittaker (Gateshead, 1981). 12 On Lawson see E.J. Whittaker, *Thomas Lawson 1630–1691: north country botanist, Quaker and schoolmaster* (York, 1986). 13 John Ray, *Catalogus plantarum Angliae, et insularum adjacentium ... Editio secunda* (London, 1677). 14 An extremely useful concordance between the polynomials cited by Threlkeld to their modern equivalents is in Nelson (ed.), *The first Irish flora*, pp 13–119. Nomenclature here follows the fourth edition of Clive Stace's *New flora of the British Isles* (Stowmarket, 2019).

C H

and Pain in the Joints; and præfcribed for an Antipodagrick to *Charles* the Fifth, by the Phyficians of *Genua*. It ftands in greater Reputation among Authors for opening Obftructions, than the *Stinking Orrach*.

CHELIDONIUM MINUS, Chelidonia rotundifolia minor, *Pilewort*, or the *Leffer Celandine*, Irifh ᵹꞃᴀɴɴ ᴀꞃᴄᴀɪɴ. I have feen this Flower in *March* 27. 1726. under the Hedges between *Roper's-reft* and *Dolphin's-barn*; its yellow Flowers look beautiful before the Grafs be up, for in Summer it cannot be found eafily. It is praifed for the Hæmorrhoids, and for preferving the Teeth and Gumms from Rottennefs.

CHRYSANTHEMUM SEGETUM Bellis Lutea folijs profundè incifis major, *Corn Marygold*, Irifh ᴃᴜɪꞁᴀɪɴ ᴃᴜɪꞁᴇ and ꞁᴇꞁᴀɴ. It is in fome Place a Peft to the Corn, and Mannour-courts do amerce carelefs Tenants, who do not weed it out before it comes to Seed.

CHRYSANTHEMUM SEGETUM NOSTRAS FOLIO GLAUCO MULTI-SCISSO MAJUS, FLORE MINORE. The Leaves are glaucous like Garden *Poppy*, and much cut. Found once near the Cart Road at the End of *Inifacore-hill*, flanting the Hill, and in a muddy Bank of a Ditch

C 4   in

5.3 Threlkeld's account for the early-flowering *Ficaria verna* (formerly *Ranunculus ficaria*) (lesser celandine), *Synopsis stirpium Hibernicarum* (Dublin, 1726), Sig. C4r. Image courtesy of the National Library of Ireland, LO 13501.

names italicized. Occasionally remarks on the growth characteristics or seasonality of each species are included before concluding with an itemization of its medicinal uses, and sometimes its culinary virtues or practical utility. Greek script was employed occasionally. The inclusion of dates of discovery of plants by Threlkeld was a belated addition and relate to the period from 1721 but mostly 1725–6 while he was preparing his manuscript for publication.

The supplementary habitat inclusions, sometimes reinforced by phrases such as 'I saw' or 'We came upon', indicate a direct personal knowledge and understanding of the circumstances in which the plants grew naturally. Where the ecological content is second-hand, this is indicated by comments such as 'sent from' or 'gathered in'. Some species accounts are skeletal and others more detailed embellished or interlaced with sideswipes at contemporary botanists, incorporating in some instances provocative taxonomic, political and religious allusions.

The bulk of each species account is written in English rather than in Latin (unlike the Latin descriptions of plants in the 1724 edition of Ray's *Synopsis*).[15] As Threlkeld's dedication and preface are also in English, this indicates that his outreach was primarily for the benefit of herbalists and others who had no access to or need of Latin.

THRELKELD'S ORBIT

Threlkeld lived in Mark's Alley, off Francis Street in Dublin (Fig. 5.4).[16] Access to natural habitats was relatively easy, on foot or horseback. In his book he set down the localities of interesting, rare or unusual species, although the sites of many commoner plants were usually not included.

The surviving topographical records of these rarer species provide a good overview of the places he visited. Short walks brought him via Islandbridge to Chapelizod or the Phoenix Park (the Deer Park).[17] Here he encountered the plants of dry sandy unimproved grassland, particularly on the slopes associated with the down-cutting of the River Liffey through the lime-rich glacial till along the stretch from Conyngham Road. Further to the west he would have surmounted Knockmaroon Hill and descended onto the wooded stretches of the Liffey along the Strawberry Beds and onwards to Lucan.

Southward he would have come to Inchicore, Dolphin's Barn, Crumlin, Harold's Cross, and Walkinstown, the esker at Greenhills and beyond. Trips northward led towards Broadstone, Cabra, Stoneybatter, Grangegorman, Glasnevin, Cardiff's Bridge and Finglas.

Travelling south towards the coast would take in Baggotrath, Ballsbridge, Merrion and the mouth of the River Dodder. Trips through Summerhill to

---

15 The 1724 edition of Ray's *Synopsis*, did, however, include many locality details in English. 16 Threlkeld, *Synopsis*, Preface, Sig. c3v. 17 For plants in the Phoenix Park see P.A. Reilly, *Wild plants of the Phoenix Park* (Glasnevin, 1993) and J.A. McCullen, *An illustrated history of the Phoenix Park: landscape and management to 1880* (Dublin, 2011).

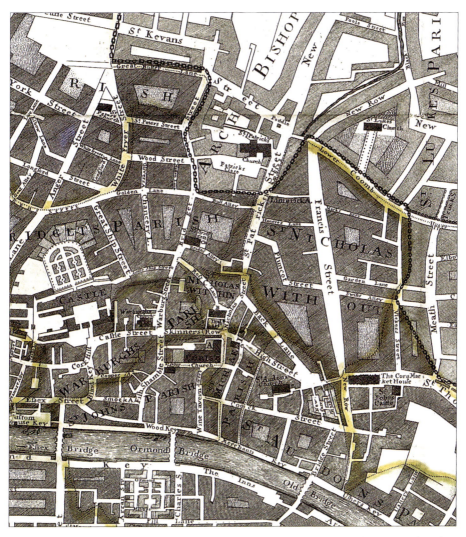

5.4 Detail from Charles Brooking's map of Dublin, 1728, showing Mark's Alley, the location of Threlkeld's Dublin home. By permission of the Royal Irish Academy. © RIA.

Ballybough at the mouth of the River Tolka led directly to the salt-marshes and mudflats of the inner bay. The initial enclosure of the intake area between Sherriff Street and the (North) Strand road was by then underway.

Excursions further afield to places such as Balscaddan in Howth via the coast road would have been undertaken on horseback. Similarly, outings along the route of the present Malahide Road led through Coolock and Balgriffin. The records from Celbridge might have come from Thomas Molyneux (1661–1733).[18] The origins of some records from Meath are more challenging.

18 For information on Thomas Molyneux see chapter 3 in this volume.

BOOKS CONSULTED BY THRELKELD

Substantial works of reference were essential components of botanists' and herbalists' personal libraries or were accessed through the benevolence of others. Then, as now, botanists in the field employed some favoured, compact summary book (a *vade mecum*), and where necessary consulted more detailed descriptions later. Threlkeld makes many references in his 'Preface' and within the species accounts to his literature sources, indicating his indebtedness to previous authors such as William Turner (1509/10–68), John Gerard (c.1545–1612), John Parkinson (1566/7–1650), Christopher Merret (1614–95) and especially John Ray, 'one of the greatest botanists of the age'.[19]

In finalizing his text before its publication in October 1726, the most up-to-date source for matters of plant description was the recently published third edition of John Ray's *Synopsis methodica stirpium Britannicarum* (London, 1724).[20] This edition, reworked and updated after Ray's death by Johann Jakob Dillenius (1684–1747), included illustrations and provided expanded descriptions of the plants with additional localities, as then known. Throughout his work Threlkeld refers to this 1724 edition of Ray's *Synopsis*, occasionally mentioning an earlier edition, instancing the illustrations of *Anacamptis pyramidalis* (pyramidal orchid) (Fig. 5.5) and another of *Linum radiola* (allseed).[21] His mention of the index at the end of the third edition of the *Synopsis*, where dubious records were kept separately, indicates direct familiarity with and use of this edition.

As a herbalist his knowledge derived from field experience, personal contacts and from possession of and access to a wide range of herbal literature. This latter function was performed by other works, many of which had appeared in the years immediately preceding the production of his *Synopsis stirpium Hibernicarum*. These include works such as Patrick Blair's *Botanick essays* (London, 1720), and much earlier, Gerard's *Herball* (London, 1597), subsequently updated by Thomas Johnson (d. 1644) in 1633 and 1636. In its layout and generous degree of illustration Gerard's *Herball* had functioned in its original and revised forms as standard references for generations of field botanists and herbalists. It was basically a translation of other works and the illustrations were largely acquired from other sources. Threlkeld personally owned a copy of one of the Johnson-revised editions and under the account of *Saxifraga tridactylites* (rue-leaved saxifrage), stated that 'There is a good Icon of it in *Gerard* Emaculated, *page* 624. where one of its former Owners had added these Words in my Copy: This is a perfect Cure for the Kings-evil, it flowers in the *Spring*, and perisheth with the Heat' (Fig. 5.6). He also commended the illustration of *Lapsana communis* (nipplewort) in the same work.[22]

19 Threlkeld, *Synopsis*, pp 23–5. 20 E.C. Nelson, 'The publication date of the first Irish flora, Caleb Threlkeld's *Synopsis Stirpium Hibernicarum* 1726', *Glasra*, 2 (1978), 37–42. 21 Ray, *Synopsis methodica stirpium Britannicarum* (1724), tab. XV, fig. 3, at p. 348, includes the illustration of *Linum radiola* ('Radiola vulgaris serpyllifolia … The least Rupture-wort, or All-seed'). 22 Threlkeld, *Synopsis*, Sig. H3v (rue-leaved saxifrage); F3v–F4r (nipplewort).

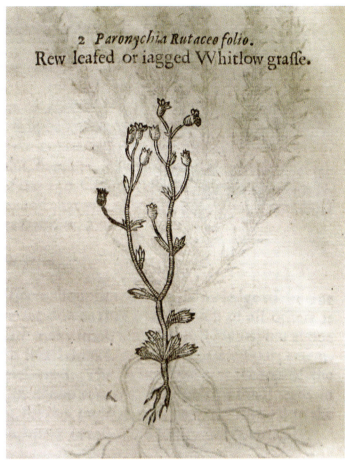

5.5 *Anacamptis pyramidalis* (pyramidal orchid) drawn by Johann Jakob Dillenius, from the third edition of John Ray, *Synopsis methodica stirpium Britannicarum* (London, 1724), Tab XVIII, opposite p. 377. Courtesy of Declan Doogue.   5.6 (*above right*) *Saxifraga tridactylites* (rue-leaved saxifrage) as illustrated in the 'enlarged and amended' second edition of John Gerard's *The herball or generall historie of plantes* (London, 1633), p. 624. By permission of the Trustees of the Edward Worth Library, Dublin. © Edward Worth Library.

Threlkeld's referencing of John Parkinson's herbal *Theatrum botanicum: the theater of plants* (London, 1640), bemoaning that the same author's earlier *Paradisus* of 1629 was not to be had easily in the Dublin of 1726, may imply that some of these (now) very expensive and rare books were in fact available to him at the time.[23] Threlkeld may have had access to some parts of the *Philosophical Transactions of the Royal Society* in which was reported the effects of the consumption of the roots of

---

23 Ibid., p. 25 of Appendix (reference of scarcity of Parkinson's *Paradisus*). Parkinson's *Theatrum botanicum. The theatre of plants* (London, 1640), is explored in Nelson's chapter on plant records in this volume (pp 45–57). The Dublin physician Edward Worth (1676–1733), whose botanical collection is examined by Elizabethanne Boran in this volume, certainly owned a copy of *Theatrum botanicum*.

5.7 *Anthriscus caucalis* (hedge parsley) as illustrated in Caspar Bauhin, *Prodromus theatri botanici* (Basle, 1671), p. 80. By permission of the Trustees of the Edward Worth Library, Dublin. © Edward Worth Library.

Glaucium flavum and which was referenced in his account of that species ('of the infatuating Force of this, read *Transactions Philosoph*. No. 242, Page 263').[24] The account in the *Philosophical Transactions* by Isaac Newton (1642–1727) reported in graphic detail the startling results of consumption of the roots of this plant on a household in Penzance, Cornwall.[25] It seems strange that Threlkeld should have refrained from using the content of this report if he had had direct sight of it and in this instance, he may well have been relying on a brief citation in Ray's *Synopsis* instead. Elsewhere, however, he had included extended commentary on the drastic effects of consuming the roots of other species such as *Oenanthe crocata* (hemlock water-dropwort) (quoting a Mr Vaughan), which was likely based on the report in the *Transactions*.[26]

Threlkeld's taxonomic readings extended far beyond Ray and other British authors and indicate a wide measure of access, if not actual possession, of a number of seminal contemporary scientific, religious and philosophical works by authors from the European mainland. Under the account of *Anthriscus caucalis* (hedge parsley) he remarked that there was a good image of this species in Caspar Bauhin's *Prodromus theatri botanici* (Basel, 1620 and 1671) (Fig. 5.7), and also comments on Bauhin's account of holly.[27] Similarly, there are several mentions of the works of Herman Boerhaave (1668–1738), Rembert Dodoens (1517–85), Joseph Pitton de Tournefort (1656–1708), and others.[28] Many of his references are not just to the various books but to the actual pages therein, perhaps indicating a level of access to literature of this quality and implying a considerable degree of support from some better-positioned benefactor.

THRELKELD'S ALLEGED PLAGIARISMS

Doubts had been expressed as to the originality of some of the botanical records and supplementary inclusions in Threlkeld's *Synopsis stirpium Hibernicarum*. These reservations derive from contemporary criticisms of the work by Dillenius, who had himself been criticized by Threlkeld throughout his text, mainly on taxonomic matters.[29] The review by Professor Michael Mitchell however confirmed that

---

24 Threlkeld, *Synopsis*, Sig. H3r (yellow horned poppy).   **25** Isaac Newton, 'An account of some effects of papaver corniculatum luteum, &c', *Philosophical Transactions*, 20:242 (1698), 263–4.   **26** Threlkeld, *Synopsis*, Sig. G8v–H1v (hemlock water-dropwort); p. 11 of the Appendix (henbane). Francis Vaughan, 'a Learned Physitian in *Ireland*, living at *Clonmell*, in the County of *Tipperary*', had sent a report on the effects of hemlock water-dropwort to John Ray, who in turn communicated the contents to Hans Sloane (1660–1753). Ray's letter, dated 1 March 1698, was published in the same issue of the *Philosophical Transactions*, 20:238, (1698), 84–6.   **27** Threlkeld, *Synopsis*, Sig. C3r.   **28** Ibid., see, for example, Sig. C3r: 'Caucalis semine aspero …' Caspar Bauhin, *Prodromus theatri botanici* … (Frankfurt am Main, Basle, 1671), p. 80; Sig. O2r: Herman Boerhaave, *Index alter plantarum quae in horto academic Lugduno-Batavo aluntur* (Leiden, 1720); Sig. B6r: Rembert Dodoens, *A nevv herbal, or historie of plants* (London, 1578), translated into English by Henry Lyte; and Sig. B6v: a 'Tournefort *English*', which possibly refers to his *Materia medica, or a description of simple medicines* (London, 1708).   **29** M.E. Mitchell, 'The sources of Threlkeld's *Synopsis stirpium Hibernicarum*', *Proceedings of the Royal Irish Academy*. Section B, 74 (1974), 1–6.

Threlkeld did indeed repeat a number of plant records published previously in editions of John Ray's *Synopsis*. The main species concerned were the unusual rayless form of *Jacobaea vulgaris* (ragwort) and *Cuscuta epiphytum* (dodder) with incorporations of supplementary anecdotal content in the English translation.[30] This material was previously published in Rays' *Synopsis*, but the sources of this material were not clearly acknowledged by Threlkeld other than in the 'Preface'.

However, Threlkeld frequently acknowledged the contribution made by others, particularly Richard Heaton in regard to *Dryas octopetala* (mountain avens) 'from the Mountains betwixt Gort and Galloway', with additional commentary regarding Lhuyd's discovery of the same species in Sligo and further remarks on its abundance in western Scotland – all clearly abstracted from Ray. Similarly, the record of *Scilla verna* (spring squill), the first formally recorded plant species from Dublin, is credited to Heaton and he also set the record straight with regard to the original finder (Heaton) of *Drosera longifolia* (= *D. anglica*) (long-leaved sundew).[31] Nowhere does Threlkeld claim to have been the discoverer of any of these earlier records. Indeed, in many instances he is at pains to cite the origins of his comments, drawing on a wide range of literature sources.

Similarly, he was effusive in his acknowledgment of the direct contribution of Dr Thomas Molyneux, who supplied him with records which were largely incorporated in the appendix. Likewise, he indicated the non-Dublin provenance of some records sent to him from the Monasterevin area – *Erica tetralix* (cross-leaved heath), *Narthecium ossifragum* (bog asphodel), *Rubus saxatilis* (stone bramble) and a species of *Polytrichum* (a hair moss), most likely from raised bogs, and *Samolus valerandi* (brookweed) from fens. *Butomus umbellatus* (flowering-rush) and *Lysimachia vulgaris* (yellow loosestrife) were also sent from the Barrow, possibly by the same unnamed provider, as the River Barrow flows through Monasterevin. Additionally, other species were sent from less clearly defined places – one example is *Lysimachia nemorum* (yellow pimpernel) brought to him, along with its Irish name, from Leinster.[32]

If Threlkeld had restricted the scope of his book to the greater Dublin area, possibly augmented by the various records or specimens consigned to him by others, then this controversy need not have arisen. His over-ambitious adoption of a concept and title so similar to that of John Ray's compelled him to include these earlier discoveries and to expand his vision far beyond his immediate sphere of competence.

---

30 Ibid., 5 and 3 respectively.   **31** Threlkeld, *Synopsis*, Sigs. C2v (mountain avens); E7v (spring squill) and I4v (long-leaved sundew). An image of squill may be found in E.C. Nelson's chapter on plant records in this volume (Fig. 2.11, p. 56).   **32** Ibid., Sigs. E3r (cross-leaved heath); B2v (bog asphodel); I5v (stone bramble); A3r (hair moss); A5v (brookweed); F1r (flowering-rush); G1v (yellow loosestrife); A5v (yellow pimpernel).

THE BOTANICAL LANDSCAPE IN THRELKELD'S TIME

Brooking's map of Dublin (Fig. 6.1, pp 118–19), issued two years after the publication of Threlkeld's *Synopsis stirpium Hibernicarum*, provides a clear picture of the proximity of semi-natural habitat to the city, but the topographical map of Dublin published around 1756 by John Rocque (*c.*1704–62) indicates in far greater detail the extent of such habitats in its immediate environs.

North of the Liffey estuary the River Tolka entered the Dublin Bay at Ballybough Bridge, where Clontarf Island had formed. The North Strand conformed to the natural curvature of the shoreline, which, further north from Raheny (Rahany) to Warren House in Kilbarrack, was still in a dynamic state. Bull Island, now a dominant physical presence in Dublin Bay, had not begun to form, although wet intertidal banks were indicated on Rocques' map. Construction of the Bull Wall, built to increase the scour of the Liffey, leading to the deposition of sand known as North Bull Island, was not to conclude for another century. Blown sand was therefore accumulating on the northern shore of Dublin Bay between Clontarf and Howth in areas that were still farmed. The shoreline was later to be consolidated by the construction of the coastal route to Howth, resulting in coastal squeeze. This in turn precipitated the eclipse of shoreline vegetation formations coinciding with the gradual attenuation of the supply of blown sand from the bay to the mainland.

South of the Liffey, Ringsend was a peninsula, jutting out into the bay to Ringsend Point. Estuarine conditions prevailed on its sheltered inner side where the mouth of the River Dodder spread widely through the area now occupied by housing estates. Early workings leading to the South Wall were at preliminary stages of planning and execution.

Further south, following the coastal routes via Ballsbridge and Merrion, various wetlands were present, as at Simmonscourt and Merrion. Some of these contained freshwater, where springs or seepage features occurred and others were brackish. The early railway system, which later impounded wetlands such as those at Booterstown, was not to be built for another century. Further south, soils which had developed on sea-washed exposures of bedrock and some sea walls enabled species characteristic of the spray zone to maintain a roothold.

Many uncommon plant species have well-defined and restricted habitat requirements. More common species with wider ecological amplitudes occupy a number of different ecological niches in the landscape. Those with narrower tolerances, especially when coupled with more precise topographical data, provide contemporary evidence indicating the presence of certain uncommon habitat-types. These rarer species often occur with others sharing similar habitat requirements. A comparison of these combinations with known present-day species-associations provides evidence of the floristic and habitat alterations which have taken place in the intervening three centuries, and *inter alia* inferentially identifies the drivers of these changes.

As is explored in the next chapter, Threlkeld incorporated substantial ecological content into his species accounts and these inclusions attest to the presence of particular habitat types providing precise evidence of the topographical position of these sites and habitat types, many of which have been lost in the intervening three centuries. The environmental conditions of other areas have been so modified that they can no longer function as suitable habitat for the rarer species as encountered by Threlkeld, though in some instances physical evidence (including the presence of some more ecologically-resilient species) still lingers in the landscape of modern Dublin.

Significantly, one of Ireland's foremost botanists, Nathaniel Colgan (1851–1919), author of *Flora of county Dublin* (Dublin, 1904), had few difficulties in accepting the validity of Threlkeld's identifications and Dublin records. A recent revision by the Dublin Naturalists' Field Club of Colgan's *Flora* reconsidered the topographical and ecological contents of each species account, and found that these were consistent with present-day habitat and geographical distribution patterns.[33]

CONCLUSION

Threlkeld's Dublin records comprise a meaningful catalogue of the state of the flora in early eighteenth-century Dublin. His summary account compares well with contemporary lists from other parts of Ireland and Britain, though weak in grasses, sedges and rushes. This makes it possible to form a view of the state of the environment, bearing in mind that his identifications were set within the developing taxonomy of the time. In many respects the composition of the natural and adventitious flora of the city and county has altered significantly in the ensuing three centuries. His base-line compilation enables a comparative retrospective to account for their present-day occurrences or apparent absences of certain species.

Botanizing in modern-day Dublin city reveals the presence of a large number of species which were not recorded by Threlkeld and were most unlikely to have been present in his time. Conversely, many others present have disappeared from their named sites, though not necessarily from the county, many as causalities of urban expansion. Others, tracking changes in landscape management have been eliminated as a result of the lowering of the water table. The conversion of hay meadows to silage grassland has eliminated most of the naturally occurring grassland species. Herbicide application has expelled many casual weeds and weeds of cultivation and has cleared the ground for other invasive newcomers. Some species, common in Threlkeld's time, still occupy the same habitat niches. A number of these were and still are largely confined to the metropolis, though recent building operations involving the movement of heavy earth-moving machinery has resulted in the transference of seeds and viable roots to new locations.

33 Declan Doogue et al., *Flora of County Dublin* (Dublin, 1998).

Caleb Threlkeld's plant records

Another group has virtually disappeared. These were predominantly species of unsavoury conditions characterized by decomposing vegetable matter, offal and animal excrement. In their natural habitats these species are still characteristic of shoreline debris, growing among cast up and decaying seaweed and other organic material. In Threlkeld's time these species extended their ranges well inland, tracking the nutrient-enriched routes and resting places of cattle and horses. Their modern equivalent habitats are decaying silage and abandoned hay bales.

Although the works on the upgraded City Basin waterworks commenced in 1721, the Grand and Royal Canals which were to augment the aquatic species of the city environs did not exist. Work on the Grand Canal commenced in 1756 and the Royal in 1790. Connecting these waterways to the Shannon and Westmeath lakes respectively resulted in the propagules (seeds, roots and viable stem fragments) of many wetland species making their way into the city.

Caleb Threlkeld thus provides his readers with a snapshot of the ecological life of Dublin in the early eighteenth century. A result of twelve years of botanizing, the *Synopsis stirpium Hibernicarum* is his attempt to 'Let the polite World know, that Arts and Sciences flourish here, and are encouraged, as much as in any other Parts of Europe'. It is more than the sum of his research; it is also a clarion call to arms, asking the reader to follow in his footsteps and to 'contribute your quota'.[34]

---

34 Threlkeld, *Synopsis*, Preface, Sig. c3v and c3r.

CHAPTER SIX

Caleb Threlkeld, Dublin's earliest plant ecologist

DECLAN DOOGUE

IN CALEB THRELKELD's time, as now, the preliminary phases of botanical exploration entailed finding, correctly identifying, naming, and recording the various plants present in an area. Additional knowledge ensued when occurrence details included supplementary habitat information set within some vegetational and spatial context. The species descriptions in various editions of John Ray's *Synopsis* had progressively incorporated some topographical and habitat details.[1] In *Synopsis stirpium Hibernicarum*, Threlkeld did not give species descriptions, relying on the scholarship of previous authors, but he appended habitat and location information, based on his direct observations, into his individual species accounts, with occasional references to prevailing weather conditions.[2] These inclusions, relating almost entirely to the plants of the Dublin area, indicate his awareness of the preferential affinity of certain species to differing habitat types.

His achievements are all the more impressive, given the developing state of knowledge of the flora in Ireland and Britain in the early eighteenth century, the scarcity of illustrated texts and the logistical difficulty in communicating with other botanists. In surmounting these difficulties he has left a body of corroborating ecological and topographical information that reduces the uncertainty when equating the present-day flora with the archaic names used in his *Synopsis stirpium Hibernicarum*. Where complications arise as to the correct modern equivalence of a small number of his species records, this is usually due to taxonomic revisions of the Irish and British floras in the intervening three centuries.[3] Some habitat information relating to a small number of rare and unusual species discovered by previous workers, such as Gédéon Bonnivert (1651–1703), Richard Heaton (1601–66), Thomas Molyneux (1661–1733), Edward Lhuyd (1660–1709) and William Sherard (1659–1728), were included, but these, with the exception of Molyneux's contributions, rarely relate to the Dublin area.[4]

In Threlkeld's day a system of habitat classification and related nomenclature had not yet evolved that would harmonize with the current vocabulary and understanding

---

1 John Ray, *Synopsis methodica stirpium Britannicarum* (London, 1680, 1696, 1724). 2 Caleb Threlkeld, *Synopsis stirpium Hibernicarum* (Dublin, 1726). 3 Declan Doogue et al., *Flora of County Dublin* (Dublin, 1998); Clive Stace, *New flora of the British Isles*, 4th edition (Stowmarket, 2019). 4 On these see E.C. Nelson, 'Records of the Irish flora published before 1726', *Bulletin of the Irish Biogeograhical Society*, 3

of plant/soil/habitat inter-relationships.[5] However, it is possible to discern in his species accounts evidence of his ability to appreciate the subtleties and nuances of landscape. Loosely defined terms for various habitat types had begun to appear in the published plant records of the time, and a number of these had been assimilated into Johann Jacob Dillenius's edition of Ray's *Synopsis*, which was to become the adopted reference work for many subsequent botanical publications.[6] Threlkeld's precise topographical records, especially of rarer species, incorporate such supplementary habitat information. In the case of commoner, unlocalized species with wider ecological amplitudes, he includes more general ecological commentaries, using familiar habitat terms in common usage in the standard texts of the time. Additionally, he sometimes employs habitat names retained from his Cumbrian days, such as plashes (a type of shallow wetland), sykes (marshy streams), closes (enclosures) and dubs (puddles) – terms seldom encountered by modern ecologists.[7]

Modern field botanists are acutely aware of the varied but consistent positions which individual species occupy in the broader ecological spectrum. Finding these species requires an appreciation of the environmental factors that determine their local distributions. Since Threlkeld's time, massive changes have come about in the greater Dublin area as land was assigned to agriculture, housing, industry and amenity. Fortunately Threlkeld's researches have created a substantial body of primary content, which is still relevant, and testifies to his competence both as a finder and recorder of plants, and as a proto-ecologist with the ability to discern and conceptually isolate some of the more clear-cut species/habitat relationships. In this sense he precedes many of the botanists of the Dublin district such as John Rutty (1698–1775), or Walter Wade (*c.*1740–1825), and Nathaniel Colgan (1851–1919), author of the *Flora of the county Dublin* (1904) who fully understood and acknowledged the significance of Threlkeld's contribution to Irish floristic studies.[8] Threlkeld's work is more meaningful and content-rich than that of his immediate followers, in that the period in which he flourished preceded the influx of future garden escapes and the arrival of many weed species whose seeds were included in imported grain.

Threlkeld's species narratives are arranged alphabetically according to their pre-Linnaean polynomials and are set within the taxonomy of the time, but where sufficient topographical information was provided, these individual accounts can also be grouped according to habitat types. In the following treatment, the scientific and English names follow Clive Stace's *New flora of the British Isles* (2019), and are linked to Threlkeld's corresponding polynomials (*via* Table 6.1), retaining a small number

---

(1979), 51–75.   **5** See, for example, J.S. Rodwell, *British plant communities volumes 1–5* (Cambridge, 1991–2000); J. Fossitt, *A guide to habitats in Ireland (reprinted with additions 2007)* (Kilkenny, 2000).   **6** Ray, *Synopsis*, ed. 3. (London, 1724).   **7** See, for example, Threlkeld, *Synopsis*, Sigs. B8r and G3v (plashes); A4r; (sykes); C3r, G3r, G8r, H6v, I2v (closes); A6r (dubs).   **8** John Rutty, *An essay towards a natural history of the county Dublin* (Dublin, 1772); Walter Wade, *Catalogus systematicus plantarum indigenarum in comitatu Dublinensi inventarum* (Dublin, 1794); Nathaniel Colgan, *Flora of the county Dublin* (Dublin, 1904).

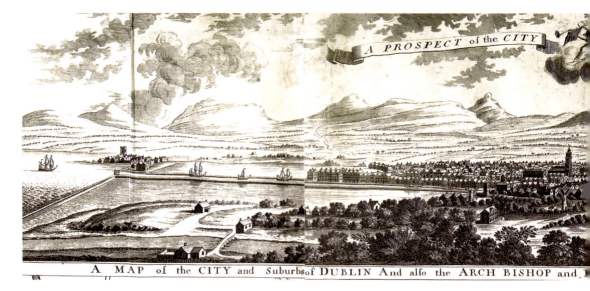

6.1 Charles Brooking's map of Dublin (1728) displaying the localities mentioned in this chapter. By permission of the Royal Irish Academy. © RIA.

of earlier (pre-1726) names, where these provide some additional clarification.[9] This concordance is founded largely on the comprehensive glossary included in Charles Nelson's 1988 edition of the *Synopsis stirpium Hibernicarum*, by the earlier synonymy in James Edward Smith's *Flora Britannica* (1800–4), in the adjudications of Nathaniel Colgan in his *Flora of the county Dublin* (1904) and corroborated by recent research by Philip Oswald and Chris Preston into the nomenclature employed in John Ray's *Catalogus plantarum circa Cantabrigiam nascentium* (London, 1660).[10]

COASTAL HABITATS

Some nationally widespread coastal species occur along the fringes of Dublin Bay and are now confined to the narrow zone between the upper tidal limits and the built environment. Although the extent of the vegetation of the littoral areas nearest the city has been heavily modified by urban development, some of the losses have been offset by the growth of North Bull Island and the recently accumulating sandy ground at Booterstown. Thus, Threlkeld's remarks regarding a common species such as *Beta vulgaris* subsp. *maritima* (sea beet), which 'grows upon the Sea Beach on both sides of the *Bay* of *Dublin*', still stand. Similarly, *Plantago coronopus* (buck's-horn plantain) recorded 'along the barren sandy Shore, copiously on both Sides of the Bay of *Dublin*' or a species of *Spergularia* (sea-spurrey), probably *S. media* (greater sea-spurrey), 'Every where near the Sea, copiously', are still present in many places on

9 Stace, *New flora*, ed. 4. 10 Caleb Threlkeld, *The first Irish flora. Synopsis stirpium Hibernicarum*, ed. E.C. Nelson (facsimile with annotations by E.C. Nelson and D.M. Synnott) (Kilkenny, 1988); J.E. Smith, *Flora Britannica* (London, 1800–4); P.H Oswald and C.D. Preston, *John Ray's Cambridge catalogue* (London, 2011). A small number of names used by Threlkeld still require resolution.

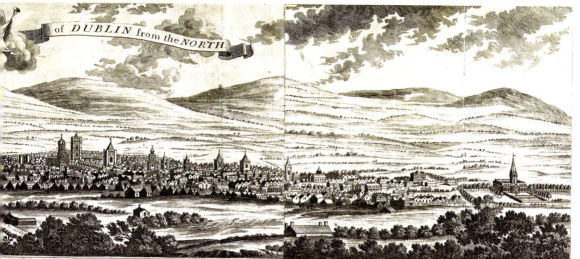

sand-covered rocks and salt marshes, respectively.[11] However, beyond a general shared association with the seashore, records of common coastal species were not localized precisely. In recent years, in common with other halophiles (species that tolerate or require salt), buck's-horn plantain and other coastal species have extended their geographical ranges in Dublin, spreading onto the salted margins of dual-carriageways and motorways.

More site-specific details are provided for species growing directly on the protruding bedrock of the coast. Threlkeld details *Armeria maritima* (thrift), 'plentifully between the *Black-rock* and *Dunlary*, upon the Scruff of the Earth, above the hard Stones' and, nearby, *Tripolium pannonicum* (sea aster), 'grows upon the shallow green Sward of the Rocks, beneath the *Black-rock*, about five Miles from *Dublin* plentifully. I never saw it at any distance from the Sea'. Another regular component of this species assemblage, in an aggregate sense, is the widespread *Cochlearia officinalis* (scurvy grass), 'Plentifully among the short Grass, below the Black-rock' and is still present here on walls in the spray zone.[12] Threlkeld distinguished two forms of scurvy grass, which may find partial equivalence in the current taxonomic interpretation of *Cochlearia officinalis* subsp. *scotica*, linked by intermediates (*C. atlantica*), to *C. officinalis* subsp. *officinalis*.[13]

Nearby he recorded *Limonium binervosum* (sea-lavender), where, with great ecological precision, he noted that 'It grows everywhere upon the Fissures of the Rocks standing into the Sea about *Dunleary*'. It is still to be found on sea walls at Merrion, at Blackrock Railway Station and on cliffs at Killiney. His comments on *Plantago maritima* (sea plantain), which was 'Large and plentiful upon Sea Banks; in some Places it is bulky, in other Places small according to the Soil', will resonate with modern ecologists who encounter it in a depauperate condition on dry sea-sprayed

---

11 Threlkeld, *Synopsis*, Sigs. B4v (sea beet); C6r (buck's-horn plantain); K5r (greater sea-spurrey).
12 Ibid., Sigs. C3r (thrift); L1v (sea aster); C5r (scurvy grass).   13 Stace, *New flora*, p. 450; T.C.G. Rich, *Crucifers of Great Britain and Ireland* (London, 1991), p. 270.

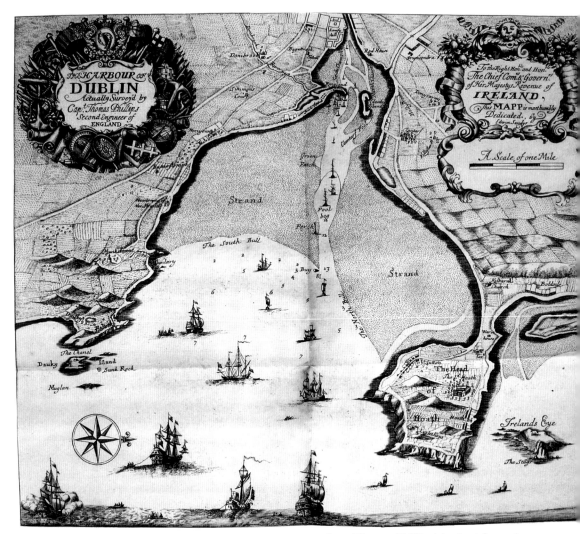

6.2 'The Harbour of Dublin actually survey'd by Capt. Thomas Phillips' (early eighteenth-century print of Phillips' 1685 map). By permission of the Trustees of the Edward Worth Library, Dublin. © Edward Worth Library.

coastal walls and contrastingly as lush individuals in salt marshes. The much rarer *Artemisia maritima* (sea wormwood) has fared less well. Threlkeld had 'Found [it] between Mirrion and the Black-rock', but its former habitats are long lost.[14] It is a species of the upper parts of some salt marshes and the spray zone on rocks and cliffs and in its former colonies on the cliffs at Sorrento in Killiney it appears to have been ousted by the invasive *Jacobaea maritima* (silver ragwort).[15] Elsewhere, it survives on

14 Threlkeld, *Synopsis*, Sigs. F6v (sea lavender); H7r (sea plantain); A1v (sea wormwood).   15 Colgan, *Flora of the county Dublin*, pp 109–10; Doogue et al., *Flora of County Dublin*, pp 357–8.

6.3 *Armeria maritima* (thrift, sea pink) can form a dense sward in salt marshes and sturdy clumps on exposed rock in the spray zone where its deep-penetrating roots anchor it in clefts, resisting wave action. © Melinda Lyons.

the south side of the Howth peninsula and in stronger colonies on the cliffs at Portrane. The site of another coastal species, *Geranium sanguineum* (bloody cranesbill), was recorded 'In a close near Simonds Court', which was built upon many years ago. This conspicuous species still forms substantial colonies on the sea cliffs at Howth and Killiney and is unlikely to have been overlooked by Threlkeld, especially in view of his reference to seeing *Silene uniflora* (sea campion) growing nearby at Balscaddan, Howth.[16]

A persuasive example of Threlkeld's acumen and ecological acuity is provided by his commentary on *Samolus valerandi* (brookweed): 'this grows between *Dunlary* and *Dawky* in moist Holes among Stones near the Sea, and sent from *Monaster-evan* in *Kildare*'. This is now a very rare species in Co. Dublin as most of its inland sites in the county are now destroyed. Small colonies survive precariously on the Dublin coast, precisely as he described, where freshwater, running off the land and percolating through the lime-rich soil overburden, lodges in shallow silt-filled depressions on rocks on the upper shore. Another species from this ecological niche, *Apium graveolens* (wild celery), is also assigned, correctly but without locality, to 'moist Places near the Sea', where it still occurs, sparingly.[17]

The detailed site citation for *Rumex crispus* (curled dock), 'In the Ditches, near the *Red-house* upon the Strand' is of interest (the Red House shows up splendidly on

---

16 Threlkeld, *Synopsis*, Sigs. E3r (bloody cranesbill); F7v (sea campion).   17 Ibid., Sigs. A5v (brookweed);

6.4 *Silene uniflora* (sea campion) can form substantial clumps close to the coast, usually a little above the spray zone. © Melinda Lyons.

Phillips' map: Fig. 6.2).[18] The species was (and still is) so common about Dublin that Threlkeld did not need to list localities. He may have come upon the more distinctive-looking taxon, *R. crispus* subsp. *littoreus*, with larger and paler fruiting bodies, which occurs on seepage lines spreading over the sand and in estuarine situations on the Dublin coast.[19]

SPECIES OF COASTAL SHINGLE

Shingle accumulates where there is a sudden reduction in the mobility of river or sea-borne pebbles, shells, coarse sand and silt, as occurs behind some obstruction or promontory. When deposited, usually by the highest tides, shingle provides a stable habitat suitable for a small number of species of free-draining, salty habitats. Threlkeld recorded the occurrence of *Glaucium flavum* (yellow horned poppy) 'Upon

A8r (wild celery).   18 Ibid., Sig. F4r (curled dock).   19 John Akeroyd, *Docks and knotweeds of Britain and Ireland* (London, 2014), p. 178.

the sandy Baich every where, and in *Clontarff Island'* and a species of the *Silene uniflora/S. vulgaris* complex (sea campion).[20] Yellow horned poppy is more typically present on pebble and shell shingle shores than on sandy beaches. Clontarf Island, which had formed in the shared estuary of the rivers Tolka and Liffey, finally disappeared in the late nineteenth century. Its eclipse was propelled by a combination of extraction of its core material and the attenuation and diversion of the replenishing supply of gravel and silty alluvium from the Liffey following the earlier construction of the Bull Wall. Alexander Williams (1846–1930), a well-known Dublin naturalist and topographical artist, had visited and illustrated the island around 1878.[21] Its former site has since been incorporated into the greatly expanded Dublin Port. On nearby shores Threlkeld recorded a typical shingle species, *Crambe maritima* (sea kale), 'Upon the Sea Beach near *Dunlary'* and, on the north side of the Howth peninsula, *Silene uniflora* 'Among the Stones near the Sea, near Ballah-na-skadan' (Balscaddan), where it is still to be seen.[22] Sea kale and yellow horned poppy are more sporadic in their recent appearances on the Dublin coast, their occurences dictated by the exigencies of winter waves conveying dormant seed to the shingle beaches. Both species have reappeared on Ireland's Eye in recent times.

SPECIES OF SALT MARSHES

In Dublin, salt marshes form as silty depositional features in the lee of developing sand spits and the sheltered upper parts of estuaries. Their vegetation cover comprises a small number of species with varying tolerances to inundation, exposure and salinity. The progressive impounding of areas at the mouths of the Liffey, Tolka and Dodder rivers reduced the amount of salt marsh habitat. Threlkeld recorded *Lysimachia maritima* (sea-milkwort) 'Plentifully near the Sea just above *Ballybaugh-bridge* near the Rivulets Side'.[23] In Co. Dublin this species occurs in the upper parts of salt marshes, especially where these are irrigated by fresh water flowing off the land. The River Tolka, issuing into the bay below Ballybough, would have diluted the saline influence of the sea to the point where sea-milkwort could maintain itself. Much of its former area is now buried beneath hard surfaces, but it has formed colonies in the nearby dune slacks on Bull Island. Indeed, many coastal plants now known from Bull Island may have derived originally from adjacent shoreline colonies, present before its formation, but now exterminated from the Clontarf seafront.

His reference to *Cochlearia danica* (Danish scurvy grass) on the estuary of the River Dodder stands out in its topographical and ecological accuracy 'Found in Flower near the Brook *Dodeer*, where it disimbogues it self into the Liffy at *Ring's-end*,

---

20 Threlkeld, *Synopsis*, Sig. H3r (yellow horned poppy).   **21** Alexander Williams, 'Bird life in Dublin Bay: the passing of Clontarf Island', *Irish Naturalist*, 17 (1908), 165–70. P.G. Kennedy, *An Irish sanctuary: birds of the North Bull* (Dublin, 1953), p. 4.   **22** Threlkeld, *Synopsis*, Sig. B5v (sea kale); Sig. F7v (sea campion).   **23** Ibid., Sig. E4r (sea-milkwort).

in the flat Marsh below the Bridge, *March* 22. this Year 1725–6'.[24] The area is now largely filled in, but early-flowering *C. danica* endures, often at the base of walls near the sea, and, in common with some other marginal halophiles, is now extending its geographical range onto motorway margins due to the use of salt in de-icing in winter.

One anomalous record, that of *Peucedanum officinale* (hog's fennel) from 'Ditches near the Sea', obtrudes.[25] This species has never been validated from Ireland and is only known in Britain from sites in south-east England in comparable estuarine situations. One potential alternative candidate, a related umbellifer, *Oenanthe lachenalii* (parsley water-dropwort), might have been the species intended. It occurs in salt marshes along the north Dublin coast.

SPECIES OF SAND DUNES

The extensive, botanically rich, sand dune systems along the north coast of Dublin at Malahide, Portmarnock, Donabate and Portrane are not mentioned by name in Threlkeld's accounts, and to visit these relatively remote places probably would have required considerable effort in his day. North Bull Island had not yet formed but his records indicate the occurrence of a number of sand dune species along the drier stretches of the shoreline.

On both sides of Dublin Bay he found *Anthyllis vulneraria* (kidney vetch) growing 'in great Beauty and Plenty upon the dry Hillocks near the Sea, both upon the South and North-side of the *Bay of Dublin*'. Similarly he recorded *Rosa pimpinellifolia* (burnet rose), 'Upon the Edge of the Brow at *Black-rock*, and near *Rahany* Mills'. The inclusion of *Cuscuta epiphytum* (dodder), from 'dry sandy banks near *Mayden Tower*, near *Drogheda*', was taken directly from Ray's *Synopsis*, having been reported by William Sherard (1659–1728). Dodder still flourishes in dry dunes on the northern side of the Boyne estuary in Co. Louth.[26]

There are very few other localized records from the north side of Dublin Bay. One is *Euphorbia paralias* (sea spurge) 'Upon the sandy Shoar between *Warren-house* and *Rahany*. It is a hardy Plant, for upon March 25. 1725 the Leaves were new sprung from its perennial root'. There is no sandy shore there now, though sea spurge is still present on the coast on parts of the nearby Howth Peninsula and on Bull Island. Similarly, *Erodium moschatum* (musk stork's-bill) might be included here, as encountered 'on the Way side leading to *Clantarf*'.[27] Though not a shore-line species, this stork's-bill has always been commoner near the coast, but has now begun to reappear, its natural pattern of occurrence overwhelmed by its inclusion in wildflower mixtures sown inland.

Most of the conspicuous species typical of dune systems, and definitely recorded *in situ* by Threlkeld, were from the south coast of Dublin, although all those he

---

24 Ibid., Sig. C5r (Danish scurvy grass).   25 Ibid., Sig. H5v (hog's fennel).   26 Ibid., Sigs. A6v (kidney vetch); I5r (burnet rose); C7r (dodder).   27 Ibid., Sigs. K7v (sea spurge); E3v (musk stork's-bill).

mentioned are still present and obvious in the dunes north of the Liffey. Dumhach Thra, the Irish toponym for Sandymount, implies the local existence of sand dunes. The subsoil in the area directly behind these dunes had been found suitable for brick making (the area was known as 'Lord Merrion's Brickfields') and associated contemporary excavations would have created much new disturbed habitat.[28] Most of the potential dunes that would have formed from the vast supply of wind-borne sand from the former Merrion shore have now been scoured away by wave action – casualties of coastal squeeze, where hard, fixed man-made surfaces have intruded onto the softer and more dynamic sandy shoreline. Accumulations of wind-blown sand from Merrion Strand still form in sheltered pockets on the outer side of the South Wall where some of these species now occur. *Salsola kali* (prickly saltwort) 'in the Mid-way between *Ring's-End* and the *Black-rock*, on a Sandy Beach' and *Cakile maritima* (sea rocket) 'found growing … near *Mirion* by the Sea-side' are still common here. However, *Eryngium maritimum* (sea holly) which occurred 'Plentifully upon the sandy Shore near the *Brick-fields*' and 'Plentifully on the bare Pasture near the *Brick-kilns*' has not been seen here for many years and is in serious decline everywhere on the Dublin coast.[29]

Less securely tied, topographically and ecologically, to the sand dunes of the time are *Trifolium arvense* (hare's-foot trefoil), 'I saw it once in the sandy Ground near *Mirian*', and *Cynoglossum officinale* (hound's-tongue) 'in Mirrion Church-yard', still to be seen there towards the end of the nineteenth century.[30] These, and others, occurred on sandy ground near the sea, but were not strictly halophiles. Nearby, Threlkeld recorded *Erodium cicutarium* (common stork's-bill) 'On the dry Banks facing *Pool-beg*'. Similarly, records from the coast, further south, of *Anacamptis pyramidalis* (pyramidal orchid) 'Upon the dry Sea-banks between Newtown and Dunlary' and of *Erigeron acris* (blue fleabane) 'Upon a dry hilly Pasture to the eastward, facing the Hutts at the *Black-rock*', refer to dry sandy ground typical of the coast, although these species are also occasional constituents of thin dry sandy unimproved lime-rich soils further inland. This inland floristic component included *Agrimonia eupatoria* (agrimony), encountered 'in the Hedges and Borders of Fields, as in the Meadows above Dunlary' reflecting its affinity for dry base-rich soils. *Torilis nodosa* (knotted hedge-parsley), found 'In dry Banks below *Ring's-end*, lying upon the Ground near the sea', has now become a very rare plant in Ireland and is surviving in small quantity, typically growing procumbently on sunny dry sandy ground at the foot of old walls near the sea.[31]

There are some taxonomic puzzles here. Threlkeld had seen a specimen of a large-flowered *Viola*, '*Pansy with a Large Yellow Flower*,' possibly *V. tricolor* subsp.

---

28 Susan Roundtree, 'Dublin bricks and brickmakers', *Dublin Historical Record*, 60:1 (2007), 63. 29 Threlkeld, *Synopsis*, Sigs. F2v (prickly saltwort); D3v (sea rocket); D4r (sea holly). 30 Ibid., Sigs. F3r (hare's-foot trefoil); C7v (hound's-tongue). Wade, *Catalogus systematicus*, p. 51, for comment on hound's-tongue. 31 Threlkeld, *Synopsis*, Sigs. E3v (common stork's-bill); H2r (pyramidal orchid); C5r-v (blue-fleabane); A3v (agrimony); C3r (knotted hedge-parsley).

curtisii (wild pansy), 'Fetch'd from the *Hill of Hoath*: its flower is large in proportion to the smallness of the Plant, the Specimen I saw scarce exceeding three Inches in height'.[32] Threlkeld had distinguished *V. arvensis* (field pansy) from *V. tricolor* but the taxonomy and related nomenclature of these species and their hybrid derivatives was unclear then and still is. He may have had a narrow concept of *V. tricolor*, possibly as that of a predominantly blue-flowered plant, and had subsequently encountered atypical examples of the sand-dune pansy in its yellow form in Howth. In his former botanizing days in Cumbria he would have known the larger-flowered, yellow *V. lutea* (mountain pansy) in upland grasslands.[33]

SPECIES OF DRY, SANDY GRASSLAND HABITATS

Many species characteristic of dry limestone soils in the greater Dublin area also occur in sand dunes or sandy/gravel glacial outwash features, which may have been their original habitat prior to the removal of woodland and the ensuing formation of grasslands. Threlkeld provides good inland topographical references for many such species. Most of the mineral soils of lowland Ireland have long since been assigned to intensive agriculture, though remnants of these dry, lime-rich features can still be identified in modern Dublin. Down-cutting rivers have carved through various strata of glacial drift, exposing their sandy and gravel-rich character, revealing their porosity, low nutrient status and limited humification. These features enable a number of calcicolous (lime-loving) species to continue, even within built-up areas, especially where the angle of repose of the exposures is sufficiently steep to prevent or retard colonization by perennial herbs and scrub. Most of these species are now confined to thin ribbons of habitat, unable to survive in the heavily fertilized pastures and silage grasslands of the greater Dublin area.

There are many instances: for example, *Centaurium erythraea* (centaury), where Threlkeld correctly identifies its preferred habitat as bare dry pastures, and knowingly indicates that 'It cannot be nourished in Gardens, for it perishes the Year it is planted, and never rises again from the Seed'. His comments on the closely-related *Blackstonia perfoliata* (yellow-wort) found 'in the Closes adjoining the green Hills near *Crumlin* plentifully' chime with his observations regarding centaury, evoking images of a now largely lost grassland flora constituted on the remnants of the lime-rich Greenhills esker, mostly quarried away for sand, levelled and grassed over and managed for amenity.[34]

Other species from this habitat type include *Daucus carota* (wild carrot) that 'We meet with it in all dry Dykes plentifully, especially about *Coulach* in *Fingall*'; with unlocalized mentions of *Trifolium campestre* (hop trefoil) 'Plentiful upon dry Banks', *T. dubium* (lesser trefoil) as a companion species, and *Polygala vulgaris* (common

---

32 Ibid., Sig. L6r (viola). **33** J.E. Whitaker (ed.), *A seventeenth-century flora of Cumbria* (Gateshead, 1981), p. 93. Geoffrey Halliday, *A flora of Cumbria* (Bolton, 1997), p. 185. **34** Thelkeld, *Synopsis*, Sigs.

6.5 *Ulex europaeus* (gorse). © Melinda Lyons.

milkwort) 'found in our dry Pastures frequently'. In the case of *Pimpinella saxifraga*, (burnet-saxifrage) he noted that 'Here are two Sorts of this, and it is bigger in the Closes near *Dunacarney*, than in the Hill sides of the *Deer Park*; but whether they differ in kind, is not so certain'. It is now well known to be very variable in the dissection of its leaves, its hairiness and stature. In the Dublin lowlands, *Ulex europaeus* (furze, whins or gorse) (Fig. 6.5) is characteristic of free-draining soils and Threlkeld had recognized the significance of its positioning 'Upon the Brows near the Liffey above *Chapel-izod* etc.' where it is linked toponymically to the Furry Glen in the Phoenix Park.[35] Other species of lime-rich grassland have fared less well. In times of far less intensive grazing he was able to detect *Alchemilla vulgaris* (lady's-mantle) – now known to be a complex of closely related apomictic taxa (producing seed without fertilization) – 'in Closes going from *Glasmuckanogue* [Grangegorman] to *Finglas* and above *Glasnevan*'.[36] These sites are long-since altered and we may never know which of its segregates occurred here. By Colgan's time, further colonies had been detected, at Knockmaroon and the Furry Glen, as well as sites in north Co. Dublin at Knocksedan and Blanchardstown.[37] It was re-discovered in the Furry Glen

C3v (centaury); C3r (yellow-wort). **35** P.A. Reilly et al., *Wild plants of the Phoenix Park* (Dublin, 1993), p. 34. **36** Threlkeld, *Synopsis*, Sigs. C8r (wild carrot); L1r (hop trefoil and lesser trefoil); H7r (common milkwort); H6v (burnet-saxifrage); E2v (furze, whins or gorse); A4r (lady's-mantle). **37** Colgan, *Flora*

by Philip Grant (as one of its segregate species, *Alchemilla filicaulis* subsp. *vestita*) in 1998 and may still be there.[38] Its erasure from the landscape is matched by the decline in *Poterium sanguisorba* (salad burnet) so familiar to Threlkeld that its localities were not listed, thus obscuring the extreme association between it and the freely draining lime-rich graves of the Liffey valley and the adjoining Phoenix Park where it still survives. A regular associate of many of these species of lime-rich soils is *Galium verum* (lady's bedstraw) and Threlkeld had it as being 'In dry barren Banks it grows plentifully about this City' and it is still a useful indicator of the presence of calcareous soils and calcicolous vegetation. In similar dry situations occurred *Sherardia arvensis* (field madder) 'In Lay-grounds' (areas left fallow), and *Convolvolus arvensis* (field bindweed) was on 'Mud Walls in *Cabera*-lane' (Stonybatter).[39]

Another indicator of more grassy vegetation on lime-rich sandy soils is *Ranunculus bulbosus* (bulbous buttercup), which still prevails about the city on surviving fragments of calcareous soils in the grounds of parks and state buildings. Threlkeld had found it growing, untypically, 'in some wet Closes between *Dannebrook* and *Ring's-end*, where I could pull up the knobby Root without breaking the Stalk, the Ground was so soft and spongy'. Two other components of this suite of ecologically well-defined species were *Linum bienne* (pale flax) 'upon the lands of *Simond's Court*' (included without further comment under the English name 'Wild Perennial Blue Flax', thus distinguishing it from the cultivated flax) and, with better environmental context, *Allium vineale* (wild onion), 'This grows upon the Bank-side of the Mill-race above *Island-bridge*, upon the back of the House where the Sign of the *Salmon* is, and in some Meadows near *Bally Griffin* in *Fingall* copiously' – all totally credible locations for this uncommon species.[40]

Plant ecologists and phytosociologists instantly recognize this suite of widespread species as being characteristic of dry, lime-rich grassland. With these may be included the much rarer *Salvia verbenaca* (clary), 'Upon the Brow below the Hospital of *Kilmainham* near the Road, and in such sandy Places about the City', which preceded more detailed records by Walter Wade in 1794 and Colgan in 1904, who recorded it nearby from the roadside by the wall of the Phoenix Park opposite Long Meadows.[41] It is now a nationally rare species, extirpated from most of its former Dublin sites. The local conjunction of other rare species such as *Lithospermum officinale* (gromwell) 'at the Foot of *Inisacore-hill*, and under the Brow above *Palmerstown Mills*' (it still survives in the Furry Glen of the adjoining Phoenix Park) and, similarly, *Origanum vulgare* (marjoram) 'between the Mill-dam and the River above *Chapple-izod-bridge*, among the Bushes in a small Islet' (where Colgan found it), now define the continuing presence of small sites of enduring high nature conservation value.[42]

---

of the county Dublin, p. 70.   **38** Reilly, *Phoenix Park*, p. 37.   **39** Threlkeld, *Synopsis*, Sigs. H6r (salad burnet); E2v (lady's bedstraw); I5r (field madder); C5v (field bindweed).   **40** Ibid., Sigs. I2v (bulbous buttercup); F6v (pale flax); A4v (wild onion).   **41** Ibid., Sig. E7v (clary); Wade, *Catalogus systematicus*, p. 9; Colgan, *Flora of the county Dublin*, p. 162.   **42** Threlkeld, *Synopsis*, Sigs. F7r (gromwell); H2r (marjoram); Colgan, *Flora of the county Dublin*, p. 141 (gromwell), pp 160–1 (marjoram).

6.6 *Centaurea nigra* (knapweed). © Pat Lenihan.

The occurrence of these and other species attests to the open and lightly vegetated character at that time of the Liffey exposures. Fragments of these gravel features are still visible on the southern side of the Phoenix Park at Conyngham Road and extend along the Strawberry Beds, where, until recently, some were quarried for sand. Sporadically, *Tragopogon pratensis* (goat's-beard) still appears: 'It grows near the Mill-race behind the Sign of the *Salmon* at *Island-bridge*, and above *Glasneven* upon a Pasture' on dry, disturbed ground mainly within areas where these superficial gravel deposits are evident. These habitat conditions also favour *Verbascum thapsus* (mullein) which 'is no very scarce Plant with us, for we have met with it several times in our Perambulations, and in particular near *Lutterel's-town*'.[43] Here, on the sunny south-facing slopes of the Strawberry Beds road, mullein still occasionally occurs and though considered by some to be a long-established relic of cultivation, it maintains

[43] Threlkeld, *Synopsis*, Sigs. K8r (goat's-beard); L4r (mullein).

130   *Declan Doogue*

a distinct ecological relationship with open gravel pits and other dry sunny spots. Similar transitory exposures were formed many years later when railways cut through some of these gravel ridges. More recently, the construction of new motorways such as the M50 (which passes over the Liffey valley gravels) intersected the remains of the Greenhills Esker at Greenhills/Tymon creating short-lived exposures where floristic remnants of the former grassland still occasionally surface in the central reservation.

To these lime-loving species may be added a *Carex* (sedge), which Threlkeld found early in the year (12 April 1725) flowering 'a little above the Mill in the Fields at *Harold's-cross*'.[44] Threlkeld recorded very few sedges or grasses, indicating his lack of familiarity with them and their reduced relevance to herbalism. However, *Carex caryophyllea* (spring-sedge) may have been the intended species, being one of the first sedges to flower, and known nearby from the Phoenix Park near the Chapelizod gate.[45]

Of the commoner dry grassland species, Threlkeld was still able to offer some pertinent comments, noting of *Hypochaeris radicata* (cat's-ear) 'is found in Pastures above *Island-bridge*'. He used the contemporary English name (taken from Ray) 'Long-rooted Hawkweed' – an English rendition of the prevailing polynomial 'Hieracium longuis radicatun' – which character enables the species to endure long periods of drought. In recent very dry summers this rosette-forming plant was one of the few species able to maintain itself in heavily mown lawns in public parks while most other species had died back. Other common grassland species included *Centaurea nigra* (knapweed), 'In some meadows it is a Pest for its Frequency', and *Pteridium aquilinum* (bracken), that 'is too rife in Barren Pastures'. To these may be added a record of *Primula veris* (cowslip) 'In the Avenue going up to Squire *Conolly's* Seat at *Castle-town*, near *Kildroughan*' (Cill Droichead or Celbridge), and *Pilosella officinarum* (mouse-ear-hawkweed) 'Upon some dry Banks in a broad Way beyond *Rathfarnham*', tracking the distribution of the glacial drift on the north side of the Dublin mountains.[46]

Threlkeld also recognized the dry open-ground character of situations where certain species occurred on less heavily vegetated ground such as tracksides and old buildings. The widespread and trampling-tolerant *Polygonum aviculare* (knotgrass) or possibly *P. depressum* (equal-leaved knotgrass), he listed 'In all gravelly places'. *Anagallis arvensis* (scarlet pimpernel) was recorded 'in fields and sandy Banks near the High-way going to *Drumcondra* it is often met with' and *Lepidium coronopus* (swine-cress) was 'upon the Way-sides to *Rathfarnham*, and in the Way under the Park Wall'. *Saxifraga tridactylites* (rue-leaved saxifrage) grew 'Upon Mr. *Grosvenor's* Malt-house, and some Houses in *Cavan-street*, and on the sandy Banks near the *Brick-fields*'. It has been undergoing something of a renaissance in recent years around Dublin, now colonizing accumulations of blown sand and urban moss mats in

---

44 Ibid., Sig. E4v ('Gramen cyperoides folijs caryophyllæis'). **45** Reilly, *Phoenix Park*, p. 56. **46** Threlkeld, *Synopsis*, Sigs. E6r (cat's-ear); E8v (knapweed); D5r (bracken); H8r (cowslip); H6r (mouse-

Caleb Threlkeld, Dublin's earliest plant ecologist

business parks and industrial estates. Here it often grows in similar early-season circumstances with *Erophila verna* (common whitlow-grass) which 'grows upon dry banks early in the *Spring*, and withers with the heat'.[47]

WET GRASSLANDS AND MARSHES

In Threlkeld's time, damp grasslands were not unusual in the Dublin area, situated mainly in the natural flood plains of substantial rivers and on spring lines and along the percolation zones of slopes. The winter-flooded water meadows associated with weirs and the flood plains of the largely unenclosed Liffey were dominant factors in determining where certain wetland plants would grow. Depressions in the landscape held water in small pools. Drains, cut into adjoining fields to release water into rivers, maintained a slightly different flora from the adjoining moist grasslands. Though diminished in recent years, the ecological value of these riverside areas endures along with their distinct suite of taller species, adding to their significant environmental contribution to the flora of the urban fringe.[48]

Threlkeld gave precise localities for a number of these notable wetland species along the Liffey, where they grew close to the river. A fern ally, *Botrychium lunaria* (moonwort), 'In the pastures of Palmerstown', has not been seen here for many years, presaging its fast-declining status in modern Ireland. The closely related *Ophioglossum vulgatum* (adder's-tongue) is correctly assigned to moist meadows, without locality, and has similarly been erased from most of its former lowland Dublin sites.[49]

Threlkeld had *Caltha palustris* (marsh marigold) 'In the small Sykes or watery plashes of moist Meadows, as in the fields between the *Barracks* and *Chappel-izod* copiously'. He provided more general habitat references, without place names, in relation to a number of commoner species that took his interest. Thus smaller species such as *Ranunculus flammula* (lesser spearword) 'In wet Meadows', *Myosotis scorpioides* (water forget-me-not), 'They are obvious enough in wet Grounds', and *Silene flos-cuculi* (ragged robin) 'In the sides of the wood of the Deer Park' still persist in wetter places in the Liffey valley and elsewhere. *Angelica sylvestris* (angelica) occurred 'By the Rivers brink, and in wet Plashes and Dubs' while *Veronica anagallis-aquatica* (blue water-speedwell) was associated by Threlkeld with 'Ditches and Rills of Water' to which may be added species of *Mentha* (mint) 'In wet Plashes'.[50]

It is more difficult to find a secure modern equivalent for Threlkeld's 'Cicutaria palustris', which he has placed under water hemlock, as growing in slow moving

---

ear-hawkweed).   **47** Ibid., Sigs. H7v (knotgrass); A5v (scarlet pimpernel); C6r (swine-cress); H3r (rue-leaved saxifrage); H3r (common whitlow-grass).   **48** On this see Hadrian Cook and Tom Williamson, *Water meadows. History, ecology and conservation* (Bollington, 2007).   **49** Threlkeld, *Synopsis*, Sigs. F7v (moonwort); H1v (adder's-tongue).   **50** Ibid., Sigs. B8r (marsh marigold); I2v (lesser spearwort); G7r (water forget-me-not); F7v (ragged robin); A6r (angelica); A5r (blue water-speedwell); G3v (mint).

6.7 *Caltha palustris* (marsh marigold). © Declan Doogue.

waters, but without stating locality.[51] This pre-Linnaean name had been assigned broadly to *Oenanthe phellandrium* and, more recently, to either *O. aquatica* and/or *O. fluviatilis*.[52] The habitat requirements discerned by Threlkeld point to *O. fluviatilis* (river water-dropwort), but this had not been distinguished at that time. Both species were to spread via the canal systems to Dublin many years later and separate colonies of *O. aquatica* (fine-leaved water-dropwort) were discovered in quarries and pools elsewhere in the county.[53] Threlkeld's 'Cicutaria palustris' may possibly be better assigned to *Helosciadium nodiflorum* (*Apium nodiflorum*) (fool's water-cress), a common and widespread umbellifer, which Threlkeld does not appear to have mentioned or to *O. crocata* (hemlock water-dropwort) which he mentioned elsewhere, giving its Irish name also, 'Dahow ban' (dathabha bán).[54]

On the flood plain proper a number of larger vigorous species that form part of tall-herb vegetation communities occurred. These are plants typical of water meadows, with corresponding high nutrient demands that are provided by the plentiful supply of alluvium. Typical species include *Eupatorium cannabinum*

---

51 Ibid., Sig. C4v (Threlkeld's 'Water Hemlock', possibly fools water-cress or hemlock water dropwort). 52 Oswald and Preston, *John Ray's Cambridge catalogue*, p. 182; M.J.Y. Foley, 'Lectotypification of Oenanthe phellandrium [β] fluviatilis Bab., basionym of O. fluviatilis (Bab.) Coleman (Apiaceae)', *New Journal of Botany*, 2:1 (2012), 73. 53 Colgan, *Flora of the county Dublin*, pp 89, 90. 54 Threlkeld,

(hemp-agrimony) 'In moist Rills, as under *Inisacore-hill* near the Liffey Banks', *Lythrum salicaria* (purple-loosestrife) that 'grows in Ditches, and in particular by a rill of Water, which comes from *Still-organ* towards the Sea through the Meadows, and at *Cardiff's-Bridge*' and two large willowherbs, *Epilobium hirsutum* (great willowherb) and *E. parviflorum* (hoary willowherb): 'These two grow in Brooks'. With them grew *Solanum dulcamara* (bittersweet): 'It grows in Wet Places about Ditches and Mill-dams, amongst the Stones'. He identified the habitat of *Valeriana officinalis* (common valerian), 'It grows in wet Places', and *Rumex conglomeratus* (clustered dock), 'In untilled watery Places', without citing localities. A consistent component of flood plain vegetation, scrambling over taller robust plants, is *Calystegia sepium* (hedge bindweed), 'among Bushes near the Liffey Side above *Chappel-izod*; it clambers up the Shrubs, and then overtops them with its Bell-flower', a description which perfectly matches the occurrence of the species where it still flourishes along the Liffey from Chapelizod to Lucan and beyond.[55]

With some insight he noted the presence of *Bidens cernua* (nodding bur-marigold) as '*Water-Hemp Agrimony with an undivided leaf*' adding 'That with a radiate Flower is frequent here' referring to the var. *radiata* of that species but without citing localities.[56] Dillenius had been previously notified of its Irish presence by Sherard ('In Hibernia certe frequentissime occurrit').[57] Various field botanists have occasionally encountered this very uncommon Dublin species over the centuries along the banks of the Liffey since, both in its typical form and as var. *radiata* with expanded ligules.[58] Threlkeld's referencing of '*Water Hemp Agrimony*' from 'moist rills, as under *Inisacore-hill* near the Liffey Banks' as 'Eupatorium cannabinum fæmina' requires comment.[59] The addition of 'fæmina' to the otherwise straight-forward and familiar polynomial has created some confusion, seeming to refer to *Bidens tripartita* (trifid bur-marigold). This equivalence was accepted by Colgan, who also agreed with the attribution of *B. cernua* to 'Eupatorium cannabinum folio non diviso'.[60] Wade saw both species on river banks between Knockmaroon and Lucan, and *B. tripartita* was discovered by Gerry Sharkey at Hynestown reservoir in 1984, but it has not been confirmed from the Liffey in Dublin since Wade's time.[61] However, by a process of elimination, it becomes evident that Threlkeld clearly had intended the much commoner *Eupatorium cannabinum* (hemp-agrimony).

With greater topographical precision Threlkeld recorded, from the low-lying lands at the mouth of the Tolka, *Stachys palustris* (marsh woundwort) 'in the Dykes near *Finglass* River above *Ballybaugh-bridge*'. To these may be added another robust riverside plant, *Lysimachia vulgaris* (yellow loosestrife), 'Sent from the River *Barrow*'.[62]

Synopsis, Sig. G8v (hemlock water-dropwort).   **55** Ibid., Sigs. D4v (hemp-agrimony); F8v (purple-loosestrife; G1v (great willowherb and hoary willowherb); D1v (bittersweet); L3v (common valerian); F4r (clustered dock); C5v (hedge bindweed).   **56** Ibid., Sig. D4v (nodding bur-marigold).   **57** Ray, *Synopsis*, edited by Dillenius, p. 188.   **58** Doogue et al., *Flora of county Dublin* (Dublin, 1998), pp 336–7. **59** Threlkeld, *Synopsis*, Sig. D4v (water hemp agrimony).   **60** Colgan, *Flora of the county Dublin*, p. 105. **61** Wade, *Catalogus systematicus*, pp 222–3; Doogue et al., *Flora of County Dublin*, p. 36.   **62** Threlkeld, *Synopsis*, Sigs. K2r (marsh woundwort); G1v (yellow loosestrife).

6.8 *Stachys palustris* (marsh woundwort). © Declan Doogue.

There is one tantalizing record here, that of 'Euphrasia major lutea latifolia palustris', which Threlkeld called the '*Great yellow Marsh Eye-bright*': 'We found it upon the North-side of the small River, beneath *Cardiff's-bridge*, among some Bushes near the wet Meadows'. This may have been *Parentucellia viscosa* (yellow bartsia) as Threlkeld had separately listed the somewhat similar *Rhinanthus minor* (yellow-rattle) with the convincing commentary that 'it withers before mowing Time', alluding to the manner in which the seeds rattle about in the capsule after flowering, especially on dry nutrient-poor grassland.[63] If the record for *Parentucellia viscosa* was correct it might indicate its early presence in a semi-natural habitat in Ireland, as it is often considered to be an accidental contaminant in grass seed in recent years. However, more recent research into the taxonomy of *Rhinanthus minor* has disclosed the existence of a number of subspecies, such as the larger *R. minor* subsp. *stenophyllus*, which is more robust than the commoner form and is strongly associated with wetland habitats.[64] This may have been the taxon encountered by Threlkeld.

63 Ibid., Sigs. D4v ('Great yellow Marsh Eye-bright', possibly yellow bartsia); H4r (yellow-rattle).   64 Stace,

Caleb Threlkeld, Dublin's earliest plant ecologist

In contrast to the general loss of wetland species, the much rarer and precisely localized species *Lycopus europaeus* (gipsywort), 'found *Rough*, in a Ditch of the *Deer Park*, but not plentifully, for I could not light upon it the next Year', still grows in the Furry Glen and other pools in the Phoenix Park and is now also scattered along the margins and lock gates of the Royal and Grand Canals.[65]

On slightly wetter ground or areas where water would have stood in summer, Threlkeld included *Typha latifolia* (bulrush) that grows 'in Meers, large Ponds and Stanks of standing Water', along with a species of *Callitriche* (water starwort) that 'grows in watry Places' and one of the *Nasturtium officinale* aggregate (water cress) which 'grows in Ditches and Rills of Water'.[66]

SPRINGS

Small springs, especially those issuing from or percolating through lime-rich soils, are rare habitats in Dublin due to the lowering of the water table and the rationalization of superficial land drains. Many such springs had a distinct associated flora but, because of drainage, culverting and piping, their waters have been disconnected from the surrounding countryside. As a result, their significant beneficial contribution to species diversity and habitat quality has been largely lost. Threlkeld's records, confirmed by subsequent field workers, attest to the occurrence of a number of lime-rich wetlands between Templeogue and Tallaght (for example at Whitestown) where species of this habitat-type survived well into the twentieth century.

One such species was the semi-aquatic *Baldellia ranunculoides* (lesser water-plantain) included by Threlkeld as 'Plantago aquatica stellata, *Star-headed Water-plantain*': 'We found this in a muddy Pit in a Pasture near *Temple-oge*, and although the *Summer* was dry, yet it was difficult enough to come at it Dry-shod, to get a fair Specimen of it'. It is now on the verge of extinction in Co. Dublin. Nearby, *Pulicaria dysenterica* (fleabane) grew 'In wet Plashes about *Temple-ogue*'.[67] Fleabane produces extremely long roots which can grow down following the falling water table – unlike most shallow-rooted species – and sometimes persists long after its former wetland habitats have been permanently degraded.

Other species of shallow pools in calcareous marshes include *Pinguicula vulgaris* (common butterwort), found 'In a Pasture between *Temple-oge*, and *Tallow*, and in a boggy Meadow belonging to *Barberstown* in the County of *Kildare*'. His mention of another characteristic member of this vegetation community, *Parnassia palustris* (grass of Parnassus), which was growing 'in the wet Ground under *Inisacore-hill*, but not plentifully', resonates with records of similar colonies growing on the slopes of the Tolka above Blanchardstown (where it survived at least up to 1976), the Ward River

---

New flora, p. 698. **65** Threlkeld, *Synopsis*, Sig. G2v (gipsywort); Reilly, *Phoenix Park*, p. 48. **66** Ibid., Sigs. L3r (bulrush); K5v (water starwort); G7v–G8r (water cresses). **67** Ibid., Sigs. H7r (lesser water-plantain); C5r (fleabane).

6.9 *Pinguicula vulgaris* (common butterwort). © Declan Doogue.

below Chapelmidway and on the wet lime-rich glacial drift of the Dodder valley.[68] Another conspicuous component of this assemblage, *Pedicularis palustris* (marsh lousewort) – 'It grows upon wet Meadows' – was not provided with localities suggesting its relative frequency at the time. Other wetlands near the city supported additional members of this distinct community. Threlkeld's records of *Lysimachia tenella* (bog pimpernel) found 'In a rotten spungy Pasture beyond *Simon's-Court*' and also 'in a broad Road beyond *Rathfarnham* in a wet Plash' where water issuing from roadside slopes irrigated the lime-rich glacial drift, neatly bracket two of its main habitat types. Similarly, *Hydrocotyle vulgaris* (marsh pennywort), 'In a Marsh Ground between the *Black-rock* and *Still-organ*', indicates the former presence of similar freshwater marshland features nearer the Dublin coast. To these may be added a reference to a species of *Chara* (stonewort), 'In the dirty Drains between *Ball's-bridge* and *Ring's-end*'.[69] Stoneworts are closely associated with lime-rich, though not dirty, waters and are regarded as reliable indicators of good quality habitat.[70]

---

68 Ibid., Sigs. H6v (common butterwort); E5r (grass of Parnassus); Colgan, *Flora of the county Dublin*, p. 76.   69 Threlkeld, *Synopsis*, Sigs. H4v (marsh lousewort); G8r-v (bog-pimpernel); C6v (marsh pennywort); D2v (stonewort).   70 On this see J.A Moore, *Charophytes of Great Britain and Ireland* (London, 1986).

RIVER BANKS

The vegetation of river banks includes a number of larger species with high water and nutrient demands, usually equipped with strong rooting systems sufficient to withstand the shearing effects of flood waters. Threlkeld did not deal with most of the taller grasses of the river margins, but did mention a few less common species with distinct flowering heads.

One of the most robust species fringing river banks is *Sparganium erectum* (branched bur-reed), where he noted that 'This grows on the Banks of the *Aonna Liffy*, in deep Water over-against the *Phoenix*' where it still flourishes. He recorded *Scrophularia auriculata* (water figwort), from a single site 'in the very River Brink of the Liffy under *Inisacore-hill*', distinguishing it from the more widespread *S. nodosa* (common figwort), included without localities, and much valued as a medicinal herb for alleviating the Kings-evil (a form of tuberculosis).[71] Both of these figworts occur along the Liffey with the much rarer *S. umbrosa* (green figwort), not distinguished in Threlkeld's time. In John Ray's alphabetically arranged catalogue of the plants found about Cambridge, published in 1660, these two very similar species were listed separately, *S. auriculata* as 'Betonica Aquatica while *S. nodosa* was grouped under 'Scrophularia Major', an arrangement to which Threlkeld conformed.[72] In his *Catalogus*, Ray stated under *S. auriculata* that 'The odour, sap, shape of the flowers, colour etc. show that this plant possesses the same properties as Figwort. What is more it so much recalls that plant in its outward appearance that they could be distinguished with difficulty other than by their roots & the shape of their leaves'.[73] Dillenius's revised and expanded third edition of Ray's *Synopsis* had rectified the matter but Threlkeld had retained the earlier nomenclature and systematics.

Large plants of *Petasites hybridus* (butterbur, known informally as false rhubarb), 'Upon the *Liffy* Banks', now form large colonies along the fringes of the Liffey, as at the Wren's Nest and elsewhere along the river, especially where the stonework associated with weirs and mills reduces the flow and scour of the river, encouraging the deposition of nutrient-rich alluvium. An outlying colony of *Chrysosplenium oppositifolium* (golden saxifrage), 'Found in a Gutter at the Mill near *Harold's-cross*', was included probably because of the unusual circumstances of its occurrence, as it was almost certainly encountered in more natural damp shaded habitats along the Liffey valley. His record of *Oenanthe crocata* (hemlock water-dropwort) from the River Tolka 'below *Finglas-bridge* upon the River Side' was confirmed from the Tolka at Cardiff's Bridge (Finglas), Ashtown and Scribblestown by Wade in 1794, and later in 1904 by Colgan and is still a feature of some stretches of the river.[74] Another

---

71 Threlkeld, *Synopsis*, Sigs. K4v (branched bur-reed); B4v (water figwort); K1r (common figwort).
72 John Ray, *Catalogus plantarum circa Cantabrigiam nascentium* (London, 1660), pp 20–1, 152. See Oswald and Preston, *John Ray's Cambridge catalogue*, pp 167–8.   73 Ibid., p. 21; translation by Oswald and Preston, *John Ray's Cambridge catalogue*, pp 167–8.   74 Threlkeld, *Synopsis*, Sigs. H5v (butterbur);

emergent species, *Alisma plantago-aquatica* (water-plantain), 'It is a fair Plant to behold when in Flowers, it grows in the Water', was widespread then and localities were not given. It has become a conspicuous feature of the marginal vegetation of the fringes of the Royal and Grand Canals but is rare elsewhere. Unusually, Threlkeld did not record *Butomus umbellatus* (flowering rush) from the Liffey where it is now a prominent component at many points along the river although it was sent to him from the River Barrow. It may be a relatively recent colonist of the Liffey, having spread successfully by vegetative means, possibly from a horticultural source. The same provider may have been the supplier of *Lysimachia vulgaris* (yellow loosestrife) for which Threlkeld offered no Dublin records but had gleaned from his correspondent(s) that both species were plants of river margins.[75]

TRUE AQUATICS

True aquatics, rooted in open water, have floating or submerged leaves and stems. Many species are small and inconspicuous and Threlkeld's listing is of the larger and more obvious species. His note of *Potamogeton natans* (broad-leaved pondweed), 'In all standing Pools copiusly', was not supplemented by localities, but then as now, the Liffey carried a range of *Potamogeton* species. *Persicaria amphibia* (amphibious bistort) was encountered in its colourful flowering state: 'This we found in some dirty deep Pools in the Pasture against the *Salmon-wyer* upon the *South* side of the Liffy; It was in its beauty above the Waters, of which we had much to do to get fair Specimen's dry shod'. In the river proper flowered a large water crowfoot, probably *Ranunculus penicillatus* (stream water-crowfoot), 'It grows in the middle of the *Liffy*, between the *Barracks* and *Island-bridge*; Its specious [showy] white Flowers look very charming, as it floats upon the rolling Streams of the *Aon na Liffy*'.[76] This species is known to be characteristic of clean-water river systems and still abounds on the Liffey on the Wicklow/Kildare boundary, but has declined in many parts of its lower reaches, a casualty of nutrient-enrichment (eutrophication).[77] At the opposite end of the water-quality spectrum, Threlkeld's pungent description of the habitat of one of the most pollution-tolerant aquatic species, *Potamogeton crispus* (curled pondweed), 'Above *Ballybaugh-bridge* in some stinking standing Water near the River, upon the North-side of it', leaves little to ecological speculation.[78]

I9v (golden saxifrage); G8v (hemlock water-dropwort); Wade, *Catalogus systematicus*, p. 81; Colgan, *Flora of the county Dublin*, p. 89; Doogue et al., *Flora of county Dublin*, p. 269.   **75** Threlkeld, *Synopsis*, Sigs. H6v (water-plantain); F1r (flowering rush); G1v (yellow loosestrife).   **76** Ibid., Sigs. H8r (broad-leaved pondweed); H5v (amphibious bistort); I2r (stream water-crowfoot).   **77** C.D. Preston and J.M. Croft, *Aquatic plants in Britain and Ireland* (Colchester, 1997), p. 65.   **78** Threlkeld, *Synopsis*, Sig. H8r (curled pondweed).

HEDGES, WOODS, AND SCRUB

A short walk westward from Threlkeld's urban home led to a rural landscape where he recorded common hedgerow shrub and herbaceous species, many of which are still present in wooded sections of large estates and institutional grounds. He seldom gave site locations and habitat details for most of the hedge-forming species but he noted *Ligustrum vulgare* (privet) 'In the Hedges near *Clantarff*, and in the Road to *Lucan*'. Trees within the city are rarely mentioned, though *Salix alba* (white willow), growing near his home by the Poddle was recorded as 'This is the greatest of all the Tribe, and grows near the Water-course upon *Crooked-staff*, a tall Tree'. Brief commentaries without localities or more ecological content were included for *S. caprea* (goat willow, or, more likely, *S. cinerea*, grey willow) and for *Quercus* (oaks) and other widespread hedgerow shrubs and trees.[79]

The distinction between the ground flora of hedges, scrub and woods was not always obvious, even at that time and the nearby churchyard of St Luke's parish church, erected in the early 1700s in the Coombe, had *Stachys sylvatica* (hedge woundwort), 'Frequent enough under Hedges and even in Saint *Luke's* Church-yard', near to his home. The then rare *Helminthotheca echoides* (bristly oxtongue), 'frequent under Hedges, and above the Barracks in a Brow to the Westward', is now fast declining in all its former Dublin sites, though it persisted in inland sites at Knockmaroon Hill until at least 1866 and is now found mainly in nutrient-rich disturbed situations near the coast.[80]

In formerly scrubby areas between Inchicore Hill, Roper's Rest, Kilmainham and Mount Jerome he found *Hypericum androsaemum* (tutsan) growing 'among the Scrogs upon *Inisacore-hill*' and *Stellaria holostea* (greater stitchwort) occurred 'Amongst Bushes … both at *Roper's-rest* and *Inisacore-hill*'. In the same area *Veronica chamaedrys* (germander speedwell) was noted where 'It grows upon *Inisacore-hill*'. Similarly, *Circaea lutetiana* (enchanter's nightshade) grew 'within three Yards of the *Mill Wheel* at *Mount Jerom* under the Bushes' and *Sanicula europaea* (wood sanicle) 'Beyond Mount *Jerom*, and in the Closes beyond *Drumcondrah*'. *Geranium robertianum* (herb Robert), still a frequent presence in hedges and older city gardens, was 'frequently met with, As under the Hedges between *Kilmainham-gallows* and *Chapel-izod-bridge*' as was *Ficaria verna* (lesser celandine), 'under the Hedges between *Roper's-rest* and *Dolphin's-barn*'. *Geranium molle* (dove's-foot crane's-bill) and *G. dissectum* (cut-leaved crane's-bill), both still familiar species on roadside verges, were also recorded, without topographical or ecological commentary. Another common species of the time was *Torilis japonica* (upright hedge parsley), 'under the Hedges about *Old Bane*, and between *Caberah* and *Cardiff's-bridge*', and is still a feature of hedgerows in rural Dublin, as is *Vicia cracca* (tufted vetch), commonly

---

79 Ibid., Sigs. F6r (privet); I6v (white willow); I7r (goat or grey willow); I1v (oaks). **80** Ibid., Sigs. E2r (hedge woundwort); B7r (bristly oxtongue).

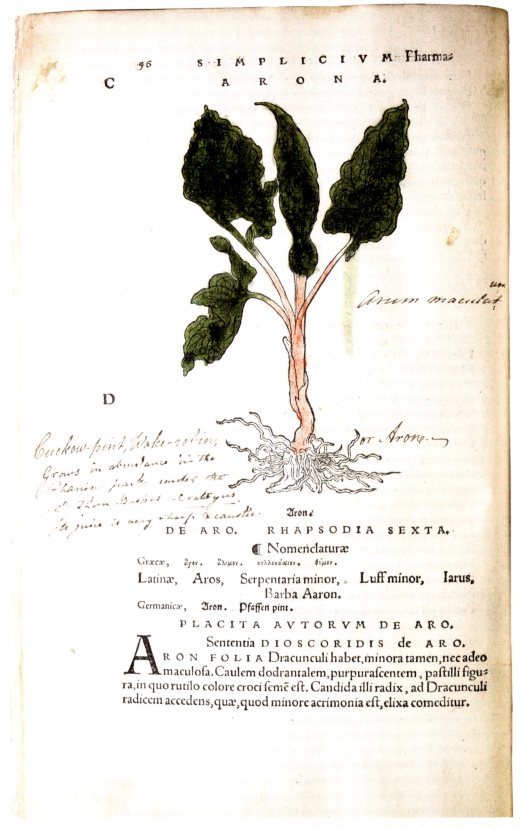

6.10 Anonymous annotation (possibly eighteenth-century) recording 'lords-and-ladies' in the Phoenix Park, where Threlkeld also found it: from Otto Brunfels, *Herbarum vivae eicones ad naturae imitationem* (Strassburg, 1532). Courtesy of the National Botanic Gardens, Glasnevin/OPW.

encountered on roadside hedgerows in high summer. Threlkeld may have recorded another species of vetch, possibly *Ervilia sylvatica* (wood vetch), 'This last has a fine blue Spike for a set of Flowers, we found it amongst Bushes near to *Dunlary*' – a very much rarer species which was recorded on many occasions scrambling in rocky scrub in the Killiney area and continues to hold on, further south on the coast in Co. Wicklow.[81] Threlkeld's remarks concerning the conspicuous inflorescence of that species resonates with similar comments of Henry Chichester Hart (1847–1908) who came upon it in great quantity on sea cliffs on the Waterford coast at the end of the nineteenth century, and where it is now much rarer.[82]

Most members of this suite of species are typical of the margins of deciduous woodland, and in common with many others maintain a presence in the hedged landscape just beyond the expanding suburbs. Threlkeld included many other familiar and common species but without localities. Thus, *Geum urbanum* (herb Bennet), which was 'under all our Hedges', is now increasing in older gardens. Other woodland margin and hedgerow species recorded with more detail include *Alliaria petiolata* (garlic mustard): 'It grows under the Hedges on the West Side of *Chappel-izod-bridge*, and in a small *islet* above the Bridge between the River and Mill Race in a Thicket of Bushes'. Other woodland species are provided with similar ecological comment. *Arum maculatum* (lords-and-ladies) was 'growing under all our shady Hedges and Woods, copiously enough in both the Counties of *Dublin* and *Wicklow*, as in the *Phoenix-park* belonging to his Majesty, and at *Kill-eager*' (Fig. 6.10). Another woodland-fringe species, now common in hedges, *Lapsana communis* (nipplewort), was 'common enough, as near the Stiles, as you go through the Fields to Temple-Ogue', and *Galium odoratum* (woodruff) was recorded flowering early: 'This year 1725, being a forward Spring it flowered in *April*, among some Bushes between *Roper's-rest* and Mount *Jerom*'. Similar seasonal allusions applied to *Veronica hederifolia* (ivy-leaved speedwell): 'Found in Seed and Flower, *Martij* [March] 30. 1724. in the Hedge of a Garden at *Stony Batter*'.[83] Most of these species are still to be found close to where he recorded them. His observations regarding flowering times (recorded mainly between 1724 and 1726) have additional relevance today, in the light of phenological observations relevant to subsequent climate change.

Although *Ranunculus auricomus* (goldilocks buttercup) – 'Flowers early in the Hedges beyond *Roper's-rest*' – may now be a thing of the past, other woodland margin species were common along the Liffey valley. *Ajuga reptans* (bugle) grew 'in the King's *Deer-park* [The Phoenix Park], and in the Woods above *Palmerstown*' and *Potentilla sterilis* (barren strawberry) could be 'found in Woods', unlocalized. One of the rarest Irish species, *Lamiastrum galeobdolon* (yellow weasel-snout), he found

---

81 Ibid., Sigs. A6r (tutsan); E6v (greater stitchwort); C3v (germander speedwell); C4v (enchanter's nightshade); I8r (wood sanicle); E3v (herb Robert); C4r (lesser celandine); E3r (dove's-foot crane's-bill); E3v (cut-leaved crane's-bill); C3r (upright hedge parsley); L5v (wood vetch). On wood vetch see also J.P. Brunker, *Flora of County Wicklow* (Dundalk, 1950), p. 104.   82 P.R. Green, *Flora of County Waterford* (Dublin, 2008), p. 177.   83 Threlkeld, *Synopsis*, Sigs. C2v (herb Bennet); A4r (garlic mustard); B1v (lords-and-ladies); F4r (nipplewort); B2v (woodruff); A5r (ivy-leaved speedwell).

'Among bushes beyond *Roper's rest* near a Cart way, where there is a Ditch on both sides'. This is still nearby, in scrub on the south side of the Liffey above Islandbridge and further upriver just into Co. Kildare at Leixlip. Though not a plant of the lime-rich lower Liffey valley, *Teucrium scorodonia* (wood sage), a species of woodland margins usually on acid soils, was mentioned as being 'In Woods and Thickets'. Other species identified correctly as being typical of woodland include *Silene dioica* (red campion) – 'In moist woods, Hedges and Ditches' – which occurs in wooded situations along the lower stretches of the Liffey, and *Neottia ovata* (twayblade), 'frequent enough in Woods'. The record for a species of old woodland, *Lathraea squamaria* (toothwort), seems ecologically implausible. Threlkeld stated that he found it 'upon a moist Acclivity, as we came up the Sea Shore from *Dunlary* to *Newton*'.[84] Both toothwort and the related parasitic *Orobanche hederae* (ivy broomrape) are still significant components of the Liffey valley woodland flora, where the latter, even extends onto shaded roadsides on the Strawberry Beds road and would hardly have been missed. The identification of some broomrape species is still difficult.[85]

Threlkeld was aware of the degraded state of the woodlands of his area and beyond. Under his account of the fern *Polypodium vulgare* aggregate (polypody), he declared that '*Ireland* is so miserably bereft of Woods, that most of what we use is imported, and *Tanners* find *Bark* dearest in the Mid-land Counties', and elsewhere in relation to oak woods stated that 'The County of *Kildare* contiguous to *Dublin* had its Name *Kill Darah*, *Hoc est Cella Quercuum*, from its abundance of *Oaks*, but through Mismanagement they are destroyed'.[86]

WALLS AND OLD BUILDINGS

By the start of the eighteenth century, the city authorities were imposing some degree of planning and organization on the urban landscape, and were already clearing older decrepit buildings, enclosing intakes from the sea and walling the lower parts of the Liffey.[87] Threlkeld had realized that certain plant species were strongly and preferentially associated with buildings, walls and wall-bases, some of which were old even in his time. Many of these were species of arid conditions, such as rock outcrops, in their original natural state, and had colonized analogous habitats occupying the shallow skin of vegetation forming on some of these man-made stone structures. Some references, such as that to the medicinal herb *Leonurus cardiaca* (motherwort), 'Found under a Wall at *Roper's Rest*', were purely topographical, but most of his observations suggest his awareness of the presence of a distinct urban-wall component in the flora. He noted *Parietaria judaica* (pellitory-of-the-wall) on the

---

84 Ibid., Sigs. I2v (goldilocks buttercup); B7r (bugle); D6v (barren strawberry); F3v (yellow weasel-snout); I7r (wood sage); F8r (red campion); B5r (twayblade); D1r (toothwort).   85 On this see Chris Thorogood and Fred Rumsey, *Broomrapes of Britain and Ireland* (London, 2021).   86 Threlkeld, *Synopsis*, Sig. H7v (polypody); I1v (oak woods).   87 On this see Colm Lennon, *Irish historic towns atlas No. 19. Dublin, part II, 1610 to 1756* (Dublin, 2008).

6.11 *Malva sylvestris* (common mallow). © Melinda Lyons.

walls of old buildings ('the oldÆdifice at *Tallow*') and *Umbilicus rupestris* (navelwort), 'Upon *May* Day 1722. I found it growing out of the Wall of a demolished Church at *Lucan*'. The record of *Ballota nigra* (black horehound), growing 'in the Church-yard in *Crumlin*, and under the Hedges about *Glasnevan*', hinted at an awareness of its association with much older habitation, evidence for which is borne out to this day, though challenged increasingly by clean-up operations directed at old buildings. *Sedum acre* (biting stonecrop), a native species of sand hills, had by then spread onto old walls to the extent that its urban localities were not listed. However, another succulent stone-crop of garden origin, possibly *Petrosedum fosterianum* (rock stonecrop) or *P. rupestre* (reflexed stonecrop), grew 'Upon the Tiles of the Houses at *Chappel-izod*' and persisted in the immediate area, including the walls of the nearby Phoenix Park, into the twentieth century.[88] *Hordeum murinum* (wall barley), now widespread throughout the city and suburbs, was only mentioned from 'Upon the

88 Threlkeld, *Synopsis*, Sigs. C1r (motherwort); H3r (pellitory-of-the-wall); L7v (navelwort); B3v (black horehound); K1r (rock or reflexed stonecrop); Colgan, *Flora of the county Dublin*, p. 269.

Sides of the Highway, and on the Walls leading to *Bagatrath*'. Another species, now mainly confined to nutrient-enriched sandy soils and lingering near the coast, was *Anthriscus caucalis* (bur chervil), 'In an old Mudd Wall at the ruined Church of *Mirian*'. He also recognized the rupestral character of *Asplenium ceterach* (rustyback) encountered in 'the Openings of Rocks, brought in Quantities out of the Country'; it is now a rare fern about the city though still to be found on old mortared walls beyond the suburbs.[89]

The combined references to *Malva sylvestris* (common mallow) and *M. neglecta* (dwarf mallow), 'These are found in Way-sides and Rubbish heaps', indicated their shared close association, even at that time, with the built environment. In recent years *M. sylvestris* has maintained its position in the environs of Dublin, growing even in the central reservations of motorways, but *M. neglecta* has declined, due to the cleaning up of graveyards and old ruins and is now largely restricted to dry gravelly places near the Dublin coast. Threlkeld's record of 'Eruca sylvestris vulgatior, Common wild Rocket' – 'It grows upon Walls, as between *Dolphin's-barn* and *Cork-bridge*' – is more difficult to assign to species.[90] Colgan thought that it might refer to *Sisymbrium irio* (London rocket), once a widespread weed about the city, especially at the base of old walls, which went into decline towards the end of the nineteenth century.[91] He presciently attributed this decline to the introduction of concreted pavements, not anticipating the future impact of selective weedkillers on so many species tied to this particular habitat. The species in question might also have been a *Diplotaxis* or some other species of salad vegetable that is commonly called rocket.

OLD WEEDS OF CULTIVATION

In Threlkeld's time there was no clear-cut distinction between the untidier parts of the city outskirts and the agricultural land beyond, and hence various species found sufficient ecological similarity between their original natural habitats and the less intensively farmed urban periphery. Here Threlkeld encountered numbers of what would now be considered urban weeds.[92] The occurrence of some of these related to the untidy state of the trackways, enriched by the dung of passing livestock. Historically, a number of these species grew in small towns and villages throughout Ireland but have become rare in recent times, eliminated now by tidying and spraying of roadside verges. Many nutrient-demanding weeds of this nature still survive nearer the coast, which was probably their more natural original habitat. *Descurainia sophia* (flixweed), growing 'among Rubbish, and upon some of the low Thatched Cabbins at the end of *New-street*, near *Black-pits*', now persists in the sandy fallow lands about Rush in Fingal. *Lamium hybridum* (cut-leaved dead-nettle) has similarly decreased:

---

89 Threlkeld, *Synopsis*, Sigs. E7v (wall barley); G7r (bur chervil); B2v (rustyback).   **90** Ibid., Sigs. G2r (dwarf mallow and common mallow); D3v (Thelkeld's 'Common wild Rocket').   **91** Colgan, *Flora of the county Dublin*, p. 20.   **92** See Sylvia C.P. Reynolds, *A catalogue of alien plants in Ireland* (Glasnevin, 2002).

'In Kitchen Gardens it is sometimes found as a Weed, and as such plukt up'. Its close relative, *L. purpureum* (red dead-nettle), is a common garden weed nowadays. *Aethusa cynapium* (fool's parsley), which Threlkeld noted 'grows in waste and fat [very nutrient-rich, productive] Places, and Kitchen Gardens', is still a prominent feature of disturbed ground in various parts of the older suburbs, and both *Euphorbia helioscopia* (sun spurge) and *Sinapis arvensis* (charlock) remain very much with us, but the true wild pansy, *Viola tricolor* subsp. *tricolor*, 'Upon rubbish Heaps in waste ground', is a thing of the past other than on acid arable soils. Another regular component of such acid and neutral soils was *Galeopsis tetrahit* (common hemp-nettle) or its sometimes congener *G. bifida* (bifid hemp-nettle), 'We found it once near *Clantarff-wood*'. The hemp-nettles are now all but wiped out in lowland Dublin, though still present in the Naul Hills to the north and widespread though never common on the surviving vestiges of arable ground in the Dublin mountains. *Cichorium intybus* (chicory), 'Found near *Kilmainham* Hospital', might have been a relic of cultivation, even then. It is now incorporated into green manure and forage crops. Threlkeld noted that a species of melilot, possibly *Melilotus officinalis* (ribbed melilot) or *M. altissimus* (tall melilot), grew 'in some Closes (which by the Ridges appear to have been plowed) beyond *Coulack*, copiously'.[93] Both species still appear mainly on disturbed ground near the coast. Formerly prized as a fodder plant, particularly for horses, Threlkeld named it 'German Claver' (German clover). In similar situations, a species of *Lepidium* (pepperwort) appeared, possibly as a casual.

The creation of business parks and industrial estates, often on sandier free-draining ground inland and with warmer microclimates, has contributed to the survival of *Reseda luteola* (weld), in many sites nearer the city. Formerly grown for the dye it yields, Threlkeld noted that it grew 'spontaneously upon Rubbish, and fallow Fields, as near the Old Wind-Mill above *Dolphin's Barn*'. Similarly, *Barbarea vulgaris* (winter-cress), a plant of gravelly stream sides, found analogous habitat where it abounded 'in the Borders of Fields at all Quarters about the City' and it still occasionally puts in an appearance on disturbed wet sandy ground.[94] A less successful species, *Blitum bonus-henricus* (Good-King-Henry), was once cultivated as a pot-herb and persisted around old buildings.[95] Threlkeld noted that 'It grows beneath *Island-bridge* in the Pasture near the River, and in the Town of *Glasnevan* near Sir *John Rogerson*'s House'.[96] Several species, seldom seen nowadays, can persist in certain sites because of the extended viability of their buried dormant seed. When soil is disturbed, usually following the digging of foundations of buildings, the seeds of these species are resurrected briefly to germinate, grow, flower and set new seed. Threlkeld maintained a distinction between *Dipsacus fullonum* subsp. *fullonum* (wild teasel), which he reported without localities, and cultivated or manured teasel, the

93 Threlkeld, *Synopsis*, Sigs. K4r (flixweed); F3v (cut-leaved dead-nettle); C4v (fool's parsley); K7v (sun spurge); I3r–v (charlock); L5v (wild pansy); F3v (common hemp-nettle, bifid hemp-nettle); C4v (chicory); G3r (ribbed melilot).   94 Ibid., Sigs. F6v (weld); B3v (winter-cress).   95 Colgan, *Flora of the county Dublin*, p. 172.   96 Threlkeld, *Synopsis*, Sig. B5v (Good-King-Henry).

spiny fruits of which were used to raise the nap on certain fabrics (fullering). The latter, *D. sativus* (fuller's teasel,), was 'sown in the *Tenter-fields* about this City, as upon the Back of *Chamber's-street*'.[97] Teasels are still a conspicuous component of the vegetation of disturbed waste ground. Plants of uncertain origin are occasionally included in dried-flower arrangements and their seeds may have spread from this novel source to disturbed ground. More recently they have also appeared as an introduced component in some 'wild flower' and bird-seed mixtures.

CORNFIELD WEEDS

Before Threlkeld's time a number of species had become weeds of cultivation because seed-cleaning techniques had not progressed to the point where these contaminants could be separated from the similarly-sized seeds of the intended crop. In recent years the development and application of selective herbicides has eliminated many of these former cornfield species from the tilled landscape. At that time the then widespread *Glebionis segetum* (corn marigold) was considered such a menace that 'Mannour-courts do amerce [fine] careless Tenants, who do not weed it out before it comes to seed', presaging later legislation such as the Noxious Weeds Act of 1936. Threlkeld had discovered a variety of this with deeply divided glaucous leaves which he likened to those of garden poppies from 'near the Cart Road at the End of *Inisacore-hill*, flanking the Hill, and in a muddy Bank of a Ditch in *Patrick's-well-lane*'. Less threatened nowadays is *Sinapis arvensis* (charlock), 'It of the Nature of *Mustard*, it is called about the Streets of *Dublin* before the Flowers blow, by the name of *Corn-cail*, and used for boiled Sallet; it is like *Mustard* when grown up; it is too rank among Corn' due to the longevity of its dormant seed.[98] The culinary use of the unopened flower heads finds echoes nowadays in various types of broccoli.

One of the most conspicuous casualties of present-day cornfield management is *Agrostemma githago* (corn cockle) which was growing 'In a close of Wheat between [place name missing] and *Tallow*, near the *Green-hills*, and on the Lay-Land between the *Broad-Stone* and *Finglass*'. The precipitous decline of this species, along with corn marigold and *Centaurea cyanus* (cornflower), is now obscured by the inclusion of their seeds in various modern concoctions of alleged wild-flower mixtures. Other identifiable weeds of the time included *Aphanes arvensis* (parsley-piert), *Spergula arvensis* (corn spurrey), *Ervilia hirsuta* (hairy tare) – 'This is a Plague to the Corn' – and *Viola arvensis* (field pansy), all included without localities, as recurring components of the crop flora. Less easily identified are the various thistle species (*Cirsium* and *Carduus*), with which Threlkeld did not engage, stating only that 'All these Sorts grow about *Dublin*; the Descriptions are so confused and obscure, that we cannot find the Certainty (says Mr. *Ray*)'.[99]

---

97 Ibid., Sig. D1r (wild teasel, manured teasel).   **98** Ibid., Sig. C4r (corn marigold); I3v (charlock).
99 Ibid., Sigs. F8r (corn cockle).; H5r (parsley-piert); K5r (corn spurrey); L5v (hairy tare); L6r (field

6.12 *Narthecium ossifragum* (bog asphodel) is still a colourful feature of wet moorland in the Dublin mountains, though many of its sites on lowland raised bogs have not been lost. © Pat Lenihan.

Some other cornfield species are much rarer now – *Scandix pecten-veneris* (shepherd's-needle), and *Galeopsis angustifolia* (red hemp-nettle), which is now a species listed on the *Flora (Protection) Order*, were included without localities whereas *Ranunculus arvensis* (corn buttercup) was listed where 'It flowers among Corn in *May* about *Raheny* and *Kilsaughan*' (the old parish name for Kilsallaghan).[100] In some instances these species may have been associated with dry sandy open ground and their association with corn fields may have been attributed to the lightness of the crop, compared to the intense contemporary product, and the absence of chemical weed-killers at that time.

BOGS

There is little evidence to suggest that Threlkeld had any direct field contact with the distinct flora of the former great bogs of the Irish midlands. A record of *Viola palustris*

---

pansy); C2v (thistles).   100 Ibid., Sigs. H4r (shepherd's-needle); F3r (red hemp-nettle); I2r (corn buttercup). For the *Flora Protection Order*, see S.I. No. 356/2015 – *Flora (Protection) Order*, 2015:

(marsh violet) sounds first-hand: 'In moist Places it is found covered with *Moss*'. It occasionally grows in raised bogs but is mainly a plant of wet acid peaty soils on the sides of mountains. Similarly, *Vaccinium myrtillus* (whortle-berry or bilberry), 'They grow in wet boggy Ground', could have been encountered in the Dublin Mountains above Rathfarnham. *Narthecium ossifragum* (bog asphodel) had been sent to him from Monasterevan, and called to mind his experiences of it in 'rotten Mosses in *Cumberland*'. The record of another typical raised-bog species, *Erica tetralix* (cross-leaved heath), 'This grows in wet Grounds, and was sent from *Monasterevan*', was evidently also not his discovery and the record of *Drosera anglica* (great sundew), 'Plentifully in a Bogg by *Edenderry*' found by Richard Heaton, was already published. Similarly, the record of *Comarum palustre* (marsh cinquefoil), 'Common in all the Bogs in *Ireland*', was previously contributed by William Sherard to Dillenius's edition of Ray's *Synopsis*, and the record of *Andromeda polifolia* (bog rosemary) which was included in Thomas Molyneux's Appendix, 'on the bogg by Isaac-town in the County of *Meath*', was also one of Sherard's discoveries.[101] *Drosera rotundifolia* (round-leaved sundew), another typical plant of wet peaty ground, was included without ecological comment, but also occurred on the Howth peninsula and still does in the Dublin Mountains. The edible fruits of *Vaccinium oxycoccus* (cranberry) were mentioned as having been sent in great quantity to Dublin in season to be made into tarts, but again Threlkeld makes no direct reference to seeing them growing *in situ*.[102]

CULTIVATED PLANTS

A number of species were included by Threlkeld which do not form part of the natural flora of the Dublin area. At the start of the eighteenth century a clear-cut distinction was not always maintained between native and non-native species. He usually provided sufficient environmental context to enable modern researchers to form opinions as to the native status (or otherwise) of many of these equivocal species. Early historical records of this sort enable a more secure diagnosis of the identity of the intended species and the extent to which each is confined to natural or non-natural habitats.[103]

There are, understandably, some residual issues regarding the correct identification of species, for which three centuries of botanical recording does not always

---

https://www.irishstatutebook.ie/eli/2015/si/356/made/en/print, accessed 25 November 2021.
101 Threlkeld, *Synopsis*, Sigs. L6r (marsh violet); L3r (whortle-berry, bilberry); B2v (bog asphodel); D3r (cross-leaved heath); I4v (great sundew); H4v (marsh cinquefoil); Appendix, p. 10 (bog rosemary). These references to earlier sources are explored in E.C. Nelson, 'Records of the Irish flora published before 1726', 51–75 (see also E.C. Nelson, 'Irish wild plants before 1690' in this volume, pp 45–57). **102** Threlkeld, *Synopsis*, Sig. I4v (round-leaved sundew); Sig. L3v (cranberry). H.C. Hart, *The flora of Howth* (Dublin, 1887), p. 20 mentioned finding round-leaved sundew on the Howth peninsula as had Wade, *Catalogus systematicus*, p. 94: 'Inveni in paludosis, et inter muscosus aquaticus, apud Howth …'. **103** On this see David Pearman, *The discovery of the native flora of Britain and Ireland* (Bristol, 2017).

enable clearer retrospection. The record of 'Hiaracium, Pulmonaria Gallica … *French*, or *Golden Lungwort*. Under an hedge upon the top of *Inisacore-hill*' points to a species of *Hieracium* (hawkweed).[104] Two candidate species are included and illustrated in the revised edition of John Gerard's *Herball* (London, 1633). The complicated taxonomy of these species was not well understood then but it may be an example of an early colonist in Dublin, as one or more species of *Hieracium* have colonized the walls around Inchicore.[105]

Vinca major (greater periwinkle), esteemed as a medicinal herb, occurring 'Under Hedges at *Stoney-batter*', is certainly of garden origin. The same applies to *Ornithogalum umbellatum* (star-of-Bethlehem), which Threlkeld once found in 'a low meadow' adjoining the River Tolka, 'betwixt *Finglas's-bridge* and Drumcondrah'. Another surviving relic of garden cultivation, even then, might have been *Geranium pratense* (meadow crane's-bill) – 'Among Bryars and in Hedges' where it still appears occasionally, usually as a fairly obvious garden eject.[106]

At that time, as plants were being introduced into new areas, it would have been difficult to discriminate consistently between the wild and the planted. Threlkeld recorded asparagus either as a true wild plant – *Asparagus prostratus* – or possibly of garden origin – *A. officinalis* – without site information from unidentified sea coasts (its usual natural habitat) but it was not apparently seen by him *in situ*. He also included daffodils, *Narcissus*, 'In the Closes near *Clontarff*, and under the Skirts of the *Hill of Hoath*, and in some Closes near *Doulack's-well*', where they were obviously naturalized. The potherb *Smyrnium olusatrum* (alexanders) was noted as being associated with hedges and more site-specifically 'on a small Bushy Hillock near *Crumlin* Church', but clearly was not as rampant then as it has become in recent years about Dublin.[107]

Polemonium caeruleum (Jacob's-ladder), 'growing out of the Wall of a large Staircase at the Castle of *Rathfarnhan*', was included, as was *Antirrhinum majus* (snapdragon), which was on 'the high Orchard Walls belonging to Squire *Worth* at *Rathfarnhan*' and now forms self-sustaining colonies on many old walls around Dublin. The status of *Erysimum cheiri* (wallflower) was and still is ambiguous. Threlkeld noted it 'In the Brow going up to the Hospital of *Kilmainham*'.[108] The old walls of some towns, such as Carlingford, Co. Louth, are clothed with this species while others are devoid of it.

The fluctuating status of many such accidental introductions and subsequent escapes is still a matter of interest to archaeologists and biogeographers and more recently to climatologists, tracking the manner in which the distribution of various native and invasive species fluctuate in response to changing cultural movements and

---

104 Threlkeld, *Synopsis*, Sig. E6v ('French Lungwort').   **105** On this see Doogue et al., *Flora of County Dublin*.   **106** Ibid., Sigs. C4v (greater periwinkle); H2v (star-of-Bethlehem); E3r (meadow crane's-bill). **107** Ibid., Sigs. B2r (asparagus); G7v (daffodils); E6v (alexanders).   **108** Ibid., Sig. L3v (Jacob's-ladder); A7r (snapdragon). Squire Worth was Edward Worth (1672–1741), a cousin of Dr Edward Worth (1676–1733), whose botanical collection is explored in chapter 7 in this volume; Sig. F4v (wallflower).

weather patterns. In addition, the Threlkeld list throws light not only on what prevailed in the precincts of Dublin, but also provides food for thought for the species he failed to include. His basic catalogue is still well respected by active field botanists, and may be regarded not only as a substantial and significant work of its time but as a reminder of the natural skill and unaffected scholarship of a field botanist, ecologist and progenitor of close-focus recording, who flourished three hundred years ago in Dublin, not as a citizen scientist but as a fully-formed scientist citizen.

Table 6.1. Concordance of plant names.

Species names (polynomials) as used by Threlkeld (1726) arranged in alphabetical order, with corresponding current names, according to the fourth edition of Stace's *New flora of the British Isles* (2019).

In Threlkeld (1726) additional synonyms were often included in small type and generally in lower case, usually to clarify the nomenclatural linkage between his work and that of previous scholars. Most of these synonyms are not included in this listing, but a few are (indicated by *seu*), where their inclusion clarifies or amplifies certain taxonomic matters. Column 2 lists their corresponding names, according to the fourth edition of Stace's *New flora of the British Isles* (2019).

Threlkeld's *Synopsis* (1726)	Stace's *New flora of the British Isles* (2019)
ABSINTHIUM MARITIMUM	*Artemisia maritima (Seriphidium maritimum)*
AGRIMONIA VULGARIS	*Agrimonia eupatoria*
ALCHIMILLA VULGARIS	*Alchemilla vulgaris* agg.
ALLIARIA	*Alliaria petiolata*
ALLIUM SYLVESTRE TENUIFOLIUM	*Allium vineale*
ALSINE HAEDERACEA	*Veronica hederifolia*
ANAGALLIS AQUATICA, minor folio oblongo Crenato	*Veronica anagallis-aquatica*
ANAGALLIS AQUATICA, rotundifolia, Samolus Valerandi	*Samolus valerandi*
ANAGALLIS AQUATICA, sive Beccabunga	*Veronica beccabunga*
ANAGALLIS MAS	*Anagallis arvensis*
ANDROSAEMUM VULGARE	*Hypericum androsaemum*
ANGELICA SYLVESTRIS	*Angelica sylvestris*
ANTHYLLIS LEGUMINOSA	*Anthyllis vulneraria*
ANTIRRHINUM SYLVESTRE MEDIUM	*Antirrhinum majus*
APIUM PALUSTRE	*Apium graveolens*
ARUM VULGARE MACULATUM & NON MACULATUM	*Arum maculatum*
ASPARGUS PALUSTRIS	*Asparagus officinalis / Asparagus prostratus*
ASPERULA, sive rubeola montana odora	*Galium odoratum*
ASPHODELLUS LANCASTRIAE VERUS	*Narthecium ossifragum*
ASPLENIUM sive Ceterach	*Asplenium ceterach*

Caleb Threlkeld, Dublin's earliest plant ecologist

Threlkeld's *Synopsis* (1726)	Stace's *New flora of the British Isles* (2019)
BALLOTE, Marrubium nigrum foetidum, Ballote dictum	*Ballota nigra*
BARBARAEA, Eruca Lutea Latifolia Nasturtium Hybernum	*Barbarea vulgaris*
BEHEN ALBUM, Lychnis Sylvestris, quae Benalbum vulgo	*Silene vulgaris or S.latifolia*
BETA SYLVESTRIS MARITIMA	*Beta vulgaris* subsp. *maritima*
BETONICA AQUATICA, Scrophularia Aquatica major	*Scrophularia auriculata*
BIFOLIUM SYLVESTRE	*Neottia ovata*
BLITUM PERENNE	*Blitum bonus-henricus* (*Chenopodium bonus-henricus*)
BRASSICA MARINA	*Crambe maritima*
BRASSICA SYLVESTRIS	*Brassica napus or B.rapa* (reversions)
BUGLOSSUM LUTEUM, Lingua Bovis,	*Helminthotheca echioides* (*Picris echioides*)
BUGULA VULGARIS	*Ajuga reptans*
CALTHA PALUSTRIS	*Caltha palustris*
CARDIACA	*Leonurus cardiaca*
CARYOPHYLLATA VULGARIS FLORE PARVO LUTEO	*Geum urbanum*
CARYOPHYLLUS MARINUS MINIMUS	*Armeria maritima*
CAUCALIS MINOR FLOSCULIS RUBENTIBUS	*Torilis japonica*
CAUCALIS NODOSA ECHINATO SEMINE	*Torilis nodosa*
CENTAURIUM LUTEUM PERFOLIATUM	*Blackstonia perfoliata*
CENTAURIUM MINUS VULGARE FLORE PURPUREO	*Centaurium erythraea*
CHAMEDRYS SYLVESTRIS SPURIA MINOR	*Veronica chamaedrys*
CHELIDONIUM MINUS, Chelidonium rotundifolia minor	*Ficaria verna* (*Ranunculus ficaria*)
CHRYSANTHEMUM SEGETUM, Bellis Lutea folijs profunde incisis major	*Glebionis segetum* (*Chrysanthemum segetum*)
CHRYSANTHEMUM SEGETUM, NOSTRAS FOLIO GLAUCO MULTI-SCISSO MAJUS, FLORA MINORE	*Glebionis segetum* (*Chrysanthemum segetum*)
CICHOREUM SYLVESTRE	*Cichorium intybus*
CICUTARIA PALUSTRIS, Phelandrium	*Oenanthe phellandrium, O.aquatica or O.fluviatilis*
CICUTARIA TENUIFOLIA	*Aethusa cynapium*
CIRCAEA LUTETIANA	*Circaea lutetiana*
CLEMATIS DAPHNOIDES MAJOR	*Vinca major*
COCHLEARIA FOLIO SINUATO and COCHLEARIA ROTUNDIFOLIA	*Cochlearia officinalis and C. atlantica*
COCHLEARIA MARINA FOLIO ANGULOSO PARVO	*Cochlearia danica*
CONVOLVOLUS MAJOR	*Calystegia sepium*
CONVOLVOLUS MINOR VULGARIS	*Convolvolus arvensis*
CONYZA CAERULEA ACRIS	*Erigeron acris*

Threlkeld's *Synopsis* (1726)	Stace's *New flora of the British Isles* (2019)
CONYZA MEDIA	*Pulicaria dysenterica*
CORONOPUS RUELLIJ	*Lepidium coronopus* (*Coronopus squamatus*)
CORONOPUS VULGARIS	*Plantago coronopus*
COTYLEDON AQUATICA ACRIS SEPTENTRIONALIUM	*Hydrocotyle vulgaris*
CYANUS SEGETUM	*Centaurea cyanus*
CYNOGLOSSUM VULGARE	*Cynoglossum officinale*
DAUCUS VULGARIS	*Daucus carota*
DENTARIA MAJOR	*Lathraea squamaria*
DIPSACUS SATIVUS	*Dipsacus sativus*
DIPSACUS SYLVESTRIS	*Dipsacus fullonum*
DULCAMARA, Solanum lignosum	*Solanum dulcamara*
EQUISETUM FAETIDUM SUB AQUA REPENS	*Chara* sp.
EQUISETUM MUSCOSUM SUB AQUA REPENS SEMINE LITHOSPERMI	*Chara* sp.
ERICA BRABANTICA FOLIO CORIDIS HIRSUTO QUATERNO	*Erica tetralix*
ERUCA MARINA	*Cakile maritima*
ERUCA SYLVESTRIS VULGATIOR ?	*Sisymbrium irio*
ERYNGIUM MARINUM	*Eryngium maritimum*
EUPATORIUM CANNABINUM FAEMINA	*Eupatorium cannabinum*
EUPATORIUM CANNABINUM FOLIO non diviso	*Bidens cernua*
EUPHRASIA MAJOR LUTEA LATIFOLIA PALUSTRIS	*Parentucellia viscosa*
FILIX FAEMINA VULGARIS RAMOSA	*Pteridium aquilinum*
FRAGARIA STERILIS	*Potentilla sterilis*
GALEOPSIS VERA	*Stachys sylvatica*
GALLIUM LUTEUM	*Galium verum*
GENISTA SPINOSA VULGARIS	*Ulex europaeus*
GERANIUM BATRACHOIDES FLORE CAERULEO	*Geranium pratense*
GERANIUM CICUTE FOLIO MOSCHATUM	*Erodium moschatum*
GERANIUM COLUMBINUM FOLIO MALVAE ROTUNDO	*Geranium molle*
GERANIUM HAEMATODES	*Geranium sanguineum*
GERANIUM MALACOIDES LACINIATUM	*Geranium dissectum*
GERANIUM MOSCHATUM INODORUM	*Erodium cicutarium*
GERANIUM RUPERTIANUM	*Geranium robertianum*
GLAUX MARITIMA EXIGUA	*Lysimachia maritima* (*Glaux maritima*)
GRAMEN CYPEROIDES FOLIJS CARYOPHYLLAEIS	*Carex caryophyllea*
GRAMEN PARNASSI	*Parnassia palustris*

Caleb Threlkeld, Dublin's earliest plant ecologist

Threlkeld's *Synopsis* (1726)	Stace's *New flora of the British Isles* (2019)
HIERACIUM LONGUIS RADICATUM	*Hypochaeris radicata*
HIERACIUM, PULMONARIA GALLICA, seu Aurea latifolia	*Hieracium* sp.
HIPPOSELINUM, SEU SMYRNIUM VULGARE	*Smyrnium olusatrum*
HOLOSTEUM VERNUM	*Stellaria holostea*
HORDEUM SPURIUM VULGARE, Gramen Secalinum	*Hordeum murinum*
HORMINUM SYLVESTRE LAVENDULAE FLORE	*Salvia verbenaca*
JACAEA NIGRA VULGARIS CAPITATA	*Centaurea nigra*
JUNCUS FLORIDUS MAJOR	*Butomus umbellatus*
KALI SPINOSUM COCHLEATUM	*Salsola kali*
LADANUM SEGETUM QUORUNDAM	*Galeopsis angustifolia*
LAGOPUS VULGARIS	*Trifolium arvense*
LAMIUM CANNABINO FOLIO VULGARE	*Galeopsis tetrahit*
LAMIUM CANNABINO FOLIO VULGARE, Cannabis Spuria	*Galeopsis bifida*
LAMIUM LUTEUM FOLIO OBLONGO LUTEUM	*Lamiastrum galeobdolon*
LAMIUM RUBRUM	*Lamium purpureum*
LAMIUM RUBRUM MINUS	*Lamium hybridum*
LAMPSANA	*Lapsana communis*
LAPATHUM ACUTUM	*Rumex conglomeratus*
LAPATHUM FOLIO ACUTO CRISPO	*Rumex crispus* / *Rumex crispus* subsp. *littoreus*
Ledum Palustre nostras arbuti flore (Appendix p.10)	*Andromeda polifolia*
LEUCOJUM LUTEUM	*Erysimum cheiri (Cheiranthus cheiri)*
LIGUSTRUM VULGARE	*Ligustrum vulgare*
LIMONIUM MAJUS VULGATIUS	*Limonium binervosum* agg.
LINUM SYLVESTRE CAERULEUM PERENNE ERECTUS	*Linum bienne*
LITHOSPERMUM	*Lithospermum officinale*
LUNARIA MINOR RACEMOSA VEL VULGARIS	*Botyrichium lunaria*
LUTEOLA HERBA SALICIS FOLIO	*Reseda luteola*
LYCHNIS MARITINA REPENS	*Silene uniflora*
LYCHNIS PLUMARIA	*Silene flos-cuculi (Lychnis flos-cuculi)*
LYCHNIS SEGETUM MAJOR	*Agrostemma githago*
LYCHNIS SYLVESTRIS RUBELLO FLORE	*Silene dioica*
LYSIMACHIA LUTEA	*Lysimachia vulgaris*
LYSIMACHIA PURPUREA SPICATA	*Lythrum salicaria*
LYSIMACHIA SILIQUOSA HIRSUTA MAGNO FLORE	*Epilobium hirsutum*

Threlkeld's *Synopsis* (1726)	Stace's *New flora of the British Isles* (2019)
LYSIMACHIA SILIQUOSA HIRSUTA PARVO FLORE	*Epilobium parviflorum*
MALVA PUMILA FOLIO ROTUNDO	*Malva neglecta*
MALVA SYLVESTRIS VULGARIS FOLIO SINUATO	*Malva sylvestris*
MARRUBIUM AQUATICUM	*Lycopus europaeus*
MELILOTUS GERMANICA	*Melilotus altissimus / officinalis*
MENTHA AQUATICA	*Mentha aquatica*
MYOSOTIS SCORPIOIDES PALUSTRIS	*Myosotis scorpioides*
MYRRHIS SYLVESTRIS SEMINIBUS ASPERIS	*Anthriscus caucalis*
NARCISSUS SYLVESTRIS PALLIDUS CALYCE LUTEO	*Narcissus* sp.
NASTURTIUM AQUATICUM SUPINUM	*Nasturtium officinale* agg.
NUMMULARIA MINOR FLORE PURPURASCENTE	*Lysimachia tenella* (*Anagallis tenella*)
OENANTHE CICUTAE FACIE LOBELII,	*Oenanthe crocata*
OPHIOGLOSSUM	*Ophioglossum vulgatum*
ORCHIS PURPUREA SPICA CONGESTA PYRAMIDALI	*Anacamptis pyramidalis*
ORIGANUM VULGARE SPONTANEUM	*Origanum vulgare*
ORNITHOGALUM ANGUSTIFOLIUM MAJUS, Floribus ex albo virescentibus	*Ornithogalum umbellatum*
PAPAVER CORNICULATUM LUTEUM	*Glaucium flavum*
PARIETARIA	*Parietaria judaica*
PARONYCHIA RUTACEO FOLIO	*Saxifraga tridactylites*
PARONYCHIA VULGARIS ALSINEFOLIA, Bursa pastoris Loculo oblongo	*Erophila verna*
PECTEN VENERIA, Scandix vulgaris	*Scandix peten-veneris*
PEDICULARIS	*Rhinanthus minor* subsp. *minor and* subsp. *stenophyllus*
Pedicularis palustris rubra elatior (under PEDICULARIS PRATENSIS RUBRA VULGARIS)	*Pedicularis palustris*
PENTAPHYLLUM RUBRUM PALUSTRE and PENTAPHYLLUM PALUSTRE RUBRUM CRASSIS & VILLOSIS FOLIJS	*Comarum palustre* (*Potentilla palustris*)
PERCEPIER ANGLORUM	*Aphanes arvensis* agg.
PERSICARIA SALICIS FOLIO PERENNIS	*Persicaria amphibia*
PETASITES VULGARIS	*Petasites hybridus*
PEUCEDANUM	*Peucedanum officinale*
PILOSELLA REPENS	*Pilosella officinarum*

Caleb Threlkeld, Dublin's earliest plant ecologist

Threlkeld's *Synopsis* (1726)	Stace's *New flora of the British Isles* (2019)
PIMPINELLA SAXIFRAGA UNIBELLA CANDIDA	*Pimpinella saxifraga*
PIMPINELLA SYLVESTRIS and PIMPINELLA MINOR	*Poterium sanguisorba*
PINGUICULA GESNREI	*Pinguicula vulgaris*
PLANTAGO AQUATICA MAJOR	*Alisma plantago-aquatica*
PLANTAGO AQUATICA STELLATA (as) = Damasonium alisma	*Baldellia ranunculoides*
PLANTAGO MARINA	*Plantago maritima*
POLYGALA VULGARIS	*Polygala vulgaris*
POLYGONUM MAS VULGARIS	*Polygonum aviculare / P.depressum (P.arenastrum)*
POLYPODIUM MAS VULGARE and POLYPODIUM QUERCINUM	*Polypodium vulgare* agg.
POTAMOGITON FOLIJS CRISPUS	*Potamogeton crispus*
POTAMOGITON LATIFOLIUM	*Potamogeton natans*
PRIMULA VERIS MAJOR	*Primula veris*
QUERCUS VULGARIS CUM GLANDE (and QUERCUS CUM EXCREMENTOSIS FUNGOSIS)	*Quercus* sp.
RANUNCULUS AQUATICUS HEPATICAE FACIE FOLIO ROTUNDO, & CAPILLACEO	*Ranunculus penicillatus*
RANUNCULUS ARVORUM	*Ranunculus arvensis*
RANUNCULUS AURICOMUS DULCIS	*Raunuculus auricomus*
RANUNCULUS BULBOSUS	*Ranunculus bulbosus*
RANUNCULUS T[F]LAMMEUS MINOR; T[F]lammula	*Ranunculus flammula*
RAPISTRUM ARVORUM FLORE LUTEO	*Sinapis arvensis*
ROS SOLIS FOLIO ROTUNDO	*Drosera rotundifolia*
ROSA PIMPINELLE FOLIO	*Rosa pimpinellifolia*
RUBEOLA ARVENSIS CAERULEA	*Sherardia arvensis*
SALIX FOLIO EX ROTUNDITATE ACUMINATO	*Salix caprea* (or possibly *S. cinerea*)
SALIX VULGARIS ALBA ARBORESCENS	*Salix alba*
SALVIA AGRESTIS	*Teucrium scorodonia*
SANICULA	*Sanicula europaea*
SAXIFRAGA AUREA	*Chrysosplenium oppositifolium*
SCROPHULARIA NODOSA FAETIDA	*Scrophularia nodosa*
SEDUM MINUS HAEMATOIDES FLORE LUTEO	*Petrosedum fosterianum* or *P.rupestre*
SEDUM PARVUM ACRE FLORE LUTEO	*Sedum acre*
SIDERITIS ANGLICA STRUMOSA RADICE	*Stachys palustris*

Threlkeld's *Synopsis* (1726)	Stace's *New flora of the British Isles* (2019)
SOPHIA CHIRURGORUM	*Descurainia sophia*
SPARGANIUM RAMOSUM	*Sparganium erectum*
SPERGULA MARINA NOSTRAS	*Spergularia media*
SPERGULA SAGINAE SPERGULA MAJOR	*Spergula arvensis*
STELLARIA AQUATICA	*Callitriche* sp.
TITHYMALUS HELIOSCOPIUS	*Euphorbia helioscopia*
TITHYMALUS PARALIUS	*Euphorbia paralias*
TRAGOPOGON LUTEUM PRATENSE	*Tragopogon pratensis*
TRIFOLIUM LUPULINUM ALTERUM MINUS	*Trifolium dubium*
TRIFOLIUM PRATENSE LUTEUM CAPITULA LUPULI	*Trifolium campestre*
TRIPOLIUM MAJUS & MINUS	*Tripolium pannonicum* (*Aster tripolium*)
TYPHA PALUSTRIS MAXIMA	*Typha latifolia*
UMBILICUS VENERIS	*Umbilicus rupestris*
VACCINIA NIGRA VULGARIA	*Vaccinium myrtillus*
VACCINIA PALUSTRIA	*Vaccinium oxycoccus*
VALERIANA MAJOR SYLVESTRIS	*Valeriana officinalis*
VALERIANA SYLVESTRIS MINOR	*Polemonium caeruleum*
VERBASCUM MAS LATIFOLIUM LUTEUM	*Verbascum thapsus*
VICIA SYLVESTRIS MULTIFLORA SPICATA	*Ervilia sylvatica* (*Vicia sylvatica*)
VICIA SYLVESTRIS, seu Cracca Minima	*Ervilia hirsuta* (*Vicia hirsuta*)
VIOLA BICOLOR ARVENSIS	*Viola arvensis*
VIOLA MONTANA LUTEA GRANDIFLORA	*Viola lutea*
VIOLA PALUSTRIS ROTUNDIFOLIA GLABRA	*Viola palustris*
VIOLA TRICOLOR	*Viola tricolor* subsp. *tricolor*

CHAPTER SEVEN

Botany and gardens at the Edward Worth Library, Dublin

ELIZABETHANNE BORAN

IN 1723 DR EDWARD WORTH (1676–1733), an early eighteenth-century Dublin physician and bibliophile, decided to leave his collection of more than 4,000 books to Dr Steevens' Hospital, an institution of which he was a Trustee. This decision ensured the survival of his collection, one of vital importance to historians of medicine, science and of the book. At the intersection of all three subjects lies his collection of books on botany, which present us with a cornucopia of sources for early modern botany. This chapter explores the contents of Worth's 'paper garden' and investigates the factors affecting his choice of books.

In order to understand the importance of the botanical books in Worth's collection, we must first consider how it fits into his overall library. The Edward Worth Library is rightly known for its large medical collection, which is one of the few extant medical libraries of the period in Ireland.[1] However, Worth did not focus solely on his professional concerns. As one might expect, his library held many classical texts as well as historical works. It is clear that one of the most important sub-sections of his library was his scientific collection, which covers all areas of science and which, as the following chart (Table. 7.1) demonstrates, was particularly strong in the area of botany.[2]

Table 7.1. Scientific subject divisions in the Edward Worth Library.

Subject	Per cent	Subject	Per cent	Subject	Per cent
Mathematics	11.9	Paleontology	2.2	Composite	17.4
Astronomy	11.4	Botany	13.4	Veterinary	0.9
Physics	10.8	Zoology	9.7	Music	0.2
Chemistry	7.6	Engineering	6.9		
Earth Sciences	5.6	Agriculture	1.9	Total	100%

1 Elizabethanne Boran, 'Collecting medicine in early eighteenth-century Dublin: the library of Edward Worth' in John Cunningham (ed.), *Early modern Ireland and the world of medicine: practitioners, collectors and contexts* (Manchester, 2019), pp 165–87. 2 The subject divisions in this chart represent modern subject classifications.

157

7.1 Dr Edward Worth (1676–1733): portrait in oils, artist unknown. By permission of the Trustees of the Edward Worth Library, Dublin. © Edward Worth Library.

Worth's scientific collection was roughly divided between natural philosophy (58%) and natural history (42%).[3] The strong showing of natural philosophy, particularly of the areas of astronomy and mathematics, is hardly surprising, given that these were areas which were covered as part of the undergraduate curriculum. However, as Worth's mathematical collection and his obsession with Newtonian works demonstrate, his natural philosophical concerns remained a feature of his collecting throughout his life. As these figures (Table. 7.1) suggest, while overall Worth might have devoted more attention to natural philosophy than natural history, when it came to individual scientific disciplines, he strongly favoured botanical works. If we set aside the 'composite' cohort (i.e. books which either deal with 'philosophy of science' or cover more than one subject area – more usually natural history compilations), the dominance of botany is very clear indeed. This dominance is no accident, for botany was, after all, one of the porous areas between natural history and medicine which any self-respecting medical practitioner needed to know.

MEDICINAL BOTANY

Physicians played a fundamental role in the rise of botanical studies (and more generally natural history) in the early modern period.[4] We see this in the papers of the Royal Society of London and the Dublin Philosophical Society, where natural history formed a dominant subsection of reports and experiments.[5] Worth is a good example of this. In his medical studies at Leiden, he was expected to attend lectures on the natural sciences, and Leiden, following the model of the University of Padua, had established a botanical garden in 1593.[6] In Dublin Robert Huntington (1637–1701), provost of Trinity College Dublin, set up a physic garden on the campus in 1687 and it seems likely that beyond these institutional botanical gardens, physicians such as Worth may have cultivated their own personal physic gardens.[7] Throughout

3 The definition of what constituted natural philosophy and natural history in the early modern period changed over time. Patricia Reif, in a seminal article on the textbook tradition, harked back to an Aristotelian model in her definition of natural philosophy as 'a speculative science which studies the world of changing material things – celestial and terrestrial, animate and inanimate – culminating in the study of man' (Patricia Reif, 'The textbook tradition in natural philosophy, 1600–1650', *Journal of the History of Ideas*, 30 (1969), 17–32, at 20). This definition might also encompass what we would today define as 'natural history' (i.e., the branch of science dealing with animals, vegetables and minerals), which likewise was undergoing a transition in the early modern period.   4 B.W. Ogilvie, *The science of describing: natural history in Renaissance Europe* (Chicago, 2006), pp 35, 38, 46, 243.   5 K.T. Hoppen (ed.), *Papers of the Dublin Philosophical Society 1683–1709*, 2 vols (Dublin, 2008).   6 Petrus Pauw, *Hortus publicus Academiae Lugduno–Batavae, ejus ichnographia, descriptio, usus. Addito, quas habet stirpium numero et nominibus* (Leiden, 1601); Claudia Swan, 'Medical culture at Leiden university *ca.* 1600: a social history in prints', *Nederlands Kunsthistorisch Jaarboej (NKJ) / Netherlands Yearbook for History of Art*, 52 (2001), 234–6. On botanical links between Leiden and Dublin in the seventeenth and eighteenth century see E.C. Nelson, 'The influence of Leiden on botany in Dublin in the early eighteenth century', *Huntia*, 4:2 (1982), 133–48, and P.H. Kelly's chapter in this volume.   7 On the subsequent history of the botanical garden at TCD see P.S. Wyse Jackson, 'The botanical garden 1687 to 1987', *Botanical Journal of the Linnaean Society*, 95, (1987), 301–11. See also E.C. Nelson's chapter on 'The Physic Garden of Trinity College,

96 SIMPLICIVM Pharma-
Herba Paralysis.

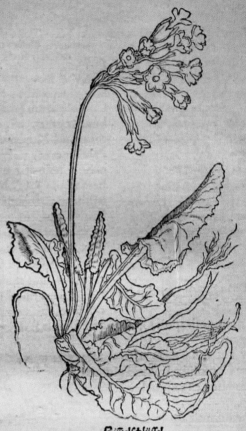

Himelschlüssel.

DE HERBA PARALYSI,
Rhapsodia XV.
❡ NOMENCLATVRAE.
Latinæ, Herba paralysis, Margarita.
Germanicæ, S. Peters schlüssel/ Himmelschlüssel/ Schlüsselblumen/ Weiss Betonien.

MVLTA SVBINDE apud autores de Paralysi herba uestiga-
uimus, plurima cum herbarijs contulimus, uerum necdum quicq̃ com-
perimus, quod ad stomachũ fecerit nostrum. Nomen ignotũ ueteribus
scriptoribus. Barbari tam inscite, tam inepte, cõfusaneeq̃ oĩa miscent, ut
maius etiam negociũ fecerint. Sic enim reliquit de ea Pandectarum rha-
Pandectarius psodus. Herba Paralysis est, cuius folia florere incipiũt tempore hyemis,
quę se extendunt in terra, quasi alba & crispa: ut Alisfagus, florem album
profert.

Botany and gardens at the Edward Worth Library, Dublin 161

the sixteenth century physicians had played a prominent role in the investigation of botanical topics and it is striking that Worth has copies of works by all the leading practitioners: Otto Brunfels (*c.*1489–1534); Leonhard Fuchs (1501–66); Pietro Andrea Mattioli (1501–77); Guillaume Rondelet (1507–66); Francisco Hernandez (1515–87); Rembert Dodoens (1517–85); Ulisse Aldrovandi (1522–1605); Andrea Cesalpino (1519–1603); Charles de l'Écluse (1526–1609); Matthias de L'Obel (1538–1616); and Caspar Bauhin (1560–1624) (Fig. 7.4, p. 167).

Preceded by the rediscovery of ancient texts, most notably the *Materia medica* of Dioscorides, the period 1530–60 witnessed northern European scholars (again, invariably physicians) investigate plants native to their locale.[8] As a result, the sixteenth century was the age of the illustrated herbal, a trend clearly visible in Worth's library. These large volumes were expensive items to produce, not only because their folio format ensured they used more paper than smaller books, but also because, by their very nature, they included a host of illustrations.

A good example is Worth's earliest herbal, Otto Brunfels' *Herbarum vivae eicones ad naturae imitationem* (Strasburg, 1532), whose woodcuts issued in 'a new epoch in the study of plants'.[9] In the words of Brunfels' contemporary, Leonhard Fuchs (whose *De historia stirpium commentarii insignes* (Basle, 1542) was likewise collected by Worth), Brunfels was 'the first of all to bring back the correct method of illustrating plants into our Germany, giving others something to imitate'.[10] As the title suggests, Brunfels and his illustrator Hans Weiditz (*fl.* 1495–1536) provided readers with 'images of living plants', such as *Primula veris* (cowslip), not stylized, unrealistic ones.

Many subsequent herbals followed the pattern laid down by Brunfels and Fuchs: a pattern clearly visible in Worth's seventeenth-century editions of two leading English writers, John Gerard (*c.*1545–1612), and John Parkinson (1566/7–1650). Today Gerard's *Herball* (Worth owned the 1633 edition edited and corrected by Thomas Johnson (*d.* 1644)) is probably better known since it has often been reprinted, sometimes in abbreviated form. It was joined in 1640 by *Theatrum botanicum* by the English apothecary John Parkinson, one of the last herbals to be collected by Worth. Rather than simply regurgitating earlier works and re-using earlier illustrations (a charge laid at Gerard's door), Parkinson's book was encyclopaedic in scope, aiming to bring together the writings of ancient authors as well as contemporary writers. The publication of two large herbals within seven years of each other highlights the continuing market for herbals in the vernacular in the mid seventeenth century, while *Theatrum botanicum* also points to the challenges inherent in summarizing the botanical knowledge then available.

Dublin' in this volume. **8** On the challenges of printing Dioscorides in the Renaissance see Alain Touwaide, 'Printing Greek medicine in the Renaissance. Scholars, collections, opportunities and challenges', *Early Science and Medicine*, 17 (2012), 371–6; on the rise of Renaissance herbals see Brent Elliott, 'The world of the Renaissance herbal', *Renaissance Studies*, 25:11 (2011), 24–41. **9** Blanche Henrey, *British botanical and horticultural literature before 1800*, 3 vols (London, 1975), i, p. 7. **10** F.G. Meyer, E.E. Trueblood and J.L. Heller (eds), *The great herbal of Leonhart Fuchs*, 2 vols (Stanford, 1999), i, dedicatory epistle. Worth's copy of Fuchs' *De historia stirpium commentarii insignes* includes annotations

Elizabethanne Boran

THE INFLUENCE OF LEIDEN

As Johnson made clear in his 1633 edition, Gerard's text owed much to the works of Rembert Dodoens, Matthias de L'Obel and Charles de L'Écluse (Carolus Clusius).[11] This triumvirate were trail-blazing, not least in their quest (begun at the end of the sixteenth and continuing into the seventeenth century) to develop botany as a subject in its own right, rather than as a medical adjunct.[12] The fact that two of these botanists were also professors of medicine at the University of Leiden is, in the context of Worth's botanical collection, important.[13] Rembert Dodoens was appointed professor of medicine at Leiden in 1582. His *Cruydeboeck* of 1554 was translated into French by L'Écluse and Worth had an edition of a Latin translation, *Stirpium historiae pemptades sex* (Antwerp, 1616).[14] L'Écluse, in turn, had been appointed to the medical faculty in 1593 and he became the first director of the Hortus Academicus of Leiden, the botanical garden of the university.[15] It was L'Écluse who was instrumental in the development of the Hortus Academicus' collection for it was he who urged the Dutch East India Company to search out specimens for its garden. L'Écluse's successors as prefect continued his work and Worth, educated at Leiden in the late 1690s, would have been very much aware of the vital importance of the garden to the university generally, and the medical faculty in particular.

The impact of Worth's medical education in Leiden and, more generally, his sojourn in the Netherlands, on his botanical collection is evident in his collection of Asian and African floras. Above all, the Worth botanical collection reflects the dominant role of the Dutch Republic and, more specifically, the rise to power of the Dutch East India Company (Vereenigde Oost–Indische Companie, or VOC) in early modern botanical exploration. The VOC not only led botanical investigations of south-eastern Asia, but also brought countless plants from southern Africa to the Hortus Medicus in Amsterdam.[16] These two loci of botanical study, the Hortus Academicus of the University of Leiden, and the Hortus Medicus of the city of Amsterdam, dominate Worth's botanical library.

---

in both Latin and English, but some of these are likely to have been added by previous owners since the endings of some Latin words have been cropped in the binding process.   11 John Gerard, *The herball or Generall historie of plantes. Gathered by Iohn Gerarde of London Master in Chirurgerie very much enlarged and amended by Thomas Iohnson citizen and apothecarye of London* (London, 1633), Sig. ¶¶¶1r. 12 Ogilvie, *The science of describing*, p. 44.   13 On Leiden see W.T. Stearn, 'The influence of Leyden on botany in the seventeenth and eighteenth centuries', *The British Journal for the History of Science*, 1:2 (1962), 137–58 and Florike Edmond, 'Town and gown: Leiden and the convergencies of European traditions' in Florike Egmond, *The world of Carolus Clusius* (London, 2010), pp 157–74.   14 Dodoens' signature may be found on Worth's copy of Guillaume Rondelet's *Libri de piscibus marinis* (Lyon, 1555). Worth also owned books belonging to another noted botanist, Joseph Pitton de Tournefort: on this see E.C. Nelson, 'Books from the libraries of Tournefort and Dodoens in Ireland' in E.C. Nelson (ed.), *History and mystery. Notes and queries from newsletters of The Society for the History of Natural History* (London, 2011), 135–6.   15 On L'Écluse see P.G. Hoftijzer, Florike Egmond, and R.P.W. Visser (eds), *Carolus Clusius: towards a cultural history of a Renaissance naturalist* (Amsterdam, 2007).   16 G. Scott and M.L. Hewett, 'Pioneers of ethnopharmacology: the Dutch East India Company (VOC) at the Cape from 1650 to 1800', *Journal of Ethnopharmacology*, 115 (2008), 338–60. On the Hortus Medicus of

Botany and gardens at the Edward Worth Library, Dublin 163

The Hortus Medicus had been set up by the city council of Amsterdam on 12 November 1682. Its early commissioners, Jan Commelin (1629–92) and Joan Huydecoper van Maarseveen (1625–1704), benefited not only from their links to the VOC, but also from the level of independence the new institution had been granted, for it was not part of the Athenaeum Illustre of Amsterdam. Commelin was responsible for a flagship project of illustrating and printing representations of the varied plants available in the Hortus. The result, *Horti Medici Amstelodamensis,* was printed by the Blaeu firm at Amsterdam in two volumes between 1697 and 1701. The publication, which Worth duly collected, graphically reflects the botanical hegemony of the aspiring Dutch state.[17]

There were also close links between the Commelin family and a similar botanical VOC initiative.[18] The VOC Governor of the Malabar, Hendrik Adriaan van Rheede tot Drakenstein (1636–91), had initiated a study of the botany of the Indian subcontinent. A huge project, the *Hortus Malabaricus* was finally published in a massive twelve-volume set, which Worth also collected.[19] Jan Commelin had been responsible for editing volumes 2–11 and part of volume 12, and his nephew Caspar Commelin (1667/8–1731) produced an index of it, *Flora Malabarica sive Horti Malabarici catalogus* (Leiden, 1696).[20] The examination of the botany of the Indian subcontinent and nearby areas in south Asia was thus made possible by this combination of forces, scholarly and military, and both the Hortus Medicus of Amsterdam and the botanical garden of the University of Leiden were its major beneficiaries.

Caspar Commelin had been responsible for the addition of a number of southern African plants into the second volume of the *Horti Medici Amstelodamensis* (which appeared in 1701).[21] The Cape of Good Hope was of vital interest to the VOC as an important way station on their voyages to Asia. In December 1651, the VOC commanders had set up a garden and began to explore the flora of the Cape area. Later commanders and governors of the VOC continued this interest for, as Scott and Hewett make clear, the VOC itself was immensely interested in the medicinal use of such plants and was keen to learn local medicinal lore from members of the Khoi-Khoi and San peoples.[22] Hundreds of living plants gathered in the hinterland of the

---

Amsterdam see D.O. Wijnands, 'The Hortus Medicus Amstelodamensis – its role in shaping taxonomy and horticulture', 4 (1987), *The Kew Magazine,* 78–91. **17** *Horti Medici Amstelodamensis,* 2 vols (Amsterdam, 1697–1701). **18** On the Commelins see D.O. Wijnands, *The botany of the Commelins* (Rotterdam, 1983). **19** On the *Hortus Malabaricus* see J. Heniger, *Hendrik Adriaan van Reede tot Drakenstein (1636–1691) and Hortus Malabaricus. A contribution to the history of Dutch colonial botany* (Rotterdam, 1986). **20** Worth bought the Index in 1729 from the auction of the Dutch collector, Goswin Uilenbroek: *Bibliotheca Uilenbroukiana, sive catalogus librorum quod collegii … Goswinus Uilenbroek, in tres partes divisus,* 3 vols (Amsterdam, 1729), iii, p. 72. **21** Worth purchased his copy of the *Horti Medici Amstelodamensis,* 2 vols (Amsterdam, 1697–1701) in 1726 for £3 10 shillings from the auction of the library of Monsieur D'Alone, which took place in London: *Bibliotheca in omni disciplinarum genere illustrissimae, sive catalogus … Being a catalogue of choice, valuable, and very scarce books, … collected by the defunct, Mr. d'Alone; … to be sold … at the shop of J. Groenewegen, and A. vander Hoeck, … on Monday the 1st of February 1725 …* (London, 1726), p. 132. **22** Scott and Hewett, 'Pioneers of ethnopharmacology', 340–60.

7.3 'Lilio-Narcissus Africanus platycaulis humilis …' (*Ammocharis longifolia* (L.) Herb.). Jan Commelin, *Horti Medici Amstelodamensis rariorum*, 2 vols (Amsterdam, 1697–1701), i, fig. 36. By permission of the Trustees of the Edward Worth Library, Dublin. © Edward Worth Library.

Botany and gardens at the Edward Worth Library, Dublin   165

Cape of Good Hope were sent to the Amsterdam Hortus Medicus during the period 1682–1710.[23] Many of these plants were illustrated in Commelin's *Horti Medici Amstelodamensis*.

Worth collected works by other authors who likewise had connections both to the botanical garden at Leiden and the Dutch East India Company. One of the most important of these was Paul Hermann (1646–95), a German physician and botanist who later became director of the Leiden botanical garden.[24] Worth owned a copy of Hermann's *Paradisus Batavus* (Leiden, 1698), a description of plants in the Leiden Botanical garden. The 'Batavus' of the title could be read in two ways: as a reference to the ancient name of the Netherlands itself, or as an oblique reference to Batavia (Java), the location of the overseas headquarters of the VOC, and the origin of some of the botanical specimens.

Though clearly Worth's botanical collection was heavily influenced by his education at the University of Leiden (at just the time some of these multi-volume works were being produced), he did not limit his collection solely to the regions explored by the VOC. He also paid attention to botanical works about the plants of the Levant and other parts of the eastern Mediterranean, the earliest being Johann Vesling's *De plantis aegyptiis observationes*, printed at Padua in 1638; to this was added Joseph Pitton de Tournefort's *Relation d'un voyage du Levant* (Amsterdam, 1718) and Johann Christian Buxbaum's 1728 list of plants of modern Turkey.[25] Again, there were Leiden links here: Vesling (1598–1649) was a German botanist who had studied medicine at the universities of Leiden and Bologna.[26] Buxbaum (1693–1730), likewise, had studied at Leiden, though in his case his educational trajectory had been decidedly German: he had studied at Leipzig, Wittenberg and Jena before travelling to Leiden.[27]

THE NAMING OF PLANTS

Worth's education at Leiden influenced his botanical collection in other ways. We have seen the dominance of the medicinal approach to botany and Worth's allegiance to the publications outlining the botanical gardens at both Leiden and Amsterdam, but there were other trends in Leiden which are reflected in his collection. As mentioned previously, the investigations of Dodoens and L'Écluse, though originating from a search for plants of medicinal value, gradually had broadened out to investigate plants in their own right. The emphasis began to move from the

---

23 Wijnands, *The botany of the Commelins*, p. 5.   **24** Pieter Baas, 'The golden age of Dutch colonial botany and its impact on garden and herbarium collections' in Ib Friis and Henrik Balslev (eds), *Tropical plant collections: legacies from the past? Essential tools for the future?* (Copenhagen, 2017), p. 56.   **25** Johann Christian Buxbaum, *Plantarum minus cognitarum centuria I complectens: plantas circa Byzantium & in Oriente observatas* (St Petersburg, 1728).   **26** Erich Hintzche, 'Vesling, Johann' in C.C. Gillispie (ed.), *Dictionary of scientific biography* (New York, 1976), xiv, pp 12–13.   **27** E.I. Kolchinsky, 'The role of eighteenth-century Russian expeditions in the development of natural history', *Proceedings of the California Academy of Sciences*, 55, Supplement II, no. 8 (2004), 106–16.

medicinal to the naming and classification of plants. There were elements of this in Worth's copy of *Horti Medici Amstelodamensis*, but as the sheer abundance of Asian, African and American plants hitherto unknown to European botanists became clear, so too did the problem of nomenclature. That Worth was interested in the naming of plants is clear from a sub-section in his collection, that moves away from studying plants in the medicinal strait-jacket of the sixteenth-century herbal, and the superbly illustrated floras of the seventeenth century, to the decidedly more textual and less visual publications of the later seventeenth and early eighteenth century.

The reason is not hard to understand – illustrating one small nation's native flora was a challenging task. Illustrating the sheer cornucopia of plants becoming known to botanists in Europe in the early modern period was simply not possible. The avalanche of information clearly necessitated a new approach and new forms of classification came into being. Worth's collection predates the works of Carl Linnaeus (1707–78), which dominated botany in the second half of the eighteenth century, and instead allows us to witness the various possibilities on offer to a keen botanist in the early eighteenth century. One might say that classification, as opposed to describing, really began with the Italian botanist Andrea Cesalpino (1519–1603), whose system based on fruit and flower, although ignored in his own time, greatly influenced later botanists.[28] *Pinax theatri botanici* (Basel, 1623) compiled by the Swiss botanist Caspar Bauhin (Fig 7.4) included over 6,000 names for different plants but, though it was widely used, it did not provide a satisfactory classification.[29] Works by Robert Morison (1620–83), John Ray (1627–1705), Augustus Quirinus Rivinus (1652–1723), Joseph Pitton de Tournefort (1656–1708) and Sebastien Vaillant (1669–1722), in the latter part of the seventeenth and early eighteenth centuries, refocused on the problems of classification.[30] Works by all these authors were collected by Worth.[31]

Worth owned a number of works devoted to the botany of the New World. Undoubtedly one of the most important was Francisco Hernandez's *Nova plantarum* (Rome, 1651), which catalogued the flora of New Spain (Mexico), and Worth also had such books as Charles Plumier's *Description des plantes de l'Amerique* (Paris, 1693) and Jacques Philippe Cornut's *Canadensium plantarum* (Paris, 1635). Hernández (1515–87), a Spanish physician, had been sent to Mexico by Philip II of Spain (1527–98), specifically to search out plants of medicinal use since it was believed that cures for the new diseases afflicting early modern Europe might well be found in newly conquered dominions.

---

28 On Cesalpino see C.E.B. Bremekamp, 'A re-examination of Cesalpino's classification', *Acta Botanica Neerlandica*, 1:4 (1953), 580–93.   29 Anna Pavord, *The naming of plants: the search for order in the world of plants* (London, 2005), pp 359, 373, 382.   30 See Pavord for discussions of their contributions.
31 Robert Morison, *Plantarum umbelliferarum distributio nova* (Oxford, 1672) and *Plantarum historiae universalis Oxoniensis seu herbarum distributio nova*, 2 vols (Oxford, 1715); John Ray, *Synopsis methodica stirpium Britannicarum* (London, 1690); *Historia plantarum species hactenus editas aliasque insuper multas noviter inventas & descriptas complectens*, 3 vols (London, 1686–1704). Augustus Quirinus Rivinus, *Introductio generalis in rem herbariam*, 2 vols (Leipzig, 1690). Joseph Pitton de Tournefort, *Institutiones rei herbariae*, 3 vols (Paris, 1700); *Corollarium institutionum rei herbariae* (Paris, 1703); *Contractus sub forma tabularum sistens institutiones rei herbariæ* (Frankfut am Main, 1715). He also possessed Sébastien Vaillant, *Discours sur la structure des fleurs, leurs differences et l'usage de leurs parties* (Leiden, 1718).

7.4 Caspar Bauhin (1560–1624), portrait from Pietro Andrea Mattioli, *Opera quæ extant omnia: hoc est, commentarij in VI. libros Pedacij Dioscoridis Anazarbei de medica materia* (Basle, 1598), Sig. 2*6v. By permission of the Trustees of the Edward Worth Library, Dublin. © EdwardWorth Library.

Worth was equally interested in Western European floras and had a wide-ranging collection which included works describing the plants found in France, Spain, Italy, Switzerland and the Holy Roman Empire, such as Jacques Barrelier's *Plantae per Galliam, Hispaniam et Italiam observatae* (Paris, 1714), Paolo Boccone's *Icones et descriptiones rariorum plantarum Siciliæ, Melitæ, Galliæ, et Italiæ* (Oxford, 1674) and Giulio Pontedera's Italian flora, *Compendium tabularum botanicarum* (Padua, 1718). He was likewise interested in local floras, such as Joachim Camerarius' *Hortus medicus et philosophicus* (Frankfurt, 1583), which listed plants found in the area of Nuremberg and the Harz mountains.

GARDENS AND FLORAS

As we have seen, Worth also bought works on specific gardens. Just as he had collected works on the academic and civic botanical gardens of Leiden and Amsterdam, so too did he collect works on botanical gardens linked to universities elsewhere. From Italy, he had works on the famous botanical gardens at the universities of Pisa and Padua, the first academic botanical gardens in Europe, which had been created in 1544 and 1545 respectively.[32] Likewise his collection of works on French gardens concentrated on institutional gardens such as the famous Jardin du Roi in Paris, and the royal gardens of Montpellier and Blois.[33]

Alongside these explorations of institutional gardens were a couple of works on private gardens. The first was Pietro Castelli's description of the plants in Cardinal Odoardo Farnese's garden at Rome: *Exactissima descriptio rariorum quarundam plantarum quae continentur Romae in horto Farnesiano* (Rome, 1625), which Worth purchased in 1729 from the auction of a Dutch collector, Goswin Uilenbroek (1658–1740).[34] Undoubtedly Worth's most important description of a private garden was his magnificent *Hortus Eystettensis*, first published in 1613, which was a pictorial record of the plants in the garden of the Prince Bishop of Eichstätt Johann Konrad von Gemmingen (1561–1612), illustrating more than 600 different plants. Worth bought the edition of 1640, printed at Nuremberg, that, like its predecessor, was an enormous tome. It was probably the most expensive book illustrating flowers of its time, containing 367 copper engravings which had been undertaken by a team of six engravers led by Wolfgang Kilian (1581–1662) from Augsburg. Divided into sections for Winter, Spring, Summer and Autumn, botanical accuracy was often sacrificed to

---

32 Worth had two works on the botanical garden of the university of Padua: Jean Prevost, *Hortulus medicus selectioribus remediis* (Padua, 1681) and Giulio Pontedera, *Anthologia, sive, De floris natura libri tres, plurimis inventis, observationibusque, ac æreis tabulis ornati accedunt ejusdem Dissertaiones XI ex iis, quos habuit in Horto publico paptavino anno 1719, quibus res botanic, & subinde etiam medica illustrator* (Padua, 1720); and one work on the garden at Pisa: Michelangelo Tilli, *Catalogus plantarum horti Pisani* (Florence, 1723).
33 Dionys Joncquet, *Hortus Regius* (Paris, 1665); Pierre Magnol, *Hortus Regius Monspeliensis, sive catalogus plantarum quae in Horto* (Montpellier, 1697); Robert Morison, *Hortus Regius Blesensi* (London, 1669).
34 *Bibliotheca Uilenbroukiana*, i, p. 48.

Botany and gardens at the Edward Worth Library, Dublin 169

decorative effect. The text was the work of a Nuremburg apothecary Basil Besler (1561–1629) who was in charge of the Eichstätt garden after the original designer, Joachim Camerarius, died in 1598. Besler was commissioned by the bishop to undertake this book, probably around 1600, though he claimed in the first edition of 1613 that he had intermittently spent sixteen years on the project.[35]

On a much smaller scale, another seasonally organized text, the *Hortus Floridus* of Crispijn van de Passe (1589–1670), not only provided Worth with a beautifully illustrated florilegium, but also gives us some indication of garden design since each season is preceded by a plate of a garden representing the relevant season.

GARDEN DESIGN

Garden design is also represented in works such as Worth's copy of Johann Christopher Volkamer's *Nürnbergische Hesperides* (Nuremberg, 1708). Included in this fascinating book about the cultivation of citrus fruits are depictions of different types of gardens in the city of Nuremberg. Worth's two-volume copy includes a fascinating panorama of garden layouts, albeit as backdrops. Such garden designs by default might also be found in architectural books in Worth's library, for example Johann Bernhard Fischer von Erlach's *Entwurff einer historischen architectur* (Leipzig, 1725). Worth did, however, collect one book which was explicitly devoted to garden design: Paolo Bartolomeo Clarici's *Istoria e coltura delle piante …* (Venice, 1726). In this work Clarici went into detail about the garden he had designed at the Villa Sagredo (Fig. 7.5) at Marocco (in the Contado of Venice).

In the main, however, Worth's collection holds relatively few books on garden design. The same is true for his collection of books on gardening, for, though Worth had a stupendous collection of botanical items, he appears to have bought few books on the practice of gardening. Perhaps the most famous was the sixth edition of Sir Hugh Plat's *The Garden of Eden* (London, 1675). The subtitle of the work points to its practical approach: '*or, an accurate description of all flowers and fruits now growing in England, with particular rules how to advance their nature and growth, as well in seeds and herbs, as the secret ordering of trees and plants*'. Plat's book was essentially a text for people interested, as he said himself, in the 'Practical and Operative part of Nature, whereunto but a few in many Ages have attained'. It had been 'wrung out of the earth by the painful hand of Experience' and was a clearly presented handbook for the active gardener, who wanted concrete advice on subjects such as 'how to destroy caterpillars'.[36]

Did Worth follow Plat's advice? We just don't know. He did collect a few books on the cultivation of particular plants: for example, he had a copy of the Dublin reprint of the revised fourth edition of Stephen Switzer's *A compendious method for*

---

35 Wilfrid Blunt, *The art of botanical illustration* (London, 1950), pp 95–7. 36 Sir Hugh Plat, *The Garden of Eden* (London, 1675), Sigs. A6r; A7r; and pp 151–2.

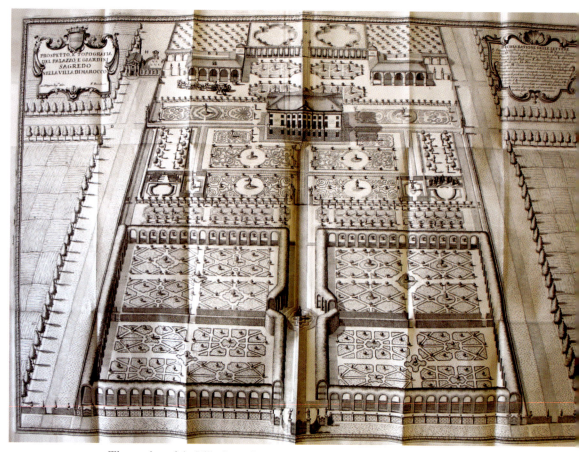

7.5 The garden of the Villa Sagredo at Marocco, illustrated in Paolo Bartolomeo Clarici's *Istoria e coltura delle piante …* (Venice, 1726), foldout plate. By permission of the Trustees of the Edward Worth Library, Dublin. © Edward Worth Library.

the raising of the Italian brocoli, Spanish cardoon, celeriac, finochi, and other foreign kitchen-vegetables (London and Dublin, 1729), and John Evelyn's *Sylva, or a discourse of forest-trees, and the propagation of timber in His Majesties dominions* (London, 1679). However, the text on kitchen vegetables was the only book by the prolific Switzer that Worth purchased, and the copy of Evelyn's *Sylva* had been bought by his father, John Worth (1648–88), rather than himself. True, Worth would have had access to other advice on gardening in some of his botanical items, but the proliferation of large illustrated folios and the relative dearth of practical handbooks on actual gardening techniques strongly suggest that Worth was an armchair gardener rather than an active one.

Worth's collection of books on botany and gardening was, therefore, governed by his professional medical concerns and his academic education. Coupled with these, there were two other factors that influenced his collecting: a) his financial resources, which allowed him to amass a large collection of highly illustrated – and hence costly – books; and b) his all-encompassing passion for the book as object. We know that Worth inherited lands from his father, John Worth, who had been dean of St Patrick's Cathedral, Dublin, and he also benefited from a bequest from a wealthy uncle, William Worth, second baron of the exchequer, who died in 1721. Worth's own medical practice in Werburgh Street in Dublin was lucrative – particularly given the relative dearth of medical professionals in Dublin at this time.[37] Perhaps the greatest proof of his financial liquidity is the wonderful library he left to Dr Steevens' Hospital.

The contents of Worth's library amply reflect not only his privileged financial status but also his passion for the book as object for his library holds an outstanding collection of gold-tooled volumes dating from the sixteenth to the early eighteenth centuries and spanning bookbinding styles in a host of European countries. For Worth, the book was as much a display item as a text to be read. His collection of auction catalogues show that he was a typical connoisseur collector, eager to buy rare printings and fine bindings.[38] Plotting Worth's acquisition of botanical items over his lifetime is difficult as his extant collection of sale and auction catalogues provide (relatively) reliable information only for the last ten years of his life (1723–33). Before that, we can isolate the inherited part of his collection by tracking his father's signature on books, but for purchases between his father's death in 1688 and the earliest auction catalogue of 1723, there is a dearth of information. The auction catalogues provide us with both positive and negative evidence: they can show us what items he bought (or was at least interested in), but also, by tracking them against the extant collection, we can see what books are in the collection but are not marked in the catalogues (which may indicate that he had already acquired them by 1723). The auction catalogues are immensely valuable as sources because they suggest that many of his botanical items were probably bought before 1723 (since they are not marked in the auction catalogue cohort). At the same time, the catalogues indicate that Worth's passion for botany continued into the latter years of his life. For example, it is likely that he bought his copy of Caspar Commelin's *Horti Medici Amstelædamensis* (Leiden, 1706) and Otto Brunfels' *Herbarum vivae eicones* (Strasburg, 1532) from the auction of the library of an unknown 'eminent Physician', which took place in Dublin in 1731, just two years before Worth's death.[39]

---

37 On this see James Kelly, 'The emergence of scientific and institutional medical practice in Ireland, 1650–1800' in Greta Jones and Elizabeth Malcolm (eds), *Medicine, disease and the state in Ireland, 1650–1940* (Cork, 1999), pp 21–39; James Kelly, 'Domestic medication and medical care in late early modern Ireland' in James Kelly and Fiona Clark (eds), *Ireland and medicine in the seventeenth and eighteenth centuries* (London, 2010), pp 109–36; John Cunningham (ed.), *Early modern Ireland and the world of medicine: practitioners, collectors and contexts* (Manchester, 2019). **38** On Worth as a collector see Elizabethanne Boran, 'Dr Edward Worth: a connoisseur book collector in early eighteenth-century Dublin' in Elizabethanne Boran (ed.), *Book collecting in Ireland and Britain, 1650–1850* (Dublin, 2018), pp 80–193. **39** *A catalogue of choice physick books &c. of an eminent physician deceas'd. To be sold by auction…. The 2d of April, 1731…* (Dublin, 1731), pp 20–1.

Equally, his copy of the auction catalogue of the library of Samuel van Huls (1655–1734), which took place at The Hague in 1730, includes a large number of items that Worth marked as interesting (though he did not acquire all of them).[40] Worth's annotations in his copy of the three-volume auction catalogue of the library of Samuel van Huls, a former mayor of The Hague and a noted art collector, reflect his approach to buying botanical books.[41] Van Huls' library was a massive affair, providing Worth with wonderful opportunities for extending his already extensive botanical collection. His annotations in this catalogue demonstrate that Worth was more interested in folios and quartos than the smaller botanical books available at the 1730 auction and that pattern is replicated in his books on botany and gardening more generally. Not for him cheap octavos on gardening techniques, such as the best-selling Clement Markham's *A way to get wealth*, which went through sixteen editions after its initial publication in 1623. When Worth bought a text by John Parkinson, it was, as we have seen, his encyclopaedic *Theatrum botanicum*, rather than the more down to earth *Paradisi in sole, paradisus terrestris, or, a garden of all sorts of pleasant flowers*, first published at London in 1629. Giving Worth the benefit of the doubt one can argue that he might not have been able to track down Thomas Hill's *A most briefe and pleasaunte treatise, teachyng how to dresse, sowe, and set a garden*, which was first published about 1558, but the fact that there is no copy of Hill's (as Dydymus Mountaine) *The gardeners labyrinth* (which was reprinted eight times between 1577 and 1660) is certainly suggestive.

Supply could not have been an issue when it came to books on gardening printed in Dublin. As Máire Kennedy points out, in the 1710s and early 1720s the Dublin printer George Grierson reprinted some popular English texts on gardening.[42] The first was Charles Evelyn's *The lady's recreation* (Dublin, 1717), and the same year saw Grierson publish it again with two tracts by John Laurence (1668–1732), *The clergyman's recreation: shewing the pleasure and profit of the art of gardening* and *The gentleman's recreation* (both hugely popular works in England), and, as a fourth part, an appendix 'explaining the motion of sap, and generation of plants' by Richard Bradley (1688–1732), professor of botany at the University of Cambridge. This combined text, *New improvements of planting and gardening, both practical and philosophical* (Dublin, 1717), obviously found a ready market in Dublin because Grierson published it again the following year and in 1719 he renamed it *Gardening improv'd* (Dublin, 1719). Grierson subsequently printed a fourth edition, Bradley's *New improvements of planting and gardening* (Dublin, 1720–1).[43] All of these books were in small octavo formats and, like Caleb Threlkeld's *Synopsis stirpium*

---

40 *Bibliotheca Hulsiana, sive catalogus librorum quos magno labore, summa cura & maximis sumptibus collegit Vir Consularis Samuel Hulsius...* 3 vols (The Hague, 1730), i, pp 109–11; ii, pp 325–8. **41** On Samuel Van Huls see Mirjam M. Foot, 'An eighteenth-century Dutch patron of bookbinding', *Quærendo*, 41 (2011), 193–207. **42** Máire Kennedy, 'Botany in print: books and their readers in eighteenth-century Dublin', *Dublin Historical Record*, 68:2 (2015), 193–205. **43** On Bradley's publications see John Edmondson, 'Richard Bradley (*c.*1688–1732): an annotated bibliography, 1710–1818', *Archives of natural*

Hibernicarum (Dublin, 1726 and 1727), were clearly intended as practical guides. Worth did not buy any of them.[44] Nor was he tempted to subscribe to or purchase larger format botanical and gardening texts printed at Dublin, works such as John Laurence's *A new system of agriculture* (Dublin, 1727) or the 'pyratically printed' edition of Philip Miller's *The gardeners dictionary* (Dublin, 1732).[45]

Instead, Worth concentrated on richly illustrated herbals of the sixteenth and seventeenth centuries, and magnificent floras and catalogues of botanical gardens of the seventeenth and early eighteenth centuries. Many of these were richly bound and were clearly intended as display objects, rather than guides to cultivation techniques. Worth's books on gardens, and more generally his wonderful botanical collection, thus tell us much about his education at Leiden, his professional interests in medicinal botany, and his identity as a collector of rare items, but unfortunately they shed little light on what he might actually have been planting in his garden in Werburgh Street in Dublin.[46]

---

history, 29: 2 (2002), 177–212. **44** The only text published by Grierson on plants which Worth acquired was, significantly, Sir John Colbatch's *A dissertation on mistletoe* (Dublin, 1720), which he clearly bought for its medicinal information. Worth did not buy other octavos on botany and gardening reprinted in Dublin such as Benjamin Townsend's *The complete seedsman* (Dublin, 1726), and Philip Miller's *The gardener's kalendar* (Dublin, 1732). **45** Henrey, *British botanical and horticultural literature*, iii, p. 89, entry 1102. **46** More information about Worth's botanical collection is available at an online exhibition, curated by the author and Dr Emer Lawlor: https://botany.edwardworthlibrary.ie, accessed 25 April 2022.

CHAPTER EIGHT

'If you have a garden in your library, nothing will be wanting': botany and gardens in the collections of Marsh's Library, Dublin

SUSAN HEMMENS

THREE YEARS BEFORE HIS DEATH, the Roman philosopher Cicero, excluded from active public life by the machinations of imperial politics, wrote to the satirist, linguist and agriculturist Marcus Terentius Varro (116–27 BCE), seeking a visit to discuss philosophy. 'Si hortum in bibliotheca habes', he wrote, 'deerit nihil'. This appealing quotation, connecting the library and the garden, forms the epigraph to this chapter, and appears in the earliest printed work in Marsh's Library, a Milan edition of Cicero's letters to his friends, dating from 1472.[1] The garden is found in symbol and metaphor on the shelves of the Library, reflected in the anthologies which gathered and cultivated ideas.[2] The utility of plants in medicines, whether old or new, was echoed by the prospect of economic utility in the gathering of exotica for interest and profit, as was the investigation of improved methods of cultivation. Plants also held a key to understanding the generation of form in the embryo, and the garden became an essential tool of the early modern natural philosopher, alongside the repository and laboratory. All of these aspects of botanical studies are to be found on the shelves of Marsh's Library, illustrating the developments in natural history which took place in the early modern period.

Marsh's Library was built at the expense of Narcissus Marsh (1638–1713) and established by an act of the Irish parliament in October 1707.[3] Enclosed on three sides by the library building itself was a 'A Garden for the use of the Library Keeper' (Fig. 8.1). To provide a core for the Library, Marsh purchased the library of the English bishop, theologian and controversialist Edward Stillingfleet (1635–99), from Stillingfleet's son James.[4] Arriving in Ireland in 1705, the books were classified and

---

1 *Marci Tullii Ciceronis epistolarum familiarium* (Milan, 1472), IX, 4: 'Si ortu in bibliotecha habes deerit nihil'.   2 For a discussion of botanical metaphors which were in general use in published work see Leah Knight, *Of books and botany in early modern England: sixteenth-century plants and print culture* (Farnham, 2009), pp 1–5.   3 Marsh was educated at Oxford, appointed as provost of Trinity College Dublin in 1679, and advanced in the Church of Ireland to become archbishop of Dublin in 1694, and finally archbishop of Armagh in 1705. The act establishing 'A Public Library Forever' was passed in the Irish parliament in October 1707. See Muriel McCarthy, *Marsh's Library: all graduates and gentlemen* (Dublin, 2003), ch. 1.   4 The books were brought to Ireland in 1705, although it appears that they were not shelved in the

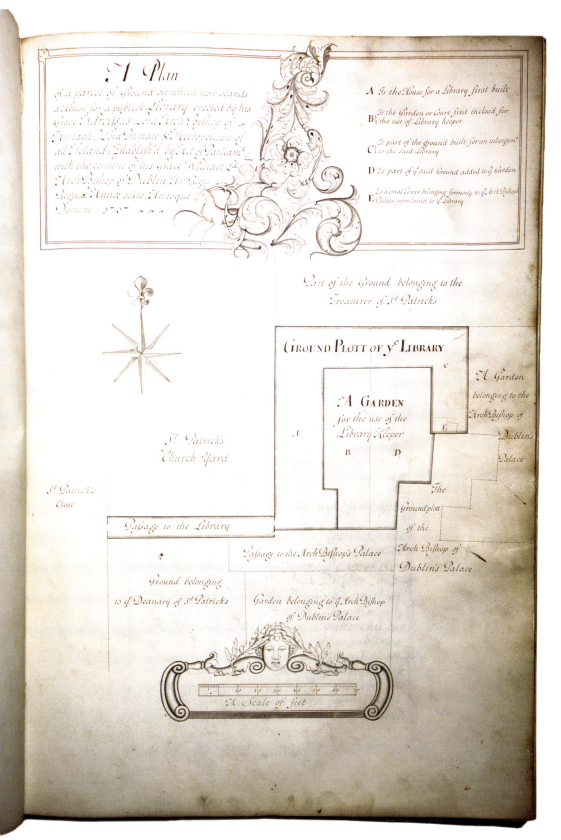

8.1 Ground plan of the Library contained in the Visitations Book, Marsh's Library. By permission of the Governors and Guardians of Marsh's Library. © Marsh's Library.

arranged on the shelves by Marsh's first librarian, the Huguenot refugee Elie Bouhéreau (1643–1719), whom Marsh had met in late 1698 and described as 'an ingenious and well-learned man'.[5] Bouhéreau's own books came to the Library under the terms of his appointment by royal warrant of June 1701.[6] His accounts for 20 October 1704 show that he paid £2 13s. 0d. 'Pour mettre le Jardin en état'; one can only assume that this was the garden at Marsh's.[7] Marsh's books were added to the Library as provided by his will.[8] In Marsh's personal collection, the botanical books are largely to be found under the category 'Historia naturalis, cum Medicis, Geographis et Peregrinatoribus' (J).[9] The distribution of publication dates within this category, as in the other parts of Marsh's collection, show that he continued to acquire books while resident 'out of the way of learning' where he felt himself to be on the periphery of the learned world.[10] Earlier acquisitions ranged from the revised edition of John Gerard's *The herball* (London, 1633) to Caspar Bauhin's *Pinax* (Basle, 1624). The fourth core collection belonged to John Stearne (1660–1745), bishop of Clogher, and represents only a part of his extensive library, some books having gone to the curates of his diocese; some, including his manuscripts, to Trinity College Dublin; and the remainder to Marsh's.[11] Later additions to the Library included John K'Eogh's *Botanalogia* (Cork, 1735), given by the Dublin banker and alderman John Macarell (*fl.* 1735), shortly after publication. This copy was later recorded as missing (presumed stolen) and replaced with the current copy.[12]

Library itself until the act establishing the Library was passed: see Bodleian Library, Oxford, MS Smith 52, fos. 119–20: Marsh to Thomas Smith, 3 November 1705. **5** Bodleian MS Smith 52, fos. 71–4: Marsh to Thomas Smith, 17 December 1698. Bouhéreau arranged to get a copy of *Bibliotheca librorum novorum* from Utrecht for Marsh's use. A set of twelve volumes from 1697–99 remains on the shelves in Marsh's own collection. **6** Bouhéreau's appointment was recorded on 11 June 1701: 'Royal warrant dated Kensington to the Lords Justices of Ireland to insert in the Civil List of Ireland the salary of 200l. [pounds] per an. for Elias Bouhereau as Library Keeper at Dublin … the said Bouhereau also has a collection of books valued at 500l. [pounds] which he is willing to put into the said library …' *Calendar of Treasury Books, 1700–1701* (London, 1938), xvi, p. 281. https://www.british-history.ac.uk/cal-treasury-books/vol16/pp276-285, accessed 8 February 2022. For an account of his library, see Philip Benedict and Pierre-Olivier Léchot, 'The library of Élie Bouhéreau: the intellectual universe of a Huguenot refugee and his family' in Muriel McCarthy and Ann Simmons (eds), *Marsh's Library, a mirror on the world: law, learning and libraries, 1650–1750* (Dublin, 2009), pp 165–84. **7** Marsh's Library MS Z2.2.2, entry for 20 October 1704; Marie Léoutre, Jane McKee, Jean-Paul Pittion and Amy Prendergast (eds), *The diary (1689–1719) and financial accounts (1704–17) of Élie Bouhéreau*, (Dublin, 2019), p. 400. **8** Marsh's bequest excluded duplicates, and his manuscripts were largely left to the Bodleian Library, Oxford. Some of his books may have been shelved as soon as the second gallery was ready in 1709, as Marsh indicated was his intention. Bodleian Library, Oxford, MS Smith 52, fos. 85–6: Marsh to Thomas Smith, 4 May 1700. **9** 'Natural history, with Medicine, Geographies and Travels'. This heading is given by Bouhéreau in the earliest extant shelf catalogue of Marsh's Library, 'Catalogus impressorum bibliotheca publicae Dublinensis' (*c.*1719), p. 630. 'J' relates to the shelving arrangement. **10** Bodleian, MS Smith 52, fos. 67–8: Marsh to Thomas Smith, 30 August 1698. **11** Toby Barnard, 'Bishop Stearne's collection of books and manuscripts' in McCarthy and Simmons (eds), *Marsh's Library*, pp 185–202. Stearne developed a garden at his episcopal palace at Clogher: Edward Malins and the Knight of Glin, *Lost demesnes: Irish landscape gardening 1660–1845* (London, 1976), p. 127. **12** Recorded in Marsh's Library donations book, 1730–40. See Marjorie Leonard and Jason McElligott (curators), *Hunting stolen books: an exhibition in Marsh's Library* (Dublin, 2017).

BOTANY IN CLASSICAL ANTIQUITY

Natural history, as conceived in the Renaissance and developed in the pre-Enlightenment, emerged from a general background in classical antiquity. The humanist scholars who edited the classical writers portrayed themselves as having retrieved the older learning, set in place by the Greeks. Sometimes their search after knowledge reached further, to ancient Egypt or to biblical lands, occasionally with something of a hermetic glamour. Classical sources were drawn upon to support and extend the story of the fall and redemption of humanity read in the books of nature and scripture.[13] Early modern reception of the botany of the ancient Greek world is represented in Marsh's by editions of the writings of the Roman naturalist Pliny the Elder (Gaius Plinius Secundus, 23–79 CE).[14] Also prominent among the ancients were two Greeks, Theophrastus of Eresos (371–287 BCE); and the highly influential Dioscorides (Pedanios Dioskouridēs, *c*.40–90 CE), whose *materia medica* was disseminated together with texts by the early medical writers Hippocrates and Galen on the characteristics and utility of plants.[15]

Later accounts of plants, of gardens, of cultivation and of the usefulness of botanical products mediated the concepts of the ancients in ways characteristic of each era of scholarship. The intersecting influences at play in the learned world are evident in the relationships of editors and commentators, as seen in many examples from the collections in Marsh's. One of Stillingfleet's copies of Pliny's works was a Geneva edition of *Historia mundi* based on that by the sixteenth-century French scholar, botanist and physician Jacques Daléchamps (1513–88), who had studied medical botany in Montpellier under the physician and naturalist Guillaume Rondelet (1507–66).[16] This edition contained commentary from other writers, including the Czech humanist Sigismund Gelen (1497–1554).[17] As Susanna De Beer has shown, Daléchamps' work on the medical botany of Pliny influenced his *Historia*

---

13 For overviews of these developments see Brian Ogilvie, *The science of describing: natural history in Renaissance Europe* (Chicago, 2006); Paula Findlen, *Possessing nature: museums, collecting, and scientific culture in early modern Italy* (Berkeley, 1994); J.J. Bono, 'The two books and Adamic knowledge: reading the book of nature and early modern strategies for repairing the effects of the fall and of Babel' in J.M. Van Der Meer and S.H. Mandelbrote (eds), *Nature and scripture in the Abrahamic religions: up to 1700* (Leiden, 2008), pp 299–340.   14 Anthony Grafton, 'The New Science and the traditions of Humanism,' in Jill Kraye (ed.), *The Cambridge companion to Renaissance humanism* (Cambridge, 1996), pp 203–23, 214. 15 Ogilvie, *Science of describing*, ch. 3, claims that Dioscorides was the more influential of the two in the Renaissance. See also W.T. Stearn, 'From Theophrastus and Dioscorides to Sibthorp and Smith, the background and origin of "*Flora Graeca*"', *Biological Journal of the Linnean Society*, 8 (1976), 285–98; and J.E. Raven, *Plants and plant lore in ancient Greece* (Oxford, 2000).   16 See Florike Egmond, 'Into the wild: botanical fieldwork in the sixteenth century' in A. MacGregor (ed.), *Naturalists in the field* (Leiden, 2018), pp 166–211. Daléchamps was thus an inheritor of the medieval Montpellier school of medicine, represented in Marsh's by a manuscript compilation dating from the late thirteenth or early fourteenth century (on which see further below).   17 *C. Plinii Secundi Historiae mundi libri XXXVII*, edited by Jacques Daléchamps, with notes by Sigmund Gelen and Hernán Nuñez de Toledo y Guzmán (Geneva, 1615). Gelen became a corrector at the printing house of Frobenius in Basel when hostility towards humanism deprived him of university support. See Francis Dvornik, *The Slavs in European history and civilization* (New Brunswick, 1962), p. 293.

generalis plantarum, present in Latin in Stearne's collection and in French among Bouhereau's books.[18] Stillingfleet also owned a 1685 Paris edition of Pliny's *Naturalis historiae* by the Jesuit scholar Jean Hardouin (1646–1729).[19] Bouhéreau's copy of *Historia naturae* is an earlier Paris edition printed by Jehan Petit (*fl.* 1492–1532), in 1532, which had belonged to the French physician, scholar and bibliophile François Mizière (*d.* 1620).[20] The plants of the Near East, reputedly the location of the Garden of Eden, featured in Stillingfleet's copies of *Papyrus* by Melchior Wieland (also known as Melchiorre Guilandino) (*c.*1520–89), a German physician who became superintendent of the botanic garden at Padua. In describing these plants, Wieland reworked material from Pliny.[21]

Both Theophrastus and Dioscorides were transmitted in a similar manner. John Stearne's copy of Theophrastus' *Opera omnia* from 1613 was edited by the Leiden scholar Daniel Heinsius (1580–1655). This celebrated Dutch humanist studied under the biblical scholar and chronologist Joseph Justus Scaliger (1540–1609), whose father, Julius Caesar Scaliger (1484–1558), had been instrumental in removing from the Aristotelian canon some spurious material relating to the study of plants. Stillingfleet's collection includes a heavily annotated copy of *In libros duos, quo inscribuntur de plantis, Aristotele autore* (Paris, 1556), in which the elder Scaliger had further employed his philological skills to remove the accretion of error resulting from generations of inaccurate transmission.[22] The *materia medica* of the Greek physician Dioscorides was widely influential, remaining a reference work into the seventeenth century. Bouhéreau, who was a practising physician as well as a divine, owned an edition by Pietro Andrea Mattioli (1501–77), whose identification of the plants used by Dioscorides was aided by woodcuts.[23] John Stearne possessed an edition in Spanish by Andrés de Laguna (1499–1559), printed in Antwerp in 1555, previously owned by Thomas Ramsay (probably one of a family of physicians) and containing many annotations.[24] Marsh's own collection included a Strasbourg edition

---

18 Susanna de Beer, 'The world upside down: the geographical revolution in humanist commentaries on Pliny's *Natural history* and Mela's *De situ orbis* (1450–1700)' in Karl Enenkel and Henk Nellen (eds), *Neo-Latin commentaries and the management of knowledge in the late Middle Ages and the early modern period (1400–1700)* (Leuven, 2013), pp 139–97, at p. 158. For general commentary on Daléchamps see C.B. Schmitt, 'Daléchamps, Jacques' in C.C. Gillispie (ed.), *Dictionary of scientific biography* (New York, 1971), iii, pp 533–4. 19 A smaller format edition by the classical scholar Johann Friedrich Gronovius (1611–71) published in Leiden (1669) is among the books missing from Stillingfleet's collection. 20 For Jean (Jehan) Petit, see Philippe Renouard, *Imprimeurs parisiens, libraires, fondeurs de caractères et correcteurs d'imprimerie, depuis l'introduction de l'imprimerie a Paris (1470) jusqu'a la fin du XVIe siècle* (Cambridge, 2011), reprint, p. 293. Mizière is noted as 'Médecin. – Bibliophile et collectionneur d'objets d'histoire naturelle et d'antiques' in the database of the Bibliothèque Nationale: https://data.bnf.fr/fr/10222174/francois_miziere/, accessed 8 February 2022. 21 S.J. Forbes, 'Collections and knowledge: constancy and flux in a sixteenth-century botanic garden', *Studies in the History of Gardens and Designed Landscapes*, 36:4 (2016), 245–60. 22 Jill Kraye, 'Philologists and philosophers' in Jill Kraye (ed.), *The Cambridge companion to Renaissance humanism* (Cambridge, 1996), pp 142–60, at p. 147. 23 Wilfrid Blunt and W. T. Stearn, *The art of botanical illustration: an illustrated history* (Woodbridge, 1994), pp 57–9. 24 Ramsay appears to have been in medical practice in the vicinity of Londonderry, Co. Londonderry, *c.*1661. Stearne's copy of *Opera omnia Arnaldus Villanova cum Nicolai Taurelli annotationibus* (Basel, 1585), which had also been in the possession of Dr Alexander Ramsay, contains a loose note dated 1661 from an

of 1665 by the Augsburg city physician Johannes Moibanus (1527–62), which was brought to the press by the Swiss naturalist Conrad Gessner (1516–65), after Moibanus' death.[25] An edition by Jean Antoine Sarrasin (1547–98), a professor of medicine at Montpellier, printed in Frankfurt in 1598, is found in both Bouhéreau's and Stillingfleet's collections.[26] Pittion has noted that an innately conservative medical outlook ensured that many medical collections contained texts from earlier generations, and even where later editions existed, the earlier ones were retained.[27] Reception in the foundation collections of Marsh's Library serves to emphasize the status of classical treatises as core texts, with the apparatus of later scholarship enhancing their continuing usefulness.

MEDICINAL BOTANY AND THE RISE OF THE HERBAL

The lengthy history of medicinal 'simples' produced from plants gathered from nature or grown in the physic garden is also evident among the collections in Marsh's. The earliest example is a manuscript on vellum of medical texts related to the medieval school at Montpellier. Dating from the first half of the fourteenth century, it appears to have been from the collection of the Irish antiquarian and oriental scholar Dudley Loftus (1618–95).[28] Marsh purchased Loftus' manuscripts, and these were retained in Dublin as provided by Marsh's will, unlike his oriental manuscripts which were bequeathed to the Bodleian Library in Oxford.[29] The earliest known description of the manuscripts in Marsh's contains the somewhat vague listing 'Liber medicinalis antiqua incerti authoris', which also appears in a seventeenth-century hand on the manuscript, and in the listing of Loftus' manuscripts in the 1697 union catalogue of manuscripts attributed to Marsh's friend and correspondent, Edward Bernard (1638–97).[30] More recently, this manuscript has been recognized by O'Boyle and Nutton as a significant collection of Montpellier medicine.[31] Fig. 8.2. shows the

apothecary in Derry, William Long, about a prescription made by Ramsay. It is possible that some of the medical books in Stearne's collection came from the library of his father, also John Stearne (1624–69), who founded the Royal College of Physicians in Ireland. **25** Ann Blair, 'Conrad Gesner et La publicité un humaniste au carrefour des voies de circulation du Savoir' in Annie Charon, Sabine Juratic and Isabelle Pantin (eds), *L'Annonce faite au lecteur: la circulation de l'information sur les livres en Europe (16e–18e Siècles)* (Louvain, 2017), pp 21–55. Open access version available at http://nrs.harvard.edu/urn-3:HUL.InstRepos:41474028, accessed 8 February 2022. **26** 'Sarrasin (Jean-Antoine)' in Ferdinand Hoefer (ed.), *Nouvelle biographie générale: depuis les temps les plus reculés jusqu'à nos jours ...* XLIII (Paris, 1854–66), pp 341–2. **27** Jean-Paul Pittion, 'Medicine in print in the early modern period: medical books in Marsh's Library, Dublin' in Danielle Westerhof (ed.), *The alchemy of medicine and print: the Edward Worth Library, Dublin* (Dublin, 2010), pp 57–74. **28** On Dudley Loftus see Elizabethanne Boran, 'Loftus, Dudley (1618–95), Oriental scholar and jurist', *DIB*. **29** Colin Wakefield, 'Arabic manuscripts in the Bodleian Library: the seventeenth-century collections' in G.A. Russell (ed.), *The 'Arabick' interest of the natural philosophers in seventeenth-century England* (Leiden, 1994), pp 128–46. **30** The manuscript is listed as no. 925.76 in Edward Bernard, *Catalogi librorum manuscriptorum Angliae et Hiberniae in unum complecti* (Oxford, 1697), *Pars altera*, ii, p. 50. **31** Cornelius O'Boyle and Vivian Nutton, 'Montpellier medicine in the Marsh Library, Dublin', *Manuscripta* 45–6 (2003), 109–32.

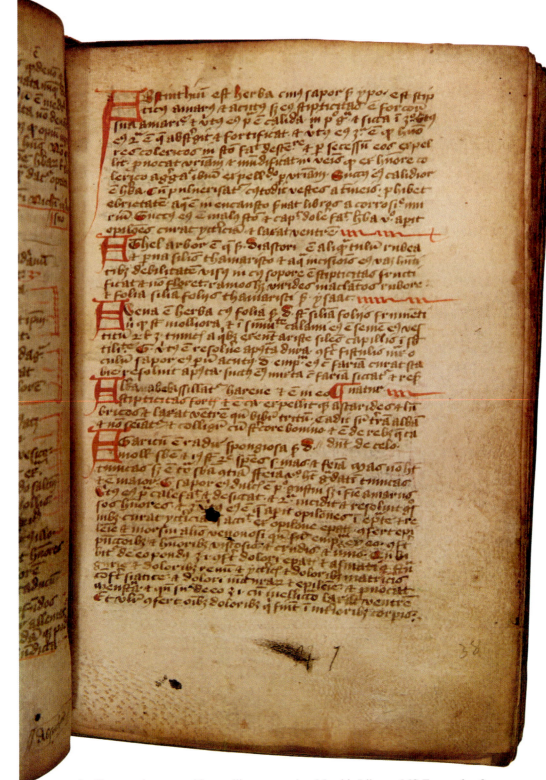

8.2 Fourteenth-century Montpellier manuscript: Marsh's Library, MS Z4.4.4, fo. 38r.
By permission of the Governors and Guardians of Marsh's Library. © Marsh's Library.

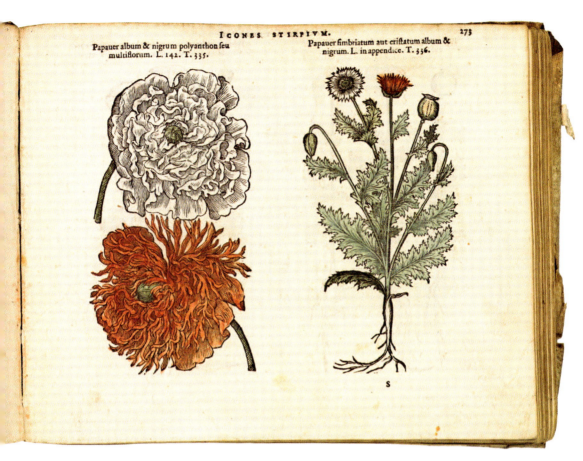

8.3 Poppies as illustrated in Mathias de L'Obel, *Icones stirpium* (Antwerp, 1591), p. 273. This image depicts a cultivated variant of *Papaver somniferum* (opium poppy) with deeply divided (fimbriated) petals (right), and (left) two so-called 'double flowered' garden poppies with numerous extra 'petals' (upper) and with numerous extra fimbriated 'petals' (lower). The colouring is likely to have been added by an owner rather than by the author. By permission of the Governors and Guardians of Marsh's Library. © Marsh's Library.

opening of an otherwise anonymous list of remedies which is associated with that of Serapion, a twelfth-century medical writer. The list shown commences with absinthe (possibly *Artemisia absinthium*), which is described as a herb whose juice is styptic.[32]

Readers sometimes added their own descriptions, identifications and recommendations for remedies to printed herbals, giving vernacular names with which they were possibly more at ease, and occasionally references to other works, and to remedies.[33] Two editions of the herbal produced by the German physician Leonhart

---

[32] Styptic implies it was employed in staunching the flow of blood.   [33] The copy held in Marsh's Library of Leonhart Fuchs, *Histoire de plantes* (Paris, 1549), is heavily annotated in several different hands and languages. It belonged to John Stearne, and may possibly have been inherited from his father, the physician John Stearne (1624–69).

Fuchs (1501–66), one from Marsh's collection (Paris, 1543), the other from John Stearne's library (Paris, 1549), show evidence of heavy use. The pages are annotated by hands which are possibly from different periods; they are worn, dog-eared, and water-stained to an extent not very typical of books in these collections.

The Mechlin physician Rembert Dodoens (1517–85), whose *Purgantium* (Antwerp, 1574) is also found in John Stearne's collection, was in the tradition of those Flemish herbalists whose writings were printed by Christophe Plantin (1620–89) in Antwerp and were rapidly disseminated.[34] As Elliott points out, Fuchs set the standards for the description of plants, including species from the Americas, which were followed by Dodoens, Pena, L'Obel and Charles de L'Écluse (Clusius) (1526–1609) in a long tradition which is well represented in Marsh's, particularly among Bouhéreau's books.

Illustration, as well as description, was probably intended to aid in identification of plants, although, as has been noted, this aim was only achieved if both illustration and identification were accurate. Colour was occasionally added, as in a copy of *Icones stirpium*, printed in Antwerp in 1591 from Bouhéreau's collection (see Fig. 8.3). The text is attributed to Mathias de L'Obel (1538–1616), a Flemish physician, whose *Stirpium adversaria nova* (London, 1571), produced in collaboration with the Provencal botanist Pierre Pena (1535–1605), is also in the Library.[35] Emphasizing the links between classical and later herbal medicine, fictitious images of Dioscorides and Theophrastus, together with Ceres and Pomona, and the deity (as represented by the tetragrammaton), appear on the engraved title page of Thomas Johnson's 1633 London edition of John Gerard's *Herball*, a copy of which is in Marsh's own collection. Johnson, whose letter to the reader described Theophrastus as having fathered botany, was much less kind to Gerard, appending a list of mistakes to the prefatory letter to the reader.[36] Although it did not compete for popularity with Nicholas Culpeper's *English physician*, Gerard's book was one often found in the colonies of North America.[37] The tradition of herbals continued until the early eighteenth century, and John Stearne's collection included the last of those popular in the Anglophone world, William Salmon's *Botanologia* (London, 1710).[38]

EARLY MODERN BOTANY AND CABINETS OF CURIOSITIES

Gathering of facts by experiment and observation characterized the period at which the collections in Marsh's were brought together. As Daston has shown, the description and classification of the natural world was also an essential component of

---

34 Brent Elliott, 'The world of the Renaissance herbal', *Renaissance Studies*, 25:1 (2011), 24–41. **35** *Icones stirpium* is in an unusual oblong format, its limp vellum binding filled with sheets of printed waste of varying sizes and hand-coloured illustrations. Ogilvie, *Science of describing*, p. 73, notes that L'Obel's book was a popular field manual. **36** Ogilvie described Johnson as 'the tireless corrector of Gerard's mistakes: *Science of describing*, p. 93. **37** R.P. Stearns, *Science in the British colonies of America* (Chicago, 1970), p. 63. **38** The library copy is volume 1 only, and is signed 'John Clogher', indicating that Stearne owned it while he was bishop of Clogher. For more on botanical books printed in Ireland

natural philosophy and formed part of the understanding of the nature and properties of fact. Once objects had been added to a repository, the physical arrangement of the items – some beautiful, some rare and unusual, all engaging – stimulated the impulse to classify and engaged the observation of functional and ontological relationships between items.[39] The foundation collections of Marsh's Library all contain works that demonstrate the multi-faceted nature of collecting in the early modern period. Stillingfleet owned a copy of the works of the Bologna collector, Ulisse Aldrovandi (1522–1605), among which was *Dendrologiae naturalis scilicet arborum historiae libri duo* (1668), edited by Aldrovandi's collaborators. The description of each plant conforms to a pattern, naming the plant itself, its parts, its classical and scriptural references, and its usefulness as food or medicine, enhanced with many detailed images. According to Findlen, the design of Aldrovandi's villa encouraged him to engage the humanistic ideal of knowing himself through knowledge of his collection, emblematized in the building.[40]

Travel, as well as correspondence, cemented relationships in the Republic of Letters, and learned travellers sought out cabinets of curiosities and museums, some of which became famous. A later superintendent of Aldrovandi's botanic garden at Bologna, Giacomo Zanoni (1615–82), received a party of visitors including the naturalist John Ray (1627–1705), from the Royal Society in 1664.[41] Zanoni's work on rarities, with a particular focus on the regional, *Istoria botanica* (1675), was owned by Stillingfleet, as were John Ray's own works on the classification of plants. Ray also had associations with the Cistercian Paolo Silvio Boccone (1633–1704), whose work on the rarities of the Mediterranean region was published at Oxford in 1674. Stillingfleet acquired both this work and another of Boccone's books, *Récherches et observations naturelles,* published by Jansson in Amsterdam in the same year, a copy of which was also owned by Bouhéreau.

For those who could not travel to see the collections of wonders brought together in the great collections of Europe, books served to make them even more widely known. Examples included those cabinets assembled by Ferrante Imperato (1550–1625), in Venice and Francesco Calzolari (1522–1609), in Verona, both of whom were apothecaries.[42] Publications describing the contents of Imperato's museum were owned by both Stearne and Marsh, while Stillingfleet acquired the account of Calzolari's collection, and that of the Royal Society, by its curator Nehemiah Grew (1641–1712). For these collectors, as for the Royal Society whose museum was described by Grew, fascination with 'the singular and the anomalous' saw monstrous plants distinguished from the normal.[43]

and Britain before 1800 see Blanche Henrey, *British botanical and horticultural literature before 1800*, 3 vols (Oxford, 1975). See also E.C. Nelson, 'Works of botanical interest published before 1800 held in Irish libraries', *Occasional papers of the National Botanic Gardens, Glasnevin* (1984). **39** 'Facticity in science has a history, and these early facts resemble those honored by later generations only in part.' See Lorraine Daston, 'The moral economy of science', *Osiris*, 10 (1995), 2–24, at 16. **40** Findlen, *Possessing nature*, pp 302–3. **41** C.E. Raven, *John Ray, naturalist: his life and works* (Cambridge, 1986). **42** Findlen, *Possessing nature*, pp 37–8. **43** L.J. Daston, review. '*The factual sensibility*. Edited by Oliver Impey, Arthur MacGregor, and R.F. Ovenell', *Isis*, 79:3 (1988), 452–67.

8.4 Paul Contant, *Le bouquet printanier* (La Rochelle, 1600), introductory plate. By permission of the Governors and Guardians of Marsh's Library. © Marsh's Library.

The French apothecary Paul Contant (1562?–1629?) wrote a preliminary treatise on his cabinet, later producing a much more complete description of his collection in the *Le jardin et cabinet poétique* (Poitiers, 1609). *Le bouquet printanier* (1600), which is in Bouhéreau's collection, was printed by Jerome Haultin in La Rochelle. It is a unique example of this work, which is related to Contant's later publication on his

8.5 Daniel Rabel, *Theatrum florae* (Paris, 1620), engraved frontispiece. By permission of the Governors and Guardians of Marsh's Library. © Marsh's Library.

cabinet of curiosities.[44] At the base of the detailed introductory plate of plants, Contant's punning motto 'Du don de Dieu je suis contant' appears. The plate depicts flowers arranged as if in a vase, which are numbered as a key to the poems that follow. The 'bouquet' conveys the significance of the plants for beauty and fragrance, as well as their usefulness in medicine (Fig. 8.4).

Rarities and exotica were prized, as were the floral elements of Contant's *Bouquet*, for their qualities of novelty and of beauty, as well as for their contribution to knowledge. In Stillingfleet's collection, the French court painter Daniel Rabel's exquisite *Theatrum florae* (Paris, 1620) preserves the delicate beauty of the specimens he recorded (Fig. 8.5).[45] Illustrated catalogues of plants such as this, and the *Hortus floridus* of Crispijn de Passe (*c.*1590–*c.*1664) were designed 'not for the apothecaries' dusty cabinets, but for the lady's garden'.[46] This aspect of the cultivation of plants echoes Marie Meurdrac's reflection on the provision of plants in the Garden of Eden, described in the book of Genesis as being for the delight of humankind, as well as for their uses as food and medicine.[47]

NAMING PLANTS

Leonard Plukenet (1641–1706), gardener to Queen Mary II of England (1662–94), combined two aspects of botany in his publications, those of rarity and arrangement. As Alette Fleischer argues, both nature and knowledge were tamed in the early modern period, by capturing plants in ordered gardens and knowledge in ordered books.[48] Plukenet's publications were owned by John Stearne, whose collection of works on plants and gardening is somewhat more extensive than those of the other foundation collectors in Marsh's. He also possessed Robert Morison's Oxford flora, published in 1715. This book was of interest to Thomas Molyneux (1661–1733) of the Dublin Philosophical Society, who inquired of Edward Lhwyd (1660–1709) as to Morison's progress in writing the book.[49] The title of this book emphasizes the

---

44 For an account of a modern edition of the longer publication by Contant see Alain Cullière, Review, '*Le jardin et cabinet poétique (1609)*, by Paul Contant, Myriam Marrache-Gouraud, Pierre Martin, and Jean Céard', *Bibliothèque d'Humanisme et Renaissance*, 68:2 (2006), 445–8. The reviewer deplores the omission of a reference to the copy of the *Bouquet* held in Marsh's. **45** Lucia Tongiorgi Tomasi, *An Oak Spring flora: flower illustration from the fifteenth century to the present time* (New Haven, 1997), pp 69–73. **46** Victoria Dickenson, *Drawn from life: science and art in the portrayal of the New World* (Toronto, 1998), p. 95. **47** Marie Meurdrac, *La chymie charitable et facile en faveur des dames* (Paris, 1666). The second edition is in Bouhéreau's collection. In the preface to the second section (p. 44), Meurdrac writes 'La Genese nous apprend que le Vegetal fut le premier crée pour les delices, & le service de l'homme dans son estat de Grace. Il contribua à ses plaisirs par l'embellissement du Paradis terrestre, dont il estoit tout l'ornement; & depuis sa disgrace, il en eut besoin comme de medicament …'. For a further exploration of early modern concepts of fragrance, see Holly Dugan, *The ephemeral history of perfume: scent and sense in early modern England* (Baltimore, 2011). **48** Alette Fleischer, 'Gardening nature, gardening knowledge: the parallel activities of stabilizing knowledge and gardens in the early modern period' in Hubertus Fischer, Volker R. Remmert and Joachim Wolschke-Bulmahn (eds), *Gardens, knowledge and the sciences in the early modern period* (Dordrecht, 2016), pp 289–304. **49** On Molyneux's botanical interests

Botany and gardens in the collections of Marsh's Library, Dublin   187

arrangement of plants according to their affinities: Morison aimed to remedy the deficiencies in arrangement he perceived in the earlier works of Bauhin, Daléchamps and Ray.[50]

For the divines whose collections made up Marsh's Library, the most fundamental expression of order in the natural world was represented by the creation narrative in the book of Genesis, where the orders of nature were called into being on successive days, and Adam was given the first task of naming the creatures. Classical taxonomy of plants had been established by Theophrastus, following Aristotle, who divided plants into trees, shrubs and herbs. Refinement of taxonomy assumed an importance in the early modern period, and various systems were proposed.[51] The study of languages supported the search to reverse the chaos of Babel and retrieve the ordered naming of animated nature. Edward Stillingfleet collected *Etymologicon* by Stephen Skinner (1623–67) which has a strong botanical component.[52] Stillingfleet also acquired the substantial polyglot *Index nominum plantarum universalis, multilinguis* (Berlin, 1682) by Christian Mentzel (1622–1701), personal physician to Friedrich Wilhelm (1620–88), Elector of Brandenburg and Duke of Prussia. Mentzel produced this work as the result of an extensive correspondence with travellers in the Indies, and as a collaboration with his son, Johann Christian.[53]

Marsh acquired *Pinax theatri botanici* (Basel, 1624) by the Swiss botanist Caspar Bauhin (1560–1624). This work, a precursor to the Linnaean system of botanical nomenclature, has more recently been shown to be closely related to the Aristotelian philosophical concepts of species and genus.[54] John Stearne held among his collection *Institutiones rei herbariae* (Paris, 1719), the posthumous third edition of the work of the French botanist Joseph Pitton de Tournefort (1656–1708), whose concept of species and genus was much closer to that in use in the post-Linnaean world.[55] Tournefort's successor at the Jardin du Roi (later the Jardin des Plantes), Antoine de Jussieu (1686–1758), was responsible for the 1719 edition. He rejected the concept of sexual reproduction in plants, which had been advanced in 1694 by the German botanist Rudolf Jakob Camerarius (1665–1721).[56]

---

see chapter 3 in this volume.   **50** The full title of Morison's work is *Plantarum historiae universalis Oxoniensis seu herbarum distibutio nova, per tabulas cognationis & affinitatis ex libro naturae observata & detecta* (Oxford, 1715). For an account of its publishing history see Scott Mandelbrote, 'The publication and illustration of Robert Morison's *Plantarum historiae universalis Oxoniensis*', *Huntington Library Quarterly*, 78:2 (2015), 349–79.   **51** For discussion see Ogilvie, *Science of describing*, pp 182–92.   **52** John Considine, 'Stephen Skinner's *Etymologicon* and other English etymological dictionaries 1650–1700', *Studia Etymologica Cracoviensia*, 14 (2009), 123–51.   **53** Alix Cooper, 'Latin words, vernacular worlds: language, nature, and the "Indigenous" in early modern Europe', *East Asian Science, Technology, and Medicine*, 26 (2007), 17–39.   **54** For an account of the *Pinax* see Ogilvie, *Science of describing*, pp 182, 218–19; and for another view see A.J. Cain, 'Rank and sequence in Caspar Bauhin's *Pinax*', *Botanical Journal of the Linnean Society*, 114:4 (1994), 311–56.   **55** Scott Atran, 'Origin of the species and genus concepts: an anthropological perspective', *Journal of the History of Biology*, 20:2 (1987), 195–279.   **56** On Camerarius see A.G. Morton, *History of botanical science: an account of the development of botany from ancient times to the present day* (London, 1981), chapter 7: 'Camerarius to Linnaeus: the recognition of sex in plants and the exploration of the world flora (1694 to 1753)'.

Camerarius was familiar with the works by the Italian microscopist Marcello Malpighi (1628–94), whose study of plant anatomy and development was just one among many to raise queries about plant reproduction.[57] In *Origines sacrae*, Stillingfleet drew upon the work of Malpighi and that of Francesco Redi (1626–97), to refute the concept of spontaneous generation. Stillingfleet cited Malpighi more generally, with works of William Harvey (1578–1657), John Ray, Robert Boyle (1627–91), Antoni van Leeuwenhoek (1632–1723), and others in his wider arguments against atheism.[58] John Stearne also collected Malpighi's work on plant anatomy and development. Owned by Bouhéreau in French translation as well as by Stillingfleet, Nehemiah Grew's study of the anatomy of plants, presented to the Royal Society, coupled botany with other aspects of natural philosophy and found a wide circulation.

BOTANY AND CULTIVATION

Early modern accounts of techniques of cultivation were closely linked to the culture of utility and improvement, in both the domestic and the colonial contexts.[59] The works of classical authors were drawn upon to engage ancient knowledge in support of improving practice. Stillingfleet owned Marcus Porcius Cato's (234–149 BCE) *De re rustica* in a 1514 Venice collection which included works by Cicero's correspondent Marcus Terentius Varro (116–27 BCE), Lucius Columella (4–*c*.70 CE) and Rutilius Palladius (*c*.fourth–fifth century CE), produced by the famous printing house of Aldus Manutius (*d.* 1515). A *Geoponika*, which apparently dealt with similar material but from Greek sources, is recorded as missing from the shelves of Marsh's own collection. *Re rustica* was held in all four foundation collections, in several editions reflecting successive generations of scholarship.

Travellers were questioned about the natural products of the countries they visited. Robert Boyle's 'General Heads for a Natural History of a Country, Great or small' was originally published in the *Philosophical Transactions of the Royal Society*, and later as a monograph, the posthumous 1692 edition of which was owned by Edward Stillingfleet. The motivation underlying these queries was not only philosophical curiosity but also the potential utility of products found in the process of exploration. The taking of natural histories could also form a basis for improvement in a colonial context. In the context of Ireland, Gerard Boate's natural history of Ireland (London, 1652), which was also in Stillingfleet's collection, was edited by Samuel Hartlib (*c.*1600–62), 'For the Common Good of *Ireland*, and more especially, for the benefit of the Adventurers and Planters therein'.[60] The title page

---

57 Ibid., p. 215. **58** Sarah Hutton, 'Science, philosophy and atheism: Edward Stillingfleet's defence of religion' in Richard H. Popkin and Arjo J. Vanderjagt (eds), *Scepticism and irreligion in the seventeenth and eighteenth Centuries* (Leiden, 1993), pp 102–20. **59** Toby Barnard, *Improving Ireland? Projectors, prophets and profiteers, 1641–1786* (Dublin, 2008); Sarah Irving, *Natural science and the origins of the British empire* (London, 2015), pp 110–13. Irving discusses John Locke's concepts of improvement and its application to the colonial context. **60** Gerard Boate, *Ireland's naturall history being a true and ample description of*

also advertises the improvements which could be made by manuring the 'Fruitfull parts and profitable grounds'. Fertile and profitable colonial lands could also be acquired on the other side of the Atlantic. Daniel Denton's account of New York, published in 1670, which is found in Stillingfleet's extensive travel collection, was calculated to show the suitability of the land for cultivation by colonists, describing 'the fertility of the soyle, healthfulness of the climate, and the commodities thence produced'.[61] Plants and their native habitats in Great Britain occupy the majority of the second edition of *Pinax rerum naturalium Britannicarum, continens vegetabilia, animalia, et fossilia, in hac insula reperta inchoatus* by the Royal Society fellow Christopher Merrett (1614–95). Merrett also covered animals and minerals in a broad view of natural history, a view which would have been of interest to Marsh and his fellow-members of the Dublin Philosophical Society (1683–1709). Variation of the created order in different localities was a topic of lively interest for seventeenth-century natural philosophers. The collection of works such as this supported their search to observe 'matters of fact' in natural history, which Hans Sloane (1660–1753), Irish-born physician and naturalist, secretary of the Royal Society of London from 1693 and its president from 1727, declared to be 'more certain than most others, and in my slender Opinion, less subject to Mistakes than Reasonings, Hypotheses, and Deductions are'.[62]

Seventeenth-century improvements in cultivation of both kitchen and pleasure gardens were encouraged by those who, like the Royal Society, saw themselves as following the precepts of Francis Bacon (1561–1626). John Stearne's collection included *Systema horti-culturae or the art of gardening* (the 1677 edition) by John Worlidge (1640–1700). Fig. 8.6 shows a round garden, recommended by Worlidge as 'very good for Fruit, the Winds being not so severe against a round, as against a streight Wall … the Borders of the round Walk, and the cross Walks being sufficient for Flowers and Plants of Beauty and Delight'.[63] Stearne's copy of the same author's *Systema agriculturae* was among those items stolen from the Library.

For those with greater ambitions, the elegance and mathematical arrangement of French garden design of the era of Louis XIV were desirable.[64] John Evelyn (1620–1706), natural philosopher, landowner, diarist and scholarly virtuoso, translated the works of Nicolas de Bonnefons (*fl.* 1655) and Jean-Baptiste La Quintinie (1626–88) into English, bringing French design and cultivation methods to his peers among the landowners in the Royal Society, and to a wider public. Bonnefons had been *premier valet du roi* to Louis XIV; La Quintinie was a lawyer who found fame as the creator of the kitchen garden at Versailles and as a result was raised to the ranks of the

---

its situation, greatness, shape, and nature (London, 1652), title page.   **61** Daniel Denton, *A brief description of New-York: formerly called New-Netherlands with the places thereunto adjoyning, together with the manner of its scituation, fertility of the soyle, healthfulness of the climate, and the commodities thence produced* (London, 1670), title page.   **62** Hans Sloane, *A voyage to the islands Madera, Barbados, Nieves, S. Christophers and Jamaica* (London, 1707), Sig. B1v.   **63** John Worlidge, *Systema horti-culturae or the art of gardening* (London, 1677), p. 15.   **64** Volker R. Remmert, 'The art of garden and landscape design and the mathematical sciences in the early modern period' in Hubertus Fischer et al., *Gardens, knowledge and the*

8.6 John Worlidge, *Systema horti-culturae or the art of gardening* (London, 1677), p. 17. By permission of the Governors and Guardians of Marsh's Library. © Marsh's Library.

Botany and gardens in the collections of Marsh's Library, Dublin 191

nobility.[65] A speciality of these French gardeners was the cultivation of tender plants, such as melons. French gardening is also represented in Bouhéreau's collection by Pierre Morin's *Remarques nécessaires pour la culture des fleurs* (Paris, 1670).[66] As a member of the Royal Society, with its Baconian roots, Evelyn sought to publish his concepts of improvement in an accessible form, setting out a 'Kalendarium hortense' appended to his *Sylva, or discourse of forest trees* (London, 1670) with tasks for every month of the year.[67] His works were popular and ran to several editions: *Sylva* was collected by Stillingfleet in its first and Marsh in its third edition (1664 and 1679 respectively).

CONCLUSION

From its foundation, Marsh's Library contained works of botanical interest in considerable variety brought together in the original collections. The use made of these botanical books in the early decades of the Library's existence is more difficult to assess, as reader records from that time do not survive (if, indeed, they were kept at all). As Jason McElligott has discussed, the registers of missing books can stand as a partial substitute for records of reading.[68] McElligott showed that thefts tended to concentrate on those books in the vernacular rather than in the scholarly languages of Latin, Greek or Hebrew. Books on natural philosophy in all its guises were also especially attractive to the light-fingered among the Library's readers. Among botanical works stolen, the English translation of the account of the elder (*Sambucus nigra*) and its medicinal uses by the German physician Martin Blochwitz (*c.*1602–29) is missing from Marsh's collection – tellingly, the Latin version remains on the shelf in Stillingfleet's collection.[69] The Oxford nurseryman Ralph Austen's *Observations on Sir Francis Bacon's Natural History as it relates to fruit-trees, fruits and flowers* (Oxford, 1658) was stolen from Stillingfleet's collection, as well as Kenelm Digby's *Discourse on the vegetation of plants* (London, 1661) which had gone missing from the same section by 1766. Missing also are the *Hortus floridus* by Crispijn de Passe, mentioned earlier for its beauty, and a more practical treatise by Leonard Mascall (*d.* 1589), *The country-man's new art of planting and grafting* (London, 1651).[70] These thefts indicate

---

sciences in the early modern period, pp 9–28.   **65** Angus Vine, 'Evelyn, John' in Garret A. Sullivan and Alan Stewart (eds), *The encyclopedia of English Renaissance literature* (Cambridge, 2012), i, p. 327.   **66** For an account of this work, which was based on a seedsman's catalogue, and its author, see Prudence Leith-Ross, 'A seventeenth-century Paris garden', *Garden History*, 21:2 (1993), 150–7. It is tempting to think that Bouhéreau might have consulted this book when considering how to put the garden at Marsh's in order in 1704.   **67** The volume also contained a treatise (*Pomona, or, an appendix concerning fruit-trees in relation to cider*) on apples and the making of cider, with a diagram of an improved cider-press.   **68** Jason McElligott, 'Hunting stolen books in nineteenth- and twentieth-century Dublin' in Marjorie Leonard and Jason McElligott (curators), *Hunting stolen books: an exhibition in Marsh's Library* (Dublin, 2017), pp 3–7.   **69** Martin Blochwitz, *Anatomia sambuci: quae non solùm sambucum & huiusdem medicamenta* (Leipzig, 1631) and the 1670 English translation, *Anatomia sambuci: or, The anatomie of the elder* (London, 1670).   **70** Marsh's Library, Dublin, MS 1766: 'Classical Catalogue of missing books'.

the interests of at least some of the early readers in Marsh's, whose depredations have left us with the only record of their reading.

In the four foundation collections brought together in Marsh's Library, concepts of botany embraced the classical world, medicine and herbals, taxonomy and collection, growth and development. The intersecting interests of the collectors are evident in their ownership of similar works, with divergence of editions provided by geography and language as much as by different emphases of interest or route of acquisition. All four sought to read the books of nature and of scripture in an effort to understand the hidden truths of creation. The garden provided a microcosm in which the bounty of Providence could be experienced: the library, a microcosm in which the knowledge of creation could be explored. With this rich ground, the early modern collectors whose libraries came together in Marsh's truly seem to have wanted little more for the cultivation of ideas.

CHAPTER NINE

Pleasure gardens and gardening for pleasure in the Fagel collection at Trinity College Dublin

REGINA WHELAN RICHARDSON

'Til now it's been a joy to me to write
Of fruitful trees and of wild laneways;
Of how one grafts with bud or twig,
And how one nurtures trees and grows new plants,
Of how the beehive can delight the senses,
And how one's homegrown produce tastes the best;
Of how to trap wild animals in a snare,
And fish in little ponds without a care,
In brief the woodland scene and country life
Have been my inspiration and delight.[1]

A GATHERING OF BOTANICAL wonder is to be found within a Dutch library collection that has formed part of the famed Old Library of Trinity College Dublin for over two centuries. The fortunes of war and the upheaval of revolution in Europe at the end of the eighteenth century were the forces leading to the transfer of the magnificent Fagel family library from The Hague to Dublin.[2] Economics, and attributes of foresight and decisiveness played their part in the acquisition of the unique library now known as the Fagel collection. Purchased for Trinity College in 1802, this library was assembled over a period of a century-and-a-half by several generations of the Fagel family, many of whom held high public office in the Dutch Republic, to become one of the most distinct and important private libraries in early modern Europe.

Hendrik Fagel the Younger (1765–1838), who had inherited the library, was on a diplomatic mission in London when the Liberty Tree was raised in Dam Square in Amsterdam, on 19 January 1795 and the Batavian Republic proclaimed. French

---

1 Passage from Jacob Cats (1577–1660), 'Ouderdom, buyten-leven, en hof-gedachten op Sorgvliet' in *Alle de werken van Jacob Cats*, 2 vols (Amsterdam, 1700), ii, p. 418. The Dutch country house poem is a genre in itself and a source of information on gardens. It illustrates the attachment the owners felt to their estates and this poem gives a flavour of Cats' life at his country house of Sorgvliet. Translated by Alice Schutte and the author.   2 Peter Fox, 'The Fagel collection: from Den Haag to Dublin' in T.R. Jackson (ed.), *Frozen in time: the Fagel collection in the Library of Trinity College, Dublin* (Dublin, 2016), pp 73–92.

193

revolutionary forces waiting in the wings seized the opportunity of the ensuing uncertainty and unrest to take over the country. As *greffier*, or chief minister to the States General of the Netherlands, Fagel was now effectively exiled in England and in order to raise money to support himself and his dependents he determined to sell the family library. It was due to go up for auction at Christie's on 1 March 1802, when the Erasmus Smith Foundation made an offer on behalf of Trinity College Dublin in advance of the sale. This was accepted, thus increasing the College's library holdings by forty per cent and ensuring the survival of the Fagel library almost intact.[3] Wide ranging in subject area and format, there are over 20,000 volumes, mainly in Latin, French, Dutch and English, and almost 3,000 sheet maps. The material ranges from 1460 to 1799 with the greater volume of material published and assembled in the eighteenth century and is of international scope. Christie's had published a comprehensive catalogue in advance of the sale of which a number of copies are still in existence.[4]

Through the prism of the Fagel collection I would like to present a vista of a world of gardens, horticulture and botany in the Dutch Republic during the late seventeenth and early eighteenth centuries. European baroque garden style proved to be very influential in Britain and Ireland during this period. Its 'Dutch' version came to England when the head of state of the Dutch Republic, Stadholder William of Orange (1650–1702), acceded to the English throne in 1689 as King William III, and some of its defining features would travel onwards to be implemented in Irish gardens.[5] Dutch immigration into Ireland, as described by Rolf Loeber in his article on Dutch influence in seventeenth- and eighteenth-century Ireland, also played a part.[6] Vandra Costello has referred to 'the great influence of the Dutch on the design, buildings, planting and appearance of the Irish landscape during the seventeenth century'.[7] The focus of this contribution is therefore on the Dutch prototype for such gardens, the gardens of the *buitenplaatsen*, or private country estates, and the gardening activities of the Fagel family. This is revealed through their beautifully illustrated botanical books, manuals of gardening, works of natural history, manuscripts, and engravings of views of Dutch country houses and gardens (Fig. 9.1). The Fagel library and other private libraries of the early modern period played an important role in facilitating research and knowledge. And while famous botanic gardens such as those in Amsterdam and Leiden drove new knowledge and

---

3 Vincent Kinane, 'The Fagel collection' in Peter Fox (ed.), *Treasures of the Library: Trinity College, Dublin* (Dublin, 1986), p. 160.   4 Samuel Paterson, *Bibliotheca Fageliana, a catalogue of the valuable and extensive library of the Greffier Fagel, of the Hague* (London, 1802).   5 J.C. Loudon, referring to its adherents in Ireland, wrote 'in King William's time, knots of flowers, curious edgings of box, topiary works, grassy slopes, and other characteristics of the Dutch style had come to notice' – quoted in Edwards Malins and The Knight of Glin, *Lost demesnes: Irish landscape gardening, 1660–1845* (London, 1976), p. 7. See also Keith Lamb and Patrick Bowe, *A history of gardening in Ireland* (Dublin, 1995), p. 25. On Anglo-Dutch gardens see John Dixon Hunt and Erik de Jong (eds), *The Anglo-Dutch garden in the age of William and Mary* (London, 1988).   6 Rolf Loeber, 'An introduction to the Dutch influence in 17th and 18th century Ireland', *Quarterly Bulletin of the Irish Georgian Society*, 13 (1970), 13–24.   7 Vandra Costello, 'Dutch influence in seventeenth-century Ireland: the duck decoy', *Garden History*, 30 (2002), 177–90.

Pleasure gardens and gardening for pleasure in the Fagel collection   195

research, many private gardens too were important sources of information for artists, botanists and plant collectors working in the natural sciences. We can see several of these gardens and their owners referenced in the botanical works of the time. In the seventeenth century, the Dutch Republic became the hub of the European book trade, which made it convenient for the Fagels to source a wide selection of works on botany, horticulture, garden architecture and design.[8] Their sumptuous, illustrated books, many hand-coloured, were not solely luxury items for occasional perusal but were also in use as reference works for information and discovery relating to the function of their professional lives and leisure occupations.

PLEASURE GARDENS

Among the signs of material prosperity in the Dutch Golden Age was the appearance in the landscape of country houses with carefully planned and beautiful gardens, built by prominent citizens and a new wealthy merchant class. Increasingly into the mid seventeenth century these *buitenplaatsen* were constructed and developed by a new urban administrative élite, forming a distinctive country living culture.[9] Within the composite nature of the country estates the gardens were of supreme importance. The *lusthof*, or pleasure garden, in its ideal form, looked to the ancient Greek ideal of Arcadia, and aspired to restore the garden to an approachement of the garden of Eden. In this way God could be praised through the fashioning of a garden celebrating the natural world, which he created. Many contemporary horticultural works are prefaced by long poems extolling the pursuit of gardening in praise of the divine. The Dutch pleasure gardens were dedicated to leisure time, the elegant burgher villas were associated with pleasure, rather than production. They were the summer retreats of urban dwellers, built to afford enjoyment and healthy living, and to reflect the status of their owners.

In this golden age of Dutch gardens, skilled architects, designers and botanical illustrators flourished within the visual arts and the botanical sciences. It was also the era of extensive Dutch exploration and travel, which transformed the nature and visual aspect of the gardens at home. This was manifested in the larger privately owned, the princely, and the botanic gardens of Amsterdam, Leiden and Utrecht. William III had a personal interest and developed several of his gardens to a high degree of excellence, the most famous of which is Het Loo in the Dutch Baroque style. The private gardens were places of recreation, of entertainment and of social interaction. Here one might converse with friends, make business connections, find opportunities for romantic dalliance, or discuss religion in a non-controversial and

---

8 The botanical outreach of the Dutch Republic is reflected in the 'paper gardens' of the Edward Worth Library and Marsh's Library, Dublin: see chapters by Elizabethanne Boran and Susan Hemmens in this volume.   **9** Martin van de Broeke, '*Het Pryeel van Zeeland': buitenplaatsen op Walcheren 1600–1820* (Hilversum, 2016), p. 494.

9.1 A variety of gardening tools is on display, with key, and the buildings on the left suggest an orangery and hothouses. The figure in the foreground may depict its German author Johann Herman Knoop (1706–69), renowned for his work on pomology. *Beschouwende en werkdadige hovenier-konst* (Leeuwarden, 1753), tab. III following p. 310. © The Board of Trinity College Dublin.

Pleasure gardens and gardening for pleasure in the Fagel collection   197

tolerant manner (Fig. 9.2). Music was to be heard, whether a single flautist playing for a small group in a berceau, a chamber-style orchestra performing in the open area for a social event, or dance music for a ball in one of the garden buildings; such insight can be gleaned from contemporary illustrations in the Fagel collection. Proud owners commissioned detailed engravings of their houses and elaborate gardens, and collections of views were also compiled by publishers with a view to sale to the public. The Fagel family had many of these prints in their library, showcasing large and small estates whose carefully designed and tended gardens are an integral part. Meticulously detailed drawings show gardens laid out with parterres and flowerbeds, trees and shrubs, sheltered walks and ornamental water.

FEATURES OF THE GARDENS

Formal design combined with variety were key features of the Dutch gardens, and French and Italian influences were widespread. Elements of the local topography such as the flat landscape, the abundance of water, and the windy conditions led to creativity and adaption from which a special Dutch character evolved. Water features such as canals and lakes, ponds and fishponds, some with domestic and foreign waterfowl, are a recurring feature, and fountains and cascades are also characteristic. In particular, geometric and compartmented layouts, pyramidal topiary, and boundary and decorative hedges abound. Johann Hermann Knoop (1706–69) declared his opinion in his book on the art of gardening, *Beschouwende en werkdadige hovenier-konst* (Leeuwarden, 1753), that the geometrical garden is based on the one hand on botanical science and on the other hand on geometry and architecture.[10] The numerous and varied elements of the gardens are shown in engraved prints, books, manuals of gardening and garden design, and in contemporary paintings. Family and visitors could take their ease in arbours and berceaux, promenade in colonnades and mazes, and stroll among trees in shady avenues and bosquets. They could enjoy decorated pots and urns displaying colourful and scented plants, and admire statuary placed centrally, in fountains, or within niches in hedges which were planted to give the illusion of garden rooms. Finely wrought lattice gates gave access to the different sections. The Dutch parterre tended to be colourful, jewelled with flowers and sometimes with coloured stones; grass parterres defined by box hedges were also popular. A French publication on the flower garden suggests spring flowers for parterres, including daffodils, anemones, hyacinths and tulips.[11]

---

10 See L.H. Albers, 'The perception of gardening as art', *Garden History*, 19 (1991), 163–74.   11 R.A. Fréard du Castel, *L'école du jardinier fleuriste* (Paris, 1764). See also Carla Oldenburger-Ebbers, 'Notes on plants used in Dutch gardens in the second half of the seventeenth century' in John Dixon Hunt (ed.), *The Dutch garden in the seventeenth century* (Washington, DC, 1990), pp 159–73. Exactly these plants were cultivated at Kilruddery, and receipts for purchase from continental nurseries survive: Sheila Pim, 'History of gardening in Ireland' in E.C. Nelson and Aidan Brady (eds), *Irish gardening and horticulture* (Dublin, 1979), pp 45–69, at 49–50. I am grateful to E.C. Nelson for this reference.

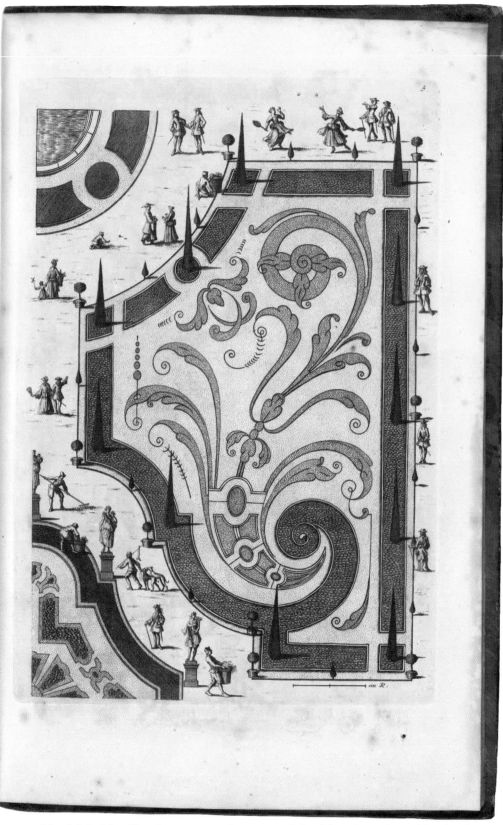

9.2 The delightful staffage figures among the parterres bring life to the gardens with a closely observed representation of human activity: *Tractaat der Lusthoff* (Leiden, 1720), plate III.
© The Board of Trinity College Dublin.

Pleasure gardens and gardening for pleasure in the Fagel collection   199

Dézallier d'Argenville (1680–1765) gave advice in *La théorie et la pratique du jardinage* (Paris, 1709) as to suitable trees such as *Ulmus* (elm), *Tilia* (lime), *Aesculus hippocastanum* (horse chestnut) and *Taxus baccata* (yew), distinguishing between those for the wilder wooded areas and the walks within the gardens.[12] Orchards and espaliers were widespread with fruit trees bearing both native and non-native fruits for alimentary and decorative purposes. Advice on their cultivation, pruning and grafting techniques and associated tools, and control of pests and diseases was prominent within the published works. These include English author Batty Langley's *Pomona, or, the fruit-garden illustrated* (London, 1729). Kitchen gardens grew produce for the house, and beehives were to be found nearby. Citrus trees came to be cultivated in orangeries in the Netherlands towards the latter half of the seventeenth century when they were enthusiastically grown and prominently displayed by professional and amateur horticulturists alike, symbols of gardening success and high status. Orangeries were a feature of Italian and French large gardens and palaces, and in the Netherlands they were developed to a high degree of technical expertise, enhancing the garden in multiple ways. Citrus trees were grown in containers, fulfilling a decorative function and allowing easy transportation of the plants to overwinter inside the orangery. The Fagels owned several books on citrus plants including the classic French work by Jean-Baptiste de la Quintinie (1626–88), director of the royal fruit and vegetable gardens of Louis XIV (1638–1715): *Instruction pour les jardins fruitiers et potagers, avec un traité des orangers, suivy de quelques réflexions sur l'agriculture* (Amsterdam, 1692).

CLINGENDAEL AND SORGVLIET

Within the many series of prints of estates in the Fagel collection are two outstanding gardens, those of Clingendael and Sorgvliet near The Hague.[13] The gardens of Clingendael (begun in 1671) were designed in French baroque style and were a model for the development of garden design in Holland. French garden prints were also in circulation and provided a source of inspiration for many French style gardens; the owner of Clingendael, Philips Doublet (1633–1707), had a series of these prints in his extensive library. The depictions of the Clingendael estate by Daniel Stopendaal (1672–*c*.1726), made about 1690 (Fig. 9.3), are introduced by double page spreads presenting a bird's eye vista of the estate in the landscape. The view out to the North Sea shows the dunes of the coastal area on the road from The Hague to Scheveningen where the estate lay. These panoramas are followed by close observational drawings detailing many of the elements mentioned above. One such is an orangery close to the house, entered from a decorative parterre through a lattice gate, with a central pond and fountain, surrounded by citrus plants in pots.[14]

12 [A.J. Dézallier d'Argenville], *La théorie et la pratique du jardinage* (Paris, 1709), part 2, ch. 5, pp 132–45.
13 Held in a volume of engravings, brought together and bound by the Fagels in the eighteenth century: [*Views of country houses, gardens, etc., in the province of Holland*].   14 See Carla Bezemer-Sellers, 'The Bentinck garden at Sorgvliet' in Hunt (ed.), *The Dutch garden in the seventeenth century*, pp 99–129.

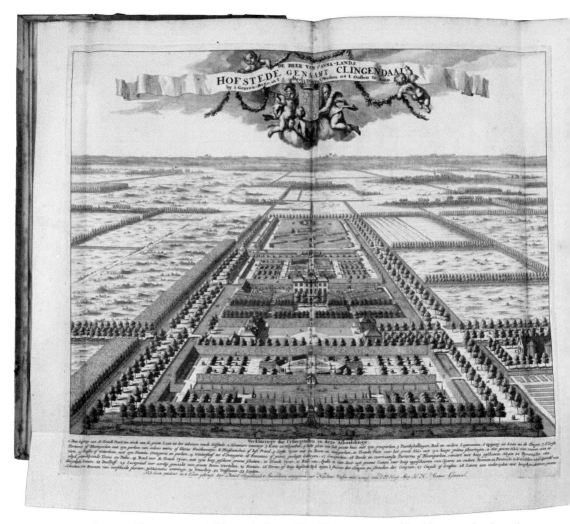

9.3 The magnificent estate of Clingendael near The Hague, presented in this engraving in a vista from east to west, shows the influence of French baroque garden design and architecture. *De Heer van St. Anna-lands Hofstede genaamt Clingendael, by 's Graven-Hage; in 't geheel van 't Oosten van 't Westen de zien* (Amsterdam, c.1690) is bound in a folio of engravings entitled *Views of country houses, gardens, etc., in the province of Holland*. © The Board of Trinity College Dublin.

Perhaps the most impressive view in a series of prints commissioned by the Bentinck family in the late seventeenth century is the magnificent semi-circular orangery at Sorgvliet. The original house and garden were begun in the 1640s by poet and politician Jacob Cats (1577–1660), who named it Sorgvliet, signifying a carefree place. The subsequent owner Hans Willem Bentinck (1649–1709), first earl of Portland, enlarged and re-fashioned the gardens, mainly but not exclusively in French style. The orangery was built about 1676 in Italian Renaissance style, probably designed by Maurits Post (1645–77). The central pond and the arrangement of the

Pleasure gardens and gardening for pleasure in the Fagel collection 201

trees complement the form of the architecture, and entry by a small bridge over a watercourse is an appealing part of the design.

The vital role of the team of gardeners required for the upkeep of the grounds is clearly acknowledged in contemporary illustrated sources. These gardeners are included in the views of the gardens, or on the title pages or frontispieces. They are depicted neither as incidentals nor relegated to the background, but frequently given prominence to the fore of the composition, active in a variety of tasks and using or carrying the tools of their trade. Figures of women engaging in gardening tasks are also shown. The frontispiece of *De Nieuwe naauwkeurige Neederlandse hovenier* (Leiden, 1713) shows a house in the background, with a couple taking a stroll in the garden surrounded by numerous gardeners conspicuously raking, clipping, carrying baskets etc. A Dutch treatise published in 1737 gives a picture of the activities and skills required for the upkeep of the Dutch country estate in the early eighteenth century.[15] The title page promises:

> special notes on the design of magnificent and ordinary country houses, summer residences, plantations and surrounding ornaments. In order to best create the above; and to prepare the grounds well; to mend what is broken, and to plant fruit trees and tree-lined lanes and dig large bodies of water, ditches and ponds. In addition instructions concerning the pruning and propagation of fruit trees and wild trees, in particular a good explanation on how to produce an abundance of grapes in the open air and in greenhouses. As well as: how to guarantee, in our cold climate, the growth of pineapples, lemon, lime and orange trees and other plants from warmer climates. And also: tested methods for the cultivation of root vegetables and chard. All this information was compiled and illustrated over fifty years in a detailed way.[16]

THE GARDEN AT NOORDEINDE

Two members of the Fagel family emerge as dedicated gardeners and plantsmen, being actively involved in gardens and gardening; they are Gaspar (Caspar) Fagel (1634–88) and François Fagel the Elder (1659–1746). Their range of gardening manuals shows that they were keen to be informed on the practical aspects of horticulture, to instruct their gardeners and garden designers and possibly to get down to some manual labour themselves. Book illustrations of their time show figures clad as gentlemen working in the garden alongside occupational gardeners, appearing to give instruction and perhaps exchanging advice. Evidence is not based on the presence of the books alone; as will be seen, documents within the collection along with other archival and contemporary printed sources attest to the fact that these two

15 Pieter de la Court van der Voort, *Byzondere aenmerkingen over … landhuizen, lusthoven, plantagien…* (Leiden, 1737).   16 Translation from the Dutch courtesy of Miriam and Roelien van der Molen.

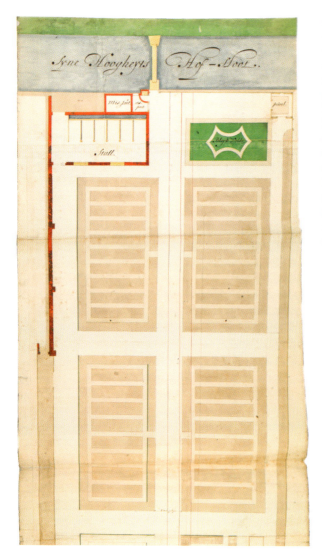

9.4 Sections of the plan of the ground floor and garden of the Fagel house in The Hague (*c.*1706), showing two of the four planting beds. The stables, rubbish and ash pits, bleaching area and arbour are indicated where the garden extends to the canal bordering the Noordeinde palace. An elegant gentleman, François Fagel the Elder (?), contemplates the plans. (Fagel Portfolio 14:0 63/1; Abbott 920). © The Board of Trinity College Dublin.

Pleasure gardens and gardening for pleasure in the Fagel collection 203

family members took an active part in the development and cultivation of their gardens. Hendrik Fagel the Elder (1706–90) was likewise interested enough to make a list of his collections of 'plantations, trees, plants and crops, and flowers'.[17]

The original architectural plans of about 1706 for the renovation of the Fagel home in the fashionable Noordeinde district of The Hague give a unique insight into the ideas and ideals of *greffier* François Fagel the Elder for his house and garden.[18] The plans are attributed to renowned French architect Daniel Marot (1661–1752), one of a number of Huguenot refugees who settled in The Hague, and who greatly influenced Dutch architecture, landscape and interior design. The garden backed onto the Noordeinde palace, bounded by a canal. An annexe was built to house the library, which was in the process of being expanded by François and this linked the house to the magnificently decorated garden pavilion, the Dome of Fagel, also designed by Marot and now part of the royal palace gardens. Cutting a dash in his plumed hat and elegant attire, a gentleman, most likely François, is portrayed in an attractive vignette forming part of the plans (Fig. 9.4). These indicate an orangery on the first floor where citrus and other delicate plants could be cultivated, and extensive planting beds. It is likely that the women of the extended Fagel family living in the house would have engaged with the cultivation and use of practical and decorative produce of the garden and orangery within the domestic sphere. Jan Commelin's *Nederlantze Hesperides* (Amsterdam, 1676), translated into English in 1683, advises on 'the management, ordering and use of the limon and orange trees, fitted to the nature and climate of the Netherlands'.[19] Commelin reminds his readers that such citrus fruits were not solely decorative but might also be used in 'physick, housekeeping and perfuming'.[20] There were some attempts to grow such citrus fruits in Ireland about the end of the seventeenth century.[21]

TULIPS

Arrangements of cut flowers enhanced domestic interiors and the Fagels may have looked for ideas on how to display them in books such as Ferrari's *De florum cultura* (Rome, 1633) with its floral arrangements and ingenious designs for water-retaining vases. The art of indoor flower arranging is seen to advantage in the signature blue and white Delftware of Holland and in Chinese porcelain vases, as depicted in an arrangement painted by Maria Sybilla Merian (1647–1717), in her work on European insects, *De Europische insecten* (Amsterdam, 1730).[22] Delft Blue or Chinese motifs also

17 Theo Thomassen, '"To put in order": how the greffiers Fagel documented themselves as men of politics, men of religion and men of the world' in Jackson, *Frozen in time*, p. 22. 18 See John Loughman, 'Tulips and building plans: primary material from the Fagel collection' in Jackson, *Frozen in time*, pp 49–71. 19 Jan Commelin, *The Belgick, or Netherlandish Hesperides* (London, 1683), title page. 20 Ibid., p. 177. 21 Pim, 'History of gardening', p. 48; E.C. Nelson, 'Some records (*c.*1690–1830) of greenhouses in Irish gardens', *Moorea*, 2 (1981), 21–8; Costello, *Irish demesne landscapes*, p. 91. 22 Maria Sybilla Merian, *De Europische Insecten* (Amsterdam, 1730), tab. CLXVIII.

9.5 Johan Barents (?), 'Viceroy', Fagel tulip catalogue (*c.*1637–41), watercolour and gouache (TCD MS 1706/1, fol. 6). © The Board of Trinity College Dublin.

Pleasure gardens and gardening for pleasure in the Fagel collection 205

decorated the special tulip vases, and ceramic flower pyramids, which were developed in the seventeenth century to a unique design, with single stems of the costly flowers placed in individual spouts. A detailed planting plan for a tulip bed in the Fagel garden, made on 16 October 1718, may have been influenced by a recently published manual giving advice on gardening in the French style, with a chapter on the cultivation of tulips.[23] Cultivars of tulip such as the so-called bizarres (*bizarden*) – with flowers variegated or streaked with red on a yellow background – which appear on the plan were described in this manual. The author proclaims that any gardener who leaves it until the beginning of the month of November to plant their tulip bulbs is to be considered lazy. But to delay until December is positively negligent as the bulbs should have been placed in the ground in October!

The Fagel tulip catalogue is an illustrated manuscript linked to the famous Alkmaar tulip auction of 5 February 1637.[24] This took place just before the tulip bulb market crashed at the height of 'tulipmania', when trade in tulip bulbs was conducted at inflated prices through futures contracts. These tulip books, or albums, are catalogues of flowers in watercolour and gouache that were commissioned by commercial growers as sales catalogues to illustrate the different varieties of tulips for prospective buyers. In some cases they were albums commissioned by wealthy growers to record the flowers in their gardens. The first painting in the Fagel album is the legendary 'Semper Augustus', with red and white flamed petals, a bulb of which could command an asking price in excess of the value of a fashionable house on the canal banks in Amsterdam.[25] The purple and white 'Viceroy' is also depicted (Fig. 9.5); one bulb was paid for in kind and included on the list of goods traded were one thousand pounds weight of cheese, eight fat pigs, two hogsheads of wine, a complete bed, and a silver beaker.[26] A similarly 'broken' or flamed flower in the same colours is the intriguingly named 'De Paus van Roomen' (the Pope of Rome). The loose documents which accompany the album indicate that the catalogue was used by the Fagels in a practical way when planning and planting their garden – these include receipts for flowers bought by the Fagels and printed records of bulb auctions.

THE GARDEN AT LEEUWENHORST

Gaspar Fagel held the position of Grand Pensionary, the highest-ranking official of the province of Holland, from 1672 to 1688. He rented an estate at Leeuwenhorst, in south Holland, and here he created a garden of renown.[27] A classic manual for Dutch

---

23 Trinity College Dublin (TCD), MS 1706/6: Planting plan for a tulip bed in the garden of the Fagel House in the Hague, 16 October 1718; Jean du Vivier, *Le Jardin de Hollande* … (Leiden, 1714), pp 49–71. **24** *Alckmaarse lusthoff van tulpaanen, ofte verkooping van een parteÿ tulpaanen, binnen Alckmaar den 5 February 1637*: TCD, MS1706/1. The tulip catalogue and associated documents are now available to view on the TCD digital repository: https://digitalcollections.tcd.ie/catalog?utf8=%E2%9C%93&search_field=all_fields&q=Alckmaarse+lusthoff+van+tulpaanen, accessed 10 February 2022.   **25** James Joyce may have had this tulip in mind when he described flowerbeds set with 'eccentric ellipses of scarlet and chrome tulips' in the Ithaca episode of Ulysses: James Joyce, *Ulysses* (London, 1960), pp 839–40. **26** Wilfred Blunt, *Tulipomania* (London, 1950), pp 15–16.   **27** See Elizabeth den Hartog and Carla

gardeners, *Den Nederlandtsen hovenier* was dedicated to him during his lifetime.[28] He was part of a network of amateur horticulturists growing exotics, some exchanging seeds, bulbs and plants, along with knowledge and expertise. This network also brought in professional collectors and his garden was visited by famous botanists such as Paul Hermann (1646–95) and Richard Richardson (1663–1741), naturalists such as Jacob Breyne (1637–97), and garden curators such as John Watts (*fl.* 1670–1701). Many of the plants he grew were referenced in the great botanical works of the time. It is believed that Gaspar Fagel was the first to have brought a tropical epiphytic orchid, *Brassavola nodosa* (lady-of-the-night), a native of Central America and northern South America, into cultivation in western Europe. An engraving of this orchid, imported from the island of Curaçao, was published in Paul Hermann's *Paradisus Batavus* (Leiden, 1698).[29] The drawing was done from the life, 'ad vivam', in Fagel's garden, 'in Horto *Fageliano*', and was one of nine plants mentioned here from that garden. Hermann was medical officer to the Dutch East India Company (VOC) in Sri Lanka, and later director of the famous botanic garden at the University of Leiden. As Den Hartog and Teune note, Hermann recorded in his notebook details of the plants which he saw in the gardens he visited; he included a list of plants from Fagel's garden, and Fagel sent him seeds and specimens for his herbarium.[30] This underlines the importance of these growers in giving access to their gardens to botanists and illustrators, thus facilitating the accurate recording and dissemination of knowledge of the new exotics.

Fagel is sure to have had one or more hothouses as the orangery could not provide the best conditions necessary for growing tropical plants. The Dutch led the development of the hothouse, pioneered at the botanic garden of the Hortus Medicus Amsterdam in 1682. Hot stoves, under-floor heating, light and ventilation were key elements enabling the pineapple and other exotic plants to be grown in north-western Europe. Several of the horticultural works in the Fagel collection have detailed technical drawings of hothouses and heating methods.

Ananas comosus (pineapple) was among the many exotic plants recorded as growing in Gaspar's garden, which included *Cinnamomum* species (cinnamon), and *Camellia sinensis* (tea). Some 258 different plants from Asia, Africa and the Canary Islands, North and South America, the Caribbean, and southern Europe, especially the Mediterranean, are recorded in various sources.[31] Botanists travelled to the colonies for first-hand encounters with exotic plants; some were commissioned by the VOC or other bodies to seek and gather information and specimens to advance discovery and knowledge of useful plants for medicinal, trade and other purposes.

Teune, 'Gaspar Fagel (1633–88): his garden and plant collection at Leeuwenhorst', *Garden History*, 30 (2002), 191–205.   **28** Jan van der Groen, *Den Nederlandtsen hovenier* (Amsterdam, 1669). Unlike the majority of the works mentioned here, this book is not part of the Fagel collection in TCD.   **29** Paul Hermann, *Paradisus Batavus* (Leiden, 1698), p. 187 [recte p. 207 as there are errors in pagination].   **30** Den Hartog and Teune, 'Gaspar Fagel', 195.   **31** Elizabeth den Hartog, 'Leeuwenhorst, een tuin van wereldformaat gezien door de ogen van Pieter Teding van Berkhout', *De zeventiende eeuw*, 24 (2008), 234–36. https://www.dbnl.org/tekst/_zev001200801_01/_zev001200801_01_0019.php, accessed 10 February 2022.

Pleasure gardens and gardening for pleasure in the Fagel collection   207

These were collected and carefully packed for transportation to Europe with a view to propagation for the botanic gardens of the Dutch Republic, and for the gardens of the Stadholder William of Orange. The garden of the settlement of the VOC at the Dutch Cape Colony in southern Africa was a rich source of rare plants, bulbs and seeds while under the governorship of Simon van der Stel (1639–1712) and later his son Willem Adriaan (1664–1733). Simon van der Stel's report to the VOC of his expedition to the copper mountains of Namaqualand in 1685 is among the manuscripts in the Fagel collection, illustrated with images of the plants and animals he encountered on his journey.[32] In 1688 he made a shipment of seventeen cases of trees and plants to the stadholder's gardens, the Hortus Medicus in Amsterdam, and Gaspar Fagel. As occurred in Ireland, requests were made to individuals abroad to send specimens home.[33] Catharina Juliana Seep sent a basket of bulbs and a box of seeds to Fagel from Cartagena in north-western South America (present-day Columbia) in 1688; the accompanying letter states that the plants had never before been seen in Holland.[34]

After his death in December of that year, Gaspar Fagel's collection of plants was sold to William III, who had them transported to Hampton Court Palace Garden in England, where they formed part of Queen Mary's collection. William had commissioned an illustrated record of the garden and plants at Leeuwenhorst beginning in 1685 and ceasing on Fagel's death in 1688.[35] More than 120 plants are depicted in watercolour, including numerous cultivars of *Tulipa* (tulip) and *Dianthus caryophyllus* (carnation), irises, palms, a few American cacti and some succulents from Africa. Many are shown in ornate containers. Several different *Tropaeolum* species including *T. majus* (garden nasturtium) are displayed to lovely effect. *T. majus* was then a new plant in European gardens, the species is native to the northern Andes and is now a very familiar annual in Irish gardens. There is also a full-page illustration of *Arbutus unedo* (strawberry tree). Unfortunately, Gaspar Fagel's library does not form part of the Fagel collection having been auctioned and dispersed after his death. The sales catalogue of that auction on the 17 October 1689 in The Hague contains many titles on botany and gardening, some of which are replicated in the Fagel collection.[36]

---

32 TCD, MS 984: Simon van der Stel, 'Dagh registergehoudenop de voiagie gedaen naer der Amacqua Land' […] First entry: 25 August 1685. The journal was published by Gilbert Waterhouse: *Simon van der Stel's journal of his expedition to Namaqualand, 1685–6. Edited from the ms. in the Library of Trinity College, Dublin, by Gilbert Waterhouse* (London, 1932). **33** Costello, *Irish demesne landscapes*, p. 78, notes that the Dublin Philosophical Society sent to Holland to ask not just for seeds but that market gardeners be sent to Ireland so that new techniques might be introduced. On the Dublin Philosophical Society and botany in early modern Ireland see Patrick Kelly's chapter in this volume. **34** Den Hartog and Carla Teuna, 'Gaspar Fagel', 195. **35** Florence, Biblioteca Nazionale, MS Pal.6.B.B.8.5 (available online at https://archive.org/details/bncf-honselaerdicensis-images/page/n2/mode/1up, accessed 10 February 2022); Stephen Cousyns, 'Hortus Regius Honselaerdicensis'. For an interpretation of the allegorical frontispiece and the plants depicted there see Hunt and de Jong, *The Anglo-Dutch garde*n, pp 288–9. **36** *Catalogus instructissimae & exquisitissimae bibliothecae illustrissimi viri Gasparis Fagel* (The Hague, 1689).

RIVERSIDE COUNTRY LIVING

In the Netherlands, riverside locations were popular for the building of country houses and the rivers Amstel and Vecht were convenient routes for inhabitants of the city of Amsterdam, who often travelled by boat. *Hollands Arcadia* (Amsterdam, 1730) is the expressive title of a compilation of picturesque views of country houses along the Amstel by Abraham Rademaker (1677–1735), with engravings by Leonard Shenck (*fl.* 1720–46). An earlier work by artist and engraver Daniel Stopendaal, *De Zegepraalende Vecht* (Amsterdam, 1719), takes us on an intriguing journey on the river Vecht, landing at pleasure grounds, country houses and villages along its route. The photograph-like views with their detailed illustrations focus on the country houses and on the design of the gardens. Their small scale, and position vis-à-vis the river, brings these houses close to the life of the river and the people, be they inhabitants of the locality, travellers, workers, or owners of the estates and their visitors. In one view a beggar gets alms from a traveller; both can enjoy some of the visual pleasures of the gardens as gates of wrought iron, and low or dipped boundary hedges allow a passer-by to see into the garden with its many adornments and delights. Swans are plentiful on the river, and on garden ponds and canals, providing a very picturesque aspect. Activities on and alongside the river merge – fishermen working for a living hauling in their nets, boatmen transporting baskets of vegetables or navigating on boats laden with barrels, alongside leisurely parties enjoying themselves in pleasure boats or on landings and viewing platforms. The villas are frequently shown in close proximity to farmland with people haymaking, women carrying pails, and animals grazing in the fields. On riverside paths pedestrians, carriages, anglers, wagons of hay, people on horseback, children playing, and the ubiquitous dogs; all are depicted side by side engaged in their daily pursuits, be they work or pleasure. Bound together with the *Zegepraalende Vecht* is a similar book extolling the delights of country living on the polders near Amsterdam; these reclaimed lands were also suitable sites for the *buitenplaatsen*.[37] A country house and farmland near Wassenaar on the outskirts of The Hague was purchased in 1708 by Hendrik Fagel (1669–1728) and was included in the inheritance of his grandson Hendrik Fagel the Younger.[38]

Several notable gardens portrayed in these works belonged to women, many of whom were widows, and two on the river Vecht are outstanding. They were created by the talented and innovative women Agnes Block (1629–1704) and Magdalena Poulle (1626–99).[39] Block bought her own land along the River Vecht during the first

---

37 Daniel Stopendaal and Mattheus Brouerius, *Het verheerlykt watergraefs of Diemer-meer by de stadt Amsterdam* (Amsterdam, 1725).   38 His namesake Hendrik Fagel the Elder (1706-1790) extended the property in 1738 by the purchase of the adjacent Westerhoek farm, and in 1757 the Waalsdorp country estate. This owner planted the grounds extensively, including trees on the access roads, and a planting plan is preserved from this time. H.H. Heldring, *Inventaris van het archief van Oostduin, Arensdorp en Waalsdorp … Haags Gemeentearchief 0172-0101* (The Hague, 2017): https://www.archivesportaleurope.net/ead-display/-/ead/pl/aicode/NL-HaHGA/type/fa/id/0172-01, accessed 10 February 2022.   39 See Marisca Sikkens-de Zwaan, 'Magdalena Poulle (1632–99): a Dutch lady in a circle of botanical collectors',

Pleasure gardens and gardening for pleasure in the Fagel collection   209

year of her widowhood in 1660. She is believed to have been the first to successfully grow a fruit-bearing pineapple plant in Europe, and her garden and pineapple are celebrated in a portrait with two children and her second husband at Vijverhof in 1670.[40] The garden included an orangery, hothouses, orchards and an aviary, and a view of the garden forms the background to the painting. As well as drawing and painting in watercolours herself, she invited noted Dutch botanical artists to come to Vijverhof and portray plants in her collection, producing around four florilegia. Poulle, a plantswoman with a flair for innovative garden design, had an outstanding garden with orangery and hothouses at Gunterstein, which she had bought as a ruined castle estate in 1680. *Myrtus communis* (myrtle), *Jasminum officinale* (jasmine) and double-blossomed *Nerium oleander* (oleander) were among the many plants she grew in a garden which had an important place in the development of the estates along the Vecht. She commissioned a book of fifteen etchings of her garden, *Veues de Gunterstein* (*c*.1690), which include her famous dragon fountain, referencing the guardian of the mythical garden of the Hesperides (Fig. 9.6).[41]

THE BOOKS AND THE GARDENS

The horticultural literature we encounter in the Fagel library was an important source of information, providing advice and guidance for the creation and maintenance of the gardens. The Fagel sale catalogue arranges the main part of the works on botany and horticulture under the headings 'Agricultura et Horticultura' and 'Regnum Vegetabile' (almost 200 titles).[42] Many practical manuals and treatises on gardening attest to the interest of the Fagel family in carrying out the practice of gardening. Classic works on botany, horticulture and garden design by French, Italian, German, English and other European authors, as well as those of the Netherlands were collected. Among the writers represented were La Quintinie, Claude Mollet (*c*.1564–*c*.1649), Giovanni Battista Ferrari (1584–1665), Herman Boerhaave (1668–1738), Breyne, Abraham Munting (1626–83), Knoop, Stephen Switzer (1682?–1745), Carl Linnaeus (1707–78), and famous Dutch botanists Jan (1629–92) and Caspar Commelin (1668–1731). Books and prints with illustrations of gardens could inspire, with ideas for plants, garden design, and landscape architecture. Works of natural history also had their place, for example, the superbly illustrated *Metamorphosis insectorum Surinamensium* by Maria Sybilla Merian (1647–1717), where the insects in varying stages of development are shown on the plants with which they are associated.[43]

Garden History, 30 (2002), 206–20.   40 *Agnes Block, Sybrand de Flines* by Jan Weenix [1694?] (Amsterdam Historische Museum).   41 Joseph Mulder, *Veues de Gunterstein* (Amsterdam, *c*.1690). This is held in a volume of engravings, brought together and bound by the Fagels in the eighteenth century: [*Views of palaces and gardens in Holland, etc.*].   42 Paterson, *Bibliotheca Fageliana*, pp 171–3; 179–86. 43 M.S. Merian, *Metamorphosis insectorum Surinamensium*, 3rd edition (Amsterdam, 1719).

9.6 Magdalena Poulle's orangery and greenhouse at Gunterstein. 'L'orangerie et sa serre, with the dragon fountain in the centre of the garden, engraving, *c.*1690' is bound with other engravings in a volume entitled *Views of palaces and gardens in Holland etc.* © The Board of Trinity College Dublin.

Herbals were important for home medication at that time and there are several in the Fagel library. Scottish author Elizabeth Blackwell (née Blachrie) (*d.* 1758) compiled *A curious herbal* and published it in weekly numbers in London in 1737.[44] The 500 illustrations were hand-drawn, engraved and coloured by herself. *A curious herbal* is represented in the Fagel collection in a later expanded edition in Latin and German.[45] Flemish physician and botanist Rembert Dodoens (1517–85) wrote his famous herbal in old Flemish, which was first published in Antwerp in 1554. The Fagels had three copies of the Dutch language edition *Cruydt-boeck* (Amsterdam, 1644), showing an ideal garden within the title frame which is coloured differently in

---

[44] Blanche Henrey, *British botanical and horticultural literature before 1800*, 3 vols (Oxford, 1975), ii, pp 230–6; iii, pp 9–11. [45] Elizabeth Blackwell, *Herbarium Blackwellianum emendatum et auctum* (Nuremberg, 1750–73).

Pleasure gardens and gardening for pleasure in the Fagel collection 211

two of the hand-painted copies. This is the most extensive edition with additions by the eminent botanist Charles de L'Écluse (1526–1609), who had established one of the earliest botanical gardens at Leiden in 1593; the Fagel collection holds several of his works including his *Rariorum plantarum historia* in the 1601 edition. The wonder of the discovery of new plants is reflected in many other works on rare and exotic plants, such as Jan Commelin's *Horti medici Amstelodamensis* (Amsterdam, 1697–1701). Medicinal plants and the associated knowledge of indigenous populations were greatly sought after in the colonies; their properties were recorded, illustrations made, and plants shipped home for propagation. An important work by the Spanish physician Francisco Hernández, *Rerum medicarum Novae Hispaniae thesaurus* (Rome, 1641), is a guide to Mexican plants, animals and minerals with medicinal properties, illustrated with woodcuts.

Another exceptional book in use by the Fagels describes the plants in the famed botanical garden of Johann Konrad von Gemmingen (*d.* 1612), the bishop of Eichstätt in Germany.[46] The Fagel edition is the black-and-white version with text, intended as a reference work; the exquisite monochrome engravings lose nothing in comparison with the luxury coloured version. An eighteen-page manuscript index to the flowers was discovered loose within the covers, beautifully written in a copperplate hand, possibly by François Fagel the Elder.[47] This alphabetical catalogue complements the seasonal arrangement of the florilegium in which the plants were drawn as they bloomed throughout the four seasons, with boxes of freshly cut flowers being sent every week from the garden to Nuremberg to be sketched from life. We can follow their blooming seasons beginning in spring, when the fritillary or snake's head comes out, a popular subject in paintings of the Golden Age. These can be seen today growing wild in the famous Haagse Bos forest of The Hague, some, perhaps, descendants of garden escapees from the grounds of the princely country seat of Huis ten Bosch, the house in the forest.[48]

CONCLUSION

According to the sKBL (Dutch Castles, Historic Country Houses & Rural Estates Foundation), 551 historic country house complexes remain of the estimated 6,000 which were built between 1600 and 1920.[49] Along with Clingendael and Sorgvliet, the demesne of Huis ten Bosch still stands, and is now the residential palace of the Dutch royal family. Clingendael houses the Netherlands Institute of International Relations and Sorgvliet is the official residence of the prime minister of The

---

46 Basil Besler, *Hortus Eystettensis* ([Nuremberg], 1613). **47** [Manuscript index] accompanying Hortus Eystettensis. **48** Views of Huis ten Bosch are held in a volume of engravings, brought together and bound by the Fagels in the eighteenth century: [*Views of country houses, gardens, etc., in the province of Holland*]. **49** Further information can be found on the sKBL website https://www.skbl.nl/ and that of the Netherlands Bureau for Tourism and Congresses https:// www.holland.com/global/tourism/ holland-stories/castles-and-country-houses.htm, accessed 10 February 2022.

Netherlands.[50] Vijverhof is no longer in existence but Gunterstein is still in the hands of Poulle's descendants. A boutique hotel and restaurant occupies a wing of the Fagel house, including the garden where the gallery housing the library formerly stood.

All these gardens live on in the paper gardens of the Fagel library, which, in common with other outstanding private libraries and gardens of the time, were a source of inspiration and information to men and women active and interested in botany and horticulture. As the working library of an affluent urban family living in The Hague, keenly interested in acquiring knowledge and in the interpretation of the contemporary world, the Fagel collection gives us an insight into the public and private world of the Dutch Republic.[51] In doing so it sheds reflected light on Irish gardens of the period, for the European baroque style apparent in these gardens spread beyond the Dutch Republic and into the gardens of early modern Britain and Ireland. Gardens considered to have 'Dutch' features included those of Doneraile Court, Stillorgan and Stradbally, and Carton demesne.[52] Gardens are dynamic and often re-fashioned to reflect changing tastes; some of these lost views are to be seen in contemporary paintings and drawings. The scene in a painting of Howth Castle *c.*1740, with its parterres, statuary, and canal with swans, would not have been out of place in one of the gardens so beautifully depicted in the Fagel collection in the Library of Trinity College Dublin.[53]

---

50 The grounds of Clingendael may be visited but little trace of the original gardens survive. **51** Guidance on consultation may be found on the Fagel collection website, and researchers should apply to the Department of Early Printed Books and Special Collections, Trinity College Dublin. Some of the beautiful works in the Fagel collection may be viewed online via the Fagel collection website and TCD Library's Digital Collections Repository. Works mentioned in the body of the text are the editions held in the Fagel collection in TCD, unless otherwise stated. The Fagel family archive is held in the National Archives of the Netherlands: *Inventaris van het archief van de familie Fagel, 1513–1927.* Nationaal Archief: 1.10.29 https://www.nationaalarchief.nl/onderzoeken/archief/1.10.29, accessed 10 February 2022. **52** On this see Loeber, *An introduction to the Dutch influence*, p. 13 and Finola O'Kane, *Landscape design in eighteenth-century Ireland: mixing foreign trees with the natives* (Cork, 2004), pp 90–1; 93–8. **53** Edward Malins and Patrick Bowe, *Irish gardens and demesnes from 1830* (New York, 1980), plate 28; Costello, *Irish demesne landscapes*, plate 1 and cover. To find out more about gardens in the Fagel collection see 'Orchids and orangeries: aspects of private gardens in the late 17th-century Dutch Republic', an online exhibition curated by the author, which is available at https://artsandculture. google.com/story/orchids-orangeries-aspects-of-private-gardens-in-the-late-17th-century-dutch-republic-trinity-college-dublin-library/yQWhu5Y5dgplJA?hl=en, accessed 25 February 2022.

CHAPTER TEN

The Physic Garden at Trinity College Dublin, in the early eighteenth century

E. CHARLES NELSON

THE UNIVERSITY OF DUBLIN, established in 1592, has had a teaching garden – variously called the physic(k) garden, hortus medicus or botanic garden – for more than three centuries, at first on the main campus in the centre of Dublin when the principal role was medical education, and later in different southern suburbs. The best known of these gardens, the one established in 1806 at Lansdowne Road, Ballsbridge, was among the finest gardens in Ireland during the nineteenth century and it had an unrivalled international reputation for its significant plant collections.[1]

Three centuries ago, on the south side of the campus of Trinity College, abutting Nassau Street and a little beyond where Frederick Street joins it, there was a modest, walled and well-ordered garden, the Physic (or Anatomy) Garden (Fig. 10.1). It was '250 feet long, and 50 feet broad', and was laid out neatly with a grid of rectangular beds, as was the established pattern for such gardens, most probably edged by clipped box hedges and separated by gravelled paths.[2] Beyond the eastern wall was tree-lined College Park. Immediately ahead at the northern end of this enclosed garden was the two-storey Anatomy House where professors of the college's medical school and their students dissected cadavers. The western boundary was formed by a wall, so the Physic Garden could not be seen from the Fellows' Garden.[3]

This particular garden was not the first of the university's teaching gardens; the earliest had been established in 1687 on a different part of the campus. Medical training in the seventeenth and eighteen centuries included the study of botany. Aspiring physicians had to know their plants and what the medicinal properties of each plant were reckoned to be. Most importantly, they had to be able to recognize

1 For accounts of the gardens associated with Trinity College Dublin (TCD), see, for example, P.S. Wyse Jackson, 'The story of the Botanic Gardens of Trinity College Dublin, 1687–1987', *Botanical Journal of the Linnean Society, London*, 95 (1987), 301–11; E.C. Nelson, 'Botany, medicine and politics in eighteenth century Dublin and the origin of Irish botanical gardens', *Moorea*, 6 (1987), 33–44; E.C. Nelson, '"Reserved to the Fellows"': four centuries of gardens at Trinity College, Dublin' in Charles Holland (ed.), *Trinity College Dublin and the idea of a university* (Dublin, 1991), pp 185–222.   2 Edward Hill, *An address to the students in physic* (Dublin, 1803), p. 7.   3 See, for example, Joseph Tudor, 'A prospect of the Library of Trinity College Dublin, Le Point de Veue de la Bibliotheque du College de la Trinité a Dublin' in *Six views of Dublin* (London, 1753), plate 6; [Samuel Byron, Isometric drawing, TCD, MUN/MC/9]: reproduced in Holland, *Trinity College Dublin*, p. 213, fig. 43.

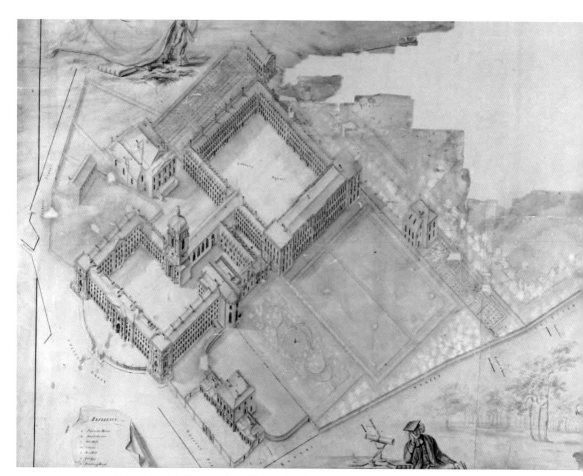

10.1 Detail of a 'bird's-eye view' (isometric drawing) by Samuel Byron of the south-western corner of Trinity College campus in 1780, with the Anatomy House and Physick Garden (centre right), and the Library and Provost's House (lower left). © The Board of Trinity College Dublin.

those such as the native *Euphorbia hyberna*, familiar at that time as 'Makinboy' (*meacan buí*, Irish spurge), and *Conium maculatum* (hemlock), which were poisonous and potentially deadly.[4] Where better to learn than in a garden devoted entirely to the cultivation of a diverse collection of those 'herbs' that were then used in the medicines dispensed by physicians or apothecaries or sold by herb-women who called their wares through the streets and alleys of the city.

The Physic Garden on Nassau Street was established after the Anatomy House was completed. On the occasion of the opening of this new medical teaching facility on 16 August 1711, Dr Henry Nicholson (*c.*1681–*c.*1721), 'Professor in Botanie',

---

4 'Makinboy' is discussed by E.C. Nelson's 'Irish wild plants before 1690' and P.H. Kelly's 'The Molyneux brothers, the New Science and the Dublin Philosophical Society in the late seventeenth century' in this volume, pp 52–3 and 73, respectively.

delivered a botanical lecture. He must have overseen the Physic Garden and built up its collections of plants for a few years at least. Nicholson certainly wrote on 18 October 1711 to the English botanist James Petiver (1663/4–1718) saying that he had 'undertaken to furnish a Physick garden here, w[ch] is about setting up by the college of Dublin, wth plants & seeds of all sorts as many as I can procure: & they have obliged me to this task by nominating me their Professor in Botanie'.[5] Significantly, Henry Nicholson had studied medicine at the University of Leiden in Holland, and, as will be shown, the plant collection in the University of Dublin's garden in the 1720s included plants that came from Dutch gardens.[6]

Nicholson engaged Petiver in correspondence for several years because he was much concerned to get new plants. 'I dont know a properer person to apply myself to', he wrote in October 1711, 'than you who understand the matter so well. If you'l please to be so kind to order, at some seed shops or gardeners, small specimens of exotick seeds, of the quantity of 2 or 300 several species such as you may judge are scarce to be had commonly in Ireland'.[7] Nicholson also had contacted people in several parts of Ireland asking them to gather native Irish plants for cultivation in the Physic Garden (Fig. 10.2). However, Nicholson left the college before 1716 and moved to London and there is no mention in the college's records of any professor of botany between 1715 and 1724. During this period, William Maple, 'a very Ingenious Gentleman and usefull to us and well received', was evidently looking after the Physic Garden.[8]

Not surprisingly, the building of Thomas Burgh's splendid new library close to the north-western corner of the Anatomy House, which Burgh had also designed, was to cause significant disruption on the college's campus.[9] The college's muniments confirm that between 1715 and 1720 a physic garden was actively maintained and also that a new garden was being prepared in 1723. In the financial quarter beginning in April 1723 a total of £73 was spent 'for the new garden' and other money was expended on such works as 'digging ye foundation of ye physick garden wall'.[10]

Two letters dating from the early 1720s independently confirm the establishment of a new physic garden on the campus. Although not dated, a letter written by Lady Dorothy Rawdon (*d.* 1733) describing her visit to the college in July 1722 contains a description of the rudimentary state of the new garden as well as relevant advice about donating plants for its collections. '[W]e were entertained a few days agoe at the Colledg and saw all the Mathemakicall Apartment', she commented, continuing that

---

5 British Library, Sloane MS 4065, fo. 4, quoted in E.C. Nelson, 'The influence of Leiden on botany in Dublin in the early eighteenth century', *Huntia*, 4 (1982), 133–46, at 136.   6 Nelson, 'The influence of Leiden', 136; E.C. Nelson, 'Botany and medicine; Dublin and Leiden', *Journal of the Irish Colleges of Physicians and Surgeons*, 22 (1993), 133–6.   7 British Library, Sloane MS 4065, fo. 4.   8 E.St.J. Brooks, 'Henry Nicholson, first lecturer in botany and the earliest physic garden', *Hermathena*, 83 (1954), 3–15, at 4.   9 Anne Crookshank, 'The Long Room' in Peter Fox (ed.), *Treasures of the Library, Trinity College Dublin* (Dublin, 1986), pp 16–28, at p. 19.   10 TCD, MS P4/27/42: Bursar's vouchers.

METHODUS PLANTARUM,

IN

Horto Medico,

COLLEGII DUBLINENSIS,

JAM JAM

Disponendarum;

In duas partes divisa; quarum prima
de Plantis, altera de Fruticibus &
Arboribus agit.

In Usum Studiosorum Academicorum.

Autore *Henrico Nicholson,* M. D.
𝕭𝖔𝖙𝖆𝖓𝖎𝖈𝖊𝖘 𝕻𝖗𝖔𝖋𝖊𝖘𝖘𝖔𝖗𝖊.

D V B L I N I:
Typis *A. Rhames,* M DCC XII.

10.2 Henry Nicholson, *Methodus plantarum, in horto medico, Collegii Dublinensis* (Dublin, 1712), title page. © The Board of Trinity College Dublin.

The Physic Garden at Trinity College Dublin

> Mr. Maple desir'd me to tell you that the ground for the Physick Garden is not yet ready, and he has no desire to run the Hazard of looseing the Plants you offer him by two removes. They shew'd me the spot of ground laid out for that purpose, which is not att all in order as yet. When 'tis prepar'd they will thankfully receive your contribution. They have gott 20 sorts of Alos [*sic*] from Holland, some of them the finest I ever saw and when they increase I believe you may be sure of them.[11]

More significant is a letter that William Stephens (*c.*1683–1760) penned on 4 May 1724 to Dr James Jurin (1684–1750), the recently elected secretary of the Royal Society in London. After apologizing for the 'interruption of our correspondence', Stephens explained that this was due 'on my part, by the erection of a physick Garden here, which the university have done me the honour, to put under my Inspection, and has really employed all my empty hours, for near these twelve months past'.[12]

The work on the relocated Physic Garden was completed by the following spring by which time it was well-stocked with interesting plants, and the college was aware that it had an asset it could show to the general public. On 8 May 1725 an advertisement appeared in the *Dublin Weekly Journal* stating that:

> The Physic Garden at Trinity College will be opened on Monday 1 June 1725, and a Course of Botany will be there begun to continue every Monday, Wednesday and Friday. Tickets will be delivered at the College and at William and John Smith's, Booksellers on Blind Quay.[13]

Probably only the keenest folk came that first open-day and lecture in June 1725, for Dublin had been lashed with rain since the middle of May. On open-day there was 'much thunder' and 'much rain all day'. The 'great showers of hail' a few days later cannot have left gardens in a happy state. As it turned out June 1725 was cold and wet throughout Europe; parts of England had snow showers on Midsummer Day, and 'great Numbers of sheep and cattle perished'. Ireland, however, 'tho bad [was] not so severely us'd'.[14]

The college continued to advertise public lectures in botany in 1726 (Fig. 10.3), evidently keen to draw in a crowd.[15] Luckily for the college, the first few days of May 1726 were fair, even warm, with sunshine and the day of the first lecture in the Physic Garden was sunny. However, the rest of May 1726 was unsettled with 'Sultry showers & much Thunder'. Again, Ireland suffered less than other parts of Europe. Mid-summer in Dublin was changeable, with showers and rain: it rained all night on 21 June.[16]

---

11 Huntingdon Library, San Marino, California, MS HA 15638, fo. 1a. A partial transcript of this letter is in TCD, MS 3741. See also Nelson, 'The influence of Leiden', 138–9.　**12** Royal Society, MS EL.S2.43: William Stephens to James Jurin, 14 May 1724.　**13** *Dublin Weekly Journal*, 8 May 1725, p. 24.　**14** [Isaac Butler], 'The diary of weather and winds 1716–1734', https://www.slideshare.net/dubcilib/ diary-of-weather, accessed 16 February 2022, fos. 200–1. See M.G. Sanderson, 'Daily weather in Dublin 1716–1734: the diary of Isaac Butler', *Weather*, 73 (2018), 179–82.　**15** *Dublin Weekly Journal*, 16 Apr. 1726, p. 215; 23 Apr. 1726, p. 220.　**16** [Isaac Butler], 'The diary of weather and winds 1716–1734', fos. 226–7.

> **ADVERTISEMENT.**
>
> THE Botany Lecture *at the* Physick Garden *at* Trinity College, *will begin on* Wednesday *the* 18th. Day of May, 1726. *and will be continued every* Friday, Monday *and* Wednesday *The Subscribers are desired to Enter their Names with* John Finigan *at the* Physick Garden, *who shall attend for that Purpose every Day from Ten to Twelve in the Morning, and from Three to Six in the Afternoon.*
>
> *Just publish'd,*

10.3 Advertisement for a series of botany lectures at the Physic Garden in *The Dublin Weekly Journal*, 23 April 1726. Courtesy of Dublin City Library and Archive.

William Stephens (Fig. 10.4), having been educated in Dublin, enrolled as a student of natural philosophy at the University of Glasgow in January 1715, remaining for a little over a year before moving to Holland where, like Henry Nicholson, he matriculated in the medical faculty at the University of Leiden. Stephens studied under Herman Boerhaave (1668–1738) at Leiden for two years and successfully defended the thesis 'De elixir proprietatibus' for which he was awarded his doctorate on 15 July 1718. He was elected a Fellow of the Royal Society of London on 1 December 1718. Stephens returned to Ireland and in 1724 obtained the degrees of bachelor and doctor of medicine from the University of Dublin. As in Nicholson's case, these qualifications were necessary before Stephens could obtain a fellowship of the King's and Queen's College of Physicians; he was elected a Fellow in 1728.

One of Stephens's first tasks after he became professor of botany at Trinity College and had completed supervising the establishment of the new Physic Garden was to prepare a catalogue (Fig. 10.5) of its collection of plants. On 22 April 1726 he wrote to Thomas Dale (1700–50), secretary of the Botanical Society of London, asking if the society would like to have a copy of the catalogue. On 21 June Dale replied that the society would 'receive your catalogue with pleasure and willingly supply you as far as lies in their power with whatever you shall have occasion for'. In view of the change of site in 1723, Dale's next remarks are interesting: he wrote that 'altho your garden is but in its infancy att present, I entertain great hopes of seeing it Shortly much superior to its neighbours Under the direction of One of your learning and affection for science'. Dale concluded with 'hearty wishes that Botany may flourish both in your College and country'.[17]

---

17 Natural History Museum, London, Manuscript minute book of the 'Botanical Society of London, 1724–26'. On this see P.I. Edwards, 'The Botanical Society (of London), 1721–1726', *Proceedings of the Botanical Society of the British Isles*, 5 (1963), 117–18; and Nelson, 'The influence of Leiden', 140.

10.4 William Stephens, portrait in oils, artist unknown. By permission of the Trustees of the Edward Worth Library, Dublin. © Edward Worth Library.

Catalogus Plantarum in Horto Dubliniensi

Classis Prima

Belladona majoribus folijs et floribus I: R: H: 17.
Solanum Melanocerasos C: B: P: 166.

1 Lilium convallium album C: B: P: 304. Lilium convallium vulgo I: B: 3.531. Lilium Convallium Dod. 205.

2 Polygonatum latifolium vulgare C: B: P: 303. Polygonatum vulgo Sigillum Solomonis I: B: 3.529.

3 Ruscus Myrtifolius aculeatus I: R: H: 79. Ruscus I: B: 1.579. Ruscum Dod: 744.

2 Gentiana alpina magno flore I: B: 3.523. Gentianella alpina latifolia et angustifolia flore magno C: B: P: 187.

6 Convolvulus maritimus nostras rotundifolius Mor: Hist: Oxon: 2.11. Soldanella maritima minor C: B: P: 295. Brassica marina sive Soldanella I: B: 2.166.

— Convolvulus major I: B: 2.154. Convolvulus major albus C: B: P: 294

— Convolvulus minor vulgaris Park: 171. Convolvulus minor arvensis C: B: P: 294. Helxine Cissampelos multis seu Convolvulus minor I: B: 2.157.

— Hujus Varietates habemus flore albo et flore albo cum purpureo umbilico C: B: P: 294. 5.

— Convolvulus angustissimo folio nostras cum Auriculis Pluck: Alm: 116 Tab: 24. Fig. 3.

— Convolvulus Indicus flore violaceo H: Eyst: Convolvulus purpureus folio subrotundo Campanula Indica I: B: 2.165.   215.

— Convolvulus Indicus flore albo H: R: Par:

— Convolvulus Indicus flore albo purpurascente semine albo.

— Convolvulus Indicus flore tenui longo pulcherrime rubro

— Convolvulus Siculus annuus coeruleus minimis capsula floris binis foliolis cincta M: H: 2.46.

10.5 The first page of William Stephens's 'Catalogus Plantarum in Horto Dublinensis'.
Image courtesy Natural History Museum, London.

The catalogue was tabled at the Society's meeting on 22 October 1726, and at the meeting on 3 December the Botanical Society's secretary was ordered to write to Stephens:

> … with great pleasure I Obey the orders of the society in sending you a parcel of seeds which they find wanting in your garden. There are some mention'd in your catalogue which are not in our garden here, & others which by the names seem to be new. I trouble you with a catalogue Of them, & you will oblige the society in sending seeds of them, that they may be rais'd under our own view.

The letter continued, expressing hope that further lots of seeds could be sent before the following spring, and that 'the news of your good success in the teaching of our Science Of the improvement of the garden, will be always very acceptable to the Society'.[18]

As a record of plants deliberately cultivated in Ireland at this period Stephens's inventory is unique.[19] No other garden was catalogued in such detail before 1800 when the earliest of the lists of the plants in the Dublin Society's Botanic Gardens (now the National Botanic Gardens) at Glasnevin was published.[20] Stephens's catalogue is remarkably detailed, listing over 500 taxa; many entries comprise multiple polynomial synonyms of each plant. The sources quoted by Stephens include many of the authoritative works of the period, the most frequently cited being Rembert Dodoens's *Stirpium historiae pemptades* (Antwerp, 1583), Johann Bauhin's *Historia plantarum universalis* (Yverdon, 1650–1), Caspar Bauhin's *Pinax theatri botanici* (Basle, 1671), Robert Morison's *Plantarum historiæ universalis Oxoniensis* (Oxford, 1715) and John Ray's *Historia plantarum* (London, 1686, 1688, 1704) and, for species found in the wild in Ireland and Britain, Christopher Merrett's *Pinax rerum naturalium Britannicarum* (London, 1667) or the third edition of Ray's *Synopsis stirpium Britannicarum* (London, 1724) that had been edited by Johann Jacob Dillenius (1684–1747), professor of botany at Oxford with whom Stephens had contact. Some polynomials that appear in Stephens's listing were probably unpublished, simply labels used by the gardens from which presumably Stephens had obtained the particular plants. The profusion of synonyms in the catalogue allows 'identification' but as there are no extant herbarium specimens from the Trinity College Physic Garden the equation of the antique polynomials with modern scientific names always entails an amount of guesswork and lingering uncertainty.

It is obvious from the inventory that in 1726 the Physic Garden was thriving and, although small by comparison with such gardens as the University of Leiden's garden

---

18 Natural History Museum, London, Manuscript minute book of the 'Botanical Society of London, 1724–26'.   19 Natural History Museum, London, MSS BANKS COLL STE: The catalogue is titled 'Catalogus Plantarum in Horto Dublinensis', and on the fly leaf is an annotation reading, in part, 'This catalogue of the plants growing in the Public Garden at Dublin was sent by Dr. William Stephens …'. Although not a fully 'public garden', as we would understand that term, the manuscript is certainly a catalogue of the Physic Garden of Trinity College.

in Holland, had a fine collection of plants. It is difficult to summarize the 'Catalogus Plantarum in Horto Dublinensis' but as well as cultivars (cultivated varieties) of such garden flowers as *Narcissus*, *Primula* and *Tulipa* (daffodils, primroses, tulips), numerous common medicinal plants were cultivated including *Digitalis purpurea* (foxglove), *Papaver somniferum* (opium poppy), *Carum carvi* (caraway), both white- and blue-flowered *Borago officinalis* (borage), *Cuminum cyminum* (cumin), *Cannabis sativa* (hemp), *Hyoscyamus niger* (henbane), *Hyssopus officinalis* (hyssop) and *Paeonia* cf. *officinalis* (peony). There were numerous plants which today we would call culinary herbs – in Stephens's day many also doubled as medicinal herbs: *Petroselinum crispum* (parsley), both plain and variegated *Salvia officinalis* (sage), *Salvia rosmarinus* (rosemary) and the gold-variegated variety, *Thymus vulgaris* (thyme), *Origanum majorana* and *O. vulgare* (marjoram, oregano, respectively) and several Mentha species (mints). Given the confined and relatively small space occupied by the Physic Garden, it is not surprising that there were no trees named in the catalogue, not even the native *Arbutus unedo* (strawberry tree), nor any large shrubs. As well as flowering plants, thirteen ferns and fern allies were listed, among which were *Osmunda regalis* (royal fern), *Ceterach officinarum* (rustyback) – its modern name signifying its former use as a medicinal plant – *Asplenium scolopendrium* (hart's-tongue) which is the commonest fern in Dublin city today, *Ophioglossum vulgatum* (adder's-tongue) and four different *Equisetum* (horsetails) probably representing three modern species.[21]

The plants catalogued by Stephens included annuals such as *Senecio vulgaris* (groundsel) and *Urtica urens* (small nettle). There were three different plants labelled 'Dens leonis', one being *Taraxacum* (dandelion) and the others probably *Hieracium* (hawkweed). We categorize those plants as weeds and ruthlessly eradicate them when they spring up in our gardens but this was a teaching garden where there were no weeds. Stephens also noted *Aegopodium podagraria* (ground elder), the earliest record of this ineradicable invader in an Irish garden. His contemporary Philip Miller (1691–1771), 'gardener to the botanick garden at Chelsea', advised that this was 'fitter for a Botanick or Physick Garden, than for Gardens of Pleasure' because it 'is an abiding Plant, which multiplies very fast by its Root, which is very apt to spread far underground; for which reason it should never be planted in a good Garden'.[22] It was first recorded occurring outside gardens as a 'wild plant' by J.T. Mackay in his catalogue published in 1825: 'Plentiful in Mr. Gregory's demesne, Phoenix Park', he reported with the comment, 'Often a troublesome weed in Gardens'.[23]

At this period, Trinity College had other garden plots on its campus including a vegetable garden to supply the kitchen for the sustenance of fellows and scholars. Yet, as befits an educational garden, you could have gathered a healthy meal in the Physic

---

20 E.C. Nelson, 'A select annotated bibliography of the National Botanic Gardens, Glasnevin, Dublin', *Glasra*, 5 (1981), 1–20 at 6–9, 10, 13–14; E.C. Nelson and E.M. McCracken, *The brightest jewel: a history of the National Botanic Gardens, Glasnevin, Dublin* (Kilkenny, 1987), p. 53.   **21** E.C. Nelson, 'Ferns in Ireland, wild and cultivated, through the ages' in J.M. Ide, A.C. Jermy and A.M. Paul (eds), *Fern horticulture: past, present and future perspectives* (Andover, 1992), pp 57–86.   **22** Philip Miller, *The gardeners dictionary* (London, 1733), Sig. I1r.

10.6 *Aloe variegata* (now *Gonialoe variegata*), one of Stephens's acquisitions from Holland, as illustrated in Jan and Maria Moninckx's *Altas*, *c*.1699–*c*.1706. © Allard Pierson, University of Amsterdam, hs. VI G 6.

Garden too, in season. Garden peas, leeks, various onions, lettuce and at least one kind of cabbage were cultivated, according to Stephens's manuscript, as well as 'Papas americanum' (*Solanum tuberosum*, potato) of which another of Stephens's contemporaries, Caleb Threlkeld (1676–1728), remarked:

> This agreeable Root (for it agrees to Fish, to Flesh, to other Herbs, as in *Cole-canon*, and that either Roasted, Boiled, Parched, Smothered or Fryed by it self, or with other Meat) is highly prized by us for its great usefulness in Food, without which innumerable poor must starve, the greatest Parts of our Lands being pasturage.[24]

The most noteworthy plants among those catalogued were species which are not frost-hardy and could only have survived a 'normal' Irish winter protected from frost. There is almost no other evidence that the Physic Garden contained a hothouse or even an unheated greenhouse, yet there must have some provision for the safe-keeping of plants from subtropical regions such as the Cape of Good Hope. Even with a hothouse, growing melons successfully requires great skill, and there were at least six members of the squash family in Stephens's list.[25] As well as *Cucumis sativus* (cucumber) and *Ecballium elaterium* (squirting cucumber) which is a native of the Mediterranean region and poisonous, there were three different varieties of *Cucumis melo* (melon), *Lagenaria siceraria* (bottle gourd or calabash) and *Cucurbita* cf. *pepo* (pumpkin). Another extraordinary inhabitant was *Solanum aethiopicum* (bitter tomato, Ethiopian eggplant) – the ripe fruit, looking like a segmented tomato, is edible but this plant is not grown much outside Africa now.

There is one document that may confirm the use of hot-beds in frames in the Physic Garden before Christmas 1724. An invoice dated 26 June 1725 reads: 'To 16 cartloads of Tanners barke w[ch] I forgot to charge along with y[e] carrage y[e] last Christm[s] ... this is over & above y[e] 4 loads w[ch] was then bestowed upon Dr Stephans'.[26] The only possible use for such a large quantity of tanner's bark is in creating hot-beds for the cultivation of such tropical and subtropical plants as *Ananas comosus* (pineapple) (Stephens did not include that novelty in his catalogue) or melons, so using tanner's bark to provide a heated, or at least frost-free, environment under glass for tender plants is certainly likely. The ideal place for such frames and hot-beds would have been against the south-facing wall of the Anatomy House but we lack evidence for this and none of the maps of the campus showing the Anatomy House and adjoining garden has any indication of such structures.

Reinforcing the notion that there had to be at least glass-covered frames that could be 'heated' – or kept frost-free – is the cluster of plants from southern Africa

---

23 J.T. Mackay, *A catalogue of the plants found in Ireland* (Dublin, 1825), p. 30; P.A. Reilly et al., *Wild plants of the Phoenix Park* (Dublin, 1993), pp 11, 39 [in error as 'Mackay 1806']. 24 Caleb Threlkeld, *Synopsis stirpium Hibernicarum* (Dublin, 1726), Sig. K3v. 25 On a history of melons in cultivation in Ireland, see E.C. Nelson, 'Of melon pits and melon feasts', *The Irish Garden*, 26:2 (2017), 56–9. 26 TCD, MS Bursar's vouchers, P4/29/29, quoted in Nelson, 'The influence of Leiden', 145, fn. 52.

The Physic Garden at Trinity College Dublin

that undoubtedly came to Dublin from Holland and most probably from Leiden. Its hortus medicus had one of the richest collections of exotic plants at the time, including countless frost-tender species brought from the Dutch colony at the Cape of Good Hope. Some of the African plants in the Physic Garden are quite familiar to present-day gardeners but they would have been great novelties in the 1720s. Lady Rawdon, in her letter already quoted, had exclaimed about seeing '20 sorts of Alos from Holland' – Stephens accounted for ten different 'Aloe Africana' and a single 'Aloe Americana', probably *Furcraea foetida* from the Caribbean and tropical South America.[27] The African aloes included *Aloe glauca* (blue aloe) and *A. variegata* (partridge-breast aloe) (Fig. 10.6), nowadays often grown as house-plants. The scientific names (polynomials) that Stephens used link the Dublin plants to watercolours painted in Amsterdam by the renowned Dutch botanical artists Jan Moninckx (*fl.* 1670–1714) and Maria Moninckx (1673–1757) which were used as the basis for engravings published in books by the merchant and botanist Jan Commelin (1629–92) and his nephew Caspar Commelin (1668–1731), a physician and accomplished botanist.[28] Another African succulent *Cotyledon orbiculata* will survive outside in the most favoured Irish gardens (for example, gardens situated on Howth Head), but it is rather unlikely that the Physic Garden's staff would have known this. Moreover, they probably did not try these plants outdoors – the specimens would have been too precious, and immensely time-consuming to replace. The collection also contained cacti including *Opuntia folio oblongo, media* or the 'Cochineal Fig-tree' (probably *Opuntia ficus-indica*), the plant commonly cultivated as a 'source' of cochineal.

Among the sixteen plants listed under 'Geranium' were three *Pelargonium* species (then named 'Geranium Africanum') with polynomials tagged 'H:L:Bat.' – the initials stand for 'Hortus Lugdunum Batavorum', the Latin name for Leiden's hortus medicus. These surely enthralled not just with their colourful blooms but also their scented foliage. Judging by their polynomials, these were *Pelargonium zonale, P. capitatum* and *P. alchemillioides.* Leiden was also the source of the glaucous-foliaged *Melianthus major* (honeyflower), another native of southern Africa. Cultivated out-of-doors nowaday, the honeyflower is much more likely to have been kept in a pot and kept in moveable cold-frames over winter but trundled out into the garden with the other exotica in the summer.

Having sent the manuscript copy of his catalogue to the Botanical Society in London, Stephens initiated an exchange between the Trinity College Physic Garden and, as the Botanical Society had no permanent premises, the Society of Apothecaries' Physic Garden at Chelsea. In exchange for the catalogue, the society sent about 180 packets of seeds to Dublin, and the list of these indicates that among

27 Huntingdon Library, San Marino, California, MS HA 15638, fo. 1a. See also Nelson, 'The influence of Leiden', 139.　28 D.O. Wijnands, *The botany of the Commelins. A taxonomical, nomenclatural and historical account of the plants depicted in the Moninckx atlas and in the four books by Jan and Casper Commelin on the plants in the Hortus Medicus Amstelodamensis 1682–1710* (Rotterdam, 1983), passim.

seedlings which could have been raised were *Cercis canadensis* (redbud) and *Gleditsia triacanthos* (honey locust) both from North America, at least half a dozen more *Pelargonium* species, *Ranunculus muricatus* from Crete and even *Brassica oleracea* (red cabbage). The lengthy Latin polynomials used confirm that the seeds came from the Chelsea Physic Garden.

While medicinal value or botanical curiosity may have been the principal characteristics of the TCD Physick Garden's collection in 1726, as already noted, Stephens did not ignore the 'ordinary', the plants that were familiar and popular garden plants in Ireland at that time. He noted 'Tuliparum varietates plurimae' (many varieties of tulip) and made similar remarks about many varieties of primroses and auriculas. There were double-flowered and variegated clones of *Vinca minor* (periwinkle), and the double-flowered variants of *Caltha palustris* (marsh marigold), *Anemone hepatica* (liverwort) and *Saponaria officinalis* (soapwort) – remarkably most of the plants of soapwort now occurring in the wild in Ireland are this variant. It was a garden of curiosities, not just for young trainee physicians but for anyone fond of gardening so it is understandable the Physic Garden was occasionally opened to the public.

William Stephens's last known contact with the London Botanical Society was a letter penned on 6 February 1727.[29] The society that only ever comprised around two dozen young men folded around this time and no more was heard of it. That day, perhaps Professor Stephens had gone indoors to shelter from 'a little rain' and took up his pen and wrote to Thomas Dale thanking him for the dozens of packets of seeds, safely received.

Henry Nicholson explicitly stated that he engaged local people to gather native plants for the Physic Garden. William Stephens probably did the same. However, there is no way to tell from the catalogue what plants were of wild, local origin; provenances are not provided by Stephens. We can safely assert that 'Tithymalus Hibernicus' (*Euphorbia hyberna*, Irish spurge) came from western Ireland. It is also highly likely that such species as *Drosera rotundifolia* (round-leaved sundew) and the native orchid *Neottia ovata* (common twayblade) were collected for Stephens in the wild. The sundew would have required damp sphagnum peat to thrive in the Physic Garden. The inclusion of common twayblade, the only orchid among the plants being cultivated, is intriguing – eight decades later, in 1804, the twayblade was among sixteen hardy native orchids growing in the Glasnevin Botanic Gardens.[30]

The practice of teachers taking students on walks or excursions to see plants growing in the wild was uncommon at this period. Professors of botany, like Herman Boerhaave in Leiden, relied on the plants cultivated in their university physic gardens for practical demonstrations. It is unlikely that Henry Nicholson and William Stephens were any different. Thus, having native 'simples' in the Physic Garden was necessary to allow students to experience the plants that they might, literally, have only heard about. In his *Synopsis stirpium Hibernicarum*, published in October 1726,

---

29 Natural History Museum, London, Manuscript minute book of the 'Botanical Society of London, 1724–26'.　**30** E.C. Nelson and Brendan Sayers, *Orchids at Glasnevin* (Dublin, 2003), pp 2, 6, fn. 4.

The Physic Garden at Trinity College Dublin

Caleb Threlkeld recorded some of the calls of the herb-folk and the hawkers of Dublin.[31] We may picture him walking through the streets and narrow alleys, curious to see what the country-people had in their carts and barrows and delighted if occasionally he found a new herb being hawked by the herb-women. He tells us about sheaves of *Artemisia maritima* (sea wormwood) brought from the coasts of Meath and Louth for the Dublin ale-house keepers to 'make their *Purl*, great Consumption of which is made in Winter Mornings'. He discovered a Dublin herb-woman selling *Ajuga reptans* (bugle) in mistake for *Betonica officinalis* (wood betony), a plant that he had not seen growing wild in Ireland. Bud-laden stems of *Sinapis arvensis* (charlock) were sold by the women in Dublin 'by the Name of *Corn-cail*' and was 'used for boiled Sallet'. *Teucrium scorodonia* (wood sage) and *Anthyllis vulneraria* (kidney vetch) called 'stanch' were also among their wares.[32] Examples of each of these plants were cultivated in the Physic Garden.

The herb-folk were not always co-operative. *Osmunda regalis* (royal fern) came to Dublin in quantity for sale and Threlkeld saw 'fair Specimens of it among the Herb Folk in *John's-lane*' but they would not disclose the localities where they collected it. They feared that interlopers 'may nim their Profit, Monopolies being natural to self-ended Men'.[33] As noted, this was among the ferns in cultivation in the Physic Garden, but its original source is unknown.

Like his predecessor Henry Nicholson, William Stephens published a book that is related directly to the plants cultivated in the Physic Garden, and clearly demonstrates the influence of Herman Boerhaave on his students. Thanking John Martyn (1699–1768) of the London Botanical Society for a copy of his *Tabulae synopticae plantarum officinalium* (London, 1726), 'a work of that kind so extremely necessary that I don't see how students can readily come att a regular knowledge of plants without Some such memorandum', Stephens remarked that he had 'yearly dictated something of that kind to the lads under my care since I began to teach'.[34] He published these dictated notes under the title *Botanical elements: published for the use of the Botany School in the University of Dublin* (Dublin, 1727), making it clear that he did this to:

> avoid the trouble of dictating yearly so many pages to the students of Botany, it being impossible to expect, that they should acquire a distinct and permanent knowledge of the method of botany, by a bare attendance upon one lecture without something farther to assist their memories.[35]

Botanical elements (Fig. 10.7) was based on *Institutiones rei herbariae* (Paris, 1700) by the French botanist Joseph Pitton de Tournefort (1656–1708), but it is not just a

31 E.C. Nelson, 'Introduction' in Caleb Threlkeld, *The first Irish flora. Synopsis stirpium Hibernicarum*, ed. E.C. Nelson (facsimile with annotations by E.C. Nelson and D.M. Synnott) (Kilkenny, 1988), p. xiv, passim. See also chapters in this collection. 32 Threlkeld, *Synopsis*, Sigs. A1v (sea wormwood); B7r–v (bugle); I3v (charlock); I7r (wood sage); A5v (kidney vetch). 33 Ibid., Sig. D5v (royal fern). 34 Natural History Museum, London, Manuscript minute book of the 'Botanical Society of London, 1724–26', p. 12. 35 William Stephens, *Botanical elements* (Dublin, 1727), Sig. A3r.

BOTANICAL

ELEMENTS:

Publiſhed for the USE of the

BOTANY SCHOOL

IN THE

Univerſity of *DUBLIN*.

Propterea quia quæ de terris nunc quoque abundant
Herbarum genera, ac Fruges arbuſtaque lata,
Non tamen inter ſe poſſint complexa creari:
Res ſic quaque ſuo ritu procedit, et omnes
Fœdere naturæ, certò diſcrimina ſervant.

Lucret. lib. 5.

DUBLIN:

Printed by S. POWELL, for G. RISK, G. EWING,
and W. SMITH, Bookſellers, in *Dame's-ſtreet,*
M DCC XXVII.

(11)

Plants the *Piſtill* is not of this Form, but a round Head, as in thoſe Plants whoſe Seeds are naked, ſuch are *Ranunculus, Strawberry,* &c. But the oblong Form being moſt general, the Name of *Piſtill* is univerſally retained : And it is eſteemed the Female Part of the Plant.

§ 22.

From the Bottom of the *Piſtill* between that and the *Flowerſtem,* or from the inſide Bottom of the Flower-leaves, ariſe ſeveral ſmall Threads ſtanding erect, and terminated in a Button compoſed of two Lobes encloſed in one common Membrane. Theſe ſurround the *Piſtill* and are called the *Chives;* before the Flower-leaves open theſe are longer than the *Piſtill,* afterwards the *Piſtill* outgrows them, the Buttons of the *Chives* are found covered with a Duſt of a particular Colour, which at certain Seaſons is ſhed into the Mouth of the *Piſtill,* and is ſuppoſed to impregnate the Eggs, which lie at the Bottom of the *Piſtill :* The *Chives* are reckoned the Male Parts of Plants.

§ 23.

That Part of the Flower which ſurrounds the *Chives* and the *Piſtill,* is the moſt obvious and glaring Part of the whole Flower ; it is called the Flower-leaf, and is more univerſally changed both in its Form and Colour, than any other Part of Plants ; the Variety of Shades and Lights that appear in this part in many Plants, make them perhaps ſome of the moſt beautiful Productions of Nature ; and ſo much and univerſally admired, that it is almoſt incredible what Pains and Ex-

C 2   pence

10.7 William Stephens, *Botanical elements* (Dublin, 1727), title page and p. 11. By permission of the Trustees of the Edward Worth Library, Dublin. © Edward Worth Library.

simple recitation of Tournefort's ideas. Stephens so constructed the book that by using the 'tables' a student could take any unknown plant and assign it to its 'proper class and range it among its congeners'. He left blank pages so that the owner could insert 'families not here mentioned … in their proper places'. In the text, he explained the method of classification used, and detailed the contemporary understanding of the functions of various plant organs. Most significantly, Stephens acknowledged that plants had male and female sexual organs; of the stamens, he stated that the 'dust [pollen] of a particular colour which at certain seasons they shed is supposed to impregnate the eggs which lie at the bottom of the pistill'.[36] At that time few botanists would have been so confident about this; the influence of Stephens's years at Leiden being taught by Boerhaave is evident!

36 Ibid., Sig. A4v and p. 11.

10.8 *Euphorbia hyberna*, Irish spurge: hand-coloured engraving by Johann Jacob Dillenius, *Hortus Elthamensis* (London, 1732), ii, tab. CCXC. It shows a stem from a plant supplied to James Sherard by William Stephens from the College Physic Garden. Sherardian Library, one of the Bodleian Libraries, University of Oxford, Sherard 644, Pl. CCXC.

Stephens concluded *Botanical elements* with a classification of the plant kingdom, the characteristics of each 'tribe' and its constituents given in simple English statements, not in Latin as was more usual in botanical publications of the period. His manuscript catalogue was also arranged systematically according to the arrangement explained in *Botanical elements*.

At least until he was appointed lecturer in chemistry on 17 February 1733, Stephens maintained his botanical interests and continued to curate the Physic Garden. Accounts for the second quarter of 1729 include the item: 'Dr Stevens for plants for the Physick garden £20', a huge sum.[37] That year he is known to have distributed 'roots' of *Euphorbia hyberna* (Irish spurge) to the wealthy apothecary James Sherard (1666–1738) who had a garden at Eltham in Kent. *Hortus Elthamensis* (Oxford, 1732), written and illustrated by Professor Dillenius, included an engraving of *E. hyberna*, acknowledged to have come from William Stephens (Fig. 10.8).[38] In October 1730, when John Mulloy was travelling through London to Leiden, Stephens had Mulloy deliver some more rootstocks of the Irish spurge to Philip Miller at Chelsea.[39]

In his letter of May 1724 to James Jurin, William Stephens expressed the hope that he could:

> turn the Garden when finished, to the advancement of natural knowledge … ; I am but too Sensible, that a bare recital of names, the too common subject of Botany, cannot tend much to the improvement of Philosophy, but a set of experiments, accurately made upon the properties of vegetables, and especially the officinals, is what I would hope, may be of service to our Profession.[40]

No document is known recording any such experiments, yet Stephens's handwritten catalogue, albeit 'a bare recital of names' but one that yields to analysis, with his *Botanical elements*, show that the small enclosed physic garden on the campus of Trinity College Dublin was part of the network of botanists and gardens centred on the University of Leiden which 'had [the most] sustained and continuous record of service to botany'.[41]

---

37 TCD, MUN/V/57/2: Bursar's quarterly accounts. By one measure the purchasing power of £20 in 1729 is the equivalent of around £2,770 or €3,100 in 2021. **38** J.J. Dillenius, *Hortus Elthamensis seu plantarum rariorum quas in horto suo Elthami in Cantio coluit vir ornatissimus et praestantissimus Jacobus Sherard* (London, 1732), ii, pp 387–8, tab. CCXC. **39** Mulloy was one of Stephens' students: according to G.D. Burtchaell and T.U. Sadleir (eds), *Alumni Dublinenses* (London, 1924), p. 604, John Mulloy (Molloy), aged 16, matriculated on 17 July 1722; Scholar 1726; B.A. 1727; B.Physic 1729. He matriculated in the faculty of medicine at Leiden, aged 24, on 25 November 1730: W.N. Du Rieu (ed.), *Album studiosorum academiae Lugduno Batavae MDLXXV–MDCCCLXXV* (The Hague, 1875), p. 931. Royal Society, MS EL.S2.45: William Stephens to Philip Miller, 28 October 1730. **40** Royal Society, London, MS EL.S2.43: William Stephens to James Jurin, 14 May 1724. **41** W.T. Stearn, 'The influence of Leiden on botany in the seventeenth and eighteenth centuries', *Leidse Voordrachten*, 37 (1961), 7–42; E.C. Nelson, 'Botany and medicine; Dublin and Leiden', *Journal of the Irish Colleges of Physicians and Surgeons*, 22 (1993), 133–6.

CHAPTER ELEVEN

Gardening at Mitchelstown: John K'Eogh's
Botanalogia universalis Hibernica (Cork, 1735)

E. CHARLES NELSON

Βοτάνη, FODDER, GRASS, HERBS: -λογία, knowledge: hence botanology is the knowledge of plants or, as one mid-seventeenth-century author wrote, it was talk about the virtue of herbs in the same sense that astrology was about the influence of the stars.[1] Botanology has dropped out of use: botany is the name of the science of plants. When the title page of John K'Eogh's book, subtitled *'A general Irish HERBAL'*, was typeset by the printer and publisher George Harrison (*d.* 1754) of Meetinghouse Lane, Cork, in 1735, an 'a' was mistakenly used to link the two Greek elements – *BOTANALOGIA* was a glaring typesetter's error and was not corrected (Fig.11.1), though elsewhere inside, as in the running heads and preface, botanology was correctly spelled.[2] Judging by the make-up of *Botanalogia universalis Hibernica* (hereafter simply referred to as *Botanalogia*), the main text and indexes were printed first, followed by the 'front end' – dedications, preface and list of subscribers as well as the title page. This was not unusual and, of course, allowed the listing of the 369 people who had subscribed for copies. Thus, K'Eogh was able to give an apology at the end of the subscribers' list, although the four-line paragraph was also replete with typographic errors.[3]

John K'Eogh (*c.*1681–1754) was the second son of a renowned scholarly cleric also called John K'Eogh (*c.*1650–*c.*1725), who fathered twenty-one children of whom only six survived into adulthood. The younger John was born in Strokestown, Co. Roscommon, and educated by his father – 'I never had any other Master, until I went

---

1 *OED* notes that the first time the term 'botanology' appeared in print was in Philip King's *Surfeit to ABC* (London, 1656), p. 33, where he noted that 'Some talk of the virtue of herbs, others of the influence & effect of stars, Botanology and Astrology'. 2 C.E. Sayle, *A catalogue of the Bradshaw collection of Irish books in the University Library Cambridge*, 3 vols (Cambridge, 1916), ii, pp 830–1, listed eight works printed by Harrison, of which K'Eogh's was the second. Harrison also published the weekly newspaper *The Medley* from 1738. 3 John K'Eogh, *Botanalogia universalis Hibernica, or, a general Irish herbal calculated for this kingdom, giving an account of the herbs, shrubs, and trees, naturally produced therein, in English, Irish, and Latin; with a true description of them, and their medicinal virtues and qualities. To which are added, two short treatises one concerning the Chalybeat, waters, Shewing their origin, situation, medicinal virtues, &c. Another of the prophylactic, or hygiastic part of medicine, Shewing how health may be preserved, and distempers which human bodies are subject to, prevented* (Corke, 1735), Sig. C3v: 'In the Preface, Page the 6th, after Charity, there are ommitted these three Words viz, (Humilty, the, two) By reason of the Author's distance from the Press, there are some other Errors committed by the Printer which I hope the

231

BOTANALOGIA
UNIVERSALIS
Hibernica,
Or, A General IRISH
HERBAL
Calculated for this KINGDOM,
GIVING AN
ACCOUNT
Of the *Herbs Shrubs*, and *Trees*, Naturally Produced therein,
in *English*, *Irish*, and *Latin*; with a true Description of
them, and their *Medicinal* Virtues and Qualities.

To which are added, Two Short
TREATISES.
One Concerning the *Chalybeat, Waters*, Shewing their *Origin*,
Situation, *Medicinal Virtues*, &c.
Another of the *Prophylactic*, Or, *Hygiastic* Part of *Medicine*,
Shewing how *Health* may be preserved, and *Distempers*
which human Bodies are subject to, prevented.

Authore Joh, K'Eogh, A. B. Chaplain to the Rt. Hon. the
Lord KINGSTON.

*He causeth the Grass to grow for the Cattle, and the Herb for
the Service of* Man. Psal. 104. 14. V.

CORKE, Printed and sold by GEORGE HARRISON
at the Corner of Meeting house Lane, 1735.

11.1 John K'Eogh, *Botanalogia universalis Hibernica* (Cork, 1735), title page. By permission
of the Governors and Guardians of Marsh's Library. © Marsh's Library.

Gardening at Mitchelstown 233

to the College' – in the school that he had established at Strokestown.[4] Aged 24, John K'Eogh matriculated in Trinity College Dublin, on 20 July 1705, the same day as his younger brother Michael, and obtained his bachelor of arts degree six years later.[5] In the preface to *Botanalogia,* he wrote:

> Perhaps you might be so curious to ask the Question, how I should arrive at such knowledge in Medicine, it not being my Province … but in answer to this, I tell, you, that I Studyed the Science of Physick for above ten years before I was Ordained, and had thought of Commencing Dr, but I changed my mind.[6]

He could have studied medicine at Trinity College Dublin, but there is no record of his doing so. There is, however, a gap of twelve years between his graduation and his next known appearance in public records. In 1723, John K'Eogh married Ann, daughter of Dr Henry Jennings, and they had three sons (only one of whom, Michael, was still living in 1748) and three daughters.[7] Following his father's and older brother's vocations, he was ordained in the Church of Ireland becoming chaplain to James King, 4th Baron Kingston (1693–1761), and also obtaining the living of the parish of Mitchelstown in Co. Cork. John K'Eogh died in 1754, aged 73.[8]

Botanalogia was one of three 'curious' works written by K'Eogh. In 1739, he himself published *Zoologica medica Hibernica* and, in 1748, *A vindication of the antiquities of Ireland and a defense thereof against all calumnies and aspersions cast on it by foreigners;* both were printed by Samuel Powell (*fl.* 1731–75), of Crane Lane, Dublin, and had Dublin imprints.[9] Like *Botanalogia,* these books had lengthy lists of subscribers whose payments presumably covered the costs of printing.[10]

Reader will excuse'.   **4** John K'Eogh, *A vindication of the antiquities of Ireland … To which is added … An appendix, giving a brief account of the original descent of the principal Milesian families in Ireland* (Dublin, 1748), pp 144 and 146.   **5** G.D. Burtchaell and T.U. Sadleir (eds), *Alumni Dublinenses* (London, 1924), p. 463. Michael graduated in 1710.   **6** J. K'Eogh, *Botanalogia*, Sig. B2v.   **7** According to 'Irish diocesan and prerogative marriage licence bonds indexes 1623–1866, diocese of Cashel and Emly', Public Record Office of Ireland, p. [253], Ann (not Elizabeth) Jennings and John K'Eogh were married in 1723: www.findmypast.co.uk, accessed 7 July 2019. The reference to Michael K'Eogh may be found in K'Eogh, *A vindication*, p. 148.   **8** Helen Andrews, 'John K'Eogh (*c.*1681–1754), clergyman and naturalist' in 'John K'Eogh (*c.*1650–*c.*1725), clergyman and scholar', *DIB*; J.G. O'Hara, 'John Keogh (1680/81–1754), Church of Ireland clergyman and author of scientific and medical tracts' in 'John Keogh (*c.*1650–1725)', *ODNB*.   **9** John K'Eogh, *Zoologia medicinalis Hibernica: or, a treatise of birds, beasts, fishes, reptiles, or insects, which are commonly known and propagated in the kingdom: giving an account of their medicinal virtues, and their names in English, Irish, and Latin. To which is added, a short treatise of the diagnostic and prognostic parts of medicine …* (Dublin, 1739): 'And to be had at JAMES KELBURN'S, Bookseller, at the *Three Golden Balls* in *George's-lane*'. *Zoologia* contains numerous bizarre receipts for cures variously effected by animals and their internal organs, and a small amount of information concerning plants; for example (p. 64), 'Garments are defended from them [moths] by lavender, flowers, rosemary, mints, wormwood, stoechas, and water germander, also by oil of spike'. Powell, Samuel I (*fl.* 1731–75), printer in Dublin, in Mary Pollard, *A dictionary of members of the Dublin book trade, 1550–1800* (London, 2000), pp 467–9. On *Zoologia*, see also E.C. Nelson, 'John K'Eogh's *Zoologia medicinalis Hibernica* (1739) and the duplicitous "Bernard Mandeville" re-issue (1744)', *Archives of Natural History*, 48 (2021), 402–5.   **10** 283 individuals were named in *Zoologia* and 373 were named in *A vindication*.

Intended to provide 'true Description[s]' of the herbs, shrubs and trees 'naturally produced' in Ireland, *Botanalogia* was certainly not a scientific flora providing information about Ireland's native plants and where they grew, nor was it simply a herbal of the 'usual medical type'.[11] It also was a garden catalogue and cultivated plants dominate the inventory. As K'Eogh commented:

> *When I was writing on this Subject, I had the Advantage daily of Viewing the Gardens belonging to the Right Honourable James Lord Baron of KINGSTON; wherein were Contained near two hundred different Species of Herbs and Trees. I was not acquainted with any Garden, which could shew so many, this was no small advantage, or Conveniency to forward this Undertaking.*[12]

In only forty-four of the 503 entries does K'Eogh indicate a locality where his subject can be found growing wild (Table 11.1, pp 246–8), whereas almost 140 of the plants are stated to be 'planted in gardens' or 'manured' or 'cultivated' or have some other indication that they were found in gardens. Thus, *Botanalogia* contains some nuggets of information about what a well-stocked Irish garden, at least one attached to a large house, contained in the 1730s. For the rest, there are no precise explanations about habitats or garden use for around 300 plants. On the other hand, it needs to be noted that K'Eogh's experience of Irish gardens was clearly rather limited because there certainly existed at that period several containing many more than a mere 'two hundred different … Herbs and Trees'. And, while the majority of his subjects are flowering plants and ferns, John K'Eogh included clubmoss and horsetails with a few mosses as well as a sparse miscellany of lichens ('Rock Liverwort', 'Ash colour'd ground Liverwort', 'Tree Lungwort', 'Cup-Moss'), fungi ('Jews-ear', 'Mushrome' and 'Spunk') and several marine organisms including algae ('Sea-girgle', 'Sea Moss or Coralline', 'Sea Wrack', 'Sea Thongs', 'Slauke' and 'Spunge'), none of which would have been cultivated.[13]

'It grows in the Lord Kingston's Garden in Mitchelstown' is an infrequent refrain in K'Eogh's book glossing only these plants: *Arbutus unedo*, 'Herb Aloe', 'Honey Tree', lemon, liquorice, myrtle, orange, saffron, scorzonera and tobacco. The less specific tag 'it grows in gardens' is much more common and together these comments allow us to reconstruct what was grown in the Mitchelstown demesne before 1735. The castle and garden that K'Eogh knew have long since vanished. The castle of his time was demolished in 1768 to make way for a Georgian mansion, which in turn was knocked down in 1823 and replaced by a Tudor-style house that was completely destroyed by fire in 1922. As for the garden, it was re-modelled in the late eighteenth and early nineteenth centuries, and finally dismantled and parcelled out in the 1920s and 1930s after the Civil War and the formation of the Irish Free State.[14]

---

11 K'Eogh, *Botanalogia*, title page.   12 Ibid., Sig. B1v.   13 Plant entries in K'Eogh's *Botanalogia* are arranged alphabetically by the English name used by him.   14 D.V. Henning, 'The demesne at Mitchelstown, Co. Cork', *Irish Geography*, 1 (1947), 97–101.

11.2 The restored eighteenth-century orangery at Marino Point, Cork. © E. Charles Nelson.

John K'Eogh leaves no doubt that there was a well-maintained and productive garden at Mitchelstown Castle in the early 1730s. This included a glasshouse although the building would not have looked like a present-day all-glass greenhouse.[15] While K'Eogh did not state that the Michelstown Castle glasshouse contained orange trees, he implies as much:

> Orange Trees grow Plentifully in forreign Countries, but of late years they have been transplanted here, which now by the Industry, and cultivation of curious Gentlemen, are in some Gardens brought to perfection. I have seen about seventy, or eighty, taken off of one Tree, in the Right Honourable the Lord *Kingstons* Garden at *Mitchelstown*, as good as any I have seen brought hither from Spain, or the West Indies.[16]

Citrus × *aurantium* (orange) trees were appropriate inhabitants of such a greenhouse, which would better have been called an orangery because it surely was built of brick,

---

15 E.C. Nelson, 'Some records (*c*.1690–1830) of greenhouses in Irish gardens', *Moorea*, 2 (1983), 21–8.
16 K'Eogh, *Botanalogia*, p. 89.

11.3 '*Aloes Vulgaris sive Sempervivum marinum*' (*Aloe vera*), as illustrated in the second edition of John Gerard's *Herball* (London, 1633), p. 507. By permission of the Trustees of the Edward Worth Library, Dublin. © Edward Worth Library.

had a roof tiled with slates not glass, and was probably fronted by double-casement windows (Fig.11.2). The orange trees will have been grown in large tubs that could be trundled out in summer to stand in the open air.

Oranges were not the only citrus fruits which 'by a little care and industry' flourished at Mitchelstown – unsurprisingly there were lemons too: '*Lemon-trees* are preserved in this Country by several curious Gentlemen, in Green houses, from the Inclemency of the Air, there are some of them to be seen in the Gardens of *Mitchelstown*'. K'Eogh added, presumably from personal experience, that the leaves of *Citrus* × *limon* (lemon) have 'a very fragrant smell'.[17]

Working out what the plant was that K'Eogh listed as 'Herb Aloe or Sea Houseleek' that also grew in 'my Lord *Kingston's* Green house', was aided by the Latin polynomial that K'Eogh also used, '*Aloes Vulgaris sive Sempervivum marinum*'.[18]

17 Ibid., p. 70.   18 Ibid., p. 3.

11.4 *Crocus sativus*, saffron. © Dr Sally Francis.

This was copied straight from John Gerard's famous herbal (Fig. 11.3), originally published more than a century earlier, in which this aloe was described: 'Hearbe Aloe hath leaves … very broad, long, smooth, thick, bending backewards, notched in the edges, set with certain little blunt prickles'.[19] This is identified as *Aloe vera*, a species from south-western Asia and long in cultivation. It is very possible it was growing in Mitchelstown during the early 1730s.

Outdoors, the Mitchelstown garden was planted with a range of medicinal and culinary herbs and vegetables for the kitchen. K'Eogh informed his readers that 'Licorice' (*Glycyrrhiza glabra*) formed good roots 'as thick as a Mans finger, which is extraordinary pleasant to the tast'.[20] The locally-grown liquorice was much better than any that was imported, rather like imported lemons which, K'Eogh noted, were never fully ripe.

Crocus sativus (saffron) (Fig. 11.4) grew 'to perfection' in Lord Kingston's garden, while *Scorzonera hispanica* (scorzonera), also known as Spanish or black

19 John Gerard, *The herball or general historie of plantes … very much enlarged and amended by Thomas Johnson* (London, 1633), pp 507–8. 20 K'Eogh, *Botanalogia*, p. 70.

salsify or viper's grass, grew to 'great perfection'. The root of scorzonera was used as a vegetable and in medieval times the plant was believed to be a cure for snakebite although K'Eogh makes no mention of this. The red styles would have been harvested from the saffron crocus flowers and then dried for later use in the kitchen and medicinally. Another plant 'particularly' grown in the Mitchelstown demesne was *Nicotiana tabacum* (tobacco), but K'Eogh makes no comments on its uses apart from his usual catalogue of medicinal ones: 'it prevents *Quinsies, Catarrhs, Megrims, Apoplexys*, and *Epidemical distempers* which proceed from the Malignity of the Air. Being externally applyed it cures *Itch, Scabs, Tetters*, and several other cuticular Eruptions'. The seeds of *Smyrnium olusatrum* (alexanders) which 'grows upon Rocks by the Sea side … [and] is commonly preserved in Gardens … mixt with Tobacco, and the fume received by pipe, into the mouth, eases tooth-ach', according to K'Eogh.[21]

Occasionally K'Eogh makes asides about other gardens that presumably he had visited, perhaps with Lord Kingston. *Myrtus communis* (myrtle), for example, was used for hedges at Lord Inchiquin's house at Rostellan on the eastern shore of Cork Harbour. Unconsciously illustrating the difference a relatively few miles can make in the climate of gardens, K'Eogh mentioned that myrtle was not grown outdoors but in the greenhouse at Mitchelstown. *Colutea arborescens* (bladder senna or bastard senna) flourished in Robert Fennel's garden near Mitchelstown – Fennel and William O'Brien, fourth earl of Inchiquin (1700–77), both subscribed for copies of K'Eogh's herbal.[22]

'Arbute', *Arbutus unedo*, the native Irish strawberry tree, was exported from Co. Kerry in quantity in the seventeenth and eighteenth centuries because there are numerous records of it flourishing in Irish gardens as far removed from Killarney as Glenarm in County Antrim.[23] John K'Eogh may have seen it in west Cork or Kerry if he travelled there. However, his description is derived from John Gerard's *The Herball*:

> This is a small tree, not much bigger than a Quince tree, the body thereof is covered with a reddish bark, which is rough and scaly, the Leaves are, broad, thick, and serrated, the flowers are white, small, & grow in clusters, after which cometh the fruit like Strawberries, green at first, but afterwards yellowish, and at last red when ripe.[24]

K'Eogh blundered by writing that *Arbutus* flowers in Spring – although there is a very small chance that the spring-blooming *Arbutus andrachne* from the eastern Mediterranean was grown at Mitchelstown, but it was not known in British gardens before the 1760s.

---

21 Ibid., p. 105 (saffron); p. 110 (scorzonera); p. 123 (tobacco); pp 3–4 (alexanders).   22 Ibid., p. 80 (myrtle); p. 112 (senna).   23 E.C. Nelson, *An Irish flower garden replanted* (Castlebourke, 1997), pp 11–13; E.C Nelson and W.F. Walsh, *Trees of Ireland, native and naturalized* (Dublin, 1993), plate 9.   24 K'Eogh, *Botanalogia*, p. 5; Gerard, *The herball*, pp 1495–6: Gerard said that the flowering time was July and August.

11.5 'Great Dragons ... Dracontium majus', called '*Geiredarrig*' in Irish, according to John K'Eogh, is a native of the Mediterranean region and only grows as a garden plant in Ireland. *Dracunculus vulgaris* (dragon arum) © E. Charles Nelson.

One strange entry is for 'Honey-tree' for which K'Eogh provided the Latin name *Melianthus* and presumably invented the Irish moniker '*Crann Mallugh*' (no-one else has ever used this name). His enigmatic description includes the information that it bore a yellow flower 'which when gone, is succeeded by a Lump of Congealed *Honey*'. Whatever this tree was, K'Eogh averred that it grew 'commonly in My Lord *Kingstons* Gardens in *Mitchelstown*, where it is brought to great Perfection, with very little Cultivation or Industry'.[25] A frequent difficulty with early-eighteenth-century lists of plants is that it is impossible to find the modern counterparts and to

25 K'Eogh, *Botanalogia*, p. 62. *Melianthus* is the name of a South African genus of shrubs and sub-shrubs, and *M. major* was cultivated in the Physick Garden of Trinity College Dublin in 1726. However, it does not have yellow flowers, nor is it a tree, so is most unlikely to have been the tree growing at Mitchelstown.

complicate matters further, in the case of K'Eogh's *Botanalogia*, he was sometimes confused by Latin names!

For the rest, we have to accept that the oft-repeated 'it grows in gardens' referred not only to Mitchelstown, but to Irish gardens in general. Among K'Eogh's more interesting comments are these. *Vitis vinifera* (grape), he noted, was planted in 'some gardens, but seldom [come] to any great perfection.' In his era, *Populus alba* (white poplar or abele) was 'planted about Mansion houses for Shelter, being of a quick growth'. *Castanea sativa* (Spanish chestnut or sweet chestnut) was 'frequently planted in Gardens, and Parks'. *Solanum tuberosum* (potato), K'Eogh observed, is a 'very nourishing healthy food, which appears by the strong [health], and robust Constitutions, of a vast number of the Natives who are almost intirely supported by' potatoes which hints that perhaps he did not much care to eat them himself.[26]

As today, borage, cabbages and peas, chervil, comfrey, dill, fennel, leeks and onions, parsley and sage were all cultivated outdoors, while basil, cucumbers and gourds are likely to have been in the greenhouse or orangery. Almond, apple, walnut and fig trees were also noted. Plants that now would be considered purely of ornamental value – but were formerly also used medicinally – included *Cupressus lusitanica* (cypress) favoured because it was evergreen, peonies of several kinds, hollyhock, jasmine, daffodils and lilies. K'Eogh noted white, red and damask roses. There were numerous other plants that he mentioned without saying that they were cultivated, but which can only have been known to him as garden plants, including 'Great Dragons … Dracontium majus' that was called '*Geiredarrig*' in Irish, he claimed. There is no description, and K'Eogh's remarks that the green leaves were 'applyed to Green Wounds' to heal them is taken from Gerard.[27] The plant is the dramatic, foetid *Dracunculus vulgaris* (Fig. 11.5), a native of the Mediterranean region known to have been grown in the Trinity College Physic Garden in 1726. Another species from Mediterranean habitats, also cultivated in the college Physic Garden, was *Ecballium elaterium* (squirting cucumber) – K'Eogh reported that the Irish name was '*Garenive*'. He noted it was grown in gardens and used to alleviate among other complaints earache and gout. According to *Botanalogia*, this bitter cucumber was found 'in several places … as in *Moycarnon* [Moycarn] in the County of Roscommon'.[28] No Irish botanical work has mentioned it since!

For reports like that of *Ecballium elaterium*, John K'Eogh has been dammed as unreliable, especially because his accounting of wild plants is sometimes suspect, not aided by the inaccurate typesetting which often makes his text, including the names of places and plants, incomprehensible. The relatively large number of dubious records in *Botanalogia* do give cause for concern: Henry Chichester Hart (1847–1908) warned that K'Eogh's records 'should never be quoted unconfirmed' and stated that

---

26 Ibid., p. 126 (vines); p. 1 (white poplar); p. 29 (chestnuts); p. 98 (potatoes). **27** Gerard, *Herball*, p. 833. **28** Ibid., pp 40–1 (great dragons); p. 36 (squirting cucumber). On squirting cucumber, see E.C. Nelson, *An Irishman's cuttings. Tales of Irish garden and gardeners, plants and plant hunters* (Cork, 2009), p. 11.

'study of [K'Eogh's] localities reveal great unreliability'.[29] John K'Eogh's reputation was first seriously dented by comments from Thomas Dix Hincks (1767–1857) in his 1840 essay 'On early contributions to the flora of Ireland; with remarks on Mr. Mackay's *Flora Hibernica*':

> The work of K'Eogh is scarcely deserving of notice ... His botanical knowledge ... may not have been such as to justify the insertion of plants merely on his authority, though it might direct attention to look for them.[30]

Considering the entries in *Botanalogia* that mention a locality within Ireland, whether a county, barony or townland (Table 11.1, pp 246–8), there are a number of obvious points. First, none of the records is for any of the eastern counties and, particularly, there is no mention of Dublin in *Botanalogia*. K'Eogh cannot have been interested in botany when he was studying at Trinity College, and if he did proceed to study medicine there, he apparently ignored plants despite the fact that for students of physic the study of botany was usually obligatory in the early eighteenth century. Second, the largest number of his localities (23) are from Co. Clare, especially from the Barony of Burren (18), an old subdivision of the county that lies within the area commonly called the Burren today.[31] Hincks assumed that the many Burren records meant K'Eogh was a native of County Clare. As Hincks pointed out in 1840, K'Eogh made mistakes because some of the plants certainly are not, and never could have been, denizens of that limestone land including 'Garden Endive ... Endiva, et Scariola' (? *Cichorium* sp. or *Lactuca* sp.), 'Goat's Rue ... Galega' (? *Galega* sp.), 'Ground Pine ... Chamæpity' (? *Ajuga chamaepitys*), 'Hedge Hyssop ... Gratiola' (? *Gratiola officinalis*), 'Palma Christi ... Cataputia major' (? *Ricinus communis*), 'Winter Savoury ... Satureia hortensis vulgaris' (? *Satuerja montana*) and 'Swallow-wort ... Asclepias, vincetoxicum' (? *Vincetoxicum hirundaria*). Yet, having excluded these, there remain around fifteen plants that are known from the area including *Filipendula vulgaris* (dropwort) – 'It grows in Gardens and wild in the *Barony* of *Burrin*, in the *County* of *Clare*' – and K'Eogh was reporting for the first time.[32] He may not have mistaken *Thalictrum flavum* (common meadowrue) or *T. minus* (lesser meadowrue), both of which occur in Co. Clare, but because he chose to use a confusing set of names, especially the Latin polynomial 'Ruta sylvestris sive Harmala', his record has been doubted – his description, if made in the field, suggests *T. flavum*.[33]

---

29 H.C. Hart, 'Remarks on the second edition of "Cybele Hibernica" with reference to the flora of Co. Donegal', *The Irish Naturalist*, 9 (1900), 27–44, at 37 and 39.   30 T.D. Hincks, 'On early contributions to the flora of Ireland; with remarks on Mr. Mackay's Flora Hibernica', *The Annals and Magazine of Natural History*, 6 (1840), 1–12, 126–35, at 8.   31 E.C. Nelson and W.F. Walsh, *The Burren; a companion to the wildflowers of an Irish limestone wilderness* (Aberystwyth and Kilkenny, 1991), pp 5–7; David Cabot and Roger Goodwillie, *The Burren* (London, 2018), pp 1–3.   32 K'Eogh, *Botanalogia*, pp 42–3 (garden endive); p. 53 (goat's rue); p. 56 (ground pine); p. 64 (hedge hyssop); p. 91 (palma Christi); p. 108 (winter savoury); p. 120 (swallowwort); p. 41 (dropwort). On dropwort, see Nelson, *An Irishman's cuttings*, p. 11. 33 Ibid., p. 105 (wild rue). Polynomials from the seventeenth century are often of uncertain application,

E. Charles Nelson

Among the noteworthy Burren plants that K'Eogh recorded was *Ceterach officinarum* (rusty-back fern). He described it succinctly and provided habitat information that is exemplary:

> Spleenwort, Ceterach, or Miltwast ... The Leaves are almost the length of a Mans Finger, and about half and Inch broad, of a greenish colour, on the upper side, and brownish beneath ... It grows in shaded and stony places and upon old stone Buildings, but particularly in great plenty in the *Barony* of *Burrin*.[34]

He knew *Crithmum maritimum* (rock samphire) grew on rocks 'by the Sea side very plentifully in the Isles of Aaron, and in the west of the County of Clare' – no-one knowing western Clare and the Aran Islands could fault those details.[35] Writing about *Adiantum capillus-veneris* (maidenhair fern), K'Eogh stated that:

> The leaves are small, round, and serrated, the stalks are black, shining, and slender, near a foot high, it grows on stone walls, and Rocks, the best in this Kingdom, is brought from the rocky mountains of Burrin in the *County* of *Clare*, where it grows plentifully, from thence it is brought in sacks to *Dublin*, and sold there.[36]

Thus, there seems little doubt that John K'Eogh had spent some time in the Burren region noticing its plants and some of their uses. He should be credited with first records for, as well as *Filipendula vulgaris* (dropwort), *Ajuga reptans* (bugle), *Eryngium maritimum* (sea holly), *Solidago virgaurea* (goldenrod), *Thymus praecox* (wild thyme), *Verbascum thapsus* (mullein), *Saxifraga hypnoides* (mossy saxifrage), *Ceterach officinarum*, *Verbena officinalis* (vervain), and probably *Thalictrum flavum* (common meadowrue).[37] Contrariwise, his failure to mention such widespread and abundant Burren specialities as *Gentiana verna* (spring gentian) and *Dryas octopetala* (mountain avens) that were observed between Gort and Galway by Richard Heaton (1601–66) in the 1640s is hard to explain unless K'Eogh knew of no medicinal applications for them.[38]

Surprisingly, K'Eogh only named Mitchelstown as the habitat of two plants. *Hyoscyamus niger* (henbane), a poisonous relative of *Solanum*, is fleeting in sandy or rocky places and is most often associated with ruined dwellings. Of the distinctive

---

but it may be pointed out in K'Eogh's defence (as did Hincks, 1840, p. 8) that *Ruta sylvestris major* and *Ruta sylvestris minor* and numerous variants upon *Ruta sylvestris* were all listed as synonyms of species of *Thalictrum* in the great nomenclator by Caspar Bauhin, *Pinax theatri botanici* (Basle, 1671), pp 335–6. **34** K'Eogh, *Botanalogia*, p. 116. **35** Ibid., p. 107. **36** Ibid., p. 74. **37** K'Eogh is credited with the first record of dropwort by D.A.Webb and M.J.P. Scannell, *Flora of Connemara and the Burren* (Cambridge, 1983), p. 60; see also E.C. Nelson, *An annotated topographical checklist of the flowering plants, conifers, ferns and fern allies of the Burren region* (Outwell, 2000), p. 34; Webb and Scannell, *Flora*, passim. **38** On Irish plant records in the seventeenth century see E.C. Nelson's 'Irish wild plants before 1690' in this volume.

11.6 *Aegopodium podograria* (bishopsweed or goutweed) is a pernicious weed of gardens and is now ubiquitous in Ireland especially in the south-east corner and the catchment of Lough Erne. Preferring lime-rich soil it is not so common where soils are peaty and acidic.
© E. Charles Nelson.

wall-dwelling *Umbilicus rupestris* (pennywort), he wrote: 'It grows upon old stone walls, and in great Quantity upon old Buildings in *Mitchelstown*, flowering in *May*'.[39] Again, personal observation cannot be doubted.

It is frequently said that K'Eogh 'copied' or 'borrowed' material from Caleb Threlkeld's book *Synopsis stirpium Hibernicarum* published nine years earlier, but that is to judge and convict him by twenty-first-century scholarly standards. Caleb Threlkeld (1676–1728) also was accused of 'unacknowledged' use for exactly the same reason – they omitted declarations of their sources, perhaps for simple economy.[40]

39 K'Eogh, *Botanalogia*, p. 85.   40 *cf.* M.E. Mitchell, 'The sources of Threlkeld's *Synopsis stirpium Hibernicarum*', *Proceedings of the Royal Irish Academy*, 74B (1974), 1–6; E.C. Nelson, 'Records of the Irish flora published before 1726', *Bulletin of the Irish Biogeographical Society*, 3 (1979), 51–74. See also Declan

Present-day authors of botanical works including floras are expected to adhere to rigorous standards and provide 'chapter-and-verse' for every individual record of a species's occurrence. Such strict rules did not apply in the seventeenth and eighteenth centuries. As it is, none of the localities in K'Eogh's *Botanalogia* repeat anything in Threlkeld's work, so either K'Eogh saw the plants himself or he had other sources of information. The Kerry reports of *Arbutus* and 'savin' most probably came from a paper by the Dublin physician Dr Thomas Molyneux (1661–1733) published in the *Philosophical Transactions of the Royal Society of London* in 1696 – Threlkeld had also 'silently' used that source.[41]

An intriguing byway among K'Eogh's localities is that given for the troublesome introduced weed *Aegopodium podograria* (bishopsweed, goutweed) (Fig. 11.6) that he reported growing 'wild on *Killough-hill*, near *Cashell*, in great abundance'.[42] That hill had a widespread reputation in the eighteenth century as a 'Small hill yt produced all plants whatsoever that are Native of Ireland'. The Welsh antiquarian and botanist Edward Lhuyd (1660–1709) had made a special trip in the 1680s to this hill situated close to Cashel, Co. Tipperary, but was disappointed to find little of interest: 'Soe much for ye Irish Traditions wch of all Nation's come the nearest Perhaps to a dream'. The legend of 'Botany Mountain' persisted into the late eighteenth century being noticed by Arthur Young (1741–1820) in his *A Tour in Ireland, 1776–1779*: 'The rich sheep pastures, part of the famous Golden Vale, reach between three and four miles from Cashel to the great bog by Botany Hill, noted for producing a greater variety of plants than common'.[43]

The Reverend John K'Eogh's *Botanalogia* is a greatly misunderstood work. It is not an original scientific flora, although it contains some localized original records for wild plants: '*this Undertaking will also … [shew] you in what County, Barony, or Place thereof [where] you may find such, and such* Herbs, *for some* Herbs *grow in one County, &c. which [are] not in another*'.[44] It was clearly intended as a *vade mecum* for literate men and women living in Ireland containing summaries of the purported medicinal uses of plants that would have been cultivated in their gardens, repeating cures and remedies that were contained in the publications of apothecaries and herbalists such as the Londoners John Gerard (1546–1612) and Nicholas Culpepper (1616–54).

A very particular example can be given to show John K'Eogh's reliance on his predecessors' books. *Euphorbia hyberna* (Irish spurge) called makinboy was probably

---

Doogue's chapter on Threlkeld's sources in this volume. **41** Thomas Molyneux, 'A discourse concerning the large horns frequently found under ground in Ireland, concluding from them that the great American deer, call'd a moose, was formerly common in that Island: with remarks on some other things natural to that country', *Philosophical Transactions*, 19:227 (1696), 498–512, at 510–11; E.C. Nelson, 'Records of the Irish flora published before 1726', 55. See also P.H. Kelly's chapter on the Molyneux brothers involvement in the Dublin Philosophical Society in this volume. **42** K'Eogh, *Botanalogia*, p. 15. 43 Quotations are from a letter by Lhuyd, now National Library of Wales, Aberystwyth, Peniarth MS 427, fos. 450–1, and from Arthur Young, *A tour in Ireland, 1776–1779* (Dublin, 1780), ii, p. 285. For more on 'Botany Mountain' see E.C. Nelson, 'Botany Mountain, Ireland: 1690s–1990s: or, Edward Lhuyd and an Irish myth', *BSBI News*, 63 (1993), 21–2. **44** K'Eogh, *Botanalogia*, Sig. A4r.

Gardening at Mitchelstown

the most famous Irish plant in the early eighteenth century. This spurge was then thought to be unique to Ireland, particularly the south and west. British botanists and gardeners were keen to acquire plants. The *Botanalogia* entry reads: 'Mountain or knotted rooted SPURGE, Hib. *Makinboy*, or *Makinbeigh au thle*, Lat. Tithymalus Hibernicus Montanus'. K'Eogh informed readers that 'It grows in abundance near *Anakirk* in the County of *Limerick*'.[45] After that statement, K'Eogh lapsed in general commentary about 'All kinds of *Spurges*', without providing any description of 'Makinboy'. There is nothing new and it is noteworthy that K'Eogh did not repeat the 'old Fable' recounted by Threlkeld that 'this [spurge] carried about a Man's Cloaths will purge him'. '[A]ll the *Tithymals*', warned Threlkeld, 'are sharp, excoriate the Guts, and are to be used with great Caution, if at all inwardly'.[46] Instead K'Eogh chose to repeat the medicinal properties and remedies for all spurges from Gerard's herbal, including the potentially lethal 'The Juice put into hollow Teeth … asswage[s] the Tooth-Ache' without Gerard's explicit warning: 'The iuice or milke is good to stop hollow teeth, being put into them warily, so that you touch neither the gums, nor any of the other teeth in the mouth with the said medicine'.[47]

Although in recent decades John K'Eogh's herbal has received renewed attention in the context of ethnopharmacology and herbal medicine, it is doubtful that there is anything novel and uniquely Irish in *Botanalogia*.[48] That said, even if his potions and cures were copied from his predecessors, rather than reflecting local Irish traditional medicine, John K'Eogh did record numerous vernacular names that were not available to him in Caleb Threlkeld's *Synopsis stirpium Hibernicarum*, the only earlier botanical publication of Irish origin.[49] K'Eogh included Irish names deliberately:

---

45 Ibid., p. 118. R.W. Scully, 'Plants found in Kerry, 1890', *Journal of Botany British and Foreign*, 29 (1891), 143–8, at 146 wrote 'Hitherto the only record for Limerick rested on the authority of K'Eogh, who stated in 1736 [*sic*] that the spurge grew abundantly near Anakirk. However, neither Anakirk nor the spurge have been found in the county for the last 150 years, and I have much pleasure in showing that K'Eogh was most probably correct in his record, though Anakirk is undoubtedly a misprint or error of some sort'. Anakirk is believed to be a misprint for Rinekirk, on the Maigue River near Adare: Nathaniel Colgan and R.W. Scully, *Contributions towards a Cybele Hibernica* (Dublin, 1898), p. 315. **46** Caleb Threlkeld, *Synopsis stirpium Hibernicarum* (Dublin, 1726), Sig. K7v and appendix, p. 22. In the appendix, Threlkeld added 'Dr. *Vaughan* writes thus concerning the Acrimony of *Tithymalus Hibernicus*, that a Country *Empirik* gave a Dose of it boiled in Milk to a strong clever Youth, about eight Miles from *Clonmell*, which excited a violent *Hypercatharsis* with *Convulsions*, upon which Death followed that Night before ten a Clock'. He was quoting from William Derham, *Philosophical letters between the late learned Mr. Ray and several of his ingenious correspondents* (London, 1718), p. 297. **47** Gerard, *The herball*, p. 506. **48** M.S. Carson, 'Caleb Threlkeld and John K'Eogh: the use of Irish grown plants in medicine in the early eighteenth century', unpublished typescript (A paper delivered to the Historical Group of the Royal Society of Chemistry annual meeting in Belfast, 1990). It should be noted that K'Eogh's *Botanalogia* was not one of the works extracted for D.E. Allen and Gabrielle Hatfield, *Medicinal plants in folk tradition. An ethnobotany of Britain and Ireland* (Portland, OR and Cambridge, 2004). **49** Patrick Wyse Jackson, *Ireland's generous nature: the past and present uses of wild plants in Ireland* (St Louis, 2014), pp [687–701]: 'Appendix II K'Eogh and Threlkeld names'. This invaluable comparative list does not include any names for plants of uncertain identity nor plants 'purely grown in gardens'.

> *You will gain great Advantage by having the Name of the* Herb *in* Irish, *for in case you did not know it, or where you might find it, only repeat that name in* Irish, *to one of your little* Botanists, *and he will fetch it to you presently.*[50]

Mysteriously, *Botanalogia* even contains two vernacular names that are of Manx origin: lus yn aile (as '*Lusinuil*') for 'Burnet', most probably *Sanguisorba minor* (salad burnet), and hollin-traie (as '*Holimtragh*'), literally holly of the beach, for *Eryngium maritimum* (seaholly).[51]

Eighteenth-century authors could never resist the chance to sermonize, and K'Eogh was no exception. He was prompted by the pleasant taste of home-grown liquorice and the bountiful orange trees in the greenhouse at Mitchelstown to remark: 'so you see, how by a little Industry, the most Exotic plants, may be brought to perfection in this Country, which demonstrates, what a fertile, prolific land we live in'.[52]

Table 11.1. Localities (by county) for wild plants published in John K'Eogh's *Botanalogia*

Armagh (1 sp.)		
Bog Onion (p. 89)		'Cepa palustris' (? *Allium schoenoprasum*)
Clare (23 spp.)		
Bugle, or middle Consound (p. 19)	near Corofin	*Ajuga reptans*
Dropwort (p. 41)	Barony of Burrin	*Filipendula vulgaris*
Garden Endive (pp 42–3)	Barony of Burrin	'Endiva, et Scariola' (? *Cichorium* sp. or *Lactuca* sp.)
Eringo or Sea Holly (p. 43)	Barony of Burren	*Eryngium maritimum*
Goats-rue (pp 53–4)	Mountains of Burrin	'Galega, & Ruta Capraria' (? *Galega* sp.)
Golden Rod (p. 54)	Barony of Burrin	*Solidago virgaurea*
Ground Pine (p. 56)	Mountains of Burrin	'Chamæpitys, & Iva Arthritica' (? *Ajuga chamaepitys*)
Hedge Hyssop (p. 64)	Barony of Burrin	'Gratiola' (? *Gratiola officinalis*)
Juniper-tree (p. 67) *	Mountains of Burrin	*Juniperus communis*
True Maiden Hair (p. 74)	mountains of Burrin	*Adiantum capillus-veneris*
English Mercury (p. 79)	Barrony of Tullagh	*Chenopodium bonus-henricus*
Mother of Thyme or Wild Thyme (p. 82)	Mountains of Burrin	*Thymus praecox*
Mullein or Hightaper (p. 84)	Barony of Burrin	*Verbascum thapsus*
Palma Christi or the greater spurge (p. 91)	Barony of Burrin	'Cataputia major, vel Ricinus' (? *Ricinus communis*)
Wild Rue (p. 105)	Barony of Burrin	*Thalictrum flavum* or *T. minus*

* indicates plants that were reported by K'Eogh for more than one county.

50 K'Eogh, *Botanalogia*, Sig. B2r.   **51** N.J.A. Williams, 'A note on John K'Eogh's *Herbal*', *Eighteenth-Century Ireland/Iris an dá chultúr*, 2 (1987), 198–202.   **52** K'Eogh, *Botanalogia*, p. 70.

Gardening at Mitchelstown

Clare (23 spp.) *(continued)*		
Wild Rue (p. 105)	Barony of Burrin	*Thalictrum flavum* or *T. minus*
Samphire (p. 107) *	west of the County of Clare	*Crithmum maritimum*
Saracens Consound (p. 108) *	Corofin	*Senecio fluviatilis*
Winter Savoury (pp 108–9)	Mountains of Burrin	(? *Satureja montana*)
White Saxifrage or stone break (p. 109)	Barony of Burrin	*Saxifraga hypnoides* (or, perhaps, *S. rosacea*)
Spleenwort, Ceterach, or Miltwast (p. 116)	Barony of Burrin	*Ceterach officinarum*
Stone Bramble (p. 118)	Cratulagh [Cratlow]	*Rubus saxatilis*
Swallow-wort (p. 120)	Mountains of Burren	'Asclepias, vincetoxicum, & Hirundaria' (? *Vincetoxicum hirundaria*)
Garden Thyme (p. 123)	Mountains of Burrin	*Thymus praecox*
Cork (3 spp.)		
Wild Columbine (p. 32) *	Curraghs near Kilbullane [Kilbolane]	*Aquilegia vulgaris*
Henbane, or common black Henbane (p. 60)	about Mitchelstown	*Hyoscyamus niger*
Navelwort or Wallpennywort (pp 85–6)	Mitchelstown	*Umbilicus rupestris*
Galway (5 spp.)		
Wild Columbine (p. 32)	near Cloontueskart [Cloontueskart, Co. Roscommon]	*Aquilegia vulgaris*
Juniper-tree (p. 67) *	near Ardraghen [Ardrahan]	*Juniperus communis*
Samphire (p. 107) *	Isles of Aaron [Aran Islands]	*Crithmum maritimum*
Saracens Consound (p. 108) *	Pallace [Pallas]	*Senecio fluviatilis*
Sow Bread (p. 115) *	Rathfarin, Letrim [Barony of Leitrim], and Mileek	*Cyclamen hederacea*
Vervein (p. 125–6)	Kiltartan	*Verbena officinalis*
Kerry (2 spp.)		
Arbute, or Strawberry tree (pp 5–6)	–	*Arbutus unedo*
Savin (p. 108)	Islands of Loughlane [Lough Leane]	*Juniperus communis*
Limerick (4 spp.)		
Dwarf-elder, Dane-wort or Wall-wort (p. 42)	near Galbally	*Sambucus ebulus*
Water Germander (p. 52)	banks of the Shannon near Limerick	*Teucrium scordium*
Hellebore, Great Bastard black Hellebore, Bears-foot or Sellerwort (p. 60) *	Slieve Baghtine, and near Drumcullagher [Dromcolliher]	*Helleborus foetidus*
Mountain or knotted rooted Spurge (p. 118)	Anakirk [? Rinakirk]	*Euphorbia hyberna*

* indicates plants that were reported by K'Eogh for more than one county.

E. Charles Nelson

Table 11.1. Localities (by county) for wild plants published in John K'Eogh's *Botanalogia* *(continued)*

Roscommon (4 spp.)		
Long Birthwort (p. 14)	Briole [Breeole], Barony of Athlone	(? *Aristolochia* sp.)
Wild Cucumber (p. 36)	Moycarnon [Moycarn]	*Ecballium elaterium*
Spindle Tree or Common Prickwood with Red Berries (p. 116)	Slievebane [Slieve Bawn]	*Euonymus europaeus*
Sow Bread (p. 115) *	near Belanasloe [Ballinasloe], and Mountalbat [Mount Talbot]	*Cyclamen hederacea*
Tipperary (6 spp.)		
Adder's-tongue (p. 1)	Barrony of Dugharrow	*Ophioglossum vulgatum*
Wood Betony (p. 13)	Tullagh, Barony of Onagh [Owney]	*Stachys sylvatica*
Bishops Weed (p. 15)	Killough-hill, near Cashell	*Aegopodium podograria*
Moon-wort (pp 80–1)	between Burgess, and Killaloe	*Botrychium lunaria*
Mountain Sage, or Garlic Sage (p. 107)	Mountains near Tullagh	*Teucrium scorodonia*
Tutsan or Park Leaves (p. 124)	'Colonel Dawsons Woods'	*Hypericum androsaemum*

* indicates plants that were reported by K'Eogh for more than one county.

CHAPTER TWELVE

Gothic features in eighteenth-century Irish landscapes

VANDRA COSTELLO

THE BUILDING OF gothick-style structures was a common feature on Irish eighteenth-century demesnes. Before embarking on any discussion of the gothic landscape in Ireland, it is necessary to consider the meaning of the term gothic. As a rule, but not uniformly, the spelling gothick (with a 'k') refers to a pastiche, a building made to look medieval with pointed arches, lancet or ogee windows and other gothic flourishes. The traditional spelling, gothic, is used to describe a genuine example of a building dating from the medieval period. Both pastiche gothick and ancient gothic ruins were incorporated into demesne landscapes in Georgian Ireland.

The gothick-style house first appeared in the late eighteenth century, most famously when Horace Walpole (1717–97) built Strawberry Hill in Twickenham, England, a battlemented medieval pastiche, between 1749 and 1778. The style became extremely fashionable at the end of the century and this trend accelerated in the nineteenth. Before gothick houses became fashionable, gothick-style buildings began to be used as ornaments in Irish demesnes, some the genuine article, and others sham ruins designed to appear antiquated. From these beginnings, gothick touches were added to the simplest and most mundane of buildings, from summer houses to ice houses.

Writing in 1756, the English architect Isaac Ware (*c.*1704–66) defined gothick as:

> A wild and irregular manner of building, that took place of the regular antique method of the time when architecture, with the other arts, declined. The *Gothick* is distinguished from the antique architecture, by its ornaments being whimsical, and its profiles incorrect.

He thought that the craze would be short lived, continuing that:

> The inventors of it probably thought they exceeded the *Grecian* method, and some of late have seemed by their fondness for *Gothick* edifices, to be of the same opinion; but this was but a caprice, and, to the credit of our taste, is going out of fashion again as hastily as it came in.[1]

---

1 Isaac Ware, *A complete body of architecture: adorned with plans and elevations, from original designs* (London, 1756), pp 19–20.

249

12.1 Leixlip Castle on the River Liffey in Jonathan Fisher, *Scenery of Ireland* (1795), plate 7. By permission of the Governors and Guardians of Marsh's Library. © Marsh's Library.

Ware was mistaken in this assumption, for gothic touches such as latticework, mullions, ogee arches, lancet windows and pointed arches were liberally applied to buildings for many years to come.

So why did the gothic become so popular in the late eighteenth century? A combination of several factors converged to form a trend and instil a taste for the gothic. One influence was the grand tour, during which travellers, usually aristocrats, viewed the elaborate high gothic cathedrals of continental Europe.[2] From the late eighteenth century the grand tourists began taking a greater interest in the medieval past of Europe. In the early years of the grand tour a uniformly classical view tended to be taken.[3] However, as Rosemary Sweet observed, 'as the medieval period and its achievements came into sharper focus, itineraries within and between the towns and

---

[2] For example, in the diary of an unknown female member of an Irish party on the grand tour in the Low Countries in 1771 the traveller comments on the 'remarkable beautiful gothic spire to the Town House': PRONI, Foster Massereene Papers, D207/27/49: 6 August 1772. [3] Rosemary Sweet, *Cities and the grand tour: the British in Italy, c.1690–1820* (Cambridge, 2012), p. 250.

cities of Italy changed. New associative meanings and different aesthetic ideas began steadily to modify the dominant classical paradigm of the eighteenth-century tour, well before the end of the Napoleonic wars'[4] Sweet identified another aspect to the growth of interest in the Middle Ages, the academic and antiquarian attempt to establish a 'system' of gothic architecture, to order it, in a similar way to the methodical ordering of classical architecture.[5]

Another influence was the gothic novel, which became popular in the late eighteenth and early nineteenth centuries. This contributed to the desire to create a more romantic, fantastic landscape, to which the gothic was ideally suited. One famous Irish gothic writer was the Reverend Charles Maturin (1780–1824), who wrote *Melmoth the Wanderer* (Edinburgh, 1820), about a man who makes a pact with the devil.[6] But he also wrote a short ghost story, posthumously published, 'Leixlip Castle' (Fig.12.1), a house that he declared had 'a character of romantic beauty and feudal grandeur, such as few buildings in Ireland can claim' and which he described as possessing 'all the sequestered and picturesque character that imagination could ascribe to a landscape a hundred miles from, not only the metropolis but an inhabited town'.[7]

A further impetus for erecting buildings in a gothic rather than a classical mode was to make a statement of the owner's taste and regard for history. The gothick style had the potential to satisfy Irish landowners of all political and religious shades; it could be either a subtle nod to the 'old' religion – Catholicism – or equally a patriotic, Protestant statement honouring Britain's past. Sham, or genuine, gothic ruins could be taken as an emblem of the destruction of Catholicism and the supremacy of the Protestant religion, or as a continuation of and association with Catholicism. On a more prosaic level it could represent nothing more than a desire to be fashionable and create a picturesque-looking scene.

As with other stylistic forms the Whig/Tory dichotomy does not prove a reliable gauge as to taste in Ireland, just as politicians could not so easily be placed in either category. Gothicism was embraced with gusto by landowners of all complexions in Ireland during the eighteenth century and beyond. The obsession with the gothic was part of a wider trend, the search for the sublime – a thrilling mix of awe and terror, and the picturesque. These were two of the three strands of landscape aesthetics which preoccupied philosophers for most of the Georgian period, the third being 'beauty'. Beautiful landscapes were exemplified by the parks of Lancelot 'Capability' Brown (1716–83): smooth undulating expanses of grassland, irregularly shaped lakes and serpentine rivers interspersed with classical buildings.

Edmund Burke (1729/30–97) first formulated the theory of sublimity in nature in 1757. In *A philosophical inquiry into the origin of our ideas of the sublime and*

---

4 Ibid., pp 249–50.   5 Ibid., p. 250. See also James Essex, 'Remarks on the antiquity and different modes of brick and stone buildings in England' *Archaeologia*, 4 (1777), 73–109, at 108 and 109.   6 Charles Robert Maturin was an Irish Protestant clergyman (ordained in the Church of Ireland) and a writer of gothic plays and novels. See Patrick Maume, 'Maturin, Charles Robert', *DIB*.   7 C.R. Maturin, 'Leixlip Castle' in A.A. Watts (ed.), *The literary souvenir; or, cabinet of poetry and romance* (London, 1825),

beautiful, he described the sublime as 'Whatever is fitted in any sort to excite the ideas of pain, and danger, that is to say, whatever is in any sort terrible, or is conversant about terrible objects, or operates in a manner analogous to terror'.[8] In Ireland, the sublime landscape could be experienced on the estates of Lord Kenmare on the mountains and great lakes of Killarney, Co. Kerry, or at Lord Powerscourt's great waterfall in Enniskerry, Co. Wicklow, or Lord Bristol's Downhill whose northern boundary was steep cliffs overlooking the north Atlantic ocean in Co. Derry. In 1768 William Gilpin (1724–1804) published his popular *An essay on prints* in which he defined the picturesque as 'that peculiar kind of beauty, which is agreeable in a picture' and developed his 'principles of picturesque beauty' landscape.[9]

In 1790 Uvedale Price (1747–1829) further defined the picturesque and categorized it as a middle 'station between beauty and sublimity'. Picturesque landscapes were, in theory, anticlassical and therefore gothic ruins were perfectly suited to picturesque aesthetic. As Price put it:

> Gothic architecture is generally considered as more picturesque, though less beautiful, than Grecian; and, upon the same principle that a ruin is more so than a new edifice. The first thing that strikes the eye in approaching any building is the general outline against the sky (or whatever it may be opposed to), and the effect of the openings: in Grecian buildings the general lines of the roof are strait, and even when varied and adorned by a dome or a pediment, the whole has a character of symmetry and regularity. Symmetry, which in works of art particularly, accords with the beautiful, is in the same degree adverse to the picturesque, and among the various causes of the superior picturesqueness of ruins, compared with entire buildings, the destruction of symmetry is by no means the least powerful.[10]

Though Burke, Price and Gilpin applied considerable intellectual energy to the debate and categorization of each form of landscape, the landowning public was less concerned with ideological purity and generally proved to happily and enthusiastically combine features of both beautiful, picturesque and sublime on their demesnes according to the topography and their own whims and tastes.

Ruins, especially ivy covered and sometimes ghostly looking gothic ruins, with their sense of abandonment, were pleasingly picturesque and romantic looking. Ancient ruins also played their part in the search for the sublime. Gothic horror gave a frisson to a scene. The ruins of Muckross Abbey, Co. Kerry (Fig. 12.2), popular with tourists in search of the sublime experience, had a particular macabre appeal. They were used as a burial place, and skeletal remains could be seen by visitors

211–32, at pp 212–13.   8 Edmund Burke, *A philosophical inquiry into the origin of our ideas of the sublime and beautiful* (London, 1757), p. 13.   9 William Gilpin, *An essay upon prints; containing remarks upon the principles of picturesque beauty …* (London, 1768), p. 2.   10 Uvedale Price, *An essay on the picturesque, as compared with the sublime and the beautiful* (London, 1794), i, pp 76 and 50.

12.2 View of Muckross Abbey, on the Lake of Killarney, Co. Kerry. This aquatint of the ruins of Muckross Abbey is based on a painting by Thomas Walmsley (1763–1805/6), and was published by Thomas Cartwright in 1806 in *Miscellaneous Irish scenery*, series no. 2, plate 1. © The British Library Board, Maps K.Top.53.43.g.No.2.PL.1.

seeking a grisly thrill, particularly when viewed at night by the light of the full moon, or at sundown. Horror was provided by the piles of human bones and exposed coffins. Arthur Young (1741–1820) described Muckross as

> one of the most interesting scenes I ever saw; it is the ruin of a considerable abbey, built in Henry VIth's time, and so entire, that if it were more so, though the building would be more perfect, the *ruin* would be less pleasing; it is half obscured in the shade of some venerable ash trees; ivy has given the picturesque circumstance, which that plant alone can confer, while the broken walls and ruined turrets throw over it *The last mournful graces of decay*, heaps

254   *Vandra Costello*

of sculls and bones scattered about, with nettles, briars, and weeds sprouting in tufts from the loose stones, all unite to raise those melancholy impressions, which are the merit of such scenes …[11]

Lewis Weston Dillwyn (1778–1855) described his impressions on a visit there in 1809:

> The Ruins are for the most part covered with Ivy, & an enormous Yew spreads a deep shade over the Cloisters, which added to the sepulchral smell & the sight of, so many naked Truths filled me with such a mixture of Awe & Horror that I confess I should not then have liked to be left alone. My imagination involuntarily painted it as 'The Land of apparitions – empty shades' & such I am ashamed to confess was its effect on my Mind that it was sometime before reason could resume her entire sway.[12]

Ireland was rich in ruins and tourists seeking to inhabit the sensorial world of the romantic landscape of Ireland, be it sublime, beautiful or picturesque, were provided with illustrated guides to help them plan their journeys. Specialist books catered to those interested in visiting categories of landscape. For example, Jonathan Fisher (*fl.* 1763–1809) included in his illustrated guides gothic abbey ruins.[13] He was not alone in this, for Caroline Wyndham-Quin (1790–1870), countess of Dunraven, likewise included gothic views in her 1865 book on Adare Manor, Co. Limerick (Fig. 12.3).[14]

From the late eighteenth century onwards new houses were built, or paradoxically, old ones re-modelled in the gothick style.[15] Many ecclesiastic buildings which survived the dissolution of the monasteries were adapted for use as private houses. For example, Moore Abbey, Monasterevin, Co. Kildare, and St Wolstan's Abbey, Celbridge, also in Co. Kildare, were re-modelled as houses in 1747 and 1767 respectively, but retained their gothic features.[16]

---

11 Arthur Young, *A tour in Ireland with general observations … made in the years 1776, 1777, and 1778, and brought to the end of 1779*, 2 vols (Dublin, 1780), i, pp 442–3. See the chapter on Killarney in Edward Malins and Patrick Bowe, *Irish gardens and demesnes from 1830* (London, 1980).   **12** Trinity College Dublin (TCD), MS 967, pp 102–3: 'Journal of a tour to Killarney by L.W. Dillwyn, 1809'.   **13** See Jonathan Fisher, *A description of the lake of Killarney, illustrated with twelve prints of its most interesting views, drawn and engraved in aquatint* (Dublin, 1796); and his *Scenery of Ireland illustrated in a series of prints of select views, castles and abbeys, drawn and engraved in aquatint by Jonathan Fisher* (London, 1795). **14** Caroline Wyndham-Quin, *Memorials of Adare manor. With historical notices of Adare, by the earl of Dunraven E.R.W. Wyndham-Quin* (Oxford, 1865).   **15** The authentically medieval Malahide Castle had a gothick porch added to it: see J.N. Brewer, *The beauties of Ireland*, 3 vols (London 1885), i, p. 240. The early seventeenth-century Portumna Castle had a gothic door leading to the terrace: TCD, MS 4035, fo. 63r: 'Tour journal of Mary Beaufort 1808'. This is available online at https://digitalcollections.tcd.ie/concern/works/d217qs77m?locale=en; accessed 20 January 2022.   **16** The dissolved abbey of Mellifont in Co. Louth was leased to the Moore family, the earls of Drogheda, and was the Moores' family home until 1725. Edmund Hogan (1831–1917) notes that the house of St Wolstan's was 'built from the ruins of the abbey, after the design of Mr Joshua Allen. This Allen who was no relation of the St Wolstan Alens, but … was well known for his skill in architecture, and, amongst other things, planned the unfinished

12.3 Adare Manor and ruins: 'Desmond Castle and the Franciscan Abbey from Adare Bridge' in Caroline Wyndham-Quin, *Memorial of Adare Manor* (Oxford, 1865), plate 25. By permission of the Governors and Guardians of Marsh's Library. © Marsh's Library.

Where new houses were built on the sites of old religious houses, such as Ardfert, Adare and Muckross abbeys, the gothic ruins were retained as eyecatchers, which added romantic elements to the demesnes. Other houses such as Shelton Abbey in Co. Wicklow sought to make the house look like 'an abbey constructed in the fourteenth century, and converted, with additions, into a noble residence at a date shortly subsequent to the Reformation'.[17] At Crom Castle in Co. Fermanagh the ruins of the old castle were remodelled to create a gothick eyecatcher to be viewed from the house. Retaining an old house and adding gothick touches gave an historical veracity to a building.

The earliest, and most famous gothick house in Ireland is Castle Ward in Co. Down. The house has two fronts, one in the classical style, preferred by Bernard

house at Sigginstown, in the Co. Kildare, for the tyrannical and unfortunate earl of Strafford': Edmund Hogan, 'St. Wolfstan's, Celbridge', *The Irish Ecclesiastical Record*, 13 (1892), 248–9. 17 Brewer, *The beauties of Ireland*, i, p. 330.

12.4 Slane Castle, Co. Meath in Robert O'Callaghan-Newenham, *Picturesque views of the antiquities of Ireland*. Drawn on stone by J.D. Harding, from the sketches of R. O'C. Newenham (Dublin, 1826). Plate of Castle and Church at Slane, unnumbered. By permission of the Governors and Guardians of Marsh's Library. © Marsh's Library.

Ward (1719–81), first Viscount Bangor, and the other in the gothick, which his wife Ann (*c.*1714–89), favoured. Vast sums of money were spent on such enterprises: Cabra Castle, Co. Cavan, actually bankrupted the Foster family, and they were often considered vulgar in their execution.[18] The new Charleville Castle, Co. Offaly, designed by Francis Johnston (1760/61–1829), was regarded as 'a magnificent mansion' in the gothick style, but it stood 'in the middle of a very flat park, with a

18 For example, Prince Hermann von Pückler-Muskau (1785–1871), thought that despite the lavish £50,000 spent on Mitchelstown Castle, Co. Cork, its situation, on 'bare turf, without the slightest picturesque break, which castles in the Gothic or kindred styles peculiarly need; and the inconsiderable park' being bereft of trees, ensured that 'one ingredient was unluckily forgotten – good taste': Hermann von Pückler-Muskau, *Tour in England, Ireland and France during the years 1828, 1829: with remarks*

12.5 Rathfarnham Castle gate, July 1952. © Fr Browne SJ collection, Dublin.

large piece of artificial water to the south'.[19] Other gothick style houses were Gowran House and Jenkinstown House in Co. Kilkenny, Castle Bernard in Co. Cork, Borris House in Co. Carlow and Slane Castle in Co. Meath (Fig. 12.4).

By the latter part of the eighteenth century the gothick style had become such a fashion that it was flagged up as an enticement in advertisements to let houses.[20] It was common, when building a new house, to leave the ruins of an older house or discontinued religious building to stand as a picturesque feature in the garden. Possibly the earliest example of this trend in Ireland was at Ardfert, Co. Kerry, where Charles Smith (1715?–62) commented on the ruins of the Franciscan friary in the 1740s.[21] Even if not architecturally gothic, Norman, or later ruins were used to create a gothic atmosphere. At Castleknock demesne in Dublin, 'the remarkable ruins' of an old motte and baily were deliberately preserved.[22] Similarly, ruinous, ivy-covered buildings were utilized at Mount Juliet, Co. Kilkenny,[23] Old Court in Bray,[24] Castlerea, Co. Roscommon,[25] and Mallow, Co. Cork.[26]

(London, 1833), p. 400.   **19** Edward Wakefield, *An account of Ireland statistical and political* (London, 1812), p. 44.   **20** *Hibernian Journal*, 4 Aug. 1784.   **21** Charles Smith, *The ancient and present state of the county of Kerry* (Dublin, 1774), pp 204–5. Daniel Augustus Beaufort, however, thought Ardfert House itself, built in 1722, was 'extremely low, ill contrived and ugly ... prospect bad': TCD, MS 4030, fo. 29r: D.A. Beaufort, 'A journal of a tour of Ireland volume two', 14 August–17 September 1788'. Beaufort's two-volume journal, covering the period 3 July to 17 September 1788, is available online at https://digitalcollections.tcd.ie/concern/works/vh53wz933?locale=en; accessed 19 January 2022.   **22** William Henry Bartlett and Joseph Stirling Coyne, *The scenery and antiquities of Ireland*, 2 vols (London, 1842), ii, p. 137.   **23** Brewer, *The beauties of Ireland*, i, p. 470.   **24** TCD, MS 2568, fo. 11r.: 'O'Connor's journal through the Kingdom of Ireland'.   **25** Isaac Weld, *Statistical survey of the county of Roscommon drawn up under the direction of the Royal Dublin Society* (Dublin, 1832), p. 467.   **26** TCD, MS 967, p. 86: 'Lewis

Perhaps the most publicly visible form of gothick was its use in the approaches to demesnes, in bridges and grand entrances with their associated lodges, which immediately announced the owner's taste to a passer-by or visitor. Houses with great gothick style entrances, to name just a few, included Heywood, Co. Laois, and Belvedere, Co. Westmeath, Strokestown, Co. Roscommon, Avondale, Co. Wicklow, and Luttrellstown Castle, Co. Dublin. A great mock gothic gateway (Fig. 12.5) was built by Henry Loftus (1709–83), first earl of Ely, of Rathfarnham Castle in Dublin. A 'great admirer of the English taste', he ordered a great gothick gateway for the Rathfarnham entrance of his demesne from a company in London specializing in artificial stone.[27] The structure was said 'to promise perfect architectural elegance. The work is to be imported piecemeal and conjoined under the inspection of the artist, and the whole expense will be considerably under that of the mountain granite on his lordship's own estate within a few miles of the spot'.[28]

Castlemartyr in Co. Cork had what Daniel Augustus Beaufort (1739–1821) described as a 'large, pasteboard thin gothic gateway' which he thought, presumably because it was too flimsy, was 'a very poor imitation of gothick'.[29]

Within Georgian demesnes gothick buildings appeared everywhere. The landscaper Thomas Wright (1711–86), the author of *Universal architecture* (London, 1758), which included original designs for arbours and grottoes, was responsible either directly, or indirectly, for many gothick additions to demesnes in Ireland. Wright's work on the antiquities of Co. Louth, *Louthiana* (London, 1748), was written after a visit to Ireland at the invitation of Lord Limerick, in whose ownership Tollymore Park, Co. Down, was at this time, and to whom Wright's book was dedicated. Wright's influential hand can be seen everywhere at Tollymore.[30] The demesne's owner, James Hamilton (1694–1758), first earl of Clanbrassil, created the sturdy medieval looking barbican gate at the eastern entrance to the demesne, and gothick entrance gates to the north of the house. The gothicization was continued by his son James Hamilton (1730–98), the second earl. The magnificent gothick barn was begun around 1757 and finished in 1789 with the addition of steeple complete with bell, clock and sundial.

Other gothick buildings directly attributed to Wright include a now-demolished 'thatched hermitage and gothick tower with attached wings' at Belle Isle in Co. Fermanagh.[31] These garden buildings were illustrated by Jonathan Fisher his *Scenery of Ireland* (London, 1795). As Eileen Harris notes:

> Both buildings are attributed to Wright on the evidence of his two visits to Belleisle in August 1746, one 'to dinner' (with ... Sir St George Gore, 5th Bt, who died on 25 September 1746), and on stylistic grounds. The hermitage can be compared to a similar Avery [Library] design and to the

Dillwyn's journal of a tour to Killarney, 1809'. **27** Edward Lloyd, *A month's tour in north Wales, Dublin, and its environs. With observations upon their manners and police in the year 1780* (London, 1781), p. 87. **28** *Saunders Newsletter*, 20 Jan. 1790. **29** Brian De Breffny and Rosemay ffolliott, *The houses of Ireland* (London, 1975), p. 161. **30** The house was demolished in 1952. **31** Thomas Wright, *Arbours &*

root house at Berkeley Castle. It is not clear whether the gothic building is what Fisher described as a 'handsome cottage with a kitchen and other conveniences, in a sweet retired place' or what Arthur Young, referred to as a 'temple built on a gentle hill overlooking the lake' … Arthur Young's temple, or at any rate a building with a pronounced portico, is shown in an engraving of Belleisle, dedicated to Lord Ross, and considerably exaggerating the 'gentle slope' for dramatic effect. Fisher's view shows the 'gothic tower with attached wings': his description of the 'handsome cottage … in a sweet retired place' sounds more appropriate to the hermitage or, perhaps, to yet another ornamental building. Arthur Young visited Belleisle on 15 August 1776 and was quite carried away by '… the charming seat of the Earl of Ross'.[32]

The famous sham gothick Jealous Wall (Fig. 12.6) at Belvedere in Co. Westmeath – built by Robert Rochfort (1708–74) – is also thought to have been based on a design by Wright. Rochfort also built a gothick arch at the northern end of the park. This was designed in the style of a castellated stone gateway in a state of ruin. It has arched windows and is decorated with tufa. (An octagon house was also built about 1765. Wright included the designs for the gothick octagon house at Belvedere in his *Louthiana* of 1748.) As with houses, many old buildings were dressed up with a gothick façade as decorative garden features. At Hillsborough, Co. Down, an old artillery fort was re-modelled as a two-storey turreted gothick gazebo in the 1750s.

The placement of gothic ruins in relation to the house was of great aesthetic importance. Links and vistas were made between ruins and the house or viewing points to ensure the most pleasing effect. Efforts were made to shroud the ruins with sufficient gloom by planting trees through which vistas were cut. For example, the ruins of Muckross Abbey were surrounded by 'embowering groves' (though much of this would have been natural woodland vistas, which could be cut to improve views to and from the abbey ruins).[33] In Cork, Castlemartyr was rebuilt and laid out in the 1760s by Nicholas Halfpenny and particular attention was paid to laying out the grounds and creating the vistas around the ruined church at Ballyoughtera, Co. Cork, in a formal manner.[34] A fir walk intersected with a winding walk lined with *Sorbus aucuparia* (quickbeam or mountain ash), and a ha-ha was built north of the church and graveyard to ensure that the view was unobstructed.[35] At Ardfert in Kerry, 'several fine vistoes [*sic*]' were opened in the pleasure grounds to give views of the adjacent ruined abbey, which Charles Smith remarked 'by its gothic pillars, spacious windows, noble arches, and subterraneous vaults, adds a solemnity to the lofty avenues of *Ulmus* (elm), and other plantations which surround it'.[36]

grottoes, ed. by Eileen Harris (London, 1979), unpaginated.   **32** Ibid.   **33** Isaac Weld, *Illustrations of the scenery of Killarney and the surrounding county* (London, 1807), p. 7.   **34** PRONI, Shannon, D2707/B/7/1–21. Weekly labour accounts, giving details of work carried out on the Castlemartyr demesne. Robert Pratt to Lord Shannon (Henry Boyle, 1st earl of Shannon, 1684–1764), 29 January 1764; Robert Pratt to Lord Shannon, 9 October 1764.   **35** Ibid.   **36** Smith, *The ancient and present state of the county of Kerry*, p. 205.   **37** Sir Charles Coote, *Statistical survey of the county of Cavan drawn up under*

12.6 The Jealous Wall at Belvedere, Co. Westmeath. © Photograph by Kevin Monaghan, courtesy of Belvedere House, Gardens & Park.

Many visitors bemoaned the missed opportunity for creating a picturesque scene, or the clumsy placement of obstacles to a view. For example Sir Charles Coote (1765–1857) thought that the ruins of the old Cormy Castle on Cabra demesne were 'quite too near to have any pleasing effect, which such pieces of antiquity afford in the landscape'.[37] Daniel Augustus Beaufort thought that Lord and Lady Kenmare (Thomas Browne (1726–95), fourth Viscount Kenmare and his wife Anne) had missed an opportunity, displaying 'little taste' when they built their ornamental cottage on St Ronan's Island, 'as no part of the beautiful ruins either east or west can be seen'.[38] Arthur Young felt that a sham ruin placed out in the open on a mound of lawn at Mount Juliet was not well placed – ruins being 'more suited to retired and melancholy spots'.[39] Whereas at Woodstock in Co. Kilkenny, Samuel Lewis (1782/3–1865) felt that the ruins of Brownsford and Clowen castles, amongst the plantations, were seen to a pleasing, or 'peculiar' effect from artificial mounds along the river.[40]

the direction of the Royal Dublin Society (Dublin, 1802), p. 169.   **38** TCD, MS 4030, fo. 35v: D.A. Beaufort, 'A journal of a tour of Ireland, volume two, 14 August–17 September 1788'.   **39** Young, *A tour in Ireland* (London, 1780), p. 74.   **40** 'Inistioge' entry in Samuel Lewis, *A topographical dictionary of*

Not all gothick designs were of the sombre, gloom-inducing character beloved by those seeking the sublime experience. From its lofty beginnings in old ecclesiastical houses and churches, the gothick style filtered down to become part of the fashionable gardening idiom, with gothick whimsies appearing on mundane garden buildings and sham gothick ruins being created where none existed. Though described as gothick, many of these buildings had no more than an ornate flourish in a gothic style. Many buildings designed to look antiquated were built for dining and picnics. On Innisfallen Island, 'under a Canopy of Ash & Beech Trees', were the ruins of an abbey which Lord Kenmare converted into 'a Banqueting House for the accommodation of visitors'.[41] At Bellevue, Co. Wicklow, a gothick-style banqueting room was built in 1788 to a design by the architect Francis Sandys (*d.* 1795).[42] At Woodstock, Co. Kilkenny, a decorative two-storey banqueting house, named whimsically Mount Sandford Castle, was built amidst the trees of the steep side of the Nore valley where diners could enjoy the view of the Nore and its bridge through a large gothic window.

Many landowners happily mixed gothic and classical styles on their demesnes, which would indicate that they were more interested in the decorative value of the styles, rather than being prompted by any deep philosophical or political intentions. For example, at Heywood, Michael Frederick Trench (1746–1836) ornamented his grounds with buildings influenced by the classical Greek style and several gothick structures. These included a sham castle (*c.*1780) with materials salvaged from the medieval Aghaboe friary, an orangery, an obelisk and entrance gates all in the gothick style. One of the best known gothick buildings in Ireland is the Batty Langley folly at Castletown, Co. Kildare. This lodge was originally built as a cottage *orné* but was redesigned with a gothic façade some time before 1760. At Marino, Dublin, famous for its classical Casino, James Caulfield (1728–99), first earl of Charlemont, who returned from a nine-year tour of Europe in 1754, built a gothick-style garden house in 1762, named Rosamund's Bower. The cleric John Wesley (1703–91), on one of many visits to Ireland, thought its design was 'delightful indeed'.[43] The Bower was a tall gothick structure, designed to look like a church with stained glass windows giving views onto Dublin Bay from one side and a serpentine lake populated by wildfowl from the other.[44]

A number of Georgian gothick buildings were more ephemeral, made from tree roots and branches and thatched with heather, with the only stylistic nod to Gothicism being their pointed arches and windows. These 'rustic habitations', often referred to as moss houses or wood houses, were little more than summer houses, containing seats for resting in the shade, an example being William Ashford's Mount

---

Ireland, 2 vols (London, 1837), ii, p. 17.   **41** TCD, MS 967, p. 94: 'Lewis Dillwyn's journal of a tour to Killarney, 1809'.   **42** Sandys died at Bellevue in 1795 and by 1822 it was 'much gone to ruin', G.N. Wright, *A guide to County Wicklow* (Dublin, 1822), p. 37.   **43** John Wesley, *The works of the Rev. John Wesley, A.M.*, 14 vols (London, 1872), iv, p. 132: 16 July 1778.   **44** Edward Lloyd, *A month's tour in north Wales, Dublin, and its environs. With observations upon their manners and police in the year 1780* (London, 1781), p. 79.

Merrion, Dublin.[45] Other outwardly ornate buildings, in common with other garden structures, often had a practical function. Knockdrin, Co. Westmeath, had a gothick-style game larder, designed by Patrick Keegan (*fl.* 1820s), which also had a dining space, while Castle Blunden, Co. Kilkenny, had a gothick-style icehouse, dating from about 1750.

In conclusion, the gothick style can be traced from its origins in the search for a sense of history and continuity from the medieval past, to a fashionable decorative style, which was to become a prominent style in the Victorian era, seen in both public and domestic buildings. In Ireland, the topography and climate were particularly suited to the picturesque landscapes to which gothick flourishes added drama and a touch of antiquity to the carefully choreographed scenes.

---

45 Wright, *A guide to County Wicklow*, p. 36.

CHAPTER THIRTEEN

The nursery and seed trade in Dublin before 1800

TERENCE REEVES-SMYTH

THE RAPID EXPANSION OF Dublin as a significant metropolitan city during the eighteenth century was accompanied by a steady growth of the seed and nursery trade to meet the ever-increasing demands from its citizens.[1] By 1760 the city's population stood at around 141,000, just less than a quarter of the size of London, and, as was the case in London, the urban periphery was then surrounded by a mélange of garden nurseries, market gardens and orchards, all graphically depicted on John Rocque's famous *An exact survey of the city and suburbs of Dublin* of 1756.[2] Nearly thirty seedsmen and nurserymen were then operating in the city – a substantial rise from barely a handful at the start of the century, while by the 1790s that number had increased to around sixty-eight.[3]

The corresponding numbers of market gardeners are more difficult to assess, for unlike the seed and nursery trade, many of their names tend not to have been recorded.[4] Although the profession of market gardener and nurseryman overlapped considerably, nurserymen as a rule, unlike market gardeners, conducted trade from their own premises rather than the city markets.[5] Both nurserymen and seedsmen

---

1 The only comprehensive work of the early Dublin nursery trade to-date has been undertaken by the late Eileen McCracken, see Eileen McCracken, 'Irish nurserymen and seedsmen 1740–1800', *Quarterly Journal of Forestry*, 59:2 (1965), 131–9; 'Notes on eighteenth-century Irish nurserymen', *Irish Forestry*, 24:1 (1967), 39–58; 'Nurseries and seedshops in Ireland' in E.C. Nelson and Aidan Brady (eds), *Irish gardening and horticulture* (Dublin, 1979), pp 179–90; see also Mary Forrest, 'Nurseries and nurserymen in Ireland from the early eighteenth century to the early twenty-first century', *Studies in the History of Garden and Designed Landscapes*, 30 (2010), 323–36.   2 Patrick Fagan, 'The population of Dublin in the eighteenth century with particular reference to the proportions of protestants and catholics', *Eighteenth-century Ireland*, 6 (1991), 121–56, see 140; see also David Dickson, 'The place of Dublin in the eighteenth-century Irish economy' in T.M. Devine and David Dickson (eds), *Ireland and Scotland: parallels and contrasts in economic and social development* (Edinburgh, 1983), pp 178–9. Rocque's map was published in four sheets from a survey undertaken in 1754 and 1755, see Colm Lennon and John Montague, *John Rocque's Dublin* (Dublin, 2010). For distribution of London's market gardens, see Malcolm Thick, *The neat house gardens. Early market gardening around London* (London, 1998), pp 57–8. 3 In all, 135 different seed merchants and nurserymen have been recorded by the writer of this paper as operating at various times in Dublin during the eighteenth century.   4 By 1800 however there were sixteen named 'Fruiterers' of 'Fruit-merchants' with their own premises listed in *Wilson's Dublin Directory*, including one in Smock Alley who specialized as a 'Foreign Fruit-merchant'.   5 The market gardener grew produce for sale, the nurseryman raised plants for others to replant; see Ronald Webber, *Market gardening: the history of commercial flower, fruit and vegetable growing* (Newton Abbot, 1972), pp 65–91.

tended to locate their retail outlets in certain favoured areas of the city, notably around Capel Street, Christ Church Cathedral, Thomas Street and the Cornmarket, but it should be emphasized that the professions of seedsman and nurseryman also overlapped. At that time seedsmen sold seeds to nurserymen and the nursery trade in turn sold plants to seedsmen. Indeed, every Dublin nurseryman of the eighteenth century appears to have sold seed, frequently also including agricultural varieties, while seed merchants, who often doubled up as a grocer or fruit merchant, usually also sold roots (rhizomes, tubers, corms and fibrous rooted plants), and sometimes trees and shrubs to widen the range of goods they had for customers.[6]

The burgeoning demand for commercial horticulture in the eighteenth century was complemented by a parallel growth in private gardening. By the mid-eighteenth century there were scores of manors around the city with elaborate gardens boasting tree-lines avenues and vistas, woods and ornamental groves, parterres, as well as kitchen gardens and orchards.[7] In addition, there were numerous town houses with rear garden plots, all of which necessitated a demand not just for increasing volumes of seed and nursery stock, but an ever greater range of plant species and varieties. Indeed, the rise in available plants was extraordinary; in England, and thereby probably also in Ireland, the number of cultivated plants rose from around 1,600 in the mid-seventeenth century to 18,000 in 1839 – most of that growth having taken place during the course of the eighteenth and early nineteenth centuries.[8]

A significant driving force behind this explosion of demand for new cultivated plants was undoubtably the emergence of the 'consumer revolution', which had a profound and transforming effect on both London and Dublin society during the eighteenth century.[9] Demanding citizens increasingly wanted 'not only necessities but decencies and even luxuries', while the rich indulged in an ever rising orgy of spending – building new houses and filling them with the latest styles in furniture, fabrics, porcelain and wallpaper.[10] As Neil McKendrick observed, 'even flowers had to submit to the tyranny of fashion. Nature itself had to conform to the lust for novelty',[11] so horticulture was not exempt from the consequent 'retailing revolution', which transformed Britain, in the words of Adam Smith (*d.* 1790), into a 'nation of shopkeepers'.[12]

The consequent 'boom in exotics' became a major factor in the nursery trade during the eighteenth century, as ambitious traders were perpetually seeking the very

---

6 Malcolm Thick, 'Garden seeds in England before the late eighteenth century – II. The trade in seeds to 1760', *Agricultural History Review*, 38, pt II (1990), 109.   7 As depicted on John Rocque's *An exact survey of the city and suburbs of Dublin* (1756) and his 1760 *An actual survey of the county of Dublin* (four sheets).   8 John Harvey, *Early gardening catalogues* (London & Chichester, 1972), p. 7; J.H. Plumb, 'The acceptance of modernity' in Neil McKendrick, John Brewer and J.H. Plumb (eds), *The birth of the consumer society: the commercialization of eighteenth-century England* (Brighton, 2018), p. 324.   9 Neil McKendrick, 'Commercialization of leisure: botany, gardening and the birth of a consumer society' in McKendrick, Brewer and Plumb (eds), *The birth of a consumer society*, pp 337–78.   10 See chapter on 'Life of the rich' in Constance Maxwell, *Dublin under the Georges, 1714–1830* (London, 1956), pp 100–36.   11 McKendrick, 'Commercialization of leisure', p. 340.   12 Roderick Floud, *An economic history of the English garden* (London, 2019), p. 133; see also Carole Shammas, *The pre-industrial consumer in England*

The nursery and seed trade in Dublin before 1800

latest and most spectacular trees, shrubs and 'florists flowers' to attract customers. However, there was still limited appreciation of how such plants grew. Although the Chinese had been hybridizing roses and camellias for centuries, its considerable benefits were not appreciated in Europe until the nineteenth century, not-withstanding Thomas Fairchild's successful plant cross between two *Dianthus* species, published in 1717,[13] and the rigorous experiments in plant hybridization undertaken by Joseph Gottlieb Kölreuter in Germany from the 1760s.[14] Accordingly, eighteenth-century nurserymen in their search for novelties had to rely on new plants coming from abroad or by old methods of careful selection of colour and form.

The increase in the range of available plants during the course of the century meant that good marketing became ever more important. Initially, following the practice of other city traders, they produced broadsheets that listed stock for sale, usually placed in a prominent position inside or outside the shop, while many also would have issued printed trade cards to give to customers; later in the century catalogues were increasingly issued in pamphlet or book form.[15] While it is evident from newspaper advertisements that many Dublin nurserymen and seedsmen did produce printed catalogues from at least the mid eighteenth century onwards, very few have survived. Fortunately, this void in our knowledge can be partially filled by other means, notably by newspapers of which around 160 are recorded having begun publication in Dublin before 1760.[16] Traders who could afford it often advertised in one of more of these papers and occasionally also listed plants they had for sale. Consequently, as we shall see in this chapter, much of our knowledge of the seed and nursery trade in eighteenth-century Dublin derives from these newspaper notices, in addition to private family papers and institutional records, notably those of the (Royal) Dublin Society.

THE NASCENCE OF DUBLIN'S SEED AND NURSERY TRADE

There is an inevitable symbiotic relationship between urban consumers and their rural hinterland. As in the eighteenth century, the medieval and Tudor city of Dublin was surrounded by gardens and orchards sufficient to provide the needs of the city, while beyond these lay extensive areas of arable land. The city's population needed bread, ale and other foodstuffs, including animal feed, all of which required plenty of wheat and oats, together with lesser amounts of barley, rye and legumes (peas and beans).[17] Industrial crops, such as flax (*Linum usitatissimum*), hemp (*Cannabis sativa*)

---

and America (Oxford, 1990).   **13** Michaeal Leapman, *The ingenious Mr. Fairchild* (London, 2000), passim. **14** Joseph Gottlieb Kölreuter (1733–1806): see W.O. Focke, 'History of plant hybrids', *The Monist*, 23:3 (July 1913), 398–415.   **15** Harvey, *Early gardening catalogues*, passim.   **16** Robert Munter, *The history of the Irish newspaper, 1685–1760* (Cambridge, 1967), passim. Of the 160 Dublin papers listed, no copies of 25 survive, while over 50 are known only in one of two issues.   **17** Margaret Murphy, 'Feeding another city: provisioning Dublin in the later middle ages' in Matthew Davies and J.A. Galloway (eds), *London and beyond: essays in honour of Derek Keen* (London, 2012), pp 3–24.

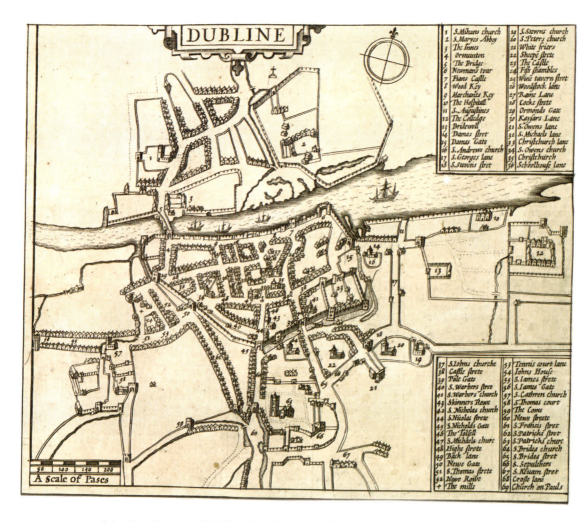

13.1 John Speed's map of Dublin, 1610. By permission of the Royal Irish Academy © RIA.

and madder (*Rubia tinctoria*), were also grown, and the city in return, in addition to providing a ready market, was able to supply manure, the only source of nitrogen prior to the seventeenth century.[18]

The ability of these market gardeners and farmers to adequately provision the city meant they had of necessity, in contrast to more rural areas, to adopt specialized and intensive management techniques. Produce also had to be stored and transported, while the gardeners and farmers needed to be able to easily acquire sufficient quantities of fresh seed and plants. This was not just a matter of saving their own

18 Margaret Murphy and Michael Potterton, *The Dublin region in the Middle Ages: settlement, land-use and economy* (Dublin, 2010), pp 287–356; also Graham Harvey, *The forgiveness of nature: the story of grass*

The nursery and seed trade in Dublin before 1800

seed; as Walter of Henley, an English friar, wrote in his widely read treatise on husbandry in *c*.1280, seed (corn) should be changed 'every year, for seed grown on other ground will bring more profit than that which is grown on your own'.[19] While we can generalize that seed and plants were traded from an early period, we can assume that much of this was done in the city markets and at fairs, alongside garden and agricultural produce. General shopkeepers would assuredly have stocked seeds, 'roots' and bulbs in small quantities, no doubt in competition with pedlars with their packs wandering the streets. Indeed, in the more refined city of the twenty-first century it is easy to overlook the former omnipresence of noisy street pedlars or hawkers at every street corner; often they were considered a public nuisance – in the 1720s Dean Jonathan Swift (1667–1745) complained of one 'crying cabbages and savoys' like a 'restless dog' who plagued him 'mightly every morning' and Caleb Threlkeld (1676–1728) likewise notes the cries of hawkers in his *Synopsis stirpium Hibernicarum*.[20] Street hawkers long had a reputation for selling seed of dubious value;[21] at the turn of the sixteenth century, Richard Gardiner, in the earliest book on vegetables published in the English language, complained bitterly of 'the great and abominable falsehood of those sorts of people which sell garden seedes' (hawkers), who commonly deceived the public by selling 'old and dead seeds for their gardens'.[22] This complaint of 'old and dead seeds' was to echo down through the ages, but it was clearly much more difficult to prosecute both town and rural pedlars, who were mobile and usually with only meagre resources than traders with fixed retail establishments.

Slips and grafts were most likely bought from nearby manorial gardens or exchanged during the medieval era; in the years prior to the dissolution, monasteries also played a key role in trading plants, particularly in introducing and distributing new fruit varieties.[23] Indeed, fruit seems to have been the first horticultural trade to have become specialized, as there had long been a keen interest in obtaining good varieties of apples, pears and cherries in particular.[24] It is worth noting that Henry VIII's 'Fruiterer' was said to have been an Irishman[25] and that by the seventeenth-century, if not long before, orchards were a familiar sight in many parts of Ireland.[26]

(London, 2001).   **19** The treatise was originally written in French and remained a standard text for centuries afterwards; translated by Elizabeth Lamond, *Walter of Henley's husbandry, together with an anonymous husbandry, seneschaucie, and Robert Grosseteste's rules* (London and New York, 1890), p. 19. **20** William Laffan (ed.), *The cries of Dublin &c. drawn from life by Hugh Douglas Hamilton, 1760* (Dublin, 2003), p. 15; on Threlkeld on hawkers see *The first Irish flora, Synopsis stirpium Hibernicarum*, ed. E.C. Nelson (facsimile with annotations by E.C. Nelson and D.M. Synnott) (Kilkenny, 1988), p. xiv. **21** Thick, 'Garden seeds in England', 106.   **22** Richard Gardiner, *Profitable instructions for the manuring, sowing and planting of kitchen gardens* (London, 1603), p. 11 (1st ed. 1599); see also Blanche Henrey, *British botanical and horticultural literature before 1800* (Oxford, 1999), i, pp 68–9.   **23** Harvey, *Early gardening catalogues*, p. 2; John Harvey, *Early nurserymen* (London & Chichester, 1974), pp 35–6. At the dissolution, monastic gardens in Ireland invariably had attached orchards: N.B. White (ed.), *Extents of Irish monastic possessions, 1540–1541, from manuscripts in the Public Record Office, London* (Dublin, 1943), passim. **24** Harvey, *Early gardening catalogues*, p. 2; Harvey, *Early nurserymen*, pp 58–9.   **25** Duncan Harrington, 'Richard Harris, "Fruiterer to King Henry VIII": some further details gleaned from documentary sources', *Archaeologia Cantiana*, 137 (2016), 295–300; see also Ronald Webber, *The early horticulturists* (Newton Abbot, 1968), pp 29–42.   **26** The Civil Survey of the 1650s documented numerous orchards

However, while fruiticulture was becoming well developed by the Tudor era, it was only during the seventeenth century that we see significant horticultural specialization as traders started to focus on supplying the ever increasing range of flowers, shrubs and trees that were becoming available.

Specialization and the emergence of professionalism in the seed and nursery trade was paralleled by the employment of skilled gardeners and the emergence of garden designers. The earliest recorded gardeners in seventeenth-century Dublin were Harry Holland (*fl.* 1605), at Trinity College Dublin and Pat McCarter (*fl.* 1635–37), who gardened at Lispopple House, near Swords, outside the city.[27] In the decades following the Restoration of 1660, following a remarkably rapid rise in the city's population,[28] the number of identified professional gardeners increases considerably,[29] while the earliest evidence of a tradesman calling himself a 'seedsman' was one Elnathan Brock 'of Hyche Street Dublin', whose will was dated 1660.[30] Some commercial seedsmen and nurserymen were clearly active in the city when in May 1686, the Viceroy, Henry Hyde (1638–1709), Lord Clarendon, in a letter to John Evelyn (1620–1706), remarked that the people of Dublin were 'curious in kitchen gardens' and that the cultivation of their 'sallets are very good and the roots generally much better than ours in England'.[31] Some of the traders whose names we know included Thomas Ashton, 'seedsman', who was made a Freeman of the City of Dublin in 1687.[32] Both John Cole and Nicholas Sheapeard are recorded as supplying the gardens of Trinity College with good quantities of vegetable seed and plants at various times between 1683 and 1685.[33] Sheapeard also furnished stock-gillyflower seeds, no doubt for the Fellow's Garden, while John Young provided an assortment of garden tools.[34] However, these individuals all appear to have been relatively small scale traders

---

across the country; in the Dublin region there were over 110 orchards large enough to merit recording: see R.C. Simington (ed.), *The Civil Surveys, AD 1654–56*, 10 vols (Dublin, 1931–61), passim. **27** For Harry Holland see E.C. Nelson and E.M. McCracken, *The brightest jewel: a history of the National Botanic Gardens Glasnevin, Dublin* (Kilkenny, 1987), p. 8; and E.C. Nelson, '"Reserved to the Fellows"; four centuries of gardens at Trinity College, Dublin' in Charles Holland (ed.), *Trinity College Dublin and the idea of a university* (Dublin, 1991), pp 185–222. For Pat Carter see Huntington Library, San Marino, California: Rawdon Papers, information from the late Rolf Loeber. **28** J.G. Simms, 'Dublin in 1685', *Irish Historical Studies*, 14:55 (1965), 216–17. Immigration from England and the Continent was responsible for much of the population increase. **29** Those late seventeenth-century gardeners whose wills were registered included Dennis Carrick (1655), Thomas Elliot (1685), Thomas Aston (1694); see Sir Arthur Vicars, *Index to the prerogative wills of Ireland, 1536–1810* (Dublin, 1897), pp 13, 78, 154. The earliest recorded female gardener was Margaret Armstrong, who worked in the Physic Garden of Trinity College (TCD, MSS Bursar's Vouchers P4/04/01); see Nelson, '"Reserved to the Fellows"', p. 188. **30** Brock's Christian name suggests he was a non-conformist. For his will dated 1660, see Vicars, *Index to the prerogative wills*, p. 56 (VIII, 84). Tokens bearing his name were recorded for the late 1650s; see *Proceedings of the Royal Irish Academy*, 4 (1850), xxxvi. According to R.H. Thompson and M.J. Dickinson (eds), *Sylloge of coins of the British Isles vol. 49. Tokens of the British Isles 1575–1750. Part VI. Wiltshire to Yorkshire. Ireland to Wales* (London, 1999), where one token is inscribed 'seedman of Hyche Street Dublin'. **31** Samuel Weller Singer (ed.), *The correspondence of Henry Hyde, earl of Clarendon and his brother, Laurence Hyde, earl of Rochester* 2 vols (London, 1828), i, p. 407. **32** 22 March 1687/88. Admitted by fine. Ancient Freemen of Dublin database, Dublin City Council: https://databases. dublincity.ie/freemen/viewdoc.php?freemenid=252, accessed 27 February 2022. **33** On the TCD gardens and gardeners see Nelson, '"Reserved to the Fellows"', pp 185–222. **34** E.C. Nelson, '"This

The nursery and seed trade in Dublin before 1800

as their names do not reoccur in documents; it is not until the early and mid-eighteenth century that we see the rise of seedsmen and nurserymen with extensive establishments serving the city.

DUBLIN'S EARLY NURSERYMEN

The enthusiasm among the upper social classes for gardening and tree planting in the decades following the Restoration, so evident in England, was also reflected in Ireland where many grandees and gentry also started to rebuild or extend their seats and enclose them in the fashionable formal parks and gardens of the era.[35] No doubt, this was purely about self-aggrandisement for some, but many others saw it as a visible manifestation of much needed rural 'improvement' in a country plagued by poor estate management and food shortages.[36] Hundreds of mansions across the country were being given formal layouts incorporating straight tree-lined avenues and vistas, flanked by geometrically laid out yards, fields and orchards, with associated blocks of woodland, ornamental groves, bosquets, parterres and other garden features.[37] To obtain the required stock for all this new planting, landowners in the decades before the close of the seventeenth century tended to buy direct from English or French nurseries as they could not obtain all that they required from Dublin. Thus in December 1653 John Perceval (d. 1665) was being supplied with a large consignment of fruit trees by London nurseryman Arnold Banbury (1598–1664/5), while his son, Sir John Perceval (d. 1686), imported forest and fruit trees from Bristol in 1682–3.[38] George Rawdon (1604–84), on behalf of Lord Conway (c.1623–83), was buying fruit trees, box and other plants from England in the 1660s,[39] and Sir John Skeffington, whose 'greatest interainmt is Planting', was importing seeds of a range of evergreen plants, trees and flowers from England in 1686.[40] However, transporting plants at this time could amount to nearly 50 per cent of the net costs;[41] in addition, plants could be damaged in transit; for example trees imported from France by Sir George Lane (c.1620–83) in the 1660s suffered badly during transport.[42] It was hardly surprising

garden to adorn with all varietie": the garden plants of Ireland in the centuries before 1700', *Moorea*, 9 (1990), 37–54, at 49–50, gives details of what seeds and plants were supplied. See also Nelson and McCracken, *The brightest jewel*, p. 9. **35** Rolf Loeber and Livia Hurley, 'The architecture of Irish country houses, 1691–1739: continuity and innovation' in Raymond Gillespie and R.F. Foster (eds), *Irish provincial cultures in the long eighteenth century: essays for Toby Barnard* (Dublin, 2012), pp 201–19. **36** David Dickson, 'Society and economy in the long eighteenth century' in James Kelly (ed.), *The Cambridge history of Ireland, 3: 1730–1880* (Cambridge, 2018), pp 154–6. **37** For a summary see Terence Reeves-Smyth, 'Demesnes' in F.H.A. Aalen, Kevin Whelan and Matthew Stout (eds), *Atlas of the Irish rural landscape* (Cork, 2011), pp 278–86; see also Vandra Costello, *Irish demesne landscapes, 1660–1740* (Dublin, 2015), passim. **38** Harvey, *Early nurserymen*, p. 41. **39** His son Arthur in 1692 famously commissioned a shipload of plants to be brought back to Ireland from Jamaica: see E.C. Nelson, 'Sir Arthur Rawdon (1662–1695) of Moira. His life and letters, family and friends, and his Jamaican plants', *Proceedings of the Belfast Natural History and Philosophical Society*, 10, ser. 2 (1983), 30–52. **40** Nelson, 'The garden plants of Ireland in the centuries before 1700', 45–9 and 53–4. **41** Harvey, *Early gardening catalogues*, p. 28. **42** Sir George Lane (later Viscount Lanesborough) was importing stock for his

therefore that landowners frequently set up their own demesne nurseries; a good example was the large nursery established by Sir Richard Bulkeley (1660–1710), at Old Bawn in south Dublin, where he grew apples, quinces, cherries, apricots and walnuts.[43]

Some general traders took advantage of the relative absence of nurseries in the early decades of the century by importing one-off shipments for sale, as for example one Raymond Penettes, 'merchant', who may have been French, was selling 'fine orange and lemon trees and roots' in St George's Lane in May 1725.[44] Around this time Charles Carter (*fl.* 1728–43), 'His Majesty's Gardener at Chapelizod' who 'having since the decease of Robert Moody his late partner carried on the seed trade by himself', was importing 'all kinds of fruit trees of the choicest French and English Collections, Forest Trees, Flowering Shrubs, Evergreen of all kinds and sizes and flower Roots'.[45]

Carter does not appear to have been a practicing nurseryman, that is to say, there is no evidence he was actually propagating his own stock. However, the city was witness to the rise of a number of successful nurserymen at this time, some drawn from the influx of immigrants into Dublin during the later seventeenth century. Among the best known was Peter Landré (1667–1747), a Huguenot fleeing the *dragonnades* in Orléans. It is not known exactly when he arrived as an émigré, but he first leased a house east of St Stephen's Green in 1709 and later acquired the lease of a grand town mansion built by Col. Cary Dillon (1627–89), later fifth earl of Roscommon, just north-east of the Green in the area between what is now Merrion Row and Hume Street. His nursery lay to the west of this house in the area now occupied by Ely Place and is shown on Rocque's 1756 Dublin map as being dominated by two short rectangular squares of trees, dissected by cross-paths. It became the city's best-known nursery and thrived until 1749 when John Landré, who had inherited the business from his late uncle a few years earlier, transformed much of the nursery ground into a 'Spring Garden, in the manner of Vauxhall, London', but after this ambitious venture failed, the land was sold for development in 1751.[46]

Landré's Stephen's Green nursery was importing fruit trees from England by 1714 and offering 'staples and rarities' as well as flower seeds, 'roots' and grass seeds. In 1723 he was importing from 'correspondents in England, Holland and France' the 'right Kinds of Trees, and new Seeds, that any Gentleman shall please to call for'. He encouraged the cultivation of fruits as good as those 'of England or France' and was successfully growing 'for Dwarf or Contra Espalier' in his own nursery.[47] The success

---

Rathcline estate, Co. Longford: see *Calendar of state papers of Ireland* (1662–4), pp 422–3; Historic Manuscripts Commission, *Calendar of the manuscripts of the marquess of Ormonde* (London, 1903), ns, 45, p. 132. **43** Toby Barnard, *Making the grand figure: lives and possession in Ireland, 1641–1770* (New Haven & London, 2004), pp 200, 421 (citing Lister Manuscript in the Bodleian Library, Oxford). **44** *The Dublin Weekly Journal*, 8 May, 1725, p. 4 and 15 May, 1725, p. 28. **45** *Dublin Intelligence*, 11 Jan. 1728, p. 3; 14 Dec. 1728, p. 3; Carter died in 1743: see Vicars, *Index to the prerogative wills of Ireland*, p. 79. **46** *Faulkiner's Dublin Journal*, 14 Oct. 1740, p. 4; 27 Jan. 1749, p. 2; 10 Feb. 1749, p. 2 and *Saunder's News-Letter*, 2 Jan. 1775, p. 3. **47** *Dublin Courant*, 21 Dec. 1723, p. 2 (notice Nov. 5). Also see *Dublin Courant*,

The nursery and seed trade in Dublin before 1800

of Peter Landré 'Gardner' (as he called himself) no doubt lay in the quality and range of his fruit and other nursery stock, but it also rested on the professional advice he provided, attracting customers from all over the country. In January 1719/20 for example, he was supplying the O'Haras at Nymphsfield (Annaghmore), Co. Sligo with stocks of peaches (three varieties), apricots, nectarines, plums (six varieties), pears (three varieties) and apples (three dwarf varieties) for the walls of their kitchen garden and in 1743–5 he provided Samuel Madden (1686–1765) with 'a catalogue of fruit trees planted in espalier hedges' for 'the upper kitchen garden' at Manor Waterhouse, near Lisnaskea, Co. Fermanagh.[48]

Landré's Dublin nursery did not long survive his death in 1747, by which time the city trade was dominated by Daniel Bullen (c.1695–1784), undoubtably Dublin's best-known eighteenth-century nurseryman. According to Joseph Cooper Walker's well known, but not always reliable, account of early gardening in Ireland, Daniel Bullen arrived in Ireland with his brother William, presumably as boys, from Westmoreland 'in the Reign of Queen Anne' (1702–14).[49] He started working for another English immigrant, Walter Roe (Rowe), who by 1711 had opened a nursery on New Street, at that time an arterial route into the city from Rathfarnham; Rowe also had a seed shop, on Christ Church Lane, which his widow retained until her death in 1745.[50] Roe's business was successful; for example, in 1722 he is recorded as selling £66 of stock, probably trees, to the earl of Meath, presumably for the Kilruddery gardens.[51] Walker's statement that Roe and Bullen were 'employed like London and Wise by the nobility and gentry in laying out their gardens' may well have been correct, but we have no direct evidence for any of their works; however, it was not unusual, nor surprising, to find nurserymen at this time laying out parks and gardens in addition to just supplying the plants.

Until the 1740s Bullen's relationship with Roe was probably as an employee managing the four-acre nursery on New Street/Circular Road. Following Roe's death however, it become Bullen's nursery, while Bullen also acquired nearby 8 Christ Church Lane as his home and seed shop, adjacent to Rowe's old shop at No. 10. Bullen's name starts to appear in estate record books from the 1750s; for example, in January 1756 he was sending seeds to William Balfour at Townley Hall, Co. Louth and the following month supplying Powerscourt, Co. Wicklow, with various vegetable seeds.[52] From then onwards Bullen was attracting customers across the country, such as Richard Edgeworth in Co. Longford in 1769.[53] One notable Bullen customer was

---

14 Jan. 1749, p. 3; 4 Feb. 1749, p. 3; 25 Mar. 1749, p. 3. **48** NLI, MS 20, 365/4 (O'Hara: 23 Jan. 1719); PRONI, D/3465/G/3/1: MIC/594/7 (Madden). See also Barnard, *Making the grand figure*, p. 424, fn. 158. **49** J.C. Walker, 'Essay on the rise and progress of gardening in Ireland', *Transactions of the Royal Irish Academy*, 4, pt. 3 (Antiquities, 1791), 3–19, fn. p13. **50** *Faulkiner's Dublin Journal*, 27 Jan. 1746, p. 4. **51** Desmond FitzGerald and John Cornforth, 'Killruddery, Co. Wicklow I', *Country Life*, 162, fn. 4176 (14 July 1977), p. 80. **52** NLI, Balfour/Townley Hall, MS 10276 (3), No. 1; NLI, Powerscourt Papers, MS 8367, folder 1, horticultural accounts, 15 March 1755. Also see Leslie Clarkson and Margaret Crawford, *Feast and famine: food and nutrition in Ireland, 1500–1920* (Oxford, 2001), pp 49–50. **53** NLI, Edgeworth Accounts, MS 1535, pp 146, 261: March (1769); 27 October (1769).

Tom (1738?–1803) and Louisa Conolly (1743–1821) at Castletown, Co. Kildare, for whom between 1763–75 were supplied with a range of forest trees, fruit trees (dwarfs and standards), roses and various other shrubs, evergreens, climbers, seeds, roots and bulbs of various sorts, plus garden tools such as pruning knives, axes, saws and bill hooks.[54]

None of Bullen's catalogues survives, but from a few rare newspaper advertisements we know that in March 1774 he was selling 'a large number of oak, beech, and elm layers, with all kinds of fruit trees, flowering shrubs, pine apple and asparagus plants' and importing garden seeds and flower roots from Holland and England.[55] In 1780, by which time he must have been at least eighty-five, he moved his seed shop to his New Street nursery[56] and in 1781 went into partnership with a much younger nurseryman, Francis Webb (*fl.* 1780–5).[57] After his death in November 1784, his nursery, now over eight acres extent, which later writers recalled had a 'hare hunt and a boat hunt in box' as an attraction,[58] was auctioned; it contained the 'greatest variety of the finest, healthy and strongest Fruit and Forest Trees' with an 'extensive collection of the most curious and beautiful Flowering Trees and Shrubs, Evergreens, Stove and Green-house Plants, with a vast quantity of Seedling Beech, &c, &c'.[59]

Bullen's name is often associated with the pineapple (*Ananas comosus*), which Walker claimed he had introduced into Ireland; if so, it probably happened in the 1730s.[60] He was still growing pineapples in the 1770s, but post 1748 was selling many through John Phelan (*fl.* 1746–89), at his shop on Christ Church Lane.[61] Phelan, who was 'bred a gardener' and trained in London under nurseryman Thomas Greening (1684–1757), had returned to Dublin in 1746 and taken over William Roe's shop on Christ Church Lane.[62] Later he named his shop 'The Sign of the Pineapple' with 'A Pine Apple Bust over the Door' and started specializing in growing pineapples himself at his nursery in Harold's Cross. The value and prestige of pineapples was then so great that he was sometimes able to rent, rather than sell, the fruit for table displays. He engaged watchmen to guard them against theft; unfortunately, on one occasion in October 1763 there was an attempt to steal 'a large quantity of pine-apples out of the hot-house', when two of his watchmen were stabbed with knives.[63]

---

54 Irish Architectural Archive, Uncatalogued Conolly Papers, Account Books, Book 1762–1767; Book 1767–1775; Book 1775–1781; see also Finola O'Kane, *Landscape design in eighteenth-century Ireland: mixing foreign trees with the natives* (Cork, 2004), pp 186–8.   55 *Saunder's News-Letter*, 25 Mar. 1774, p. 2; see also 18 Mar. 1776, p. 2.   56 8 Christ-Church Lane was acquired by Patrick Donegan, seedsman, who in 1794 was falsely calling himself 'Successor to Mr. Daniel Bullen'.   57 Messrs Bullen's & Webb's sales included fruit tree to Mount Stewart, Co. Down, in 1781: see PRONI, Londonderry Papers: D654/H1/1: Journal of accounts 1781–9.   58 Walker, 'Essay on the rise and progress of gardening', 13.   59 *Dublin Evening Post*, 6 Jan. 1787; 8 Nov. 1787, p. 2.   60 Walker, 'Essay on the rise and progress of gardening', 13; Fran Beauman, *The pineapple: king of fruits* (London, 2005), p. 104; see also E.C. Nelson, 'Some records (*c.*1690–1830) of greenhouses in Irish gardens', *Moorea*, 2 (1983), 21–8.   61 John Robertson, 'Notes on the former and present state of horticulture in Ireland', *The Gardener's Magazine*, 4 (Feb. 1830), 26–7.   62 *Faulkiner's Dublin Journal*, 27 Jan. 1746, p. 4.   63 *Freeman's Journal*, 1 Oct. 1763, p. 3; 29 Oct. 1763, p. 3; 26 Nov. 1763, p. 3; *Dublin Courier*, 30 Sept. 1763, p. 1. Also see *Belfast*

The nursery and seed trade in Dublin before 1800

By the 1760s John Phelan, though he still sometimes referred to himself as a 'Grocer',[64] had become one of the city's most successful nurserymen, importing stock from Holland and England and, unusually for an Irish nurseryman of the period, exporting to England and Wales.[65] As with Bullen none of his catalogues have survived, but we know from newspaper advertisements that in addition to fruit trees, he sold a wide range of forest trees, such as Weymouth pine (*Pinus strobus*), tulip tree (*Liriodendron tulipifera*), Spanish plane (*Platanus hispanica*), American cypress (*Taxodium distichum*), cedar of Lebanon (*Cedrus libani*), red and white Virginian cedar (*Juniperus virginiana* and *Thuja occidentalis*) and black spruce (*Picea mariana*). In the 1780s he enthusiastically promoted asparagus plants, remarking that 'it is indolent and shameful to see the number of genteel tables in the Country destitute of this most exquisite Dish'.[66] Estate records show he was fashionable among the gentry and nobility, such as the Conollys of Castletown, who he supplied from the early 1760s until at least 1773 with a wide range of stock – forest trees, shrubs, fruit trees and flowers, the latter including scarlet geranium (probably *Pelargonium inquinans*), Persian iris (*Iris persica*) and Dutch hyacinths (*Hyacinthus orientalis* cultivars), the latter including double varieties, in addition to kitchen garden seed and garden tools.[67] Another important client was Sir Patrick Bellew (1726?–95), of Barmeath, Co. Louth; it is of interest to learn that in 1775 one of John Phelan's daughters married John Bellew, a relation of Sir Patrick, who later remarked: 'I confess my pride suffers a little on account of this alliance' – an interesting reflection on the attitudes of a member of the Catholic gentry towards the social status of 'trade'.[68] Phelan provided Bellew with extensive advise on preparation, bedding, and soils, advising 'you'll probably state at all this trouble, but if you consider a diamond won't shine unless it is worked with great labour and industry'.[69] As with Landré and Bullen, Phelan's success as a nurseryman was no doubt helped considerably by his ability to advise clients, not just with 'the pruning and managing in the neatest manner, with fruit trees', but directing 'the building of stoves and fire walls', and drawing 'plans of gardens and parks and [executing] them conformable to the curious modern world, so much in practice in Great Britain'.[70]

Landscape and garden design was evidently a profitable way to make money by the early eighteenth century as the careers of English nurserymen Henry Wise (1653–1738), George London (*c.*1640–1714) and Stephen Switzer (1682–1745) would all

News-Letter, 23 Aug. 1768, p. 3; 13 Aug. 1768, p. 4; *Freeman's Journal*, 13 Aug. 1768, p. 4; see also Beauman, *The pineapple*, p. 104.   64 The announcement of his second marriage describes him as 'Grocer of Christ-church lane', see *Hibernian Journal, or, Chronicle of Liberty*, 7 Jan. 1774, p. 3.   65 *Freeman's Journal*, 13 Aug. 1768, p. 4; *Saunder's News-Letter*, 19 Feb. 1776, p. 3.   66 *Dublin Evening Post*, 27 Mar. 1783, p. 1; 1 Apr. 1783, p. 1; *Saunders's News-Letter*, 7 Mar. 1787, p. 3; 17 Mar. 1787, p. 4.   67 Irish Architectural Archive, Castletown Papers, Account Books; TCD, Conolly Papers, MS 3931–84: Tradesman's accts, 1766, 1767, 1770, 1771, 1772 and 1773; see also O'Kane, *Landscape design in eighteenth-century Ireland*, appendix 1, pp 187–8.   68 Maureen Wall, 'The rise of a catholic middle class in eighteenth-century Ireland', *Irish Historical Studies*, 11:42 (1958), 107.   69 Karen Harvey, *The Bellews of Mount Bellew: a catholic gentry family in eighteenth-century Ireland* (Dublin, 1998), p. 72.   70 *Faulkiner's Dublin Journal*, 6 Jan. 1749, p. 4.

indicate.[71] One Dublin nurseryman who seemed to excel at garden design was Robert Stevenson (*fl.* 1734–56), whose premises for the years 1734–56 lay on the east side of St Stephen's Green at 'The Orange Tree' – a shop name confusingly also used by other Dublin nurserymen.[72] In the 1740s Stevenson produced rather elaborate garden plans for Headfort House, Co. Meath, very much in the style of Stephen Switzer, with a mixture of serpentine and straight walks.[73] Also in a similar style he designed the Vauxhall-style 'New Gardens' at the Rotunda Lying-in Hospital in 1748–9, with its walks, bowling green, various bosquets, exedra or orchestra and enclosing double lines of limes; 600 elms alone were planted here in 1748.[74] No doubt he supplied all the plants, but as with other early and mid-eighteenth-century Dublin nurserymen, we have relatively few newspaper advertisements, as nurserymen at that time still relied largely on personal recommendations, by word of mouth or by letter, to gain further business.[75]

JOHNSON'S BROADSHEET AND THE CITY'S EARLY SEED TRADE

Throughout the eighteenth century Dublin's seed merchants and nurserymen imported seed from Rotterdam and London, the latter being the major seed clearing centre in Great Britain. It is often difficult to assess the balance derived from home sources; no doubt the city's market gardeners contributed a good deal to the trade, but saving one's own seed, which requires skill, can be laborious and costly with no guarantee of success. Primary sources such as original customs logs or port books are lacking to inform us about imports into the city, but fortunately Arthur Dobbs (1687–1765), then MP for Carrickfergus, went through the ledgers of the Customs House for 1720–7.[76] He did not dwell too much on the subject of garden produce, but noted that for the year ending 25 March 1726 the sum of £1,450 was spent on imports of 'garden seeds' at an average value was 2*s.* 8*d.* a pound, which sounds expensive, but indicates that 10,875 lbs (4933 kg) cleared customs, a sizable amount. Of this £800 came from England and £600 from 'Eastland' – Dobb's term for the Low Countries and Northern Europe.[77]

Dobbs made no mention of imported seeds of grasses or legumes, but flax seed, according to Dobbs, was being imported at a rate of nearly 3,000 hogheads a year, or 20,300 bushels (515,720 kg); he complained that in Ireland 'many pull their flax without saving the seed and that the wet seasons prevent others that would'.[78] Importing flax seed, or 'line-seed', had in fact been encouraged by the newly

---

71 Floud, *An economic history of the English garden*, p. 105.   **72** Hugh Henderson on Capel Street (*fl.* 1748–78); John Johnson on Corkhill (*fl.* 1700–20) and Michael Butler, well known grocer on Dame Street (*fl.* 1760–76).   **73** G.C. Taylor, 'Headfort, Co. Meath – III', *Country Life*, 79: 2046 (4 Apr. 1936), 352–8; Edward Malins and Knight of Glin, *Lost demesnes: Irish landscape gardening, 1660–1845* (London, 1976), p. 92, pl. 104.   **74** Lennon and Montague, *John Rocque's Dublin*, pp 24–5.   **75** Barnard, *Making the grand figure*, p. 215 and fn. 158.   **76** Arthur Dobbs, *An essay on the trade and improvement of Ireland* (Dublin, 1729).   **77** Ibid., pp 41, 56 and 84.   **78** Ibid., p. 33.

A CATALOGUE

OF

Garden SEEDS and Flower ROOTS,

l by *John Johnson*, Gardiner and Seedsman, at the *Orange-Tree* on *Corkhill, Dublin.*

ds of Roots.
asburgh Onion-Seed
ed *Spanish* Onion
White *Spanish* Onion
ondon Leek
eek
rot
Carrot

Parsnep
ra
all forts
ole

llad Seeds.
n Radish
adwich Radish
nish Radish
anish Radish
Lettrice
ttice
rttice
tice
rttice-Seed
tice
ice
ttice
ice
ttice
inage
ninega
ach
et

et
dive
ereo

cket

n
rel
riel

effes
resses
'd Cresses
rl'd Cresses

ervil

rarslane

rsley

ad

paragus
er
abbage
ish Cabbage
bbage
bage

ewort strip'd
avoy

ellon
ellon
llon
umber

Short Cucumber
Prickly Cucumber
Pompion
Gourd
Mekin
Symnel, all forts
Calabash, all forts.

Pot-Herb Seeds.
Endive
Succory
Borage
Buglos
Burnet
Blood-wort
Clary
French Sorrel
Double Marygold
Pot-Marjoram
Landebeef
Summer Savory
Columbine
Tanfie
Nepp
French Mallows
Orach.

Sweet-Herb Seeds.
Thyme
Hyffop
Winter Savory
Sweet Marjoram
Sweet Basil, all forts
Sweet Maudin
Rofemary
Lavender.
Baum.

Physical Seeds.
Cardus Benedictus
Scurvy-Grafs
Angelica
Lovage
Smallage
Tobacco, all forts
Dill
Common Fennel
Italian Fennel
Sweet Fennel
Caruawy
Cumin
Anife
Corriander
Gromewel
Henbane
Plantain
Nettle
Balfam
White Poppy
Cardamum
Gourd
Broom
Piony
Fœnugreek
Flaxwort
Burdock
Elecampane
Daucus
Citrul
Worm-Seed
Rue
Goats Rue
Oclus Christi
Line Seed, or Flax Seed
Marshmallow
Mustard.

Flower Seeds.
Dutch Julyflowers
Stock Julyflowers
Bloody Wallflowers
Bromton's Stockflowers
White Wallflower
Matted Pink
Mountain Pink
Double strip'd Columbine
Double Larks-heel
Upright Larks-heel
Rofe Larks-heel tipt
African Marygold
French Marygold
Snap-Dragon
Candy Tuft
Sweet Scabious
Spanish Scabious
Sweet Williams
London Pride
Capsicum Indicum
Venus Looking-Glafs
Venus Navel-wort
French Honyfuckles, all forts
Lychnis, all forts
Rofe Campian
Noli me tangere, three forts
Marvel of *Peru*
Nafturtium Indicum
Sweet Sultan, all forts
Valerian, all forts
Bellvidere
Everlafting Sunflower
Branch'd Sunflower
Canterbury Bell
Flos Adonis
Steeple Bellflower
Fox-Gloves
Ironcolour Fox-glove
Nigella *Romana*
Urtica *Romana*
Primrofe Tree
Aramanthus, all colours
Aramanthus Tricolour
Love lieth bleeding
Princes Feather
Love Apple
Thorn Apple
Double Poppy strip'd
Double Holyhock
Lobel's Catch-fly
Monks Hood
Convulvulus Major
Convulvulus Minor
Bottles of all colours
Globe Thistle
Holy Thistle
Great blue Lupines
Small blue Lupines
Yellow Lupines
White Lupines
Everlafting Lupine
Scarlet Beans
Everlafting Peafe
Dwarf Peafe
Winged Peafe
Purple Peafe
Pearl Peafe
Snails and Caterpillars
Horns and Hedghogs
Sensible Plant
Humble Plant.
A fcarlet Musk Pea from the *Indies.*

Seeds of Ever-Green and Flowering-Trees.
Cyprefs
Silver Fir
Norway Fir
Scotch Fir
Great Pine
Pinafter
Phillirea vera
Alaternus
Pyracantha
Arbutus
Arbor Indæ
Mazerian Berries
Cedar de Lebanon
Holly Berries
Myrtle Berries
Laurel Berries
Bay Berries
Juniper Berries
Yew Berries
Ever-green Oak-Acorns
Cork-Tree Acorns
Lime-Tree Seed
Cena Seed
Laburnum major
Laburnum minor
Spanish Broom Seed
Almonds
Chefnuts
Hornbeam Seed
Perfiaan Nuts from the *Indies*
Apricock Stones.

Sorts of Peafe, Beans, &c.
Edwards's Hotfpur Peafe
Green's Hotfpur Peafe
Barnes's Hotfpur Peafe
The *Indian* or *Marafat* Pea
Short Hotfpur Peafe
Long Hotfpur Peafe
Sandwich Peafe
Crown Peafe
Windfor Grey Peafe
White Rouncival Peafe
Grey Rouncival Peafe
Blue Rouncival Peafe
Green Rouncival Peafe
Maple Rouncival Peafe
Large white Sugar Peafe
Small white Sugar Peafe
Grey Sugar Peafe
White Rofe Peafe
Grey Rofe Peafe
Indian Peafe
Egg Peafe
Sickle Peafe
Gofper Beans
White Kidney Beans
Speckled Kidney Beans
Marble Beans
Indian Beans
Windfor Beans
Sandwich Beans
Canterbury Beans
Lentils.

Seeds to improve Land.
Clover Grafs
Hop Clover cleans'd
Hop Clover in the Husk
Sain-foine
La lucern
French Furz.

Dantzick Flax, or East Country Flax.

Flower Roots.
All the kinds of Picadee Ranunculus
All forts of new double Anemonies
Tuberofe Roots from *Italy*
Double white Tulip, all forts
Double yellow Tulip
Double strip'd Tulip
Poppy Anemonies
Plain Auriculus, divers forts
Double and strip'd Auriculus
Polyanthoes, all forts
Irifes, all forts
Crown Imperials
Fraxinellas, all forts
Hepatica's, double blue, and double peach Colour
Crocus's, all forts
Narciffus, all forts
Junquils, double and fingle
Piony's, all forts
Eritillaria, all forts
Hellebore, all forts
Colchicums, all forts
Cyclamen, Spring and Autumn
Bee Flower
Narciffus of *Constantinople*
Lillies, all forts
Double white Lilly
Paper white Primrofes
Lillies variegt. in the Leaf.

Sorts of Choice Trees and Plants.
Orange, strip'd and Hermophradite
Lemons
Cittrons
Pomgranate double flower
Mirtles, all forts
Silver Mirtles
Silver Rofemary
Indian Fig
Oleander, red and white
Philires, all forts
Alaternus strip'd
Cytifus, Lunatus, & Secundus Clufii
Amomum Plinii
Hollies strip'd with yellow and with white
Hedghog Holly, and other Hollies strip'd, great Varieties
Laureftinus, both forts
Laurel strip'd
Arbutus
Indian Juks, or *Adam's* Needle
Paliurs
Pyracancha
Terebinthus
Jacabea Marina
Horfe Tongue Bay
Honey Tree
Olive Tree
Cedrus Libani
Barmudy
Paffion Tree
Semper Vivens

Agnus Caftus
The true Bay of Alexander
Arbor Judæ
Platanus Orientalis & Occidentalis
Cedar of *Virginia*
Tragacantha
Horfe-Chefnut
Jeffamines, *Spanish* yellow, *Persian* white, &c.
Ciftus, all forts
Marum Syriacum
Geranium noctu Olens
Jucca Peruana
Nightfhade variegated
Mugworth variegated
Woodbine variegated
Althæa, purple, white, &c.

Fruit-Trees.
Dutch Goosberrys, the fcarlet, fmooth, and the fcarlet hairy, and the large green hairy
Large *Dutch* white Corrines
Apples, divers forts
Pears, divers forts
Plums, divers forts
Cherrys, feveral forts
Quinces, all forts
Medlers, all forts
Figs, all forts
Walnuts, all forts
Grapes of feveral forts
Peaches divers forts
Apricocks, feveral forts
Nectarines, all forts
Strawberrys, all forts
Rasberrys, all forts
Mulberrys, both forts.

Trees for Walks.
Englifh Elms
Dutch Elms
Limes
Playns
Abealis
Horfe-Chefnuts
Beach Trees
Horn Beam Plants.

Flowering Trees and Shrubs.
Rofes, divers forts
Syringos
Rofe Elder
Double bloffom Thorn
Glaffenbury Thorn
Holy Thorn
Mirtle Leav'd Thorn

Hardy Greens.
Pyramid Hollys of all forts variegated
Standard Hollys
Large Yews
Swedish Junipers
Bayes
Strip'd Filleroes
Laureftinus of all forts
Dutch Box for Edging
Variegated Box.

With many other Sorts.

ay be likewife there Accommodated with *Spades, Rakes, Hoes, Reels, Lines, Sheers, Sythes, Watering-Pots,*
Sives, *Pruning and Budding Knives ; Artichokes, Afparagus, Colliflowers, Cabbage and Tarragan Plants* : All
s of *Common Garden-Pots,* proper for the ufe of *Gardiners.*

13.2 John Johnson, *A catalogue of garden seeds and flower roots, c.*1705. © The Board of Trinity College Dublin.

established Linen Board in 1711–12 when 'with great difficulties' they imported into Dublin a large quantity of hemp seed and flax seed from Holland.[79] As the century developed it was generally acknowledged that flax seed saved in Ireland was inferior to imports from less moist climates, especially North America, which was found to suit 'light and mountain' land, while seed from Holland and Riga (Russia) was best on heavy clays.[80] Imports of flax and hemp seed gradually moved to northern ports as the linen industry, together with cordage and rope manufacturing, was most concentrated in Ulster;[81] however, between 13 January and 12 March 1785 a total of 1,179 hogheads (202,675 kg) of flax seed still arrived into Dublin, mostly from Philadelphia and New York, while 458 bushels (11,634 kg) of hemp seed also cleared Dublin customs in the same period, the latter sourced from overseas and typically loaded onto vessels out of London.[82]

Dublin's seedsmen first started to advertise regularly in newspapers during the 1730s as the numbers of traders increased.[83] Characteristically they always used the word 'fresh' for their product and to emphasize this would state it had 'just landed' from London or Rotterdam, often naming the ship itself. Variety, purity and novelty were commonly highlighted with words such as 'large and choice collection' or 'newest of the best kinds' of 'clean' seed. Building a reputation for reliability of seed quality was fundamental to customer loyalty; every year, usually in December or January, they would travel to London to select their seed and build up a relationship with suppliers. Selection required skill and experience; seed needed to be fully ripened, not too old and not adulterated with pernicious weeds.

In the promotion of both seed and plant sales, the most important practical development of the period however was the advent of the printed catalogue. Although herbalists like John Gerard (c.1545–1612) were publishing lists of plants in the sixteenth century, it was not until the 1670s that we see the first broadsheet catalogues or single printed lists in London, usually displayed inside or outside the shop. By far the earliest example to survive in Dublin was issued by John Johnson (fl. 1705), 'Gardiner and Seedsman' at 'the Orange-Tree on Corkhill', titled *A catalogue of garden seeds and flower roots*.[84] John Johnson does not appear in the published record, so the date of the catalogue is uncertain, but it is likely he was the 'gardener' of that name who left a will in 1723,[85] while it is also probable that Sarah Johnson, who had a seed shop on Cork Hill, was his widow; in 1733 she was offering 'the best kind' of

---

79 *Dublin Intelligence*, 17 Nov. 1711, p. 2; 23 Feb. 1712, p. 4 and 20 Dec. 1712, p. 2. 80 Jonathan Bell and Mervyn Watson, *A history of Irish farming, 1750–1950* (Dublin, 2008), pp 170–1. 81 W.H. Crawford, 'The evolution of the linen trade in Ulster before industrialisation', *Irish Economic and Social History*, 5 (1988), 32–53. 82 K.A. Cheer, 'Irish maritime trade in the eighteenth century: a study in patterns of trade, structures, and merchant communities' (MA, Victoria University of Wellington, New Zealand, 2009), p. 30. 83 Most prominent among these were John Jones of Cut Purse Row (c.1710–60); John and Ann Barclay with Robert Jaffray of Eustace Street (c.1733–58) and the Clibborn brothers of Meath Street (c.1734–40). 84 J.H. Harvey and Vincent Kinane, 'The earliest known printed Irish seed catalogue', *Long Room*, 38 (1993), 49–53; Barnard, *Making the grand figure*, pp 214–15. 85 Vicars, *Index to the prerogative wills*, p. 251; 'John Johnson' was made a Freeman of the city of Dublin in Easter 1702: Dublin Corporation Archives, Fr/Reg/2, p. 193. See also Harvey and Kinane, 'The earliest known

The nursery and seed trade in Dublin before 1800

ranunculus, anemones, tulips and jonquils among other things.[86] Someone pencilled '*c.*1699' into the margin of the sheet and this could be correct. However, the late John Harvey argued that a date of *c.*1709 or slightly earlier may also be acceptable in terms of the plant lists.[87]

Harvey drew attention to the close similarity of Johnson's broadsheet with one issued by Edward Fuller, successor to Lucas's famous seedshop on the Strand and believed to date around 1688.[88] Both are of similar size, layout, contents and typeface. Seeds and plants for sale are arranged in five columns and set out in categories which Harvey has demonstrated follow a formula first used around 1500 and continued in use until the 1830s.[89] These categories are

> Seeds of Roots, Sallad-Seeds, Pot-Herb Seeds, Sweet-Herb Seeds, Physical Seeds, Flower Seeds, Seeds of Ever-Green and Flowering-Trees, Sorts of Peas, Beans, &c, Seeds to improve Land, Flower Roots, Sorts of Choice Trees and Plants, Fruit-Trees, Trees for Walks, Flowering Trees and Shrubs, Hardy Greens.

The last four categories here are not included in Fuller's earlier lists, but in the other categories the number and range of plants are much the same in both with only a small number of differences, mostly some additional varieties added by Johnson none of which seem to contradict a *terminus ad quem* of around 1710 for his catalogue. At the foot of the broadsheet Johnson, like Fuller, lists garden tools and a selection of vegetable plants.

Typically for this period there are no prices attached to Johnson's list. Printing was relatively expensive and plant lists for sale often had to last a number of years during which prices may have changed; indeed, prices were liable to change seasonally reflecting availability. Even when broadsheets were largely superseded by pamphlets in the later eighteenth century there was a reluctance to include prices due in part to seasonal variations, though Harvey suggested that as many clients were wealthy, it was a matter of prestige not to count the cost;[90] a twelve-page catalogue issued in the 1780s by well-known nurseryman Edward Bray (*fl.* 1773–1815) of Merchant's Quay, did not include prices, though it did have a year of issue on its cover;[91] however, Bray (see below), like a handful of others in the later eighteenth century, very occasionally used newspapers to advertise prices, but this did not happen extensively in Dublin until well into the nineteenth century.

---

printed Irish seed catalogue', 52, fn. 7.   **86** *Pue's Occurrences*, 7 Nov. 1733, p. 2.   **87** Correspondence between John Harvey and E.C. Nelson, National Botanic Gardens, Glasnevin.   **88** J.H. Harvey, *The nursery garden* (London, 1990), p. 3. This was itself based on one issued by Lucan, dated *c.*1677: see Harvey, *Early gardening catalogues*, pp 65–74.   **89** Harvey, *Early gardening catalogues*, pp 18–19.   **90** J.H. Harvey (ed.), *The Georgian garden: an eighteenth-century nurseryman's catalogue. John Kingston Galpine* (Wimbourne, 1983), p. 10.   **91** Bray's catalogue is dated to the 1780s but the final digit is missing: E.M. McCracken, 'Nurseries and seedshops in Ireland' in Nelson and Brady (eds), *Irish gardening and horticulture*, pp 179–90, at p. 181. National Library of Ireland, Fingall Papers, MS 8036: Household, personal and miscellaneous accounts of the Plunkett family, 1620–1799.

One can appreciate from Johnson's list that he was offering quite a wide selection of stock, including medicinal and arboreal seed, while also being supplied with plant roots from nurserymen, as there is no evidence he had any nursery ground of his own. How much he ever held in ready supply is an open question. One of his categories, 'Seeds to improve Land', closely followed Fuller by including 'Clover Grass, Hope Clover cleans'd, Hope Clover in the Husk, Sain foine, La Lucern, French Furz', but unlike Fuller excludes ryegrass seed, suggesting that in fact demand for grasses was limited. Indeed, in 1702 the De Veseys of Abbeyleix could find no shop in Dublin selling sainfoin (*Onobrychis viciifolia*) or ryegrass seed (*Lolium* cf *perenne*).[92] Advances in agricultural husbandry only slowly took hold in Ireland and many Irish farmers only reluctantly adopted systems of convertible (up and down) husbandry in which grassland management became central to farming, while some garden vegetables, notably turnips, were gradually adapted as fodder crops. Encouraged by the rise of farmers' societies in Ireland, the range and volume of improved grass and fodder increased during the century and these played an increasingly important role in the expanding seed business, ultimately allowing many traders to move away from relying largely on garden seed and specializing principally if not exclusively in agricultural seed.

LATE EIGHTEENTH-CENTURY PROLIFERATION OF NURSERIES AND SEED
TRADERS

While the log books for Dublin's eighteenth-century port no longer survive, we are fortunate that a custom's official called Richard Eaton (*fl.* 1785) left us daily details of the imports and exports for the first three months of 1785.[93] Grouped by commodity, his 'List' allows us to gain a valuable glimpse of the state of the city's seed and nursery trade at that time; fortunately the January–March period was when most seed imports, then classified as another 'raw material', were arriving into the country for spring planting. During this time 10,863lbs (4,927 kg) of 'garden seeds' cleared customs, but particularly noteworthy was the volume of imported agricultural seed for grasses and fodder, once so low that Dobbs did not even mention them in the 1720s (see above). Imported clover seed amounted to 67,648 lbs (30,686 kg) and trefoil 27,328 lbs (12,396 kg), while 1,904 bushels (51,818 kg) of peas and beans came from London and Bristol. Fine onion seed, totalling 2,288 kg, arrived in eight consignments from Rotterdam and three consignments from Oporto; twenty consignments were loaded in London, two in Liverpool and two in Chester. Seed of canary grass (*Phalaris canariensis*) was also being imported (6,384 lbs/2,896 kg).

92 Barnard, *Making the grand figure*, p. 215 and fn.158.   93 Richard Eaton, *A daily and alphabetical arrangement of all imports and exports at the port of Dublin, in the quarter ending the 25th March, 1785* (Dublin, [1785]).

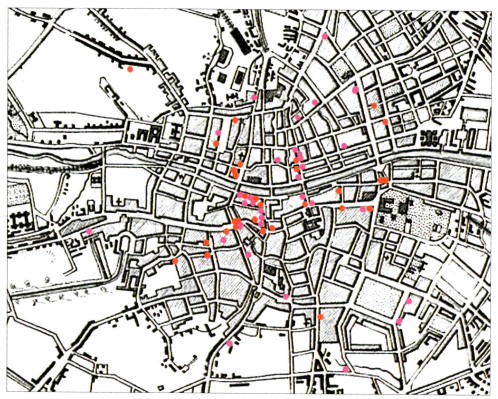

13.3 Map of Dublin seed (red) and nursery shops, 1740–1800. © Terence Reeves-Smyth.

The principal seed importers on Eaton's list were a combination of nurserymen and seedsmen. The largest importer was seedsman, James Joseph Dodd (*fl.* 1775–1800), of 72 Thomas Street, who during this time brought in from London and Rotterdam some fifteen cwt (1,680 lbs/762 kg) of which one cwt (112 lbs/51 kg) was onion seed; he also imported thirty bushels of hemp seed. Dodd had served as an apprentice to nurseryman John Phelan (*fl.* 1746–89) at Christ Church Lane, before setting up business on his own account in 1780 as a 'young beginner'; Phelan himself, now approaching the end of his career, was recorded by Eaton as having imported nine cwt (1,008 lbs/457 kg) of seed during this time. The two other significant importers on Eaton's list were Anne Hay (*fl.* 1780–90) at 'The Golden Ball', 4 Church Street (Old Church Street) and Benjamin Simpson (*fl.* 1750–1812) at 3 Corkhill. Anne Hay, who was importing six cwt (672 lbs/305 kg) of seed in addition to a hundred bushels of hemp seed (2,540 lbs) in this period, had taken over the business from her husband Edward Hay, one of the city's most prominent seedsmen, who died in 1780. Though he called himself a 'nurseryman and seedsman', Edward had no nursery ground of his own and bought in or imported all his stock, including 'White Thorn Quicks, Dutch Alders, with all kinds of Fruit and Forest Trees &c'.[94] Typically

---

94 *Dublin Courier*, 28 Feb. 1766, p. 2; *Saunders's News-Letter*, 7 Feb. 1776, p. 3.

for a specialist seedsman, Edward Hay visited London and Rotterdam annually, usually December, to buy his stock and from the early 1760s he was bringing in a wide variety of grass and garden seed and published an annual catalogue.[95] Like Hay, Simpson also imported six cwt (672 lbs/305 kg) of seed in this three-month period, but this was his first consignment, having only opened his seed shop on Cork Hill in December 1784.[96] Simpson however was already an established figure in the gardening world having served as head gardener to the first and second dukes of Leinster before setting up as a nurseryman at Inchicore in 1779. By 1792 he was claiming to have 'the most extensive' nursery in the city.[97]

Surprisingly not included among the top seed importers for early 1785 was Luke Peppard (*fl.* 1745–94) of 6 Cutpurse Row and 154 Capel Street (his warehouse), one of the best-known seed traders in the city in his own time. He started trading in the 1740s and was quickly making 'regular importations of seed' from England, Holland and Scotland, developing close relations with overseas suppliers, like James Anderson of Edinburgh. He always sought novelties; thus in the later 1770s, in addition to 'Red Clover, White Dutch Clover; Trefoil, Timothy, and Ryegrass; Lalucern, Burnett, St. Foyne', and his usual range of vegetables, flower seeds and roots, he offered the 'seeds of Early Yellow French Turnip held in such esteem by the Nobility and Gentry of France for its peculiar fine Flavour'.[98] Again in 1790 he 'just landed from Italy' the 'seed of the large mild Italian onion' that was the 'best flavoured for Onion Sauce ever was imported into this kingdom' that could be had 'no where else in Ireland'.[99]

While novelties may have attracted the attention of affluent garden owners on the look-out for something new, the city's large seed importers must have relied on wholesale for much of their business. They would have supplied not only the grocers and other small retail outlets in the city, but also the country towns, where most seedsmen and nurserymen were not in the position to import directly from London themselves. As the century progressed the number of public nurseries in rural areas increased steadily, thanks in part to the activities of the Dublin Society (Royal Dublin Society from 1820), who were particularly concerned with a lack of tree planting in Ireland and the often stated difficulty of obtaining plants in rural areas. Thus, from 1741 to 1791 the society offered a range of premiums, initially focussed on nurseries ten miles from the sea and forty from Dublin; later (from 1765) for nurseries three or more miles from a country town. During this period they paid £987 to sixty-one public nurserymen in premiums on 380 acres of new nursery land.[100]

---

95 Evidently his catalogues also contained 'proper instructions for the time of sowing', as in 1763 (*Dublin Courier*, 2 Nov. 1763, p. 2). His wife Anne was still based at their premises in Church Street in 1800, but by 1805 another Edward Hay, presumably her son, was selling from this address (*Hibernian Journal; or, Chronicle of Liberty*, 11 Feb. 1805, p. 1).   **96** *Hibernian Journal; or, Chronicle of Liberty*, 8 Dec. 1784, p. 3. **97** *Dublin Evening Post*, 26 Jan. 1792, p. 2.   **98** *Saunders's News-Letter*, 9 Feb. 1776, p. 1.   **99** *Dublin Evening Post*, 4 Mar. 1790, p. 2.   **100** McCracken, 'Notes on eighteenth-century Irish nurserymen', 39–42. See also Dublin Society, 'Premiums offered and adjudged by the Dublin Society for planting 1766–1806', *Transactions of the Dublin Society* 5, (1806), 108.

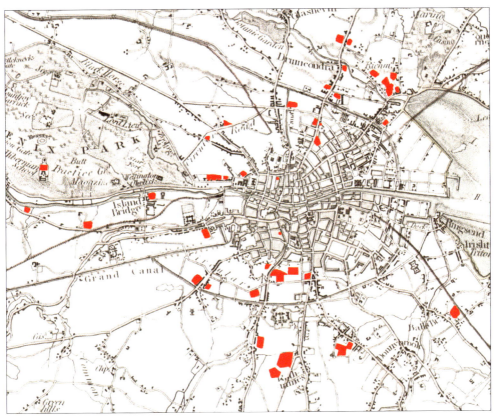

13.4 Map of Dublin's nursery grounds, 1760–1800. © Terence Reeves-Smyth.

Dublin was considered by the Dublin Society to be well served by nurseries in and around the capital; nonetheless, from 1768 to 1794 eleven Dublin nurseries also received premiums from the society, seven of which were for new or increased nursery acreages. Between 1760 and 1800 there were forty-two recorded nursery grounds serving the city, mostly located close to the south and north circular roads and accessible to the main arterial routes into the city, notably the Drumcondra Road and the Malahide/Howth Road on the north and the Rathmines Road on the south. Their sizes varied considerably; Charles (*c*.1765–1833) and Luke Toole (*c*.1777–*c*.1830) had thirty-two acres at Cullenswood; John Grimwood (*c*.1760–1837) had eighteen acres at Rathmines and another six at Portobello; both Edward Bray (*fl*. 1773–1810) and Richard Burnett (*fl*. 1776–90) each had twelve acres at Aromatic Hill and Richmond respectively; Daniel Bullen had eight acres on New Street and Benjamin Simpson eight acres at Inchicore, while most of the other nurseries varied from two to six acres extent. Some nurserymen had a number of nurseries; for example, Patrick Carroll (*fl*. 1787–1813) had one on Montpelier Hill, just north of Parkgate Street, and another at Legganhall in County Meath, while thirty-two of Dublin's nurserymen had, in addition to their nursery grounds, a seed shop in the city. During this period

Dublin had no less than sixty-one seed shops, excluding warehouses, twenty-nine of them run by seed merchants with no nursery.

Among the most prominent of the later eighteenth-century Dublin nurserymen was Edward Bray (*fl.* 1773–1815), a former apprentice of Daniel Bullen, who from 1774 had a seed shop on Merchant's Quay and from 1773 a large nursery ground at Island Bridge; he moved his ground in 1793 to 'Aromatic Hill' on the South Circular Road following the death of his partner Thomas Grafty (*fl.* 1780–6). From the start of his career he made extensive use of newspaper advertising and achieved success fairly quickly; in 1780 he was chosen to oversee the dispersal of the celebrated collection of exotics belonging to Robert Barnewall, twelfth Baron Trimleston (1704–79), which had taken forty years to build up and which included bananas and pineapples.[101]

By a stroke of good fortune, a twelve-page pamphlet that Bray produced in the 1780s still survives. *A catalogue of garden, grass and flower seeds, fruit and forest trees, flowering shrubs and evergreens, flower roots and garden tools, &c* is the earliest surviving Irish example of a pamphlet catalogue and gives us a unique insight into the choice of plants that a successful Dublin nurseryman would have been offering at that time.[102] The range included 'Forest Trees' (21 listed) and 'Flowering Shrubs and Ever-Greens' (93 listed), all of which were European, save only for Cedar of Lebanon and five species from North America. The deciduous trees included ash (3 varieties), birch, beech, purple beech, horse chestnut (4 varieties), Spanish chestnut, limes, elm (3 varieties), alder, hornbeam, scarlet maple, black and balsam, poplar, oak (5 varieties), sycamore and walnut, while his conifers included balm of Gilead, Scots pine, silver fir, spruce fir, American fir, Weymouth pine, larch, arbor-vitae, yew, cedar of Lebanon and cypress. Trees and shrubs were also offered as seed (25 varieties), while the main focus of the list comprised seeds for the vegetable or flower garden, namely peas (19 varieties), beans (12 varieties); French beans (10 varieties), 'Seeds of Roots' (23 varieties), 'Sallad seeds' (over 80 varieties), 'Pot and Sweet Herb seeds' (11 varieties), 'Physical Seeds' (9 varieties of medicinal herbs) and 'Flowering Seeds' (115 sorts), the latter including 'Tender Annuals' (11 varieties) and 'Bulbous and Tuberose [sic] Rooted Flowers' (over 21 varieties), such as auriculas, carnations, anemones, *Ranunculus* and bulbs (lilies, tulips, hyacinths, jonquils). There were eight seed types 'to improve the land'. Fruit trees, which would then have comprised an important part of a nurseryman's business, included peach (37 varieties), nectarines (14 varieties), figs (4 varieties), apricots (10 varieties), pears (40 varieties), cherries (18 varieties), apple (32 varieties), three of which were Irish, plus medlars, mulberries, quinces, gooseberries and currants, all 'new sorts' but no varieties specified.

Bray gave no prices in his catalogue, though at around the same time (1785) he did publish a price list for trees in a newspaper.[103] A number of other contemporary

---

101 *Dublin Journal* (*Faulkner's*), 3 and 14 Oct. 1780; for this remarkable collection see also: John O'Keeffe, *Recollections of the life of John O'Keeffe written by himself* (London, 1826), i, pp 5–7; E.C. Nelson, 'Some records (*c.*1690–1830) of greenhouses in Irish gardens'.   102 NLI, MS 8036.   103 *Freeman's Journal*, 8 Dec. 1785, p. 2.

A

L I S T

OF

FOREST TREES, FRUIT TREES, SHRUBS, and EVERGREENS,

For SALE, at the NURSERY GARDEN of the HIBERNIAN HOSPITAL in the *Phœnix Park*, for the Year 1781.

Lo. folder 9/98

FOREST TREES.

ENGLISH Elms, different sizes from 8s 4d to 16s 8d per Hundred
Ditto grafted on the Scotch, 25s per ditto
Birch from 8s 4d to 12s 6d per do
Dutch Alder, at 8s 4d per do to 12s 6d per do
Ash, from 4s 4d to 12s 6d per do
Flowering Ash, at 6d per Plant
Manna Ash at 6d per do
Whole leied Ash, at 1s 1d per do
Quickens Mountain Ash, at 8s 4d per Hundred
Seedling Quickens, two and three Years old at per Thousand
Horse Chesnut, at 16s 8d per Hundred
Spanish Chesnut, at 1s 1d per Plant
Yellow flowering do at 1s 1d per do
Varrigated do at 1s 1d per do
Beech, from 8s 4d to 16s 8d per Hundred
Copper leav'd, at 1s 1d per Plant
Walnuts, from 8s 4d to 16 8d per Hundred
Tacamac, 1s 5s per do
Sycamore, from 8s 4d to 16s 8d per do
Varigated or blotched at 9d per Plant
Larch, from 8s 4d to 25s per Hundred
Scotch Fir, from 8s 4d to 16s 8d per do
Spruce do, from 8s 4d to 25s per do
Silver Fir at 25s per do
Weymout Pine, transplanted at 25s per do
Stone Pine, in Potts at 6d per Plant
Oaks five Years old, at 8s 4d per Hundred
Seedling do, at 10s 10d per Thousand
Lucombe Devonshire Oak, at 1s 1d per Plant
Scarlet or Virginian Oak, 1s 1d per do
Iron Ditto, 1s 1d per do
Pine Poplars, from 8s 4d to 25s per Hundred
Black American ditto
Italian ditto, at 4d per do
Berry bearing ditto, at 6d per do
Hardy Carolina ditto, at 6d per do
Broad leav'd ditto, at 6d per do
Balsam ditto, at 6d per do
Bird Cherry at 3d per do
Weeping Willow, at 3d per do
Golden Ozier, at 3d per do
Red Mountain, Chrystal and Pasley leaved Elder at 3d per do
Varigated Elder, at 1s 1d per do

FLOWERING SHRUBS.

ARBUTUS different Sizes from 1s 1d to 1s 7d halfpenny per Plant
Rose Accacia or Robina at 2s 2d per do

Moss Roses, at 1s 1d per Plant
Compone Roses, at 1s 1d per do
York and Lancaster do at 1s 1d per do
Purple Burgundy, at 1s 1d per do
Assortment of Roses, from 3d to 6d per do
Scarlet Colluchea at 6d per do
Evergreen Cittisus at 3d per do
Spanish Broom at 3d per do
Spira Frutex at 3d per do
Scorpian Sena at 6d per do
Long-blow Honey-suckle, at 3d per do
Fly ditto, at 3d per do
Evergreen ditto, at 6d per do
Sweet Bryar, at 4s 1d per Hundred
Ditto, in small quantities at 1d per Plant
Double flowering ditto, at 1s 1d per do
Syringo or Mock Orange at 3d per do
White and yellow Jessamines at 3d per do
Shining leav'd Laurastinas at 3d per do
Common ditto, at 2d per do
Althea Frutere, four Kinds at 1s 1d per do
Red Mazerians, at 9d per do
White flowering ditto, at 1s 1d per do
Double Blossom Cherry, 1s 1d per do
Perfumed ditto, at 1s 1d per do
Double Blossom Peach, at 1s 1d per do
Double Blossom Almond, at 1s 1d per do
Dwarf Almond, at 3d per do
Single Flowering ditto, at 3d per do
Double Blossom Thorn, at 6d per do
Afarole Ditto, at 6d per do
Black American Thorn at 6d per do
Lord Ile's great Thorn, at 6d per do
Pyracantha Thorn, at 6d per do
Avia Theophrasti at 6d per do
Cockspur Thorn, at 6d per do
Purple and White ditto at 3d per do
Libarnhams Dwarfs and Standard, at 3d per do
Laccumbroom at 5d per do
White Portugal Broom, at 6d per do
Rock Rose, or Gum Cistus, at 6d per do
Gilder Rose, or Snow Ball Tree at 6d per do
Virginia Gilder Rose, at 3d per do
Citisus Secundas, at 3d per do
German and Italian Tamarisk, at 6d per do
Sumack or Buck Thorn at 6d per do
Sea Buck Thorn, at 6d per do
Dogwoods, different Kinds, at 3d per do
Varigated or Blotched Ditto, at 1s 1d per do

EVERGREEN PLANTS.

ARBUTUS from 1s 1d to 1s 7d per Plant

Shining leaved Laurastinas at 3d per do
Common Ditto, at 2d per do
Portugal Laurels at 6d per do
Portugal Laurel Seedlings at 1s 5s per Hundred
Common Ditto, from 1d to 3d per Plant
Varigated at 6d per do
Wood or Spunge Ditto, at 6d per do
Pyracantha Thorn, at 6d per do
Gold and Silver Hollies, at 1s 1d per do
Sweet Bays from 6d to 1s 7d Halfpenny per do
Seedling Ditto, at 1s 5s per Hundred
Evergreen Oaks, at 6d per Plant
Ditto at 1s 5s per Hundred
Cittisus, at 3d per Plant
Blotched and Plain Philareas at 6d per do
Junipers, from 3d to 6d per do
Cyprus, at 6d per do
Geraniums, from 6d to 1s 1d per Pot
Hollimus, or Sea Porcelain, at 3d per do

FRUIT TREES.

PEACHES in the Nursery Rows at 1s 1d per Plant
Ditto Trained, at 3s 6d per do
Ditto, in full Bearing at 5s per do
Ditto Standards or Riders trained and in full Bearing at 8s 1d Halfpenny per do
Nectarines in the Nursery, Rows, at 1s 1d per do
Ditto trained, at 3s 6d per do
Ditto Standards or Riders trained and in full Bearing at 8s 1d Halfpenny per do
Apricots, at 1s 1d per do
Ditto trained, at 3s 6d per do
Cherries, at 1s 1d per do
Ditto trained, at 3s 6d per do
Plumbs, at 1s 1d per do
Ditto, trained at 3s 6d per do
Pears of the best Sort for Wall or Standard on the Free and Quince Stocks, at 1s 1d per do
A great Variety of the best Kinds of Cyder, Kitchen and Eating Apples, on the Wilding, and Crab Stock, at 4d and 6d per do
American Pippen, at 6d per do
Gooseberries, of the best Kinds at 1s 6d per Dozen
White Red and Black Currants, at 1s 6d per do
Sweet scented Crab, at 6d per Plant
Asparagus Plants two Years old at 1s 1d per Hundred

As this Garden is calculated by the Governors more for the Health and Education of the Children in said Hospital, than for Profit, it is hoped that no Gentleman or Lady will be offended that it is ordered, that no Article shall be delivered out of the Garden until paid for.———All Orders will be recived by Major SIRR or JOHN GAHAN at the Nursery, or by Mr. BURROWES, on *Arran-quay*, who will forward them.

1781

Dublin nurserymen occasionally published very select price lists in the newspapers, notably John Grimwood (*c*.1760–1837), George Cottingham (*fl.* 1780–6), Patrick Kenny (*fl.* 1775–92), George Smitten (*fl.* 1784–1802) and the Toole brothers, but only one Dublin eighteenth-century catalogue survives that gives prices. This is a broadsheet list published in 1781 by John Gahan (*fl.* 1781–1808) of Chapelizod, for the nursery garden of the Hibernian Hospital in the Phoenix Park.[104] His price list is wide ranging and includes 'Forest Trees' (41 prices), 'Flowering Shrubs' (51 prices), 'Evergreen Plants' (19 prices) and 'Fruit Trees' (25 prices). His prices are similar and, in many cases, identical to Bray's and compare well to contemporary English nurseries, such as that of William and John Perfect of York (1777).[105]

Gahan made it clear in his catalogue, as did Bray, that no plants were to leave the nursery until they were paid for. Many other nurserymen took a similar line; George Cottingham, for example, who ran the nursery garden at the Foundling Hospital, also stated that he 'cannot execute any order without payment as the prices are reduced as low as possible in order to encourage ready money'.[106] Bray was to modify his position in the 1790s by offering six months credit 'for the purchase of 50l. [pounds] worth, twelve months for 100l. [pounds] and so in proportion to 500l. [pounds]'.[107] In truth, however, both nurserymen and seedsmen in the eighteenth century, like many other tradesmen, often had serious debt problems, as customers, who wanted their goods immediately, were often accustomed to delaying payment for months, sometimes years.[108] For their part, shopkeepers were frequently hesitant to demand payment too forcefully, lest their reputation be damaged, particularly against aristocratic clients. Failure to maintain a regular cash flow could result in bankruptcy, a fate that befell a number of Irish nurserymen and seedsmen in the eighteenth century; one notably example was Edward Murphy (*fl.* 1789–97) of Christ Church Lane, who was declared bankrupt in 1797 and had to sell his entire nursery stock in Blackrock, 'being the choicest collection of forest and fruit trees, flowering shrubs, ever-greens, flower-roots, &c, ever offered for sale in this kingdom'.[109]

Failures aside, Dublin's seed and nursery trade was in a healthy state at the end of the eighteenth century. By this stage the city had an extensive and well-developed system of canals and roads making it easier to transport weighty plants and trees to rural customers. Agricultural husbandry had improved resulting in rising sales of grass and fodder seed, whilst there was a boom in tillage, boosted in particular by post 1778 war-time demands. The last three decades of the century also saw the proliferation of country houses with their parks, woodlands, ornamental and kitchen gardens, all adding considerably to the demands on nurserymen and seedsmen, as

---

104 NLI, MS 9/98: 'A List of Forest Trees, Fruit Trees, Shrubs and Evergreens, For Sale, at the Nursery Garden of the Hibernian Hospital, in the Phoenix Park, for the Year 1781'; reproduced in J.A. McCullen, *An illustrated history of the Phoenix Park: landscape and management to 1880* (Dublin, 2011), p. 41. **105** Harvey, *Early gardening catalogues*, pp 101–16. **106** *Dublin Evening Post*, 2 Oct. 1782, p. 4. **107** *Saunders's News-Letter*, 11 Nov. (1793), p. 2; see also *Freeman's Journal*, 20 Dec. 1791, p. 1. **108** Thick, 'Garden seeds in England', 108; Floud, *An economic history of the English garden*, p. 130. **109** *Dublin Evening Post*, 19 Oct. 1797.

was the growing appearance of an affluent Dublin middle class. Among the nurserymen taking advantage of the new opportunities were the brothers Charles and Luke Toole of Kevin Street, who in 1805 acquired grand new premises at 41–42 Westmoreland Street, whilst acquiring eighty-three acres of new nursery lands at Shankill to supplement their Cullenswood grounds.[110] Their rapid increase in size at the start of the new century foreshadowed the rise of the large commercial nurseries that would come to dominate the business in the Victorian era.

110 *Freeman's Journal*, 5 Feb. 1810, p. 3.

CHAPTER FOURTEEN

Ellen Hutchins (1785–1815), botanist in west Cork: 'how did her garden grow?'

MADELINE HUTCHINS

WHO WAS THE GARDENER?

ELLEN HUTCHINS of Bantry Bay was Ireland's first well-known female amateur botanist. Alas, no portrait of her is known. She specialized in the cryptogams (non-flowering plants), particularly mosses and liverworts, as well as marine algae (seaweeds) and lichens.[1] She found many species and a significant number of these were named after her by the leading botanists of her day, in recognition of her contribution to cryptogamic botany and phycology. Ellen was prolific in her production of carefully pressed and dried specimens and generous in sharing them with fellow naturalists. She produced hundreds of accurate drawings of freshwater and marine algae, as a means of sharing knowledge and developing understanding of these organisms within the community of botanists of which she was a member. Some were engraved and published. At the request of Dawson Turner (1775–1858), an English banker and amateur botanist, Ellen produced a list of over a thousand plants found in her neighbourhood, in effect the earliest flora of west Cork.[2]

Correspondence was a key element of natural history studies during the early nineteenth century. It was a means of exchanging information and developing knowledge. Frequently, botanists who described and published new plants relied on those who observed and collected them in the field, and often these collectors lived a considerable distance away. The written accounts given by the collector of the details of the plants when 'recent' or 'fresh' were of great importance, as was the collector's ability to distinguish new plants from those already known. Correspondence between

1 On Ellen Hutchins see Madeline Hutchins, *Ellen Hutchins (1785–1815). Botanist of Bantry Bay* (Bantry, 2019); Anne Secord, 'Hutchins, Ellen (1785–1815), botanist', *ODNB*; Linde Lunney, 'Hutchins, Ellen (1785–1815), cryptogamic botanist', *DIB*; H.C.G. Chesney, 'The young lady of the lichens' in Mary Mulvihill (ed.), *Stars, shells, and bluebells: women scientists and pioneers* (Dublin, 1997), pp 28–39; and John Bevan, 'Miss Ellen Hutchins (1785–1815) and the garden at Ardnagashel, Bantry, County Cork', *Moorea*, 3 (1984), 1–10. 2 Intended for publication by the Linnean Society of London, it was not passed to the Society by Dawson Turner and remained unpublished until 1999: see M.E. Mitchell (ed.), *Early observations on the flora of southwest Ireland. Selected letters of Ellen Hutchins and Dawson Turner 1807–1814*, Occasional Papers, 12 (Dublin, 1999), pp 85–108. On Turner see Angus Fraser, 'Turner, Dawson (1775–1858), banker, botanist, and antiquary', *ODNB*.

286

14.1 Silhouette of woman writing, in the style of the early 1800s; historical re-enactor Carrie O'Flynn, silhouette by Jenny Dempsey Design, reproduced by permission of the Ellen Hutchins Festival.

Ellen and Dawson Turner of Great Yarmouth, Norfolk, England, and the Scottish horticulturist James Townsend Mackay (1775–1862) who began working at Trinity College Dublin in 1803, has survived. It tells the story of Ellen as an amateur botanist and botanical artist, and illuminates her character, health, family and her home circumstances, including her garden. She botanized from her home in Ballylickey on the shores of Bantry Bay, in the wonderful woods at Glengarriff nearby, and in the heaths, bogs, by the rivers, lakes and in the mountains around the bay. Ellen's achievements are impressive; all the more so because she was predominantly self-taught, lived in a very remote locality, suffered bouts of ill health, and was the carer for her mother and a disabled brother. She is known to have been active as a collector from 1805 and an artist from 1808, until early in 1813, when her health deteriorated and she could do no more. She died, aged just 29, in February 1815.

WHERE DID HER GARDEN GROW?

Ballylickey House (Fig. 14.2) was described by Lewis Weston Dillwyn (1778–1855), a businessman and amateur naturalist then living in Swansea, who visited Ellen in 1809:

> The House surrounded by a Plantation of Trees is delightfully situated at the head of a small Cove about three Miles North of Bantry & commands a beautiful prospect of the Bay & its surrounding Mountains.[3]

Its hinterland has a mild climate with high rainfall and a range of habitats which together produce a very rich biodiversity. In the early 1800s, Bantry Bay was difficult to reach overland, with terrible roads through mountain passes, to the extent that often travel by sea was preferred. The scenery was spectacular, but as yet there were few travellers or tourists.

Ellen lived in Ballylickey House all her life except for one significant period when she was at school in Dublin. She fell ill and while recuperating stayed with the Stokes family in Harcourt Street. Dr Whitley Stokes (1763–1845), the Hutchins family's physician, was a polymath whose wide-ranging interests included volcanoes, meteors and botany, and whose projects included translating the Bible into Irish.[4] Ellen would later describe him as her 'good friend & instructor in botany, Doctor Stokes of Dublin'.[5] However, Ellen was called home to Ballylickey, probably to look after her mother and her disabled brother Tom. A memoir written (or completed) in 1913 by Ellen's niece, Alicia Hutchins, described Ellen as dreading the return home, as it was so remote, so rural, so different from Dublin, and with no cousins her age nearby.[6] Botany was suggested as an activity by Whitley Stokes as 'it would encourage her to be out of doors and give her a quiet and interesting occupation at home'.[7] It gave Ellen a pastime and a purpose and provided a focus that counterbalanced Ellen's own ill health and her responsibilities as a carer.

Ellen grew to love her home with its setting on the bay. Along the western boundary was the Ouvane River, with a bridge and fast water over rocks as it enters

---

3 G.J. Lyne, 'Lewis Dillwyn's visit to Waterford, Cork and Tipperary in 1809', *Journal of the Cork Historical and Archaeological Society* (1986), 85–104, at 94.   4 On Whitley Stokes, see J.B. Lyons, 'Stokes, Whitley', *DIB*.   5 Trinity College Library, Cambridge (TCC), Turner Correspondence: Ellen Hutchins to Dawson Turner, 15 December 1807. See also Mitchell, *Early observations*, p. 14.   6 Representative Church Body Library (RCB), Dublin, MS 47, p. 3: Alicia Hutchins, 'Memoir of Ellen Hutchins: a botanist'. This is available online: https://www.ireland.anglican.org/cmsfiles/images/aboutus/AOFTM/2016/Feb/RCB-Library-MS47.pdf, accessed 27 February 2022.   7 Ibid., p. 4.

14.2 Ballylickey House, photograph c.1910. © Hutchins family collection.

the sea. There were woods to the east and heathlands and mountains to the north. Joseph Woods (1776–1864), an English architect and amateur botanist who accompanied Lewis Dillwyn in 1809, wrote 'there is still wood on its shores but we were told of a considerable quantity of fine timber on its banks which has been cut down within these few years'.[8] In letters to Dawson Turner, Ellen described her home setting:

> The country is poor soil, mountains & shales to the shore. There are many pretty peaceful looking spots, few more so than the little place we inhabit. The view from our door is very soft & pleasing, particularly at evening when the sun, retiring behind a beautiful mountain Sugarloaf, just gilds the high ground & leaves the little cove before us in deep soft shade, or when the moon shines bright upon it.[9]
>
> I have just turned my head about & it strikes me that few [art] collections can present a sweeter landscape than that of this moment before my eyes. Few could unite more grandeur & softness, more variety of shape & colour. What rich, soft, vivid & fading greens are at this moment before me. Blue mountains, brown hills, & green swells surround this little spot, the bay opposite & a pretty mountain river at one side.[10]

8 G.J. Lyne and M.E. Mitchell, 'A scientific tour through Munster: the travels of Joseph Woods, architect and botanist, in 1809', *North Munster Antiquarian Journal*, 27 (1985), 15–61, at 27.   9 TCC, Turner Correspondence: Ellen Hutchins to Dawson Turner, 22 September 1810.   10 TCC, Turner

290 *Madeline Hutchins*

Members of the Hutchins family still lived at Ballylickey House when Alicia Hutchins' memoir was completed in 1913, and she reported that:

> A field at Ballylickey is still called 'Miss Ellen's Garden', where she tended her plants and those sent her by Mr Mackay; and her happiest hours were spent in it and in her little boat when it was rowed beside the rocks at low tide, that she might gather the seaplants.[11]

Various suggestions have been made as to the exact site of 'Miss Ellen's Garden' (or as it was later known in the family, 'Ellen's Field'), but so far it has not been located, and with landscaping work undertaken in the twentieth century, it is probably not now possible to do so with any certainty. From her letters we know that by 1805 Ellen had a flower garden under her own care, with a large rock at the side of it which she made use of for growing certain plants. She also had a greenhouse.

WHAT DID HER GARDEN GROW?

A letter dated 22 March 1806, containing a plant list, gives us a glimpse into what grew in Ellen's garden.[12] The letter was from James Townsend Mackay, the 'gardener assistant to the botany lecturer' in Trinity College Dublin.[13] As such he was in charge of the small botanical garden then on the campus in the centre of Dublin. Mackay had visited Ballylickey House the previous summer, 1805, when on a plant-hunting trip in counties Cork and Kerry.

Mackay and Ellen went plant hunting together from Ballylickey and plants they found were published by Mackay in 1806 in his 'Systematic catalogue of rare plants found in Ireland' in the *Transactions of the Dublin Society*.[14] He included many more references to Ellen's finds in his *Flora Hibernica* (Dublin, 1836), such as his note about the 'Narrow-leaved White Helleborine' (*Cephalanthera longifolia* (narrow-leaved helleborine)) at Glengarriff, Co. Cork, 'where I first observed it, in company with the late Miss Hutchins'.[15] In the introduction to his *Flora*, Mackay acknowledged his debt to Ellen, explaining that the description of algae in the book, which had been contributed by William Henry Harvey (1811–66), had in fact been 'accomplished from the examination of a full collection in my possession, chiefly

---

Correspondence: Ellen Hutchins to Dawson Turner, 14 October 1812.   **11** RCB Library, MS 47, p. 7: Alicia Hutchins, 'Memoir of Ellen Hutchins'.   **12** Royal Botanic Gardens, Kew, Ellen Hutchins Papers: Letters 1807–1820: J.T. Mackay to Ellen Hutchins, 22 March 1806.   **13** On Mackay's time at the Physic Garden of TCD see E.C. Nelson, '"Reserved to the Fellows": four centuries of gardens at Trinity College, Dublin' in Charles Holland (ed.), *Trinity College Dublin and the idea of a university* (Dublin, 1991), pp 198–201. Chapter 10 in this volume explores the TCD Physic Garden in the early eighteenth century. **14** J.T. Mackay, 'Systematic catalogue of rare plants found in Ireland', *Transactions of the Dublin Society*, 5 (1806), 121–183. Mackay's 'Systematic catalogue' includes two plants attributed to Ellen: see E.C. Nelson, 'James Townsend Mackay's "A systematic catalogue of rare plants found in Ireland": the published versions (1806, 1807–1808) and a manuscript fragment', *Glasra*, 3 (1997), 63–84.   **15** J.T. Mackay, *Flora*

formed by the late amiable and accomplished Miss Hutchins, a lady who for many years was unremitting in her investigation of the Botany of the south of Ireland'.[16]

It seems that Mackay saw Ellen herself as a significant find, living where she did and with what he described as her 'discriminating powers and great attention' and he realized that she could be extremely useful in aiding him with the cryptogams.[17] He suggested that she study seaweeds and showed her how to make and preserve specimens. Two years later he wrote 'I am very glad you have now taken to the mosses and shall be glad of specimens of any which you don't know to be very common and also of any lichens'.[18]

Mackay's letter, dated 22 March 1806, which includes a list of plant, begins:

> I received your favour [letter] and also the box containing the plants and shells quite safe. I am very much obliged by your attention and now return the box you sent with some plants for your garden – most of them would look well upon your rock provided you have some good fresh earth to plant them in.

Mackay then listed the plants he was sending; they came presumably from the College Botanic Garden:

Cistus populifolius [*Cistus populifolius*]
— helianthimum [*sic*] var. minor [probably *Helianthemum apenninum*]
— libanotis [*Cistus libanotis*]
— ladaniferus Gum cistus or rockrose [*Cistus ladanifer*]
— roseus [? *Helianthemum nummularium*]
— mutabilis [*Helianthemum nummularium*]
— laxus [*Cistus × laxus*]
— anglicus [*Helianthemum cinereum*]
Saxifraga oppositifolia [*Saxifraga oppositifolia*]
— sarmentosa [*Saxifraga stolonifera*]
Chrysanthemum Indicum [*Chrysanthemum indicum*]
Soldonella alpina [*Soldanella alpina*]
Phlox stolonifera [*Phlox stolonifera*]
— subulata [*Phlox subulata*]
— ovata [*Phlox ovata*]
Arctotis repens [*Arctotheca prostrata*]
Rosa chinensis [*Rosa chinensis*]
— semperflorens [*Rosa chinensis*]
Vetheimia [*sic*] sarmentosa [*Kniphofia sarmentosa*]
Chelone formosa … [? *Penstemon barbatus*]

Hibernica (Dublin, 1836), p. 281.   **16** Ibid., p. x.   **17** Royal Botanic Gardens, Kew, Ellen Hutchins Papers: Letters 1807–1820: J.T. Mackay to Ellen Hutchins, 25 March 1808.   **18** Ibid.

14.3 *Fucus capillaris*, now *Gloiosiphonia capillaris*, collected by Ellen Hutchins in Bantry Bay. Image courtesy of The Herbarium. Botany Department, Trinity College Dublin.

Of these, only one, *Saxifraga oppositifolia* (purple saxifrage), is a native species in Ireland. As it does not occur in Cos. Cork or Kerry it is unlikely that it thrived in Ellen's garden.

The letter contained notes about many of the plants:

> The two roses keep flowering for the most part of the season, they may either be kept in pots of rich earth or planted out in your garden, they are hardy enough to stand our winters. The Chrysanthemum is also pretty hardy and makes a beautiful appearance in November the general season of its

flowering. It will last in flower till Christmas if the weather is not very severe – both it & the roses are readily propogated [*sic*] by cuttings.

The Cistus's are a beautifull tribe of plants & are all pretty hardy – Soldonella [*sic*] is rather tender & should be kept in a pot till you have more than one plant, when you can try it out.

I doubt not that the whole will thrive well under your fostering hand – I shall always be glad when in my power to add any plant you may wish for to your collection.

I thank you for your kind to [*sic*] offer to send me more sea plants, & am glad you find such amusement in collecting & examining them; but am afraid I give you too much trouble in drying & preparing them …[19]

From now on, for years, this was the pattern; Ellen sending Mackay specimens of seaweeds (Fig. 14.3) and plants in letters, parcels or a box, and Mackay sending Ellen plants or seeds for her garden, and specimens to add to her herbarium for identification purposes. Only a few letters survive, but from these we get two more glimpses into Ellen's garden. In September 1807, Ellen wrote to Mackay:

> I have had the pleasure to receive your last letter. I am much obliged for the various things you have sent me, and for your intention of sending me plants. I am sure I shall be delighted with the ferns. They are so interesting. You have sent me three species of Phlox; subulata, stolonifera and ovata. They have all blossomed and given me great pleasure. All the plants you sent me are growing finely.[20]

Mackay continued to send plants with detailed planting instructions; in March 1808 he wrote about another consignment:

> I heartily congratulate you on the rarities your rock produces, and will certainly fulfil my long promise of sending you some plants for it and your garden some time next week. As I intend sending you some beautiful American shrubs, you had better be getting a small bed prepared with dry turf mould from the surface of some adjacent Heath common where you see the Erica vulgaris [*Calluna vulgaris* (ling)] or cineria [*Erica cinerea* (bell heather)] thriving best. The mould should be broken down very fine. You will also want to have some fresh brown loam which should be neither too sandy nor strong clay. I dare say you may find it on some dry bank in the wood near your garden. I shall mention the particular soils for the different plants more particularly when I send them.[21]

19 Royal Botanic Gardens, Kew, Ellen Hutchins Papers: Letters 1807–1820: J.T. Mackay to Ellen Hutchins, 22 March 1806. 20 Trinity College Dublin, Herbarium (TCD): Ellen Hutchins to J.T. Mackay, 6 September 1807. 21 Royal Botanic Gardens, Kew, Ellen Hutchins Papers: Letters 1807–1820: J.T. Mackay to Ellen Hutchins, 25 March 1808.

WHY DID ELLEN HAVE A GARDEN?

Gardening suited Ellen's character, her setting and her botany. She was bright, with an active mind, and liked being busy and useful. Botany brought connections, through exchanging specimens and letters with fellow botanists, that gave Ellen a sense of usefulness in doing something for other people, which alleviated her feelings of physical isolation. Her enthusiasm for botany and the connections it gave her are amply demonstrated in her letters to Dawson Turner. Writing to him in 1809, she explained that she 'felt quite pleased when you told me your friends had robbed you of the things I sent you, as the gathering of a fresh supply will give still greater interest to a pursuit so highly delightful'.[22] In another letter she wrote 'You must not cease to ask for such plants as I can save for you because I send drawings. I shall send both with the greatest pleasure until you are acquainted with everything our rocks and shores produce'.[23] She summed up her view with 'If I can do anything for you pray tell me. Working for oneself is very dull, but to do anything for another person gives one spirit to proceed'.[24]

Ellen derived great pleasure from her garden and the process of gardening itself. In October 1809 she told Turner that:

> At present the delightful softness of the weather tempts me out & the garden requires care and preparation for winter. With us 'parting summer's lingering blooms' delay long. We have flowers till the frost comes after Christmas and even then we have but little frost.[25]

She referred to plants she found as 'little treasures' and 'exquisite little beauties' and she had some she was passionately fond of, including the butterworts:

> Pinguicula grandiflora [large-flowered butterwort], you shall have a large supply next spring, it is extremely common here. I will draw it for you, you can have no idea of its beauty from a dried specimen, of the beautiful shades & streaks in the flower. P. Lusitanica [pale butterwort] is a very elegant little plant, I wish you could have it fresh from me, I am so fond of it that I keep it in the house flowering in the Danish manner in a glass of water.[26]

The next spring, she commented to Turner that she was 'very busy planting & gardening & making alterations outside, which I delight in'.[27]

---

22 TCC, Turner Correspondence: Ellen Hutchins to Dawson Turner, 9 May 1809.   23 TCC, Turner Correspondence: Ellen Hutchins to Dawson Turner, 27 November 1809.   24 TCC, Turner Correspondence: Ellen Hutchins to Dawson Turner, 4 July 1812.   25 TCC, Turner Correspondence: Ellen Hutchins to Dawson Turner, 9 October 1809. Ellen is quoting from Oliver Goldsmith's poem *The deserted village* (1770).   26 TCC, Turner Correspondence: Ellen Hutchins to Dawson Turner, 17 September 1810.   27 TCC, Turner Correspondence: Ellen Hutchins to Dawson Turner, 8 March 1811.

14.4 *Jungermannia hutchinsiae*, a leafy liverwort, now *Jubula hutchinsiae*. W.J. Hooker, *British Jungermanniae* (London, 1816), tab. I. Image courtesy of the National Library of Ireland, LBR 58831.

The leafy liverwort, *Jungermannia hookeri* (now *Haplomitrium hookeri*, Hooker's flapwort), she described as 'another of my *darlings*'.[28] This plant illustrates the connections and friendships that botany provided for Ellen. James Townsend Mackay distributed her specimens of seaweeds, mosses, liverworts and lichens to the specialist botanists studying them. Dawson Turner was such a specialist, who was working on a major book on seaweeds and had already published a work about Irish mosses and was interested in all the cryptogams. Through their correspondence, he became Ellen's strongest friend and mentor and, despite never meeting, his friendship was significant in supporting Ellen in her difficulties with ill health and what she called family 'troubles'. Turner was also a mentor and friend to another young botanist, William Jackson Hooker (1785–1865), her exact contemporary, and he wrote of him to Ellen:

> My particular friend, Mr Hooker, who is at this moment sitting by me & working on a monograph of the genus Jungermannia, has desired me to interest myself with you to send me for him specimens of julacea, quinquedentata and curvifolia, if you find them in your neighbourhood & particularly if you find them in fruit.[29]

Ellen sent a great many specimens of rare liverworts for Hooker and found an impressive number of new ones, one of which Hooker named after her: *Jungermannia hutchinsiae* (Fig. 14.4). Another he named after Dawson Turner: *Jungermannia turneri* (now *Cephaloziella turneri*). Ellen wrote:

> Pray I beg you to thank Mr Hooker for his last letter & for the engraving of Jungermannia Turneri & the specimens he sent me. I am quite delighted with the engraving. The plant is an elegant little thing. He has done justice to its beauty. I am greatly gratified at one of mine being named after you.[30]

Mosses, likewise, were a special interest of Ellen's:

> I hope you found the mosses in the last parcel interesting. All mosses are very much so, nothing delights me more than the sight of a great rock cover'd with a variety of mosses. In winter the rich shades of green they afford are very beautiful. I have a rock in my little flower garden, the north side of which is freely covered with mosses & ferns.[31]

---

28 TCC, Turner Correspondence: Ellen Hutchins to Dawson Turner, 16 December 1812.　29 Royal Botanic Gardens, Kew, Ellen Hutchins Papers: Letters 1807–1820: Dawson Turner to Ellen Hutchins, 9 January 1808.　30 TCC, Turner Correspondence: Ellen Hutchins to Dawson Turner, 14 October 1812. The engraving was from W.J. Hooker, *British Jungermanniae* (London, 1816), tab. XXIX.　31 TCC, Turner Correspondence: Ellen Hutchins to Dawson Turner, 5 January 1810.

Ellen delighted in the sight of tiny plants under her microscope. After receiving Turner's book on Irish mosses, she wrote 'what a variety of new reflections the examination of objects so minute, so various, and so beautifully formed brings to one's mind'.[32] Later, in 1812, with the better microscope that she had acquired, Ellen wrote of spending five days examining one freshwater filamentous alga (known to Ellen as *Conferva dissiliens* but not identifiable) and described to Turner the wonders she saw.[33]

Ellen had a particular enthusiasm for roses, especially wild ones. She thought she had found a new species, but Mackay responded:

> I think your little Rose is only a variety of spinosissima [burnet rose]. It is often times very small in rocky or sandy grounds. I have several varieties of that species very dwarf with double flowers but as I only had a cutting or two of each last September my plants have done little more yet than taken root. They are the sweetest little beauties I ever beheld. One of my plants which has white flowers had one flower. When I am able to propagate them you shall have plants of all the varieties. They were first raised in Scotland by sowing seeds of the wild varieties. I have the single varieties Red, White and Striped.[34]

Two years later, she wrote to Dawson Turner about another one:

> The Rosa sent first I was always pretty sure was a distinct species, appearing to me rather to approach [*Rosa*] canina than any other. I have a very fine large specimen to send you & some smaller ones, & you shall have a grand supply next year. I could send you seeds now if you wish for yourself or any friend who would like to raise plants. Pray what name will you give it? … My new one is pretty plenty in hedges about me. [*Rosa*] Tomentosa is our most common species, very pretty it is. Is not [*Rosa*] rubiginosa rather rare? We have it.[35]

OBSERVING PLANTS

A significant aspect of Ellen's gardening was her use of her garden for research, a living extension of her herbarium of dried specimens, used for reference purposes. Ellen brought plants back from her botanizing and planted them in her garden, carefully replicating their position and growing conditions in the wild. Growing them

---

32 TCC, Turner Correspondence: Ellen Hutchins to Dawson Turner, 14 March 1808. Dawson Turner, *Muscologiae Hibernicae spicilegium* (Yarmouth, 1804).   33 TCC, Turner Correspondence: Ellen Hutchins to Dawson Turner, 7 December 1812.   34 Royal Botanic Gardens, Kew, Ellen Hutchins Papers: Letters 1807–1820: J.T. Mackay to Ellen Hutchins, 14 June 1810.   35 TCC, Turner Correspondence: Ellen Hutchins to Dawson Turner, 14 October 1812; *Rosa canina* (dog rose), *R. tomentosa* (harsh downy-rose) and *R. rubiginosa* (sweet-briar) are native Irish roses.

in this way enabled her to observe them closely, in some cases every day, as they developed their spores or flowers. An extract from one of Ellen's letters illustrates this use of her garden, and gives another insight into her enthusiasm for plants:

> Tho' I can hardly hold my pen after the fatigue of yesterday's excursion & have much to do this morning, I cannot resist the gratification it gives me to tell you of my pleasures & to enclose part of my treasures. I set out at 3 o'clock in the morning for a distant mountain lake, which I had once before visited, at a time when I did not collect plants. On the way I walked thro' a deep & curious glen, where I was delighted beyond expression at finding in a little gloomy cavern that beautiful rarity *Hymenophyllum alatum* Killarney fern [*Trichomanes speciosum*]. I could not find a single frond in fruit. I have brought home roots to plant. I placed some by a rock at one side of my flower garden where I had a morsel that I got from Killarney last year growing, so that I may expect the good roots I have now planted will flourish. I have put more in another situation. I cannot enclose you a fine specimen but have some good ones for the next parcel.[36]

Ellen was given plants and seeds for her garden by another Scottish gardener, James Drummond (*c.*1787–1863), who was the curator from 1808 to 1828 of the botanical garden established by the Cork Institution.[37] Drummond visited Ellen in 1810 while he was on a plant-hunting tour of west Cork and Kerry, and gave her plants then or sent them to her later.[38] Ellen mentions him in a letter to Dawson Turner:

> I enclose you the Hieracium [hawkweed] which I promised in my last letter. I begin to doubt that N°. 2 is *cerinthoides* of which I have a plant in the garden that was given to me by Mr Drummond at Cork, but you will be able to decide by the specimen I sent you.[39]

James Townsend Mackay also provided news of new botanical publications:

36 TCC, Turner Correspondence: Ellen Hutchins to Dawson Turner, 1 July 1812.   37 See E.C. Nelson, 'James and Thomas Drummond: their Scottish origins and curatorships in Irish botanic gardens (ca 1808–ca 1831)', *Archives of Natural History*, 17, (1990), 49–65, and E.C. Nelson, ''Mongst the green mossy banks & wild flowers', *The Irish garden*, 17 (3 Apr. 2008), 56–9, augmented and reprinted as chapter 1.6 in E.C. Nelson, *An Irishman's cuttings: tales of Irish garden and gardeners, plants and plant hunters* (Cork, 2009), pp 25–30.   38 See E.C. Nelson, 'Spiranthes romanzoffiana, Irish Lady's Tresses: (mainly) a garden history', *Pollinia*, 18 (special edition, 2018), 33–6, which mentions Hutchins and Drummond's visit to Ellen.   39 TCC, Turner Correspondence: Ellen Hutchins to Dawson Turner, 21 July 1812. Drummond's plant cannot be equated with currently recognized native species of this taxonomically complex genus. The name *Hieracium cerinthoides* L. is regarded as belonging to a species endemic in the Pyrenees.

14.5 *Arabis hirsuta* (hairy rock-cress), from J.E. Smith and James Sowerby, *English botany* (London, 1807), vol. 25, tab. 1746. © Hutchins family collection. The illustration by James Sowerby (1757–1822) showed a specimen gathered at Renvyle, Connemara, by Mackay in the autumn of 1806. Although then regarded as new to 'the British [*sic*] flora', *A. hirsuta* had been found near Bath, England, before 1634. Mackay's was the earliest published record from Ireland.

1746

May 1.1807. Publish'd by Ja.^s Sowerby London.

Turritis alpina [*Arabis hirsuta* (hairy rock-cress)], new to Britain … will soon appear in English Botany. … I enclose you a few seeds of it which you can sow immediately in your garden on a light soil. It grows on a sandy common near the sea side in Connemara perhaps you may find it on your coast next summer.[40]

Ellen valued such botanical drawings highly and saw the great significance that they had in communicating knowledge and understanding, when working at a distance from other botanists. The publications that she was contributing to contained hand-coloured illustrations of each species. For example, descriptions of algae (seaweeds and freshwater species) that she had found and her drawings of some of them are included in Lewis Weston Dillwyn's *British Confervae* and Dawson Turner's four-volume work on *Fuci* and, as we have seen, she contributed liverworts to William Jackson Hooker's *British Jungermanniae* and greatly admired his drawings of them.[41]

THE PROXIMITY OF THE GARDEN

Ellen's garden had value in providing her with plants close to hand, particularly when she became increasingly restricted in the journeys she could make:

No mother of 10 children is more bound to home than I am to this little spot by the increasing years and infirmities of my mother and the ill health of a brother who has lost the use of his limbs. They both depend almost entirely on my exertions for their amusement and health.[42]

Ellen could rarely organize cover to stay away a night or two, and when she could, she used it to go to the mountains looking for plants. 'Our dear mountains', as she called them, held a special place in her heart:

How my spirit flies to the mountains when my limbs will hardly carry me about, I was going to say the plains, but we have none. We poor Irish often boast of what we have *not*.[43]

I write in such a hurry I hardly know what I have scribbled for I am in the *very agonies* of going to the mountains. I hope to bring some things to send you.[44]

---

40 Royal Botanic Gardens, Kew, Ellen Hutchins Papers: Letters 1807–1820: J.T. Mackay to Ellen Hutchins, 26 March 1807.   **41** Lewis Weston Dillwyn, *British Confervae; or colored figures and descriptions of the British plants referred by botanists to the genus Conferva* (London, 1809); Dawson Turner, *Fuci; sive plantarum fucorum generi a botanicis ascriptarum icones, descriptiones et historia. Fuci, or, coloured figures and descriptions of the plants referred by botanists to the genus Fucus*, 4 vols (1808–19); William Jackson Hooker, *British Jungermanniae: being a history and description, with colored figures, of each species of the genus, and microscopical analyses of the plants* (London, 1816).   **42** TCC, Turner Correspondence: Ellen Hutchins to Dawson Turner, 9 October 1809.   **43** TCC, Turner Correspondence: Ellen Hutchins to Dawson Turner, 21 January 1809.   **44** TCC, Turner Correspondence: Ellen Hutchins to Dawson Turner, 9 May 1809.

An example of how far Ellen could go is in Mackay's first letter to Ellen, after his visit to Ballylickey in the summer of 1805, when he wrote 'I found the Carex [sedge] we got on Sugar Loaf [Gabhal Mhór, 574m, Caha Mountains] when crossing the Priests Leap [Léim an tSagairt, 464m, Caha Mountains]... so that you need not ascend Sugar Loaf a second time in order to fetch it'.[45] Some plants on Ellen's list are noted as found on mountain summits; *Lycopodium clavatum* (stag's-horn clubmoss), *Salix herbacea* (dwarf willow) and *Antennaria dioica* (mountain everlasting) on the summit of Knockboy (Cnoc Bui, 706m), and *Empetrum nigrum* (crowberry) and *Thymus praecox* (wild thyme) on the summit of Hungry Hill (Cnoc Daod, 685m).

Often, on account of her mother's illness, Ellen was very restricted in the time she could spend out of the house. Mackay provided a friendly comment on this:

> I am very sorry that you are likely to be so much confined and lament the cause. I hope however that your garden will afford you amusement in your leisure hours for I suppose that scarcely a bit of moss remains unnoticed by you in your immediate vicinity, but you will also have pleasure in visiting your old acquaintances near you in their native stations.[46]

Two months later he wrote 'I hope your Mother's health is better and that you have not entirely given up your botanic walks'.[47] Ellen was often ill herself, sometimes confined to bed and so prevented from getting out, and then remaining very weak and often unable to read, write or draw for weeks on end. For much of her life she suffered from a chronic abdominal disease, which could have been tuberculosis, and she describes bilious attacks, fever, headache, cough and great pain in her side.

BLURRING THE BOUNDARIES OF GARDEN AND THE WILD

Ellen chose to grow native plants in her garden, and others were there anyway, such as *Neottia ovata* (common twayblade), an orchid that grew in the lawn at Ballylickey House. The mosses, liverworts and lichens made no distinction between garden and field, or garden and woodland. Ellen reported that she had 'also found Parmelia farinacea [*Ramalina farinacea* (Fig. 14.6)] with shields [apothecia = fruiting bodies] on the upper branches of an old apple tree that was cut down'.[48] And later:

---

45 Royal Botanic Gardens, Kew, Ellen Hutchins Papers: Letters 1807–1820: J.T. Mackay to Ellen Hutchins, 10 September 1805. **46** Royal Botanic Gardens, Kew, Ellen Hutchins Papers: Letters 1807–1820: J.T. Mackay to Ellen Hutchins, 14 June 1810. **47** Royal Botanic Gardens, Kew, Ellen Hutchins Papers: Letters 1807–1820: J.T. Mackay to Ellen Hutchins, 24 August 1810. **48** TCC, Turner Correspondence: Ellen Hutchins to Dawson Turner, 7 April 1810. See 'Fruticose and filamentous lichens found in Ireland': Irish lichens, website by Jenny Seawright: http://www.irishlichens.ie/lichen-fruticose.html, accessed 15 March 2022.

302   *Madeline Hutchins*

You need not trouble Mr. Hooker for Jung. [*Jungermannia*] *resupinata* for me. … It grows in our lawn & on *my rock*. It is now in fructification. Would you like to have some? I shall put a bit into this letter that I may be sure that I am right.[49]

In the list that Ellen compiled of nearly 1,100 plants found in her neighbourhood, she often noted where she found plants and we learn a little about the garden and grounds at Ballylickey House, her immediate plant-hunting territory, from this. She listed *Orthotrichum pulchellum* (elegant bristle-moss) growing on *Salix aurita* (eared willow) and *Ribes grossularia* (gooseberry) bushes in the garden. From entries about lichens and mosses, we know that trees at Ballylickey included apple, cherry (possibly *Prunus avium*) and *Crataegus monogyna* (hawthorn). Other recorded sites of finds at Ballylickey include 'pools in the lawn', 'rock near the garden', 'in the point field' and 'marsh below the weir'.

AN UNTIMELY END

Ellen's last letter with news of her botanizing was written to Dawson Turner in April 1813:

Let me tell you how when I sat to rest my weary frame on a bank of moss I started up with pleasure at the sight of Jungermannia viticulosa [*Saccogyna viticulosa*] full of fructification & said to myself how glad Mr T. would be. I never felt more pleased at finding it, so very interesting too & connecting it so very nearly with J. trichomanis [*Calypogeia azurea*], the calyx is immersed in the earth in the same way as in that species. It is with us a very common plant.[50]

Ellen's optimistic hope in that letter that she felt 'something like the return of health' was not fulfilled, and she suffered a long illness which prevented her from undertaking any gardening or botany. The last known letter to Turner, dated 30 November 1814, ends with:

I cannot write more. I cannot read at all now or amuse my mind in any way & this is worse than pain to a mind once active & though ever struggling with disadvantages seldom unemployed. Send me a moss anything just to look at.[51]

Ellen died on 9 February 1815, shortly before her thirtieth birthday, and was buried in the Garryvurcha churchyard in Bantry. A plaque commemorating her as a

---

49 TCC, Turner Correspondence: Ellen Hutchins to Dawson Turner, 16 December 1812. **50** TCC, Turner Correspondence: Ellen Hutchins to Dawson Turner, 10 April 1813. **51** TCC, Turner Correspondence: Ellen Hutchins to Dawson Turner, 30 November 1814.

14.6 *Ramalina farinacea*. © Paul Whelan, 2022. This common lichen is a tufted, fruticose (bushy) epiphyte with branches up to 3mm wide and 7cm long, that attach to trunks and twigs of trees by solitary holdfasts.

cryptogamic botanist and natural history pioneer was unveiled there in 2015, on the bicentenary of her death, during the first Ellen Hutchins Festival. The festival is now an annual event, celebrating Ellen's story through botany, botanical art, and the landscape and biodiversity of Bantry Bay.[52]

Ellen's garden at Ballylickey played a small but significant role in her life and her botanical studies. Occupying the space nearest to the house, it was readily accessible, and satisfied her needs for plants to study and plants for their beauty. In the short time that Ellen had to botanize, her achievements were considerable, and she made a significant impression on her fellow botanists, both amateur and professional, who paid tribute to her zeal, knowledge and success. In the words of Dawson Turner 'her liberality, her pleasure in communicating knowledge, and her delight in being useful. Botany had lost a votary as indefatigable as she was acute, and as successful as she was indefatigable'.[53]

---

[52] More information is available at https://www.ellenhutchins.com/, accessed 15 January 2022.
[53] Turner, *Fuci*, iv, p. 74.

Index of plant names

SCIENTIFIC NAMES

Abies (fir), 282
Abies balsamea (balm of Gilead), 282
Acer (maple), 282
Acer campestre (field maple), 33
Acer pseudoplatanus (sycamore), 33, 94, 282
Adiantum capillus-veneris (maidenhair fern), 242, 246
Aegopodium podograria (bishopsweed, goutweed, ground elder), 222, 243, 244, 248
Aesculus hippocastanum (horse chestnut), 199, 282
Aethusa cynapium (fool's parsley), 145, 151
Agrimonia eupatoria (agrimony), 125, 150
Agrostemma githago (corn cockle), 146, 153
Ajuga chamaepitys (ground pine), 241, 246
Ajuga reptans (bugle), 141, 151, 227, 242, 246
Alchemilla filicaulis subsp. *vestita*, 128
Alchemilla vulgaris (lady's-mantle), 127–8, 150
Alisma plantago-aquatica (water-plantain), 138, 155
Alliaria petiolata (garlic mustard), 141, 150
Allium (onion), 34, 43, 224, 280
Allium schoenoprasum (chives), 246
Allium ursinum (ramsons), 74, 92
Allium vineale (wild onion), 128, 150
Alnus glutinosa (alder), 33, 43, 282
aloe, 217, 225
Aloe glauca (blue aloe), 225
Aloe variegata (partridge-breast aloe), 223, 225
Aloe vera, 233, 236, 237
Ammocharis longifolia, 164
Anacamptis pyramidalis (pyramidal orchid), 108, 109, 125, 154

Anagallis arvensis (scarlet pimpernel), 130, 150
Ananas comosus (pineapple), 201, 206, 224, 273, 282
Andromeda polifolia (bog rosemary), 148, 153
Anemone hepatica (liverwort), 226
anemones, 197, 277, 282
Angelica sylvestris (angelica), 131, 150
Antennaria dioica (mountain everlasting), 301
Anthriscus caucalis (bur chervil), 110, 111, 144, 154
Anthyllis vulneraria (kidney vetch), 124, 150, 227
Antirrhinum majus (snapdragon), 149, 150
Aphanes arvensis (parsley-piert), 146, 154
Apium graveolens (wild celery), 121, 150
Apium nodiflorum, 132
Aquilegia vulgaris (columbine), 247
Arabis hirsuta (hairy rock-cress), 298, 299, 300
Arbutus andrachne, 238
Arbutus unedo (strawberry tree), 30, 39–40, 42, 45, 47–8, 75, 76–7, 207, 222, 233, 244, 247
Arctium, 38
Arctotheca prostrata, 291
Arenaria ciliata (fringed sandwort), 78
Aristolochia, 248
Armeria maritima (thrift, sea pink), 78, 119, 121, 151
Artemisia absinthium, 44, 181
Artemisia maritima (sea wormwood), 120, 150, 227
Arum maculatum (lords-and-ladies), 140, 141, 150
Arundo donax, 33

Index of plant names

Asparagus officinalis, 149, 150; cultivated 272, 273
Asparagus prostratus, 149, 150
Asplenium ceterach (rustyback fern), 144, 150; see also *Ceterach*
Asplenium scolopendrium (hart's-tongue fern), 222
Asplenium viride (green spleenwort), 78
Aster tripolium, 156
auricula (*Primula*), 226
Avena sativa (oats), 33, 43, 265

Baldellia ranunculoides (lesser water-plantain), 135, 155
Ballota nigra (black horehound), 143, 151
Barbarea vulgaris (winter-cress), 145, 151
Beta vulgaris, 43
Beta vulgaris subsp. *maritima* (sea beet), 118, 151
Betonica officinalis (wood betony), 227
Betula (birch), 282
Bidens cernua (nodding bur-marigold), 133
Bidens tripartita (trifid bur-marigold), 133, 152
Blackstonia perfoliata (yellow-wort), 126, 151
Blitum bonus-henricus (good-King-Henry), 145, 151
Borago officinalis (borage), 44, 222
Botrychium lunaria (moonwort), 131, 153, 248
Brassavola nodosa, 206
Brassica napus, 151
Brassica nigra, 44
Brassica oleracea (cabbage), 34, 44, 224, 267; (red cabbage), 226
Brassica rapa, 151
Butomus umbellatus (flowering-rush), 112, 138, 153
Buxus sempervirens (box), 33, 43, 269, 272

Cakile maritima (sea rocket), 125, 152
Callitriche (water starwort), 135, 156
Calluna vulgaris (ling), 293
Caltha palustris (marsh marigold), 94, 131, 132, 151, 226
Calypogeia azurea, 302
Calystegia sepium (hedge bindweed), 133, 151

Camellia, 265
Camellia sinensis (tea), 206
Cannabis sativa (hemp), 34, 43, 222, 265, 276, 279
Carduus, 146
Carex caryophyllea (spring-sedge), 130, 152
Carpinus (hornbeam), 282
Carum carvi (caraway), 222
Castanea sativa (Spanish chestnut, sweet chestnut), 30, 31, 42, 240, 282
Cedrus libani (cedar of Lebanon), 273, 282
Centaurea cyanus (cornflower), 146, 152
Centaurea nigra (knapweed), 129, 130, 153
Centaurium erythraea (centaury), 126, 151
Cephalanthera longifolia (narrow-leaved helleborine), 290
Cephaloziella turneri, 296
Cercis canadensis (redbud), 226
Ceterach officinarum (rustyback fern), 222, 242, 247; see also *Asplenium*
Chamerion angustifolium (rosebay willowherb), 78
Chara (stonewort), 136, 152
Cheiranthus cheiri (wallflower), 153
Chenopodium bonus-henricus (good-King-Henry), 246; see also *Blitum*
Chrysanthemum indicum, 291, 292
Chrysanthemum segetum (corn marigold), 151
Chrysosplenium oppositifolium (golden saxifrage), 137, 155
Cichorium (chicory, endive), 241, 246
Cichorium intybus (chicory), 145, 151
Cinnamomum (cinnamon), 206
Circaea lutetiana (enchanter's nightshade), 139, 151
Cirsium, 146
Cistus ladanifer, 291
Cistus × *laxus*, 291
Cistus libanotis, 291
Cistus populifolius, 291, 293
Citrus × *aurantifolia* (lime), 201
Citrus × *aurantium* (orange), 38, 201, 233, 235, 236, 270
Citrus × *limon* (lemon), 38, 201, 233, 236, 237, 270
Clematis vitalba (traveller's joy), 50

Scientific names

Cochlearia atlantica, 119, 151
Cochlearia danica (Danish scurvygrass), 123–4, 151
Cochlearia officinalis (common scurvygrass), 78, 119, 151
Cochlearia officinalis subsp. *officinalis*, 119
Cochlearia officinalis subsp. *scotica*, 119
Colutea arborescens (bladder senna, bastard senna), 238
Comarum palustre, 154
Conferva dissiliens, 297
Conium maculatum (hemlock), 214
Convolvolus arvensis (field bindweed), 128, 151
Cornus, 30
Corylus avellana (hazel), 30, 31, 42
Cotyledon orbiculata, 225
Crambe maritima (sea kale), 123, 151
Crataegus monogyna (hawthorn), 42, 302
Crithmum maritimum (rock samphire), 44, 242, 247
Crocus sativus (saffron), 36, 44, 237, 238
Cucumis melo (melon), 224
Cucumis sativus (cucumber), 34, 43, 224
Cucurbita pepo (pumpkin), 34, 43, 224
Cuminum cyminum (cumin), 222
Cupressus lusitanica (cypress), 240, 282
Cuscuta epiphytum (dodder), 112, 124
Cyclamen hederacea, 247, 248
Cydonia oblonga (quince), 37, 38, 41, 270, 282
Cynoglossum officinale (hound's-tongue), 125, 152

Daucus carota (carrot), 34, 43; wild carrot, 126, 152
Descurainia sophia (flixweed), 144, 156
Dianthus caryophyllus (carnation), 207, 265, 282
Digitalis purpurea (foxglove), 222
Diplotaxis (rocket), 144
Dipsacus fullonum, 152
Dipsacus fullonum subsp. *fullonum* (wild teasel), 145
Dipsacus sativus (fuller's teasel), 146, 152
Draba incana (hoary whitlowgrass), 78
Dracunculus vulgaris (dragon arum), 239, 240

Drosera anglica (great sundew), 47, 48–9, 112, 148
Drosera longifolia (long-leaved sundew), 112
Drosera rotundifolia (round-leaved sundew), 148, 155, 226
Dryas octopetala (mountain avens), 49–50, 51, 78, 112, 242

Ecballium elaterium (squirting cucumber), 224, 240, 248
Empetrum nigrum (crowberry), 301
Epilobium hirsutum (great willowherb), 133, 153
Epilobium parviflorum, 154
Epipactis atrorubens (dark-red helleborine), 51
Epipactis helleborine (broad-leaved helleborine), 50–1
Equisetum (horsetails), 222
Erica cinerea (bell heather), 293
Erica tetralix (cross-leaved heath), 112, 148, 152
Erigeron acris (blue fleabane), 125, 151
Erodium cicutarium (common stork's-bill), 125, 152
Erodium moschatum (musk stork's-bill), 124, 152
Erophila verna (common whitlow-grass), 131, 154
Ervilia hirsuta (hairy tare), 146, 156
Ervilia sylvatica (wood vetch), 141, 156
Ervum, 34
Eryngium maritimum (sea holly), 125, 152, 242, 246
Erysimum cheiri (wallflower), 149, 153
Euonymus europaeus (spindle), 43, 248
Eupatorium cannabinum (hemp-agrimony), 132–3, 152
Euphorbia helioscopia (sun spurge), 145, 156
Euphorbia hyberna (Irish spurge), 34, 36, 52–3, 73, 214, 226, 244–5, 247
Euphorbia paralias (sea spurge), 124, 156

Faba, 34, 43
Fagus sylvatica (beech), 261, 272, 282
Ficaria verna (lesser celandine), 105, 139, 151

Index of plant names

Ficus carica (fig), 30, 31, 38, 41, 42, 282
Filipendula vulgaris (dropwort), 241, 242, 246
Foeniculum vulgare (fennel), 43
Fragaria vesca (strawberry), 30, 42
Fraxinus excelsior (ash), 33, 43, 92, 261, 282
Fucus capillaris, 292
Furcraea foetida, 225

Galega (goatsrue), 241, 246
Galeopsis angustifolia (red hemp-nettle), 147, 153
Galeopsis bifida (bifid hemp-nettle), 145, 153
Galeopsis tetrahit (common hemp-nettle), 145, 153
Galium odoratum (woodruff), 141, 150
Galium verum (lady's bedstraw), 128, 152
Gentiana verna (spring gentian), 50, 51, 53, 55, 242
Geranium (crane's-bill), 78; *see also* *Pelargonium* (garden geranium)
Geranium dissectum (cut-leaved crane's-bill), 139, 152
Geranium molle (dove's-foot crane's-bill), 139, 152
Geranium pratense (meadow crane's-bill), 149, 152
Geranium robertianum (herb Robert), 92, 139, 152
Geranium sanguineum (bloody cranesbill), 121, 152
Geum urbanum (herb Bennet), 141, 151
Glaucium flavum (yellow horned poppy), 111, 122, 123, 154
Glaux maritima, 152
Glebionis segetum (corn marigold), 146, 151
Gleditsia triacanthos (honey locust), 226
Gloiosiphonia capillaris, 292
Glycyrrhiza glabra (liquorice), 233, 237
Gonialoe variegata, 223
Graminae (grass family), 33
Gratiola officinalis, 241, 246

Haplomitrium hookeri (Hooker's flapwort), 296
Hedera helix (ivy), 33, 38, 43
Helianthemum apenninum, 291

Helianthemum cinereum, 291
Helianthemum nummularium, 291
Heliotropium arborescens, 34
Helleborus, 34
Helleborus foetidus (stinking hellebore), 92, 247
Helminthotheca echoides (bristly oxtongue), 139, 151
Helosciadium nodiflorum (fool's water-cress), 132
Hieracium (hawkweed), 78, 149, 153, 222
Hieracium cerinthoides, 298
Hieracium maculatum, 78
Hordeum murinum (wall barley), 143–4, 153
Hordeum vulgare (barley), 33, 43, 265
Humulus lupulus (hop), 44
Huperzia selago (fir clubmoss), 94
Hyacinthus (hyacinth), 197, 273, 282
Hydrocotyle vulgaris (marsh pennywort), 136, 152
Hyoscyamus niger (henbane), 222, 242, 247
Hypericum androsaemum (tutsan), 139, 150, 248
Hypericum hirsutum (hairy St John's wort), 92
Hypochaeris radicata (cat's-ear), 130, 153
Hyssopus officinalis (hyssop), 44, 222

Ilex aquifolium (holly), 33, 43, 94, 111
Iris persica (Persian iris), 273
Iris pseudacorus, 44

Jacobaea maritima (silver ragwort), 120
Jacobaea vulgaris (ragwort), 112
Jasminum officinale (jasmine), 209
Jubula hutchinsiae, 295
Juglans nigra (walnut), 30, 31, 42, 270, 282
Jungermannia hookeri, 296
Jungermannia hutchinsiae, 295, 296
Jungermannia resupinata, 302
Jungermannia turneri, 296
Juniperus communis (juniper), 50, 55, 77, 78, 92, 246, 247
Juniperus virginiana (red Virginian cedar), 273

Kniphofia sarmentosa, 291

Scientific names

Lactuca (lettuce), 34, 224, 241, 246
Lagenaria siceraria (bottle gourd, calabash), 224
Lamiastrum galeobdolon (yellow weasel-snout), 141–2, 153
Lamium hybridum (cut-leaved dead-nettle), 144–5, 153
Lamium purpureum (red dead-nettle), 145, 153
Lapsana communis (nipplewort), 108, 141, 153
Larix (larch), 282
Lathraea squamaria (toothwort), 90, 142, 152
Laurus nobilis (bay laurel), 43
Leguminosae, 34
Lens culinaris (lentil), 34, 43
Leonurus cardiaca (motherwort), 142, 151
Lepidium (pepperwort), 145
Lepidium coronopus, 152
Ligustrum vulgare (privet), 139, 153
Lilium (lily), 282
Lilium candidum (Madonna lily), 36, 44
Limonium binervosum (sea-lavender), 119, 153
Linum bienne (pale flax), 128, 153
Linum radiola (allseed), 108
Linum usitatissimum (flax), 34, 43, 265, 274, 276
Liriodendron tulipifera (tulip tree), 273
Lithospermum officinale (gromwell), 128, 153
Lolium perenne (ryegrass), 278, 280
Lychnis flos-cuculi (ragged robin), 94, 153
Lycopodium clavatum (stag's-horn clubmoss), 301
Lycopus europaeus (gipsywort), 135, 154
Lysimachia maritima (sea-milkwort), 123, 152
Lysimachia nemorum (yellow pimpernel), 112
Lysimachia tenella (bog pimpernel), 136, 154
Lysimachia vulgaris (yellow loosestrife), 98, 112, 133, 138, 153
Lythrum salicaria (purple loosestrife), 93, 98, 99, 133, 153

Malus (apple), 30, 42, 74, 267, 270, 271, 282, 302

Malva neglecta (dwarf mallow), 144, 154
Malva sylvestris (common mallow), 44, 143, 144, 154
Matthiola incana (stock-gillyflower), 268
Melianthus major (honeyflower), 225, 239
Melilotus altissimus (tall melilot), 145, 154
Melilotus officinalis (ribbed melilot), 145, 154
Mentha (mint), 34, 44, 131, 222
Mentha aquatica, 154
Mespilus (medlar), 282
Morus (mulberry), 282
Musa (banana), 282
Myosotis scorpioides (water forget-me-not), 131, 154
Myrtus communis (myrtle), 209, 233, 238

Narcissus (daffodil, jonquil), 149, 154, 197, 222, 277, 282
Narthecium ossifragum (bog asphodel), 112, 147, 148, 150
Nasturtium officinale (water cress), 135
Neottia ovata (common twayblade), 142, 151, 226, 301
Nerium oleander (oleander), 209
Nicotiana tabacum (tobacco), 233, 238

Oenanthe aquatica (fine-leaved water-dropwort), 132, 151
Oenanthe crocata (hemlock water-dropwort), 111, 132, 137, 154
Oenanthe fluviatilis (river water-dropwort), 132, 151
Oenanthe lachenalii (parsley water-dropwort), 124
Oenanthe phellandrium (water hemlock), 132, 151
Olea (olive), 38
Onobrychis viciifolia (sainfoin), 278
Ophioglossum vulgatum (adder's-tongue), 131, 154, 222, 248
Opuntia ficus-indica, 225
Origanum majorana, 222
Origanum vulgare (marjoram), 34, 44, 128, 154, 222
Ornithogalum umbellatum (star-of-Bethlehem), 149, 154
Orobanche hederae (ivy broomrape), 142

Index of plant names

Orthotrichum pulchellum (elegant bristle-moss), 302
Osmunda regalis (royal fern), 222, 227

Paeonia officinalis (peony), 222
Papaver somniferum (opium poppy), 181, 222
Parentucellia viscosa (yellow bartsia), 134, 154
Parietaria judaica (pellitory-of-the-wall), 142, 154
Parnassia palustris (grass of Parnassus), 135, 152
Pastinaca sativa (parsnip), 34
Pedicularis palustris (marsh lousewort), 136, 154
Pelargonium, 226
Pelargonium alchemillioides, 225
Pelargonium capitatum, 225
Pelargonium inquinans, 273
Pelargonium zonale, 225
Penstemon barbatus, 291
Persicaria amphibia (amphibious bistort), 138, 154
Persicaria vivipara (alpine bistort), 78
Petasites hybridus (butterbur, false rhubarb), 137, 154
Petrosedum fosterianum (rock stonecrop), 143, 155
Petrosedum rupestre (reflexed stonecrop), 143, 155
Petroselinum crispum (parsley), 44, 222
Peucedanum officinale (hog's fennel), 124, 154
Phalaris canariensis (canary grass), 278
Phaseolus, 34
Phlox ovata, 291, 293
Phlox stolonifera, 291, 293
Phlox subulata, 291, 293
Phragmites australis (common reed), 33, 43
Picea mariana (black spruce), 273
Picris echioides, 151
Pilosella officinarum (mouse-ear-hawkweed), 130, 154
Pimpinella saxifraga (burnet-saxifrage), 127, 155
Pinguicula grandiflora (large-flowered butterwort), 294

Pinguicula lusitanica (pale butterwort), 294
Pinguicula vulgaris (common butterwort), 135, 136, 155
Pinus pinea (stone pine), 31
Pinus strobus (Weymouth pine), 273, 282
Pinus sylvestris (Scots pine), 30, 31, 32, 41, 42, 282
Pistacia lentiscus, 31, 42
Pisum sativum (pea), 224, 265
Plantago coronopus (buck's-horn plantain), 118, 119, 152
Plantago major, 36
Plantago maritima (sea plantain), 78, 119, 155
Platanus hispanica (Spanish plane), 273
Poaceae, 33
Polemonium caeruleum (Jacob's-ladder), 149, 156
Polygala vulgaris (common milkwort), 126, 155
Polygonum aviculare (knotgrass), 130
Polygonum depressum (equal-leaved knotgrass), 130
Polypodium vulgare (polypody), 142
Polystichum lonchitis (holly-fern), 78
Polytrichum (hair moss), 112
Populus (poplar), 282
Populus alba (white poplar), 33, 240
Potamogeton crispus (curled pondweed), 138, 155
Potamogeton natans (broad-leaved pondweed), 138, 155
Potentilla palustris, 154
Potentilla sterilis (barren strawberry), 141, 152
Poterium sanguisorba (salad burnet), 128, 155
Primula (auricula, primrose), 222, 226, 282
Primula veris (cowslip), 102, 130, 155, 160, 161
Primula vulgaris (primrose), 102
Prunus armeniaca (apricot), 270, 271, 282
Prunus avium, 302
Prunus cerasus (cherry), 30, 42, 74, 267, 270, 282
Prunus × domestica (plum), 271
Prunus persica (nectarine, peach), 271, 282
Prunus spinosa (blackthorn, sloe), 30, 42

Pteridium aquilinum (bracken), 130, 152
Pulicaria dysenterica (fleabane), 135, 152
Pyrola media, 55
Pyrola minor (common wintergreen), 54–5
Pyrola rotundifolia, 55
Pyrus communis (pear), 30, 42, 74, 267, 271, 282

Quercus (oak), 94, 139, 142, 155, 282
Qercus petraea, 31
Quercus robur, 31, 42

Ramalina farinacea, 301, 303
Ranunculus (florist's ranunculus), 277, 282
Ranunculus arvensis (corn buttercup), 147, 155
Ranunculus auricomus (goldilocks buttercup), 141, 155
Ranunculus bulbosus (bulbous buttercup), 128, 155
Ranunculus ficaria (lesser celandine), 105, 151
Ranunculus flammula (lesser spearwort), 88, 131, 155
Ranunculus muricatus, 226
Ranunculus penicillatus (stream water-crowfoot), 138, 155
Rapum rapulum (turnip), 34, 43, 278, 280
Reseda luteola (weld), 145, 153
Rhamnus alaternus, 30, 42
Rhamnus cathartica (buckthorn), 31
Rhinanthus minor (yellow-rattle), 134, 154
Ribes grossularia (gooseberry), 282, 302
Ricinus communis, 241, 246
Rosa (rose), 36, 44, 265, 272
Rosa canina, 297
Rosa chinensis, 291
Rosa pimpinellifolia (burnet rose), 124, 155
Rosa rubiginosa, 297
Rosa tomentosa, 297
Rosmarinus (rosemary); see *Salvia rosmarinus*
Rubia tinctoria (madder), 266
Rubus (blackberry, bramble), 30, 42
Rubus idaeus (raspberry), 40
Rubus saxatilis (stone bramble), 55–6, 112, 247
Rumex acetosa, 44

Rumex conglomeratus (clustered dock), 133, 153
Rumex crispus (curled dock), 121, 153
Rumex crispus subsp. *littoreus*, 122, 153
Ruta graveolens, 44

Saccogyna viticulosa, 302
Salix (willow, sally), 33, 43
Salix alba (white willow), 139, 155
Salix aurita (eared willow), 302
Salix caprea (goat willow), 139, 155
Salix cinerea (grey willow), 139, 155
Salix herbacea (dwarf willow), 301
Salsola kali (prickly saltwort), 125, 153
Salvia officinalis (sage), 222
Salvia rosmarinus (rosemary), 34, 44, 222
Salvia verbenaca (clary), 128, 153
Sambucus ebulus (dwarf elder), 247
Sambucus nigra (elder), 33, 43
Samolus valerandi (brookweed), 112, 121, 150
Sanguisorba minor (salad burnet), 246
Sanicula europaea (wood sanicle), 139, 155
Saponaria officinalis (soapwort), 226
Satuerja montana, 241, 247
Saxifraga (saxifrage), 77
Saxifraga aizoides (yellow saxifrage), 78
Saxifraga hypnoides (mossy saxifrage), 78, 242, 247
Saxifraga oppositifolia, 291, 292
Saxifraga rosacea (Irish saxifrage), 247
Saxifraga spathularis (St Patrick's cabbage), 78
Saxifraga stolonifera, 291
Saxifraga tridactylites (rue-leaved saxifrage), 108, 109, 130, 154
Saxifraga × urbium (London pride), 77
Scandix pecten-veneris (shepherd's-needle), 147, 154
Scilla verna (spring squill), 56–7, 112
Scorzonera hispanica (scorzonera), 233, 237–8
Scrophularia auriculata (water figwort), 137, 151
Scrophularia nodosa (common figwort), 137, 155
Scrophularia umbrosa (green figwort), 137
Secale cereale (rye), 33, 43, 265

Index of plant names

Sedum acre (biting stonecrop), 143, 155
Sedum roseum (roseroot), 78
Senecio fluviatilis, 247
Senecio vulgaris (groundsel), 222
Sherardia arvensis (field madder), 128, 155
Silene acaulis (moss campion), 78
Silene dioica (red campion), 94, 142, 153
Silene flos-cuculi (ragged robin), 131, 153
Silene latifolia, 151
Silene uniflora (sea campion), 78, 121, 122, 123, 153
Silene vulgaris (sea campion), 123, 151
Sinapis alba (mustard), 34, 44
Sinapis arvensis (charlock), 145, 146, 155, 227
Sisum sisarum, 43
Sisymbrium irio (London rocket), 144, 152
Smyrnium olusatrum (alexanders), 149, 238, 153
Solanum aethiopicum (bitter tomato, Ethiopian eggplant), 224
Solanum dulcamara (bittersweet), 133, 152
Solanum tuberosum (potato), 224, 240
Soldanella alpina, 291, 293
Solidago virgaurea (goldenrod), 242, 246
Sorbus aucuparia (mountain ash), 42, 259
Sparganium erectum (branched bur-reed), 137, 156
Spartium junceum, 43
Spergula arvensis (corn spurrey), 146, 156
Spergularia media (greater sea-spurrey), 118, 156
Spiranthes romanzoffiana (Irish lady's tresses), 298
Stachys officinalis, 38
Stachys palustris (marsh woundwort), 133, 134, 155
Stachys sylvatica (hedge woundwort), 139, 152, 248
Stellaria holostea (greater stitchwort), 139, 153

Tanacetum vulgare, 44
Taraxacum (dandelion), 222
Taxodium distichum (American cypress), 273
Taxus baccata (yew), 17, 199, 282
Teucrium scordium (water germander), 247

Teucrium scorodonia (wood sage), 142, 155, 227, 248
Thalictrum flavum (common meadow-rue), 241, 246
Thalictrum minus (lesser meadow-rue), 78, 241, 246
Threlkeldia diffusa, 98
Thuja (arbor vitae), 282
Thuja occidentalis (white Virginian cedar), 273
Thymus praecox (thyme), 34, 44, 301, 242, 246, 247
Thymus vulgaris (thyme), 222
Tilia (lime), 274, 282
Tilia europaea (lime), 26, 33, 43, 199
Torilis japonica (upright hedge parsley), 139, 151
Torilis nodosa (knotted hedge-parsley), 125, 151
Tragopogon pratensis (goat's-beard), 129, 156
Trichomanes speciosum (Killarney fern), 298
Trifolium (clover), 278, 279, 280
Trifolium arvense (hare's-foot trefoil), 125, 153
Trifolium campestre (hop trefoil), 126, 156
Trifolium dubium (lesser trefoil), 126, 156
Trifolium repens (white clover), 34, 35, 36, 44
Tripolium pannonicum (sea aster), 119, 156
Triticum aestivum (wheat), 33, 43, 265
Tropaeolum majus (garden nasturtium), 207
Tulipa (tulip), 197, 205, 207, 222, 226, 277, 282; 'De Paus van Roomen', 205; 'Semper Augustus', 205; 'Viceroy', 204, 205
Typha latifolia (bulrush), 135, 156

Ulex europaeus (furze, gorse, whins), 38, 127, 152, 278
Ulmus (elm), 199, 259, 274, 282
Umbilicus rupestris (navelwort, pennywort), 143, 155, 243, 247
Urtica dioica (nettle), 34, 44
Urtica urens (small nettle), 222

Vaccinium myrtillus (bilberry, whortleberry), 148, 156
Vaccinium oxycoccus (cranberry), 148, 156

Vernacular names

Valeriana officinalis (common valerian), 40, 133, 156
Veratrum, 30, 34, 44
Verbascum thapsus (mullein), 129, 156, 242, 246
Verbena officinalis (vervain), 242, 247
Veronica anagallis-aquatica (blue water-speedwell), 131, 150
Veronica beccabunga, 150
Veronica chamaedrys (germander speedwell), 139, 151
Veronica hederifolia (ivy-leaved speedwell), 141, 150
Vicia cracca (tufted vetch), 139
Vicia faba (broad bean), 34, 72–3

Vicia hirsuta, 150
Vicia sylvatica, 156
Vinca major (greater periwinkle), 149, 151
Vinca minor (periwinkle), 226
Vincetoxicum hirundaria, 241, 247
Viola (pansy, violet), 36, 44
Viola arvensis (field pansy), 126, 146, 156
Viola lutea (mountain pansy), 126, 156
Viola palustris (marsh violet), 147–8, 156
Viola tricolor (wild pansy), 126
Viola tricolor subsp. *curtisii* (wild pansy), 125–6
Viola tricolor subsp. *tricolor*, 145, 156
Vitis vinifera (grape, vine), 30, 31, 38, 42, 201, 240

VERNACULAR NAMES

adder's-tongue, 131, 222, 248
agrimony, 125
aiteal (*Juniperus communis*, juniper), 54, 55
'aitin francach' (*Ulex* sp., gorse), 38
alder, 33, 279, 282
alexanders, 77, 149, 238
algae, 34, 44, 94, 115, 234, 286, 290, 291, 293, 296, 297, 300
allseed, 108
almond, 240
aloe, 217, 225, 233, 234, 236, 237
aloe, blue, 225
aloe, partridge-breast, 223, 225
anemones, 197, 277, 282
angelica, 131, 150
apple, 30, 42, 74, 191, 240, 267, 270, 271, 282, 301, 302
apricot, 270, 271, 282
arbor-vitae, 282
ash, 33, 43, 92, 253, 261, 282
ash, mountain, 42, 259
asparagus, 149, 150, 272, 273
asphodel, bog, 112, 147, 148, 150
aster, sea, 119, 156
auricula, 226, 282
avens, mountain, 49–50, 51, 78, 112, 242

bainne caoin (*Euphorbia hyberna*, Irish spurge), 36, 52–3; *see also* meacan buí
balm of Gilead, 282

banana, 282
barley, 33, 43, 265
barley, wall, 143–4, 153
bartsia, yellow, 90, 134, 154
basil, 240
bay laurel, 33, 43
bean, broad, 34, 72–3
beans, 34, 43, 265, 277, 278, 282
beech, 261, 272, 282
beet, sea, 118–9, 151
betony, wood, 227, 248
bilberry, 148, 156
bindweed, field, 128, 151
bindweed, hedge, 133, 151
birch, 282
bishopsweed, 222, 243, 244, 248
bistort, alpine, 78
bistort, amphibious, 138, 154
bittersweet, 133, 152
blackberry, 30, 42
blackthorn, 30, 42
borage, 44, 222, 240
box, 33, 43, 194, 197, 213, 269, 272
bracken, 130, 152
bramble, 30, 42
bramble, stone, 55–6, 112, 247
bristle-moss, elegant, 302
brookweed, 112, 121, 150
broomrape, ivy, 142
buckthorn, 31

Index of plant names

bugle, 141–2, 151, 227, 242, 246
bulrush, 135, 156
bur chervil, 110, 111, 144, 154
bur-marigold, nodding, 133
bur-marigold, trifid, 133, 152
bur-reed, branched, 137, 156
burnet-saxifrage, 127, 155
burnet, salad, 128, 155, 246
butterbur, 137, 154
buttercup, bulbous, 128, 155
buttercup, corn, 147, 155
buttercup, goldilocks, 141–2, 155
butterwort, common, 135, 136, 155
butterwort, large-flowered, 294
butterwort, pale, 294

cabbage, 34, 44, 224, 226, 240, 267
cailís Mhuire mhór (*Drosera anglica*, great
    sundew), 48–9
cairéad (carrot), 34
caithne (*Arbutus unedo*, strawberry tree),
    39–40, 47–8
calabash, 224
camellia, 265
campion, moss, 78
campion, red, 94, 142, 153
campion, sea, 78, 121, 122, 123, 151, 153
canary grass, 278
caorthann curraigh (*Valeriana officinalis*,
    common valerian), 40
caraway, 222
carnation, 207, 282
carrot, 34, 126–7, 152
cat's-ear, 130, 153
ceadharlach Bealtaine (*Gentiana verna*,
    spring gentian), 53
cedar of Lebanon, 273, 282
cedar, red, 273
cedar, white, 273
celandine, lesser, 105, 139, 141, 151
celery, wild, 121–2, 150
centaury, 126–7, 151
charlock, 145, 146, 155, 227
cherry, 30, 42, 74, 267, 270, 282, 302
chervil, 240
chestnut, horse, 199, 282
chestnut, Spanish, 30, 31, 42, 240, 282
chestnut, sweet, 30, 31, 42, 240, 282

chicory, 145, 151, 241, 246
cinnamon, 74, 206
clary, 128, 153
clover, 278, 280
clover, white, 34, 35, 36, 44
clubmoss, 234
clubmoss, fir, 94
clubmoss, stag's-horn, 301
cockle, corn, 146, 153
comfrey, 240
columbine, 247
cornflower, 146, 152
cowslip, 102, 130, 155, 160, 161
cranberry, 148, 156
cranesbill, bloody, 121, 152
crane's-bill, 78
crane's-bill, cut-leaved, 139, 141, 152
crane's-bill, dove's-foot, 139, 141, 152
crane's-bill, meadow, 149, 152
'crann mallugh', 239
crowberry, 301
cuach Phádraig (*Plantago major*, greater
    plantain), 36
cucumber, 34, 43, 224, 240
cucumber, squirting, 224, 240, 248
cumin, 222
currants, 282
cypress, 240, 282
cypress, American, 273

daffodil, 149, 154, 197, 222, 240, 277,
    282
damson, 30
dandelion, 222
danewort, 247
dead-nettle, cut-leaved, 144–5, 153
dead-nettle, red, 145, 153
dill, 240
dock, clustered, 133, 153
dock, curled, 121–2, 153
dodder, 112, 124
dropwort, 241, 242, 246

ealabairín (*Epipactis helleborine*,
    broadleaved helleborine), 50–1
eggplant, Ethiopian, 224
elder, 33, 43, 191
elder, dwarf, 247

Vernacular names 315

elder, ground, 222, 243, 244, 248
elm, 33, 199, 259, 272, 274, 282
endive, 241, 246
everlasting, mountain, 301

fennel, 43, 240
fennel, hog's, 124, 154
ferns, 34, 44, 142, 144, 222, 227, 234, 293, 296
fern, Killarney, 298
fern, maidenhair, 242
fern, royal, 222, 227
fern, rustyback, 144, 150, 222, 242, 247
fig, 30, 31, 38, 41, 42, 240, 282
figwort, common, 137, 155
figwort, green, 137
figwort, water, 137, 151
fir, 282
flapwort, Hooker's, 296
flax, 34, 43, 128, 265, 274, 276
flax, pale, 128, 153
fleabane, 135, 152
fleabane, blue, 125, 151
flixweed, 144, 156
flowering-rush, 112, 138, 153
forget-me-not, water, 131, 154
foxglove, 222
fungi, 34, 44, 234
furze, 38, 127, 152, 278

'garenive' (*Ecballium elaterium*), 240
'geiredarrig' (*Dracunculus vulgaris*), 240
gentian, spring, 50, 51, 53, 242
germander, water, 233, 247
gipsywort, 135, 154
glasluibh bheag (*Pyrola minor*, common wintergreen), 54, 55
goat's-beard, 129, 156
goatsrue, 241, 246
goldenrod, 242, 246
goldilocks, 141–2, 155
good-King-Henry, 145, 151, 246
gooseberry, 282, 302
gorse, 38, 127, 152, 278
gourds, 240
gourd, bottle, 224
goutweed, 222, 243, 244, 248
grape, 30, 31, 38, 42, 201, 240

grass of Parnassus, 135, 152
gromwell, 128, 153
groundsel, 222

hart's-tongue fern, 222
hawkweed, 78, 130, 149, 153, 222, 298
hawkweed, mouse-ear, 130–1, 154
hawthorn, 42, 302
hazel, 30, 31, 42
heath, cross-leaved, 112, 148, 152
heather, 261
heather, bell, 293
hedge parsley, 110, 111
hedge parsley, upright, 139, 141, 151
hedge-parsley, knotted, 125, 151
hellebore, black, 34
hellebore, stinking, 92, 247
hellebore, white, 34
helleborine, broad-leaved, 50, 51
helleborine, narrow-leaved, 290
hemlock, 214
hemlock, water, 131, 132, 151
hemp, 34, 43, 222, 265, 276, 279
hemp-agrimony, 132–3, 152
hemp-nettle, bifid, 145, 153
hemp-nettle, common, 145, 153
hemp-nettle, red, 147, 153
henbane, 111, 222, 242, 247
herb Bennet, 141, 151
herb Robert, 92, 139, 152
'hollin-traic' ('holimtragh') (*Eryngium maritimum*, sea holly), 246
holly, 33, 43, 94, 111
holly-fern, 78
holly, sea, 125, 152, 242, 246
hollyhock, 240
honeyflower, 225, 239
hop, 44
horehound, black, 143, 151
hornbeam, 282
horsetail, 222, 234
hound's-tongue, 125, 152
hyacinth, 197, 273, 282
hyssop, 44, 92, 222
hyssop, hedge, 241, 246

iris, Persian, 273
ivy, 33, 38, 43, 253, 254

Index of plant names

Jacob's-ladder, 149, 156
jasmine, 209, 240
jonquil, 277, 282
juniper, 49, 50, 54, 55, 77, 78, 92, 246, 247

kale, sea, 123, 151
knapweed, 129, 130, 153
knotgrass, 130–1
knotgrass, equal-leaved, 130

lady's bedstraw, 128, 152
lady's-mantle, 127–8, 150
lady's tresses, Irish, 298
larch, 282
leaithín (*Dryas octopetala*, mountain
    avens), 49–50
leek(s), 34, 224, 240
lemon, 38, 201, 203, 234, 236, 237, 270
lentil, 34, 43
lettuce, 34, 224
lichen(s), 234, 286, 291, 296, 301, 302, 303
lily/lilies, 240, 282, 291
lily, Madonna, 36, 44
lime (*Citrus*), 201
lime (*Tilia*), 26, 33, 43, 199, 274, 282
ling, 293
liquorice, 234, 237, 246
liverwort (*Anemone hepatica*), 226
liverworts (Marchantiophyta), 286, 295,
    296, 300, 301 see also under scientific
    names
locust, honey, 226
London pride, 77
loosestrife, purple, 93, 94, 98, 99, 133, 153
loosestrife, yellow, 98, 112, 133, 138, 153
lords-and-ladies, 140, 141, 150
lousewort, marsh, 136, 154
'lus yn aile' ('lusinuil') (*Sanguisorba minor*,
    salad burnet), 246

madder, 266
madder, field, 128, 155
madroño (*Arbutus unedo*, strawberry tree),
    40
maidenhair fern, 242, 246
makenboy (makinboy), 34, 36 fn 19, 53, 73,
    214, 244–5; *see also* Irish spurge
mallow, common, 44, 143, 144, 154

mallow, dwarf, 144, 154
maple, 282
maple, field, 33
marigold, corn, 146, 151
marigold, marsh, 94, 131, 132, 151, 226
marjoram, 34, 44, 128, 154, 222
meacan buí (*Euphorbia hyberna*, Irish
    spurge, makenboy), 34, 36 fn 19, 52–3,
    73, 214, 244–5
meacan dearg, 34, 43
meadowrue, common, 241, 242, 246
meadowrue, lesser, 78, 241, 246
medlar, 282
melilot, ribbed, 145, 154
melilot, tall, 145, 154
melons, 191, 224
membrillo (*Cydonia oblonga*, quince), 37,
    38
milkwort, common, 126–7, 155
mint, 34, 44, 131, 154, 222, 233
moonwort, 131, 153, 248
moss/mosses, 234, 286, 291, 296, 297, 301,
    302
moss, hair, 112
motherwort, 142, 151
mulberry, 282
mullein, 129, 156, 242, 246
mustard, 34, 44, 146
mustard, garlic, 141, 150
myrtle, 209, 234, 238

naranja (*Citrus × aurantium*, orange), 38
nasturtium, garden, 207
navelwort, 143, 155, 243, 247
nectarine, 271, 282
nettle, 34, 44, 254
nettle, small, 222
nightshade, enchanter's, 139, 141, 151
nipplewort, 108, 141, 153
'nonín' (nóinín, daisy), 39

oak(s), 31, 33, 42, 94, 139, 142, 155, 272,
    282
oats, 33, 43, 265
oleander, 209
olive, 38
onion, 34, 43, 224, 240, 278, 279, 280
onion, wild, 128, 150

Vernacular names

orange, 38, 201, 203, 234, 235, 236, 246, 270

orchid(s), 51, 206, 226, 301

orchid, pyramidal, 108, 109, 125, 154

oxtongue, bristly, 139, 151

pansy, 36, 44

pansy, field, 126, 146–7, 156

pansy, mountain, 126, 156

pansy, wild, 125–6, 145

parsley, 44, 222, 240

parsley, fool's, 145, 151

parsley-piert, 146, 154

parsnip, 34

pea, 224, 265

peach, 271, 282

pear, 30, 42, 74, 267, 271, 282

pellitory-of-the-wall, 142–3, 154

pennywort, 143, 155, 243, 247

pennywort, marsh, 136, 152

peony, 222, 240

pepperwort, 145

periwinkle, 226

periwinkle, greater, 149, 151

pimpernel, bog, 136, 154

pimpernel, scarlet, 130–1, 150

pimpernel, yellow, 112

pine, ground, 241, 246

pine, Scots, 30, 31, 32, 41, 42, 282

pine, Weymouth, 273, 282

pineapple, 201, 206, 209, 224, 272, 282

plane, Spanish, 273

plantain, buck's-horn, 118, 119–20, 152

plantain, sea, 78, 119, 155

plum, 30, 271

polypody, 142, 155

pondweed, broad-leaved, 138, 155

pondweed, curled, 138, 155

poplar(s), 33, 282

poplar, white, 33, 240

poppy, opium, 181, 222

poppy, yellow horned, 111, 122, 123, 154

potato, 224, 240

primrose, 102, 222, 226, 282

privet, 139, 153

pumpkin, 34, 43, 224

quince, 37, 38, 41, 270, 282

ragged robin, 94, 131, 153

ragwort, 112

ragwort, silver, 120

ramsons, 74, 92

ranunculus, florist's, 277, 282

raspberry, 40

redbud, 226

reed, common, 33, 43

rhubarb, false, 137, 154

rock-cress, hairy, 298, 299, 300

rocket, 144

rocket, London, 144, 152

rocket, sea, 125, 152

rose(s), 36, 44, 240, 265, 272, 291, 292, 293, 297

rose, burnet, 124, 155, 297

rose, Christmas, 34

rosemary, 34, 44, 222, 233

rosemary, bog, 148, 153

roseroot, 78

rustyback, 144, 150, 222, 242, 247

rye, 33, 43, 265

ryegrass, 278, 280

saffron, 36, 44, 234, 237, 238

sage, 222, 240

sage, wood, 142, 155, 227, 248

sainfoin, 278

St John's wort, hairy, 92

St Patrick's cabbage, 78

sally, 33, 43

saltwort, prickly, 125, 153

samphire, rock, 44, 242, 247

sandwort, fringed, 78

sanicle, wood, 139, 141, 155

saxifrage, 77

saxifrage, golden, 137–8, 155

saxifrage, Irish, 247

saxifrage, mossy, 78, 242, 247

saxifrage, purple, 292

saxifrage, rue-leaved, 108, 109, 130–1, 154

saxifrage, yellow, 78

sciolla earraigh (*Scilla verna*, spring squill), 56–7

scorzonera, 234, 237, 238

scurvygrass, common, 78, 119, 151

scurvygrass, Danish, 123–4, 151

sea-lavender, 119–20, 153

Index of plant names

seamair bhán (*Trifolium repens*, white clover), 35
sea-milkwort, 123, 152
'seamrog' (shamrock), 35, 36
'seámur' (*Trifolium repens*, white clover), 36
sea-pink, 78, 119, 121, 151
sea-spurrey, greater, 118–19, 156
seaweed(s); *see* algae
sedge(s), 114, 130, 301
senna, bastard/bladder, 238
shamrock (*Trifolium*), 36
shepherd's-needle, 147, 154
silverweed, 84
sloe, 30, 42
snapdragon, 149, 150
soapwort, 226
spearwort, lesser, 88, 131, 155
speedwell, germander, 139, 141, 151
speedwell, ivy-leaved, 141, 150
spindle, 43, 248
spleenwort, green, 78
spring-sedge, 130, 152
spruce, black, 273
spurge, Irish, 34, 36, 52, 53, 73, 214, 226, 229, 230, 244–5, 247; *see also* makenboy
spurge, sea, 124, 156
spurge, sun, 145, 156
spurrey, corn, 146, 156
squill, spring, 56–7, 112
star-of-Bethlehem, 149, 154
starwort, water, 135, 156
stitchwort, greater, 139, 141, 153
stock-gillyflower, 268
stonecrop, biting, 143, 155
stonecrop, reflexed, 143, 155
stonecrop, rock, 143, 155
stone-pine, 31
stonewort, 136, 152
stork's-bill, common, 125, 152
stork's-bill, musk, 124, 152
strawberry, 30, 42
strawberry, barren, 141–2, 152
strawberry tree, 30, 39–40, 42, 45, 47–8, 75, 76–7, 207, 222, 238, 244, 247
sú craobh (*Rubus idaeus*, raspberry), 40

sú na mban mín (*Rubus saxatilis*, stone bramble), 55, 56, 57
sundew, great, 47, 48–9, 112, 148
sundew, long-leaved, 112
sundew, round-leaved, 148, 155, 226
swine-cress, 130–1
sycamore, 33, 94, 282

tare, hairy, 146, 156
tea, 206
teasel, fuller's, 145–6, 152
teasel, wild, 145
thrift, 78, 119, 121, 151
thyme, 34, 44, 222, 242, 246, 247, 301
toadstool, 34, 44
tobacco, 234, 238
tomato, bitter, 224
toothwort, 90, 142, 152
traveller's joy, 50
trefoil, hare's-foot, 125, 127, 153
trefoil, hop, 126–7, 156
trefoil, lesser, 126, 156
tulip(s), 197, 203–5, 207, 222, 226, 277, 282
tulip tree, 273
turnip, 34, 43, 278, 280
tutsan, 139, 141, 150, 248
twayblade, common, 142, 151, 226, 301

'úlla caithne' (*Arbutus unedo*, strawberry tree), 47

valerian, common, 40, 133, 156
vedegambre (*Veratrum*, helleborine), 34
vervain, 242, 247
vetch, kidney, 124, 150, 227
vetch, tufted, 139
vetch, wood, 141, 156
vine(s), 30, 31, 38, 42, 201, 240
violet, 36, 44
violet, marsh, 147–8, 156

wallflower, 149, 153
walnut, 30, 31, 42, 240, 270, 282
water-cress, 91, 135
water-cress, fool's, 132
water-crowfoot, stream, 138, 155
water-dropwort, fine-leaved, 132, 151

Vernacular names

water-dropwort, hemlock, 111, 132, 133, 137, 138, 154
water-dropwort, parsley, 124
water-dropwort, river, 132, 151
water-plantain, 138, 155
water-plantain, lesser, 135, 155
water-speedwell, blue, 131, 150
weasel-snout, yellow, 141–2, 153
weld, 145, 153
wheat, 33, 43, 265
whins, 38, 127, 152, 278
whitlow-grass, common, 131, 154
whitlowgrass, hoary, 78
whortleberry, 148, 156
willow, 33, 43
willow, dwarf, 301

willow, eared, 302
willow, goat, 139, 155
willow, grey, 139, 155
willow, white, 139, 155
willowherb, great, 133, 153
willowherb, rosebay, 78
winter-cress, 145, 151
wintergreen, common, 54–5
woodruff, 141, 150
wormwood, sea, 120, 150, 227
woundwort, hedge, 139, 152
woundwort, marsh, 133, 134, 155

yellow-rattle, 134, 154
yellow-wort, 126, 151
yew, 18, 84, 199, 254, 282

General index

Abbeyleix, Co. Laois, 278
Académie des Science, 60, 71
Accademia del Cimento, Florence, 71
Adare, Co. Limerick, 245 fn 45; manor at, 254–5
Adriaan, Willem, 207
Afranca, Jorge Mendoza, 40
Africa, 162, 166, 206, 207, 239 fn 25; Cape of Good Hope, 163, 165, 224, 225; Khoi-Khoi people in, 163; San people in, 163
Aghaboe, Co. Laois, 261
Aldrovandi, Ulisse, 161, 183
Allen, Joshua, 254
America, 166, 182, 224, 273, 293; Central America, 206, North America, 182, 206, 226, 276, 282; South America, 206, 207, 225
Amsterdam, 67, 165, 183, 199, 200, 203, 210; Amstel, river, 208; Athenaeum Illustre at, 163; Dam Square at, 193; university at, 223; Hortus Medicus at, 162, 163, 165, 168, 194, 195, 206, 207; polders at, 208; Rijksmuseum at, 68; Vecht, river, 208, 209
anatomy, 72
Anderson, James, 280
animals, 41, 189, 207
Annaghmore, Co. Sligo, 271
Anne, queen of Great Britain and Ireland, 271
Anstey, Peter, 69
antiquarianism, 76, 251
Antrim, Co., 57
Antwerp, 178, 181, 182, 210, 221
apothecaries, 45, 48, 49, 58 fn 1, 61, 71, 77, 90, 97, 161, 169, 179 fn 24, 183, 184, 186, 214, 225, 230, 244

Aran, Islands, 242, 247
arbours, 197, 202, 258
Arcadia, 195
Archer, John, 85
Ardfert, Co. Kerry, 255, 257, 259
Ardnagashel, Bantry, Co. Cork, 286 fn 1
Ardrahan, Co. Galway, 247
Aristotle, 178, 187
Armagh, 246; archbishopric of, 174 fn 1; County Museum at, 65; Public Library at, 96
Armstrong, Margaret, 269 fn 29
Ashe, St George, 62, 67, 70, 71, 74, 75, 76
Ashford, William, 261
Ashton, Thomas, 268
Ashtown, Dublin, 137
Asia, 162, 163, 166, 206, 237
Aston, Francis, 74
Aston, Thomas, 268 fn 29
Astorga, Marquis of, 41
astrology, 231
astronomy, 157, 159
Athlone, Co. Roscommon, 79 fn 70, 248
Atkinson, John, 84
Atkinson, Miles, 85
Augsburg, Germany 168, 179
Austen, Ralph, 191
Austria, 75
aviaries, 209
Avondale, Co. Wicklow, 258

Babel, 187
Back Lane, Dublin, 87
Bacon, Sir Francis, influence of, 22, 61, 62, 76, 189, 191
Baggotrath, Dublin, 106, 144
Balfour, William, 271
Balgriffin, Dublin, 107, 128

Ballinasloe, Co. Roscommon, 248
Ballsbridge, Dublin, 106, 113, 136, 213
Ballybough, Dublin, 107, 113, 123, 133, 138
Ballylickey House, Bantry Bay, Co. Cork, 23, 287, 288, 289, 290, 301, 302, 303
Ballyoughtera, Co. Cork, 259
Balscadden, Dublin, 107, 121, 123
Banbury, Arnold, 269
Bantry Bay, Co. Cork, 286, 287, 288, 292, 303;
Barberstown, Co. Kildare, 135
Barclay family, Ann, 276 fn 83; Barclay, John, 276 fn 83
Barents, Johan, 204
Barmeath, Co. Louth, 273
Barnard, T.C., 19, 21, 22, 61
Barnewall, Robert, 282
Barrelier, Jacques, 168
Barrow, River, 112, 133, 138
Basle, Switzerland, 28, 110, 161, 167, 176, 221; Froben printing press at, 177 fn 17
Bath, England, 298
Bauhin family, Caspar, 110, 111, 161, 166, 167, 176, 187, 221, 242 fn 33; Johann, 221
Beaufort, Daniel Augustus, 257 fn 21, 258, 260
Bede, the venerable, 31
Belfast Natural History and Philosophical Society, 17
Belle Isle, Co. Fermanagh, 258, 259
Bellevue, Co. Wicklow, 261
Bellew family, John, 273; Sir Patrick, 272
Belvedere House, Co. Westmeath, 258, 259, 260
Bennet, Mr, 58 fn 1
Bentinck, Hans Willem, 1st earl of Portland, 200
Berkeley Castle, Gloucestershire, 259
Berkeley, George, 78, 79 fn 72
Berlin, Germany, 59, 187
Bernard, Edward, 179
Besler, Basil, 169
Birr, Co. Offaly, 47, 55
Blackrock, Dublin, 119, 120, 124, 125, 136, 284
Blackwell, Elizabeth (née Blachrie), 210

Blaeu printing press, 163
Blair, Patrick, 108
Blanchardstown, Dublin, 127, 135
Blochwitz, Martin, 191
Block, Agnes, 208
Blois, royal garden at, 168
Boardstone, Dublin, 106, 146
Boate family, Arnold, 21, 22; Gerard, 21, 22, 67, 188
Bobart, Jacob, 78 fn 67
Boccone, Paolo, 168, 183
Boerhaave, Herman, 111, 209, 218, 226, 227, 228
bogs, 21, 48, 55, 112, 135, 136, 147–8, 244, 287
Bologna, botanical garden at, 183; university of, 165
Bonnefons, Nicholas de, 189
Bonnivert, Gédéon, 100, 116
Booterstown, Dublin, 113, 118
Boran, Elizabethanne, 23
Borris House, Co. Carlow, 257
botanical gardens, 52, 159, 162, 163, 165, 168, 173, 178, 195, 211, 213 fn 1, 221, 290, 298; *see also* physic gardens
Botanical Society of Britain and Ireland (BSBI), 39
botanology, definition of, 231
Bouhéreau, Elie, 176, 178, 179, 182, 183, 184, 188
Boulter, Hugh, archbishop of Armagh, 96
Bowe, Patrick, 19
Boyle, Henry, 1st earl of Shannon, 259 fn 34
Boyle, Robert, 61, 66, 188
Brabazon, Chaworth, 6th earl of Meath, 271
Bradley, James, 64
Bradley, Richard, 172
Bray, Edward, 277, 281, 282, 284
Breeole, Co. Roscommon, 248
Brewer, Samuel, 98 fn 100
Breyne, Jacob, 206, 209
Bristol, England, 269, 278
Britain, 31, 52, 57, 71, 114, 116, 124, 189, 194, 212, 238, 274, 300
Brock, Elnathan, 268
Brooking, Charles, 107, 113, 118

Brown, Bridget, 80, 85, 86
Brown, Lancelot (Capability), 251
Brown, Robert, 98
Browne SJ, Fr, 257
Browne, family, Anne, viscountess Kenmare, 260; Thomas, 4th viscount Kenmare, 252, 260, 261
Browne, William, 53
Brownsford Castle, Woodstock, Co. Kilkenny, 260
Brunfels, Otto, 140, 159, 161, 171
Buitenplaatsen, Netherlands, gardens of, 194, 208
Bulkeley, Sir Richard, 270
Bull Island, Dublin, 113, 118, 123, 124
Bull Wall, Dublin, 113, 123
Bullen family, Daniel, 271–3, 281, 282; William, 271
Burgess, Co. Tipperary, 248
Burgh, Thomas, 215
Burke, Edmund, 251, 252
Burke, John, 38, 41
Burnet, Thomas, 67
Burnett, Richard, 281
Burren, Co. Clare, 50, 51, 53, 55, 57, 241, 242, 246, 247
Butler, James, 1st duke of Ormond, 69
Butler, Michael, 274 fn 72
Buxbaum, Johann Christian, 165
Byron, Samuel, 214

Cabbage Garden Cemetery, Dublin, 97
cabinets of curiosities, 71, 182–6
Cabra Castle (Cormy Castle), Co. Cavan, 256, 260
Cabra, Dublin, 106, 139
Cadiz, Spain, 25
Calabria, Italy, 92
Calais, France, 64
Calepino, Ambrogio, 28
Calzolari, Francesco, 183
Cambridge, 102; university of, 47, 61, 70, 172
Camerarius, Joachim, 168, 169
Camerarius, Rudolf Jakob, 187, 188
Canary islands, 31, 206
Capel family, Algernon, 64; Elizabeth, 64
Capel Street, Dublin, 264, 274, 280

Cardiff's Bridge, Dublin, 90, 106, 133, 134, 137, 139
Caribbean, 206, 225
Carlingford, Co. Louth, 149
Carlisle, 82, 83, 85; Cumbria Archives at, 83, 89; Midsummer Quarter Session at, 85
Carrick, Dennis, 268 fn 29
Carrickfergus, Co. Antrim, 274
Carroll, Patrick, 281
Cartagena, Columbia, 207
Carter, Charles, 270
Carton House, Co. Kildare, 212
Cartwright, Thomas, 253
Cashel, Co. Tipperary, 244
Castelli, Pietro, 168
Castle Bernard, Co. Cork, 257
Castle Blunden, Co. Kilkenny, 262
Castle Ward, Co. Down, 255
Castleknock, Dublin, 257
Castlemartyr, Co. Cork, 258, 259
Castlerea, Co. Roscommon, 257
Castletown, Co. Kildare, 130, 261, 272, 273
caterpillars, 169
Cato, Marcus Porcius, 188
Cats, Jacob, 200
Caucasus, 37
Caulfield, James, 1st earl of Charlemont, 261
Cavan Street, Dublin, 130
Celbridge, Co. Kildare, 107, 130, 254
Celsus, Aulus Cornelius, 30
Ceres, 182
Cesalpino, Andrea, 161, 166
Chamber's Street, Dublin, 146
Chapelizod, Dublin, 106, 127, 128, 130, 131, 133, 139, 141, 143, 270, 284
Chapelmidway, Co. Dublin, 136
Charleville Castle, Co. Offaly, 256
Chelsea, London, 222, 225, 230
Chelsea Physic Garden at, Society of Apothecaries, 225, 226
chemistry, 66, 72, 157
Chester, England, 74, 278
Christ Church Lane, Dublin, 271, 272, 273 fn 64, 279, 284
Church Street, Dublin, 279

General index

Cicero, Marcus Tullius, 174, 188
Clare, Co., 49, 51, 53, 241, 241, 247
Clarici, Paolo Bartolomeo, 169, 170
Clibborn, family, 276 fn 83
Clingendael, Netherlands, 199–200, 211
Clogher, 22, 62, 176
Clontarf, Dublin, 77, 113, 123, 124, 139, 145, 149
Clontueskart, Co. Galway, 247
Clowen Castle, Woodstock, Co. Kilkenny, 260
Clusius, Carolus *see* L'Ecluse, C.
Cole, John, 268
Colgan, Nathaniel, 114, 117, 118, 127, 128, 133, 137, 144
Coliemore, Dalkey, Co. Dublin, 57
colonization, 20, 22, 189
Columella, Lucius, 188
Commelin family, Caspar, 163, 171, 209, 225; Jan, 163, 164, 165, 203, 209, 211, 225
Congregational Fund Board, 83
Connemara, 300
Conolly family, Louisa, 272–3; Tom, 271–3
Consistory Court records, 84
Contant, Paul, 184, 186
Conway, Edward, 1st earl of Conway, 269
Conyngham Road, Dublin, 106, 129
Cook Street Meeting House, Dublin, 89
Coolock, Dublin, 107, 126, 145
Coote, Sir Charles, 260
Copernican theory, 64
Cork Hill, Dublin, 274 fn 72, 276, 279, 280
Cork, Co., 36, 48, 52, 238, 286–303; city of, 232
Cork Institution, 298
Cornmarket, Dublin, 264
Cornut, Jacques Philippe, 166
Corofin, Co. Clare, 246, 247
correspondence, importance of, 23, 69, 183, 286
Costello, Vandra, 194
Cottingham, George, 284
Cox, Richard, 76
Crane Lane, Dublin, 233

Cratlow, Co. Clare, 247
Crom Castle, Co. Fermanagh, 255
Cromwell, Oliver, 21
Cromwellian plantation, 21
Crow, Robert, 71
Crumlin, Dublin, 106, 126, 143, 149
cryptogams, 286, 291, 296
Cullenswood, Dublin, 281, 285
Culpeper, Nicholas, 182, 244
Cumberland, Cumbria, England, 80, 81, 84, 90, 104, 117, 126
Curaçao, island of, 206
Custom's House, Dublin, 274
Cut Purse Row, Dublin, 276 fn 83, 280

D'Argenville, Dézallier, 199
Dale, Samuel, 90, 98
Dale, Thomas, 218, 226
Daléchamps, Jacques, 28, 29, 39, 177, 187
Dalkey Island, Dublin, 57, 121
Dalrymple, Elizabeth, 82
Dame Street, Dublin, 274 fn 72; Crow's Nest at, 70–1
Danish mounts, 67, 76
Daston, Lorraine, 182
De Barry, Gerald (Gerald of Wales), 20, 25, 28
de Beer, Susanna, 177
de Bhaldraithe, Tomás, 28, 41, 42
de Nebrija, Elio Antonio, 30
de Vesey family, 278
Dempsey, Jenny, 287
Den Hartog, Elizabeth, 206
Denmark, 67
Denton, Daniel, 189
Derry, Co., 33, 57, 76, 103, 178 fn 24, 179 fn 24, 252
Descartes, Réne, 71
Devlin, Zoe, 54, 93
Dewhurst, Kenneth, 77 fn 65
Digby, Kenelm, 191
Dillenius, Johan Jakob, 97, 98, 108, 109, 111, 117, 133, 137, 148, 221, 229, 230
Dillon, Cary, 270
Dillwyn, Lewis Weston, 254, 288, 289, 300
Dioscorides, 98, 161, 177, 178, 182

dissenters, 80, 81, 82, 83, 84, 86, 87, 96; Synod of Munster, 89; Synod of Ulster, 88; Plunket Street Meeting House, 88; Wood Street Meeting House, 88

Dobbs, Arthur, 274, 278

Dodd, James Joseph, 279

Dodoens, Rembert, 111, 161, 162, 165, 182, 210, 221

Dolphin's Barn, Dublin, 106, 139, 144, 145

Domville, Lucy, 64

Donabate, Dublin, 124

Donegan, Patrick, 272 fn 56

Doneraile Court, Co. Cork, 212

Donnybrook, Dublin, 128

Doogue, Declan, 109, 132, 134, 136

Doublet, Philips, 199

Doulack's well, Dublin, 149

Down, Co., 57

Downhill, Co. Derry, 252

Dr Steevens' Hospital, Dublin, 157, 171

Drelincourt, Charles, 67

Drogheda, Co. Louth, 31, 38, 41, 124

Drumcolliher, Co. Limerick, 247

Drumcondra, Dublin, 130, 139, 149, 281

Drummond, James, 298

Dublin Bay, 113, 118, 124, 261

Dublin City Library and Archives, 60

Dublin Naturalists' Field Club, 114

Dublin Philosophical Society, 17, 22, 23, 58–79, 159, 186, 189, 207 fn 33; astronomy at, 72; cabinet of curiosities at, 71; herb garden at, 71; herbarium at, 71, 292; laboratory at, 71; library at, 71

Dublin printing, 20, 21, 22, 61, 71, 172, 173

Dublin Weekly Journal, 217, 218

Dublin, 22, 45, 48, 49, 77, 87, 88, 90, 91, 92, 97, 98, 99, 100, 112, 113, 114, 116, 118, 120, 122, 123, 124, 141, 142, 147, 148, 150, 170, 171, 179, 216, 227, 228, 241, 242, 244, 276, 278, 288, 290; booksellers at, 61, 217; Christ Church Cathedral, Dublin, 264; coffee houses at, 61; College of Physicians, 61, 94, 218; dissection of an elephant at, 64;

Dodder river, 57, 106, 113, 123, 136; Foundling Hospital at, Dublin, 284; fruiterers in, 263 fn 4; Liffey, river, 57, 106, 113, 123, 125, 127, 128, 129, 130, 131, 133, 137, 138, 141, 142; Medico-Philosophical Society at, 96; New Science at, 58–79; nursery trade in, 263–85; Poddle, river, 139; population, 263, 268; seed trade at, 263–85; St Patrick's Cathedral, 94, 97, 171; street hawkers, 267; surgeons at, 61; Tolka River, 107, 113, 123, 133, 135, 137, 149; university of, 60, 213, 215, 218, *see also* Trinity College Dublin

Dugharrow, Co. Tipperary, 248

Dunacarney, Dublin, 127

Dungannon, Co. Tyrone, 33

Dún Laoghaire, Dublin, 90, 119, 121, 123, 125, 141, 142

Dunmore, Co. Kilkenny, 78

Durham, Co., England, 84

Dursey Island, Co. Cork, 32

Dutch East India Company (VOC), 22, 162, 165, 206; garden at Cape, South Africa, 207, 225

Dutch Republic, 162, 193, 194, 195, 207, 212, *see also* Holland

earth sciences, 157

Eaton, Richard, 278, 279

Eden, Garden of, 178, 186, 195

Edenderry, Co. Offaly, 48, 55, 57, 148

Edgeworth, Richard, 271

Edinburgh, 99, 251, 280; Royal College of Physicians at, 87; university of, 70, 80, 87, 90

Eichstatt, Germany, garden at, 168–9

Elizabeth I, queen of England, 20, 25

Ellen Hutchins Festival, 287, 303

Elliott, Brent, 182

Elliott, Thomas, 268 fn 29

Eltham, Kent, 230

Ely Place, Dublin, 270

England, 61, 87, 102, 103, 124, 172, 217, 249, 264, 269, 270, 272, 273, 274, 280, 287

Enniskerry, Co. Wicklow, 252

Erasmus Smith Foundation, 194

Erlach, Johann Bernhard Fischer von, 169
Erne, Lough, 242
Europe, 23, 33, 36, 59, 69, 71, 75, 102, 111, 166, 193, 206, 207, 209, 212, 217, 261, 265, 274, 282; Little Ice Age, 31
Eustace Street, Dublin, 276 fn 83
Evelyn, Charles, 172
Evelyn, John, 67, 170, 189, 191, 268

Fagel family, 22; archive, 212 fn 51; François the Elder, 201, 202, 203; Gaspar, 201, 205, 206, 207; Hendrik the Elder, 203, 208; Hendrik the Younger, 193–4, 208; library of, 193–212; sale catalogue of, 209
Fairchild, Thomas, 265
Farnese, Odoardo, 168
Fennel, Robert, 238
Ferrari, Giovanni Battista, 203, 209
Findlen, Paula, 183
Fingal, Dublin, 126, 128, 144
Finglas, Dublin, 106, 127, 133, 137, 146, 149
Fisher, Jonathan, 250, 254, 258, 259
Fitzgerald family, James, 1st duke of Leinster, 280; William, 2nd duke of Leinster, 280
Fitzgerald, Desmond, 19
Flamsteed, John, 66
Fleetwood, Charles, 21
Fleischer, Alette, 186
Flinn, Bridget, 35
Fogarty, John, 51
Foley, Samuel, 72, 73
Foster family, Co. Cavan, 256
France, 31, 76, 168, 269, 270
Francis Street, Dublin, 106
Frankfurt, Germany, 75, 168, 179
Franklin, Richard, 82
Frederick Street, Dublin, 213
Friedrich Wilhelm, duke of Prussia, 187
Fuchs, Leonhard, 161, 182
Fuller, Edward, 277, 278
fullering, 146
Furry Glen, Dublin, 127, 128, 135

Gahan, John, 284
Galbally, Co. Limerick, 247

Galen, 177
Galicia, Spain, 25
Galilei, Galileo, 71
Galway, Co., 49, 50, 51, 53, 78, 96, 97, 112
garden design, 22, 169, 189, 191, 195, 209, 273; Dutch Baroque style, 195, 197–212
gardeners, 201, 215, 263
gardening manuals, 169, 170, 182 fn 35, 194, 197, 201, 205–6, 209
gardening tools, 196, 268, 272, 273, 277, 282
Gardiner, Richard, 267
Garryvurcha, Bantry, Co. Cork, 302
Gascoigne, William, 66 fn 17
Gaymans, Antoni, 74
Gelen, Sigismund, 177
Gemmingen, Johann Konrad von, bishop of Eichstätt, 168, 169, 211
Genesis, Book of, 187
Geneva, 177
Gerard, John, 78, 98, 108, 109, 149, 161, 162, 176, 182, 236, 237, 238, 240, 244, 245, 276
Germany, 31, 69, 168, 211, 265
Gessner, Conrad, 179
Gilpin, William, 252
Glasgow, Scotland, university of, 82, 87, 218
Glaslough, Co. Monaghan, 97
Glasnevin, Dublin, 106, 127, 129, 143, 145; see also National Botanic Gardens
glasshouses, 235 (see also greenhouses, hothouses, orangeries)
Glenarm, Co. Antrim, 238
Glenconkeyne, Co. Derry/Londonderry, 32, 33, 41
Glengarriff, Co. Cork, 287, 290
Golden Vale, Co. Tipperary, 244
Gómez de la Huerta, Jerónimo, 28
Gore, Sir George, 5th baronet, 258
Gort, Co. Galway, 49, 50, 53, 55, 78, 112, 242
gothick, definition of, 249
Gowran House, Co. Kilkenny, 257
Grafty, Thomas, 282
Grand Canal, Dublin, 115, 135, 138
Grangegorman, Dublin, 106, 127

Grant, Philip, 128
Great Peter Street, Dublin, 66
Great Yarmouth, Norfolk, 287
Greenhills, Dublin, 106, 126, 130, 146
greenhouses, 201, 210, 224, 235, 236, 238, 240, 246, 290; *see also* glasshouses, hothouses, orangeries
Greening, Thomas, 272
Grew, Nehemiah, 67, 73, 183, 188
Grierson, George, 172
Grimwood, John, 281, 284
Gronovius, Johann Friedrich, 178 fn 18
grottoes, 258
Gunterstein, Netherlands, 209, 210, 212

Haak, Theodore, 67, 74
ha-ha, 259
Halfpenny, Nicholas, 259
Halley, Edmund, 66, 67, 75
halophiles, 119, 124, 125
Hamilton family, James, 1st earl of Clanbrassil, 258; James, 2nd earl of Clanbrassil, 258
Hamilton, Hugh Douglas, 91
Hampton Court Palace, garden of, 207
Harcourt Street, Dublin, 288
Hardouin, Jean, 178
Harold's Cross, Dublin, 106, 130, 137, 272
Harris, Eileen, 258
Harris, Richard, 267 fn 25
Harrison, George, 231
Hart, Henry Chichester, 141, 240
Hartlib, Samuel, 21, 22, 52, 61, 188
Harvey, John, 277
Harvey, William Henry, 290
Harvey, William, 188
Haultin, Jerome, 184
Hay family, Anne, 279; Edward, 279, 280; son of, 280 fn 95
Headfort House, Co. Meath, 274
Heaton, Richard, 21, 23, 47, 48, 49, 50, 51, 53, 55, 57, 78, 100, 112, 116, 148, 242
Heinsius, Daniel, 178
Hemmens, Susan, 70
Henderson, Hugh, 274 fn 72
Henry VI, king of England, 253
Henry VIII, king of England, 267

herb sellers, 90, 91, 214, 227
herbalists, 98, 101, 102, 106, 108, 182, 244, 276
herbals, 20, 45, 47, 79, 98, 100, 108, 109, 149, 161, 166, 173, 176, 179, 181, 182, 192, 210, 231, 234, 237, 238, 245
herbarium/herbaria, 23, 67 fn 21, 70 fn 30, 71, 74, 90, 102, 104, 206, 293, 297; specimens 18, 57, 69 fn 25, 90, 221
Heritage Gardens Committees, 19
Hermann, Paul, 67, 69, 70, 74, 165, 206
Hernandez, Francisco, 161, 166, 211
Hesperides, 209
Het Loo, Netherlands, 195
Heywood, Co. Laois, 258, 261
Hibernian Hospital, Dublin, 283, 284
Hill, Thomas, 172
Hillsborough, Co. Down, 259
Hinck, Thomas Dix, 241
Hippocrates, 87, 177
Hogan, Edmund, 254
Holland, 67, 69, 199, 203, 207, 217, 218, 222, 223, 225, 270, 272, 273, 276, 280; *see also* Netherlands and Dutch Republic
Holland, Harry, 268
Hooke, Robert, 67
Hooker, William Jackson, 296, 300, 302
Hoppen, Theodore K., 59, 61, 62, 66, 70, 72, 76
hortus botanicus, hortus medicus, 68, 162–3, 165, 206–7, 225; *see also* physic gardens
hortus siccus (*horti sicci*), 23, 74 fn 54, 88, 90, 102, 104; *see also* herbaria
hothouses, 196, 206, 209, 224, 272; *see also* glasshouses, greenhouses, orangeries
How, William, 21, 47, 48, 52, 55, 57, 100
Howard, Hugh, 77 fn 64
Howth, Dublin, 57, 107, 113, 121, 123, 124, 126, 148, 149, 212, 225, 281
Huddlesceugh (Parkhead), Cumberland, 82, 83, 84, 85, 86; Parkhead Register, 83, 84
Huguenots, 87, 92, 270
Huls, Samuel van, 172
Hume Street, Dublin, 270
Hungary, 75, 76

General index

Hungry Hill, Caha Mountains, Co. Cork, 301
Huntington, Robert, 72, 159
Hutchins family, 288, 290; Alicia, 288, 290; Ellen, 23, 286–303; Tom, 288
Huyghens, Christiaan, 69
Hyche Street, Dublin, 268
Hyde, Henry, Lord Clarendon, 268
Hynestown Reservoir, Dublin, 133

Imperato, Ferrante, 183
Inchicore, Dublin, 106, 128, 133, 135, 137, 139, 146, 149, 280, 281
India, 163, 187
Iniscattery, Co. Clare, 55
Inishfallen Island, Co. Kerry, 261
insects, 203, 209
Ireland's Eye, Dublin, 57, 123
Irish Garden Plant Society, 19
Irish Manuscripts Commission, 41, 70
Isaactown, Co. Meath, 148
Islandbridge, Dublin, 106, 128, 129, 130, 138, 142, 145
Italy, 76, 168, 280
Iveragh Peninsula, Co. Kerry, 40

Jaffray, Robert, 276 fn 83
Jansson, Jean, 183
Jardin du Roi, Paris, 168, 187
Java (Batavia), 165
Jena, German, university of, 165
Jenkinstown House, Co. Kilkenny, 257
Jennings family, Ann, 233; Henry, 233
John's Lane, Dublin, 227
Johnson family, John, 274 fn 72, 275, 276, 277, 278; Sarah, 276
Johnson, Thomas, 108, 161, 162, 182
Johnston, Francis, 256
Johnston, William, 97
Jones, John, 276 fn 83
Joyce, James, 205 fn 25
Jurin, James, 217, 230
Jussieu, Antoine de, 187

K'Eogh family, John 23, 41, 79, 94, 176; 231–48; John, (c.1659–1725) father of, 78, 79 fn 70, 231; Michael, brother of, 233

Keegan, Patrick, 262
Keibergh (Caber), Cumberland, 80, 81
Kendal, Cumbria, 85
Kennedy, Máire, 22, 75, 172
Kenny, Patrick, 284
Kerry, Co., 47, 48, 52, 238, 244, 290, 292, 298; Desmond area in, 47, 53
Kevin Street, Dublin, 285
Kew House, London, 64
Kilbarrack, Dublin, 113
Kilbolane, Co. Cork, 247
Kildare, Co., 138, 142
Killaloe, Co. Tipperary, 248
Killarney, Co. Kerry, 40, 77, 238, 252, 253, 298
Killeager, Co. Wicklow, 141
Killian, Wolfgang, 168
Killiney, Dublin, 119, 120, 121, 141
Killough Hill, Tipperary, 244, 248
Kilmacduagh, Co. Galway, 49, 55
Kilmainham, Dublin, 139; Royal Hospital at, 128, 145, 149
Kilmore, Co. Roscommon, 79 fn 70
Kilruddery, Co. Wicklow, 197 fn 11, 271
Kilsallaghan, Co. Dublin, 147
Kiltartan, Co. Galway, 247
King, James, 4th baron Kingston, 233, 234, 235, 237, 238, 239
Kinsale, Co. Cork, 25
Kirkoswald, Cumberland, 80, 81, 84, 85; St Oswald's parish church at, 80
Kneller, Sir Godfrey, 63
Knockboy, Caha Mountains, Co. Cork, 301
Knockdrin, Co. Westmeath, 262
Knockmaroon Hill, 106, 127, 133, 139
Knocksedan, Swords, Co. Dublin, 127
Knoop, Johann Herman, 196, 197, 209
Kölreuter, Joseph Gottlieb, 265
Kurdistan, 37

L'Écluse, Charles de (Carolus Clusius), 78, 161, 162, 165, 182, 211
L'Obel, Matthias de, 161, 162, 181, 182
La Quintinie, Jean-Baptiste de la, 189, 199, 209
La Rochelle, France, 184
Laguna, Andrés de, 178

Lamb, Keith (Dr J. G. D.), 19
Lambay Island, Co. Dublin, 57
Landré family, John, 270; Peter, 270, 271, 273
Landsdowne Road, Dublin, 213
Lane, Sir George, viscount Lanesborough, 269
Langley, Batty, 199, 261
languages, Greek plant names, 26, 28, 34, 36, 38, 40, 106, 191, 231; Irish plant names, 25 fn 4, 26, 36, 38, 39, 40, 42–4, 58, 92 fn 78, 93, 104, 245, 246; Manx plant names, 246; Spanish plant names, 26, 28, 34, 37, 38, 40, 178
Laurence, John, 172, 173
Lawlor, Emer, 102
Lawson, Thomas, 103
Leeuwarden, Netherlands, 196, 197
Leeuwenhorst, Netherlands, 205–8
Legganhall, Co. Meath, 281
Leiden, Netherlands, 171, 198, 201, 206, 230; Hortus Academicus at, 68, 74, 162, 163, 165, 168, 194, 195, 206, 211, 221, 225; university at, 22, 64, 66, 67, 68, 69, 70, 74, 159, 162–5, 173, 178, 215, 218, 226, 228, 230
Leinster, 112
Leipzig, Germany, 169; university of, 165
Leixlip, Co. Kildare, 142; castle, 250, 251
Lenihan, Pat, 56, 129, 147
Levant, 165, 178
Levinge family, Isabel, 97; Richard, 97
Lewis, Samuel, 260
Lhuyd, Edward, 77, 78, 100, 103, 112, 116, 186, 244
Liberties, Dublin, 80, 87, 92
Linnaeus, Carl, 102, 117, 132, 166, 187, 209
Lisnageeragh, Co. Offaly, 50, 51
Lispopple House, Swords, Dublin, 268
Liverpool, England, 278
Locke, John, 62, 69, 70, 77 fn 65
Loeber, Rolf, 194, 268 fn 27
Loftus family, Adam, archbishop of Dublin, 64; Dudley, 179; Henry, 1st earl of Ely, 258
Lombard, Peter, 31

London, 22, 45, 61, 64, 66, 70, 87, 97, 99, 169, 170, 176, 182, 190, 191, 193, 199, 210, 215, 221, 229, 230, 244, 258, 269, 272, 274, 276, 278, 279, 280, 295, 298; population of, 263; Botanical Society of, 218, 221, 225, 226, 227; British Library, 253; Christie's, 194; Linnean Society of, 286; National Portrait Gallery, 63; Natural History Museum, 220; Strand, 277
London, George, 271, 273
Long, William, 179 fn 24
Longford, Co., 271
Lonicer, Adam, 75
Lough Leane, Killarney, Co. Kerry, 40, 76–7, 247
Louis XIV, king of France, 189, 199
Louth, Co., 57, 227, 258
Lucan, Dublin, 106, 133, 139, 143
Lusthof, pleasure gardens, 195–7
Luttrelstown, Co. Dublin, 129; castle, 258
Lynch, John, 41
Lyon, France, 28
Lyons, Colley, 97
Lyons, Melinda, 121, 122, 127, 143

Maarseveen, Joan Huydecoper van, 163
Macarell, John, 176
Macartney, Valerie, 49
McCarter, Pat, 268
McCracken, Charles J., 79 fn 72
McCracken, Eileen, 19, 263 fn 1
McElligott, Jason, 191
McErlean, Thomas, 18
MacGillicuddy Reeks, Co. Kerry, 40
Mackay, James Townsend, 17, 222, 241, 287, 290, 291, 293, 296, 297, 298, 301
McKendrick, Neil, 264
Madden family, John, 68, 69 fn 25; Mary, née Molyneux, 68; Samuel, 271
Madrid, Spain, 25, 28
Maiden Lane, Dublin, 87
Malabar, India, 163
Malahide, Co. Dublin, 107, 124, 281; Castle, 254 fn 15
Malins, Edward, 19
Mallow, Co. Cork, 257

Malpighi, Marcello, 188
Mangerton Mountain, Co. Kerry, 77
Manor Waterhouse, Lisnaskea, Co. Fermanagh, 271
Manutius, Aldus, 188
Maple, William, 215, 217
Marggraf, Christiaan, 67
Marino Casino, Dublin, 261
Marino Point, Cork, 235
Mark's Alley, Dublin, 80, 106, 107
market gardener, definition of, 263 fn 5
Markham, Clement, 172
Marot, Daniel, 203
Marsh, Narcissus, 22, 174, 176, 178, 182, 183, 189, 191
Marsh's Library, Dublin, 22, 103, 232, 250; botany and gardens at, 174–92
Martyn, John, 227
Mary II, queen of England, Scotland and Ireland, 186, 207
Mascall, Leonard, 191
mathematics, 157, 159
Mattioli, Pietro Andrea, 78, 161, 167, 178
Maturin, Charles, 251
Mayo, Co., 53
Meath Street, Dublin, 276 fn 83
Meath, Co., 77, 107, 227
Mechlin, Belgium, 182
Mediterranean, 165, 183, 206, 224, 238, 239, 240
Meelick, Co. Galway, 247
Meetinghouse Lane, Cork, 231
Mellifont Abbey, Co. Louth, 254 fn 16
Mentzel, Christian, 187; Johann Christian, 187
Merchant's Quay, Dublin, 277, 282
Merian, Maria Sybilla, 203, 209
Merrett, Christopher, 53, 108, 189, 221
Merrion Row, Dublin, 270
Merrion, Dublin, 106, 113, 119, 120, 125, 144
Meurdrac, Marie, 186
Mexico, 166, 211
microscope, 72, 297
Milan, Italy, 174
Miller, Joseph, 90
Miller, Philip, 94, 173, 222, 230

Mitchell, M.E., 21, 73, 111
Mitchelstown, Co Cork, 231–48, 256
Mizière, François, 178
Moibanus, Johannes, 179
Moira, Co. Down, 97
Molen family, Miriam van der, 201 fn 16 ; Roelien van der, 201 fn 16
Moll, Hermann, 60
Mollet, Claude, 209
Molyneux family, Adam, 64 ; C.C., 66 fn 19; Patrick, 97; Samuel the elder, 64, 72; Samuel the younger, 64, 70, 72, 78, 79; Thomas and William, 58–79
Molyneux, Thomas, 22, 58, 59, 61, 62, 64, 65, 66, 68, 69, 70, 73, 74, 76, 77, 78, 94–6, 116, 148, 186, 244; herbarium, 74, 94; Katharine, wife of, 77; library, 72
Molyneux, William, 58, 61, 62, 63, 64, 66, 68, 69, 70, 71, 72, 74, 76, 77
Monaghan, Kevin, 260
Monasterevin, Co. Kildare, 112, 121, 148, 254
Monelea, Co. Dublin, 97
Monincks family, Jan, 223, 225; Maria, 223, 225
Montpellier Hill, Dublin, 281
Montpellier, France, royal garden at, 168; university at, 177, 179, 180
Moody, Robert, 270
Moore Abbey, Monasterevin, Co. Kildare, 254
Moore family, earls of Drogheda, 254 fn 16
Moore, David, 17
More, Alexander Goodman, 17
Moriarty, Christopher, 45
Morin, Pierre, 191
Morison, Robert, 67, 78, 166, 186, 187
moss houses, 261
Mount Jerome, Dublin, 139, 141
Mount Juliet, Co. Kilkenny, 257, 260
Mount Merrion, Dublin, 262
Mount Sandford Castle, Woodstock, Co. Kilkenny, 261
Mount Stewart, Co. Down, 272 fn 57
Mount Talbot, Co. Roscommon, 248
Mountaine, Dydymus, see Hill, Thomas

Mountheaton (Ballyskeneagh), Co. Offaly, 51, 55
Moycarn, Co. Roscommon, 240, 248
Muckross Abbey, Co. Kerry, 252–5, 259
Mullen, Allen, 62, 73, 75
Mulloy, John, 230
Munster, 39, 40
Munting, Abraham, 209
Murphy, Edward, 284
Murray, Johann Andreas, 98
Musgrave, William, 73

Namaqualand, South Africa, 207
Naples, Italy, 59
Nassau Street, Dublin, 213, 214
National Botanic Gardens, Glasnevin, 19, 74 fn 54, 140, 221, 226
National Library of Ireland, 26 fn 6, 41, 101, 105, 283, 295
natural history, 159, 174, 188, 189
natural philosophy, 159, 183, 191, 218
Naul Hills, Co. Dublin, 145
Nelson, E.C., 20, 48, 50, 52, 54, 56, 80, 96, 102, 118
Nesbitt, John, 83
Netherlands, 69, 162, 165, 194, 199, 203, 208, 209
Netherlands Institute of International Relations, 211
New Row Without-Newgate Meeting House, Dublin, 89
New Street, Dublin, 144, 271, 272, 281
New York, 189, 276
Newcastle upon Tyne, England, 84
newspapers, 265, 276, 277, 282, 284
Newton, Sir Isaac, 59, 62, 67, 111, 159
Newtown, Co. Dublin, 125, 142
Nicholson, George, 82
Nicholson, Henry, 214, 215, 216, 218, 226, 227
Nicolson, William, 103
nomenclature (botanical), 34, 102, 104, 117, 130, 133, 137, 150, 166, 221, 225, 226, 236, 241; binomial (Linnaean) system, 102, 187
Nore, river, Co. Kilkenny, 261
North Strand, Dublin, 107, 113

Northumberland, England, 84
Nuremberg, Germany, 168, 169, 211
nurseries, English, 269; French, 269; Irish (see Dublin, nursery trade in)
nurseryman, definition of, 263 fn 5
Nutton, Vivian, 179

O'Boyle, Cornelius, 179
O'Brien, William, 4th earl of Inchiquin, 238
O'Donnell, Thomas Joseph, 41
O'Donoghue Mór, Rory, 40, 47
O'Flynn, Carrie, 287
O'Hara family of Nymphsfield, Annaghmore, 271
O'Neill, Hugh, 2nd earl of Tyrone, 33
O'Sullivan Beare, Philip, 19, 20, 21, 25–44; Zoilomastix of, 19, 20, 21, 25–44
O'Sullivan, Denis C., 41, 42
Offaly, Co. (Kings county), 55, 97
Old Bawn, Dublin, 139, 270
Old Court, Bray, Co. Wicklow, 257
Oporto, Portugal, 278
optics, 62, 66, 69
orangeries, 196, 199, 200, 203, 206, 209, 210, 235, 240, 261 (see also glasshouses, greenhouses, hothouses)
orchards, 209, 263, 264, 267
Orleans, France, 270
Ortelius, Abraham, 32
Oswald, Philip, 118
Ouvane River, Co. Cork, 288
Ovid, Publius Ovidius Naso, 87
Owney, Co. Tipperary, 248
Oxford, 168, 183, 186, 191, 221, 230, 255; Bodleian Library at, 176 fn 8, 179; botanical garden at, 52; Magdalen College at, 82; university of, 52, 61, 67 fn 21, 174 fn 1, 221
Oxford Philosophical Society, 70, 72

Padua, Italy, 165, 168; botanical garden at, 159, 168, 178; university of, 159
palaeontology, 157
Palladius, Rutilius, 188
Pallas, Co. Galway, 247
Palmerstown, Dublin, 128, 131, 141

Paris, France, 69, 178, 182, 185, 186, 187, 199, 227
Parkgate Street, Dublin, 281
Parkinson, John, 45, 46, 47, 48, 50, 108, 109, 161, 172
parterres, 197, 198, 199, 212, 264, 269
Passe, Crispijn de, 186, 191
Patrick's Well Lane, Dublin, 146
Paul, James, 84
Pemberton, Thomas, 49
Pena, Pierre, 182
Penettes, Raymond, 270
Penrith, Cumbria, 86
Penzance, Cornwall, 111
Peppard, Luke, 280
Perceval, Sir John, 269; John, father of, 169
Perfect family, John, 284; William, 284
Peter Street, Dublin, 94
Petit, Jean, 178
Petiver, James, 215
Petty, Sir William, 22, 47, 53, 61, 62, 64, 67
Phelan, John, 272, 273, 279; daughter of, 273
Philadelphia, 276
Philip II, king of Spain, 166
Philip, Thomas, 120, 122
Phoenix Park, Dublin, 106, 127, 128, 129, 130, 131, 135, 137, 140, 141, 143, 222, 283, 284
phycology, 286
physic gardens, 98 fn 100, 159, 179, 213–30, 239 fn 25, 240, 268 fn 29, 290 fn 13
Pisa, Italy, botanical garden at, 168
Pittion, Jean Paul, 179
Plantin, Christophe, 182
plants, early modern medicinal uses of, 30, 34, 41, 66, 72, 84–5, 91, 92–4, 98, 99, 100, 104, 106, 137, 142, 149, 159–61, 162, 163, 165–6, 173, 174, 179–82, 183, 186, 191, 192, 206, 211, 213–15, 218, 222, 226, 233, 237, 238, 240, 241, 244, 245, 278, 282; *see also* herbals
Plat, Hugh, 169
Pliny the Elder (Gaius Plinius Secundus), 28, 30, 38, 40, 177, 178

Plot, Robert, 70,
Plukenet, Lenard, 186
Plumier, Charles, 166
Plunkett family manuscripts, 277 fn 90
Poitiers, France, 184
polynomials (pre-Linnaean), 102, 104, 117, 130, 132, 133, 150–6, 221, 225, 226, 236, 241
pomology, 196
Pomona, 182
ponds, 135, 193, 197, 201, 208
Poolbeg, Dublin, 125
Portmarnock, Co. Dublin, 124
Portobello, Dublin, 281
Portrane, Co. Dublin, 121, 124
Portugal, king of, 72
Portumna Castle, Co. Galway, 254 fn 15
Post, Maurits, 200
Poulle, Magdalena, 208–10, 212
Powell, Samuel, 233
Powerscourt, Co. Wicklow, 271
Praeger, Robert Lloyd, 17
Pratt, Robert, 259 fn 34
Presbyterians, 87
Preston, Chris, 118
Price, Uvedale, 252
Priests Leap, Caha Mountains, Co. Cork, 301
Pückler-Muskau, Hermann von, prince, 256
Pulteney, Richard, 80, 84, 88, 97, 98

Quakers, 87, 104
Quin, Caroline Wyndham, countess of Dunraven, 254, 255

Rabel, Daniel, 185, 186
Rademaker, Abraham, 208
Raheny, Dublin, 113, 124, 147
Ramsay, Alexander, 178 fn 24
Ramsay, Thomas, 178
Ratheline, Co. Longford, 270 fn 44
Rathfarin, Co. Galway, 247
Rathfarnham Castle, Dublin, 257–8
Rathfarnham, Dublin, 130, 136, 148, 149, 271
Rathmell, Settle, North Yorkshire, 82
Rathmines, Dublin, 281

Rawdon, Sir Arthur, 269 fn 39; Lady Dorothy, 97, 215, 225; George, 269; Sir John, 97; Rawdon, John, 1st earl of Moira, 97

Ray, John, 77, 78, 90, 97, 100, 102, 103, 104, 106, 108, 109, 112, 116, 117, 118, 124, 130, 137, 146, 148, 166, 183, 187, 188, 221

Ray, Joseph, 71

Redi, Francesco, 188

Reeves-Smith, Terence, 19

Renvyle, Connemara, 298

Rheede tot Drakenstein, Hendrik Adriaan van, 163

Richardson, Richard, 97, 206

Richmond, Dublin, 281

Riga, Latvia, 276

Rinekirk, Co. Limerick, 245, 247

Ringsend, Dublin, 57, 113, 123, 125, 128, 136

Rivinus, Augustus Quirinus, 166

Robartes, Francis, 71 fn 40

Rochfort, Robert, 259

Rocque, John, 113, 263, 270

Roe (Rowe), William, 271; widow of, 271

Rogerson, John, 145

Rome, Italy, Farnese garden at, 168

Romney, John, 82

Rondelet, Guillaume, 161, 177

Roper's Rest, Dublin, 139, 141, 142

Rosamund's Bower, Marino, Dublin, 261

Roscrea, Co. Tipperary, 50, 55

Rostellan, Co. Cork, 238

Rotterdam, Netherlands, 274, 276, 278, 279, 280

Rotunda Lying-In Hospital, Dublin, 274

Royal Canal, Dublin, 115, 135, 138

Royal College of Physicians, Dublin, 94, 179 fn 24 218

Royal Dublin Society, 17, 19, 265, 280, 281; botanical gardens at Glasnevin, 221 (*see also* National Botanic Gardens); *Transactions of the Dublin Society*, 290

Royal Irish Academy, Dublin, 17, 107, 118, 266

Royal Society, London, 22, 59, 60, 62, 64, 67, 70, 71, 72, 73, 74, 76, 159, 183, 188, 189, 191, 217, 218; *Philosophical transactions*, 109, 111, 188, 244

Rush, Co. Dublin, 144

Rutty, John, 96, 117

St George, George, 96

St George's Lane, Dublin, 270

St Ronan's Island, Co. Kerry, 260

St Stephen's Green, Dublin, 94, 270, 274

St Wolstan's Abbey, Celbridge, 254

Salmon, William, 182

Sandymount, Dublin, 125

Sandys, Francis, 261

Santiago de Compostela, Spain, university of, 25; Irish college at, 25

Sarrasin, Jean Antoine, 179

Sassini, Giovanni Domenico, 69

Scaliger family, Joseph Justus, 178; Julius Caesar (his father), 178

Scheldorp, John, 67

Scheveningen, The Hague, 199

Scotland, 61, 87, 112, 280, 297

Scribblestown, Co. Dublin, 137

Seddon, Peter, 86

Seep, Catharina Juliana, 207

Serapion, 181

Seville, Spain, 30

Sex, Susan, 53

Shane, Sir Arthur, 79

Shankill, Dublin, 285

Shannon, river, 55, 115, 247

Sharkey, Gerry, 133

Sheapeard, Nicholas, 268

Sheffield, England, university of, 61

Shelton Abbey, Co. Wicklow, 255

Shenck, Leonard, 208

Sherard, James, 229, 230

Sherard, William, 97, 98, 100, 116, 124, 133, 148

Sheriff Street, Dublin, 107

Sicily, Italy, 76

Sigginstown, Co. Kildare, 255 fn 16

Silliard, Zanche, 48, 49

Simmonscourt, Dublin, 113, 121, 128, 136

Simpson, Benjamin, 279, 280, 281

Skeffington, Sir John, 269

General index

Skinner, Stephen, 187
Slane Castle, Co. Meath, 257
Slieve Bawn, Co. Roscommon, 248
Sligo, Co., 48, 77, 112
Sloane, Hans, 78, 111 fn 26, 189
Smith, Adam, 264
Smith, Charles, 257, 259
Smith, James Edward, 118
Smith family, John, 217; William, 217
Smith, Robert, 62
Smitten, George, 284
Smock Alley, Dublin, 263 fn 4
Sorgvliet, Netherlands, 199–200, 211
South Circular Road, Dublin, 271;
    Aromatic Hill on, 281–2
South Wall, Dublin, 113
Southampton, England, Pitt Collection,
    71
Sowerby, James, 298
Spain, 25, 31, 41, 168, 235
Sparwenfeldt, Johan Gabriel, 41
Speed, John, 266
Sri Lanka (Ceylon), 69, 206
Stace, Clive, 117, 150–6
Stainton, Cumberland, 84
Stanihurst, Richard, 25, 28
Staunton, George, 96
Stearne family, John, bp of Clogher, 22,
    176, 178, 181 fn 33, 182, 183, 186, 187,
    188, 189; John, father of, 179 fn 24,
    181 fn 33
Stel, Simon van der, 207
Stephens, Philip, 53
Stephens, William, 23, 98, 217, 218, 219,
    220, 223–30
Stevenson, Robert, 274
Stewart, Captain, 58, fn 1
Stillingfleet family, Edward, 174, 177, 178,
    179, 183, 186, 187, 188, 189, 191;
    James, son of, 174
Stillorgan, Dublin, 133, 136, 212
Stockholm, Sweden, 59
Stokes, Whitley, 288
Stoneybatter, Dublin, 106, 128, 149
Stopendael, Daniel, 199, 208
Stradbally, Co. Laois, 212
Strasburg, France, 171, 178
Strawberry Beds, Dublin, 106, 129, 142

Strawberry Hill, Twickenham, London,
    249
Strokestown, Co. Roscommon, 79, 231,
    233, 258
Sugar Loaf, Caha Mountains, Co. Cork,
    301
Summerhill, Dublin, 106
Swansea, Wales, 288
Sweden, 41
Sweet, Rosemary, 250, 251
Swift, Jonathan, 17, 267
Switzer, Stephen, 169, 209, 273, 274
Switzerland, 168
Sydenham, Thomas, 70, 77 fn 65

Talbot, Richard, 1st earl of Tyrconnel, 74
Tallaght, Dublin, 135, 143, 146
Tasmania, 98
Templeogue, Dublin, 135, 141
Tenterfields, Dublin, 146
Teune, Carla, 206
The Coombe, Dublin, 139
The Hague, Netherland, 172, 193, 199,
    200, 212; Fagel house at, 202, 212;
    Haagse Bos forest at, 211; Huis ten
    Bosch, 211; Noordeinde Palace at,
    201–3
Theophrastus of Eresos, 177, 178, 182,
    187
Thomas Street, Dublin, 87, 264, 279
Thomond, Co. Limerick, 38
Threlkeld, Caleb, 17, 20, 22, 41, 45, 48,
    58, 59, 67, 77, 79, 172, 224, 226–7,
    267; life of, 80–99; in Dublin, 87–97,
    106–7; family of, 81; John
    (grandfather), 81; Thomas (father),
    80, 81, 83, 85; John (brother), 85;
    Joshua (brother), 85; Thomas (cousin),
    85; and Thomas Molyneux, 94–6;
    Synopsis, publication and reception of,
    96–9, 100, 172, 243, 244, 245; plant
    records in, 100–15; sources of, 102–12;
    taxonomy of, 102, 104–6, 117;
    herbarium of, 90, 103; as plant
    ecologist, 116–56
Toledo y Guzmán, Hernán Nuñez de, 177
    fn 17
Tollymore Park, Co. Down, 258

Tolson family, Elizabeth, 86; James, 85, 86, 87; Joshua, 86; Mary, 86
Toole family, Charles, 281, 284, 285; Luke, 281, 284, 285
Tournefort, Joseph Pitton de, 111, 165, 166, 187, 227, 228
Townley Hall, Co. Louth, 271
Trench, Michael Frederick, 261
Trinity College Dublin, 17, 20, 62, 64, 66, 67, 71, 76, 78, 94, 95, 159, 174 fn 1, 176, 194, 233, 241, 268, 287, 290; Anatomy House, 213–5, 224; botany lectures at, 217–8; College Park, 213; Department of Botany at, 88, 90, 292; Fagel collection at, 22, 193–212; Fellows' Garden, 213, 268; herbarium, 23, 69, 88; Old Library, 22, 193, 212, 214, 215; Physic Garden: 23, 159, 213–30, 239 fn 25, 240, 268, 291; Provost's House, 214
Tullagh (Tulla), Co. Clare, 246
Tullagh, Co. Tipperary, 248
Turkey, 165
Turner, Dawson, 286, 287, 289, 293, 296, 297, 298, 300, 302, 303
Turner, William, 108
Tymon, Co. Dublin, 130
Tynemouth Castle, Northumberland, England, 84
Tyrone, earl of, 33

Uilenbroek, Goswin, 168
Ulster, 31, 88, 276; O'Neill clan in, 32; flight of the earls from, 32;
Uppsala, Sweden, university library of, 19, 27, 41
Ussher, family, 64
Utrecht, Netherlands, 70; university botanical garden at, 195

Vaillant, Sebastien, 166
Van Leeuwenhoek, Antoni, 60, 69, 188
Van Swanenburg, William Isaacsz, 68
Varro, Marco Terentius, 174, 188
Vaughan, Francis, 111
Vauxhall, London, 270, 274
Venice, Italy, 169, 170, 183
Verona, Italy, 183

Versailles, France, 189
Vesling, Johann, 165
Vijverhof, Netherlands, 209, 212
Villa Sagredo, Marocco, Contado of Venice, Italy, 169, 170
Villermont, Esprit Cabart de, 74
Virgil, Publius Vergilius Maro, 87
Volkamer, Johann Christopher, 169

Waalsdorp, Netherlands, 208
Wade, Walter, 117, 128, 133, 137
Wales, 273
Walker, Joseph Cooper, 271
Walkinstown, Dublin, 106
Walmsley, Thomas, 253
Walpole, Horace, 249
Walsh, Wendy F., 37
Walter, of Henley, 267
Walton, Catherine, 82
Ward family, Bernard, 1st Viscount Bangor, 255–6; Ann, Viscountess Bangor, 256
Ware, Isaac, 249
Wassenaar, Netherlands, 208
Waterford, Co., 141
Watts, John, 206
Watts, Michael, 84
Webb, David Allardice, 17
Webb, Francis, 272
Weiditz, Hans, 161
Wentworth, Thomas, 1st earl of Strafford, 255 fn 16
Werburgh Street, Dublin, 171, 173
Wesley, John, 261
West Indies, 235
Westerhoek, Netherlands, 208 fn 37
Westmeath, Co., 115
Westmoreland, England, 271
Westmoreland Street, Dublin, 285
Whitesmith, Leonard, 84, 89, 90
Whitestown, Dublin, 135
Wicklow, Co., 138, 141
Wieland, Melchior, 178
Wilde, Sir William, 66
William III, king of England, Scotland and Ireland, 194, 195, 207
Williams, Alexander, 123
Willoughby, Charles, 64

General index

Windermere, Cumbria, England, 85
Wise, Henry, 271, 273
Witherall, Robert, 71
Wittenberg, Germany, university of, 165
wood houses, 261
Woods, James, 289
Woodstock, Co. Kilkenny, 260, 261
Worlidge, John, 189, 190
Worm, Ole, 67
Worsley, Benjamin, 61, 62
Worth family, Dr Edward, 22, 109 fn 23; Edward (cousin of), 149; John (father of), 170, 171; library, 157–73; medical collection, 157; scientific collection,

157–9; trustees of, 46, 73, 75, 109, 110, 120, 158, 159, 164, 167, 170, 219, 228; William (uncle of), 171
Woudanus, Jan Cornelisz, 68
Wright, Thomas, 258, 259

York, 284
Yorkshire, 47, 82, 84
Young, Arthur, 244, 253, 254, 259, 260
Young, John, 268
Yverdon, Switzerland, 221

Zanoni, Giacomo, 183
zoology, 25, 28, 157, 233